Land Rites and Wrongs

The Management, Regulation and Use of Land in Canada and the United States

Edited by
Elliot J. Feldman
Michael A. Goldberg

A Lincoln Institute of Land Policy Book

Sponsored by the Lincoln Institute of Land Policy and the University Consortium for Research on North America

Published by the Lincoln Institute of Land Policy

International Standard Book Number: 0-89946-222-7

Library of Congress Catalog Card Number: 87-12186

Printed in the U.S.A.

The Lincoln Institute of Land Policy
26 Trowbridge Street
Cambridge, MA 02138 U.S.A.

Library of Congress Cataloging-in-Publication Data

Land rites and wrongs.

"In 1984–85 the draft papers were the vehicle for the Seminar on Canadian-United States Relations of the University Consortium for Research on North America at the Harvard University Center for International Affairs."
Bibliography: p. 283.
Includes index.
1. Land use — United States — Congresses. 2. Land use — Canada — Congresses. 3. Land use — Government policy — United States — Congresses. 4. Land use — Government policy — Canada — Congresses. I. Feldman, Elliot J. II. Goldberg, Michael A. III. Lincoln Institute of Land Policy. IV. University Consortium for Research on North America. V. Seminar on Canadian-United States Relations (1984–1985: Harvard University Center for International Affairs) VI. Harvard University. Center for International Affairs. VII. Title: Land rights and wrongs.
HD171.A15L28   1987   333.33'13'0971   87–12186
ISBN 0-89946-222-7

Written under the auspices of the University Consortium for Research on North America, a partnership of Brandeis, Harvard, and Tufts Universities, and The Fletcher School of Law and Diplomacy.

*To Harold and Ruth Goldberg, Lily, and Shira,
who likes to see her name in print.*

Contents

List of Tables

List of Figures

Preface and Acknowledgments

This book began with a concern for how democratic societies balance individual property rights with the public interest. It began, too, with an awareness of essential differences between Canada and the United States, relating both to specific issues of property rights and to the broader organization of institutions. Although each of the scholars involved in this collaborative project had different substantive empirical interests, they shared a desire to discover the range of possible solutions to common problems of land use and development in advanced industrial states, to identify the key forces shaping public policy outcomes, and to assess the balance of public and private sector activity shaping the use of land. These common concerns enabled us to fashion a team effort that would maximize the diversity of inquiry while assuring a coherence of analysis.

The essential rules of the team effort were few and simple. Each individual project was to be comparative. Each was to involve specific case material in both Canada and the United States. Each was to consider public participation and participatory mechanisms as an important basis of comparison. Each was to compare the performance of the public sector and the private sector.

The team met collectively at regular intervals over a four year period for presentations and discussions of work in progress. Roughly mid-way in our work we organized a conference with urban researchers from Montreal to assess the overall project. In 1984–85 the draft papers were the vehicle for the Seminar on Canadian-United States Relations of the University Consortium for Research on North America at the Harvard University Center for International Affairs. Each paper was presented to an audience of specialists for extended discussion. Professionals from the public and private sector, from both countries, led off discussions and provided invaluable commentary for revision. Many of the team members participated in sessions other than their own, further assuring an integrated effort. Thus the project maintained a collective character even though all team members pursued their own cases and issues.

The research for this book was conducted under the auspices of the University Consortium for Research on North America, a partnership of Brandeis, Harvard, and Tufts Universities. It was supported financially and spiritually by the Lincoln Institute of Land Policy, although some project members received other support as well. At least three major books have benefited in substantial part from the Lincoln Institute's support of this project, authored by Gordon Clark, Michael Goldberg, and Christopher Leman. In turn, those projects were aided by the National Research Council (Clark), the Forest Economics and Policy Program at Resources for the Future in Washington, D.C. (Leman), the Canadian Social Sciences and Humanities Research Council, the University of British Columbia, the Department of External Affairs, and the Real Estate Council of British Columbia (Goldberg). Mario Ristoratore's work was supported additionally by the Sachar International Scholarship and the Gordon Fund at Brandeis University, where the research reported here contributed to his doctoral dissertation. The Government of Canada and the Andrew W. Mellon Foundation supported the seminar series for the presentation of draft papers.

A great deal of research for this book was done in the field, in many states and provinces and in the federal capitals. Public officials, politicians, industry leaders, scholars and ordinary citizens gave generously of their time, knowledge, and experience. They cannot all be named here, and in many instances we would not compromise their confidence by naming them. Nevertheless, we are all very grateful for their cooperation and help.

We are particularly grateful to the experts who traveled to Cambridge to lead the discussion of each paper. Often they held (or previously had held) positions of public authority directly responsible for policies under evaluation by the project team. Professor Robert Wood of Wesleyan University, former United States Secretary of Housing and Urban Development, led the discussion of the work of Michael Goldberg comparing urban development in Canada and the United States. The Honorable Barnett Danson, Canadian Consul General and former Minister of State for Urban Affairs, led the discussion of John Brigham's research on port development. Mr. Russell Sylva, Massachusetts Commissioner of Environmental Quality Engineering, and Dr. André Marsan of Montreal's André Marsan et Associés, chemical engineering consultants, commented on the presentation of Mario Ristoratore's inquiry into the politics of toxic waste disposal. The analysis of Frank Colcord's research on center city preservation in Montreal and Boston was led by Dr. Phyllis Bronfman Lambert, Director of the Canadian Institute of Architecture in Montreal, and Mr. Edward Logue, former Director of the Boston Redevelopment Authority. Discussion of Christopher Leman's paper on forestry policy was led by Dr. Guy Lemieux, Director of Land Management in the Ministry of Energy and Resources in Quebec, and Dr. James McNutt, General Manager of the Timber Division of Container Corporation of America in Alabama. Elliot J. Feldman's paper on land use controls on the urban periphery was discussed principally by Professor Leonard Gertler, Director of the School of Regional and City Planning at the University of Waterloo and former Director of Research for the Canadian Ministry of State for Urban Affairs, and Mr. Henry Richmond, Executive Director of 1000 Friends of Oregon, the main organization sponsoring Oregon's comprehensive land use controls. Only Gordon Clark's contribution was not the subject of a seminar session, but it had been the centerpiece of a special Canadian Study Group meeting at Harvard in 1983.

In addition to this distinguished group that provided each author with detailed advice for the revision of papers, all the chapters were read by Neal A. Roberts, Esq. of Rogers and Wells, Los Angeles, Professor Lawrence Susskind of MIT, and Canadian federal Judge Barry Strayer, former federal Assistant Deputy Minister of Justice. They served as an informal advisory board for the project. Finally, Frank Schnidman, Director of Programs at the Lincoln Institute, guided the project from its inception and was crucial for the successful completion of this book. He and Arlo Woolery, the Institute's Executive Director, were indispensable in lending all manner of support for this effort and in providing for the publication of the present volume.

The home base for this research was the Harvard University Center for International Affairs. Professor Seyom Brown, who served as Acting Director of the Consortium during a leave of absence for Elliot J. Feldman to work in the United States government, helped organize and chair the seminar series. Dr. Jerome Milch helped organize the original project and contributed mightily to the concepts that guided it. Finally, Katherine Davis helped edit the book and prepare it for publication, Anne Denna oversaw final manuscript preparation, and Priscilla Battis prepared the index.

A cross-national, multidisciplinary collaborative research project may be especially prone to errors. Although we have consulted with experts on diverse subjects, as overall editors we have found it particularly challenging to identify and correct errors that remain. Nevertheless, as editors we accept responsibility for the finished product.

Elliot J. Feldman
Michael A. Goldberg

Cambridge, Mass.
July 1986

Introduction

Elliot J. Feldman and Michael A. Goldberg

The ability of governments to solve social problems is now widely debated. The regulatory and managerial functions assumed by the public sector in the twentieth century have always been criticized by those champions of private enterprise who argue that government is inefficient, overly centralized, and an inadequate substitute for the market. Recently, however, the criticism of government has been extended to the traditional virtues of the public sector, such as the ability to address questions of equity, to solve the problem of collective goods, to plan comprehensively, and to provide opportunities for participation in collective decisions.[1] Indeed, proposals for deregulation and reprivatization, once the exclusive domain of conservative critics of government, are now echoed by many disenchanted liberals who contend that public bureaucracies all too often are less effective than the private market in promoting the public interest.[2]

These arguments have been buttressed, to some extent, with empirical data. It has been shown, for example, that public regulatory agencies frequently have become tools of the private interests they are supposed to regulate, and comprehensive planning strategies may fall victim to the inability of government to coordinate its own activities.[3] However, the blanket indictment of public sector inadequacies implicit in much recent criticism, and the growing preferences for private solutions to social problems, require more evidence than has been marshalled so far. It remains too early to conclude from an insufficient empirical base that policy should follow this ideological view. Isolated studies of agency behavior illustrate the failure of government initiatives, but they do not justify the conclusion that governments cannot play an instrumental role in solving societal problems. We must understand better the nature of government success and failure before we choose simplistically between solely public or private solutions.

Despite somewhat different national experiences with government intervention, the current criticism is characteristic of all industrial countries. Comparative cross-national research helps assess the limitations as well as the capabilities of government by controlling for the peculiar influences of political structures and cultural values. The climate for government activity may affect performance, and this climate varies from country to country. Thus, cross-national research, in principle, enables comparisons of analogous cases in settings typified by higher and lower expectations for the success of government intervention.

This book constitutes one attempt to consider the role of the state, or more precisely the performance of government in dealing with the transfer, development, and use of land. Land use is a problem commonly examined by economists, lawyers and planners but rarely analyzed as a social or political issue. Here we examine government decision making and policy implementation at the levels of cities, regions, counties, states, provinces, and central federal governments in both Canada and the United States. Furthermore, we consider government performance dealing with land in the urban core, on the urban fringe, in ports, industrial zones, and in forests. We consider the roles of executive, legislative, and judicial branches of government in both countries.

Few issues cut across as wide a variety of economic, political, legal, and philosophical questions as those concerning land use. The allocation and use of land inevitably affect housing and urban development, waste management, transportation, energy, mineral extraction, forestry, agriculture, and recreation. Competing claims have economic implications and generate inevitable political conflict partly because of the finite quality of the resource and partly because of the emotional attachment to land and property in North America. Land policy, moreover, presents society with important philosophical and legal choices, such as between public and private forms of ownership and management and between development and preservation. The disposition of land is sensitive in any society, and public policy has always played an important role.

According to liberal western tradition, the function of government is to protect life, liberty and property. Liberal governments generally have limited their intervention in the land market to specified purposes, even when more extensive powers, which originated before liberal ideas took root, were available.[2] Throughout much of human history, after all, governments have exercised control over land, owning some of it outright, regulating its use in private hands, and sometimes asserting the right to confiscate it with or without compensation. The development of national markets for goods and capital contributed to major reductions in government control and typically fostered the liberal ideas and legal doctrines that cemented individual property rights.[3]

Despite the liberal traditions that inhibited public intervention everywhere (and especially in the United States), in recent years government involvement in the land market has increased throughout the advanced industrial world. Numerous tools have been developed to assist governments in controlling private land use and in managing public lands. Moreover, governments have become active consumers of land, purchasing or expropriating private lands for a growing array of specified and unspecified public purposes. In liberal societies as elsewhere, government has become again an important actor in determining the availability of land, the price at which it is exchanged, and the purposes for which it is used.[6] Yet liberal ideas regarding the protection of private property certainly persist, establishing an endless dilemma for societies and for governments as they trade off public needs against private rights.

The debate over government intervention, over public and private choices in the disposition of land, became central to public discourse in the United States during the closing year of the Carter Administration and the beginning of the Reagan Administration. Perhaps the symbol of the Carter period was the 1980 Alaska Land Act, which placed 106.2 million virgin acres—approximately one-third of the state—under varying categories of environmental protection. And just a year earlier the president had commissioned a National Agricultural Lands Study that led to policies designed to preserve farmland against development.

President Reagan's early symbol was James Watt, whom the White House had commit publicly to selling off public lands for private development. However, these apparent partisan and presidential differences can be misleading. Both developers and conservationists (or environmentalists, although they are not always the same) have looked to government intervention, especially at state levels where most land use decisions reside. Under Chapter 353 in Missouri, for example, private developers secured use of the state's power of eminent domain, utilizing public authority to amass urban land parcels for private development. And a unanimous United States Supreme Court upheld a Hawaiian law that authorizes the state to take land from one private owner and deliver it to another, attempting to solve the historical maldistribution of land where governments own 45 percent and nine private owners own another 45 percent of all the land in Hawaii.[7] The 1967 Hawaii Land Reform Act had not succeeded in solving this problem.

Massachusetts may serve as something of a microcosm in considering the shifting politics of land use in the 1970s and '80s. In 1977 Governor Michael Dukakis introduced the Agricultural Preservation Restriction Program that enabled farmers, beginning in 1980, to sell development rights to the state, providing the farmers with cash and the state with assurances the land would not be developed. By contrast, Dukakis's successor, Edward J. King, sought special legislation in 1981 that would enable the state to sell land to private developers.

The Massachusetts legislation for selling development rights on agricultural land to preserve open space followed by a year similar steps in Suffolk County, New York. By 1980 the practice had spread to Maryland, Connecticut, New Hampshire, and King County, Washington. Yet everywhere legislation designed to limit, control, or stop development has been marked by arrangements balancing the objectives of developers. In Vermont, for example, developers utilized a provision in Act 250 permitting development on parcels of ten acres or more, and legislative attempts to close the loophole failed. In 1983 the Oregon land use law was modified to encourage economic development and to oblige state agencies to accept local plans that had not been as conservationist as a state commission had desired. New Hampshire's "current use" law, giving tax breaks to farmers so they would keep farming, did not prevent farmers from selling to developers; it mostly improved the price they could get.

The intervention of government, even when provisions remain for private developers or owners, is pervasive or perpetually imminent. In Canada this rule always has prevailed because history has been on the side of collective or Crown ownership and use; the impact of the new Charter of Rights may be a new vision of individual property rights, but the cases have not yet been heard. In the United States, recent landmark judicial decisions may transform thinking about land use for the rest of this century. They plainly shift American emphasis away from the nineteenth century domination of individual property rights.

The 1984 Supreme Court decision in Hawaii held that the state's peculiar history had created unworkable and undemocratic anomalies in the land tenure system and only a broad exercise of the state's police power could serve the public interest. The Court thus compelled near-monopoly land owners to sell to tenants. Three years earlier, in *Poletown Neighborhood Council* v. *City of Detroit*,[8] the Supreme Court of Michigan upheld the obliteration of a neighborhood by a municipality for the purpose of securing a land parcel for a private corporation. The Michigan Court ruled that the private corporation, General Motors, operated in the public interest because it provided jobs, and any public interest activity could warrant expropriation.

The decision in Hawaii may come to be interpreted as uniquely suited to a particular situation, but in combination with *Poletown*, American courts seem to be saying that there are no discernible limits on the power of the state to take property and to define the public interest.

The state may force one private owner to surrender land to another; the state may take private property, alter it, and turn it over to another private owner. And under Missouri's Chapter 353, local governing bodies may give a private developer the state's power, leaving it to the private party to take the property of another citizen. Combined with a 1983 statute allowing cities to fund private redevelopment through tax increment financing, Chapter 353 is the major vehicle for urban change in Missouri.

Whatever constitutional questions might have been raised by the "giving issue," as John Brigham characterizes the process of governments acquiring property from one private owner in order to deliver it to another, after *Hawaii* and *Poletown* little is left of the public/private distinction in land acquisition or disposal. General Motors is treated as if it were a public agency; the right of private Hawaiian tenants to own property is treated as a universal public good.

The acquisition and disposal powers of government celebrated in *Hawaii* and *Poletown* have been complemented in the courts by powers to control, particularly and most impressively through planning and zoning. In *Southern Burlington County NAACP* v. *Township of Mt. Laurel*,[9] the New Jersey Supreme Court effectively invented a new unit of government and seized local powers in order to enforce state-created fair housing rights. Canadian parliaments have long exercised such powers to control urban development, as in the Manitoban creation of a regional government for Winnipeg. American legislatures may have the power to eliminate local government (for they certainly have the power to create it), but the bicameral balances and importance of local representation outweigh the party allegiance so vital in Canada. Indeed, Michael Goldberg holds the contrast between Canada's domination of parliament and the American reliance on the judiciary as one of the central distinctions between the two countries. But when the Township of Mt. Laurel used its zoning powers for socioeconomic exclusions and suburban state legislators did not object, the New Jersey Supreme Court disallowed local control and demanded consideration of "regional" criteria and needs.

The American judiciary, at least in New Jersey, might be accomplishing what in Canada is achieved by a provincial assembly. And in the United States the agenda is more manifest, with an open declaration of a social and political purpose, whereas in Canada, if like purpose there be, it is hidden in technical explanations about land management.

The *Mt. Laurel* decision goes to the heart of jurisdictional disputes among governments at the same level and deploys the superior powers of hierarchical levels. It takes American land use control for the first time into the areas of the Canadian experience with government intervention. More typically, in both systems, some attempts have been made to coordinate the interests of different governments in facing the general public with land use decisions.

Few results are clear from the 1983 New Jersey decision, and little is known more generally about the influence of intragovernmental and intergovernmental discord on the execution of land policy. Certainly if the *Mt. Laurel* objectives were legislated the state would be zoning statewide with equity, not efficiency criteria. New Jersey, and any other states following this decision, would then eliminate the urban fringe as a targeted area because planning would have to be regional to be legal.

The American development debate has followed along the lines of Canada's and has put the power of the state at the center of the controversy. The liberal consensus supporting only limited government intervention in land markets has been shattered.[10]

If the broad debate over whether the public or private sector could best serve society profits from elegant simplicity, the more specific debate now is instrumental and requires measured results. Government intervention may be debated in principle, but in practice it is almost everywhere assumed. The prevailing questions are: Whose purposes should the state serve? Which instruments would be most effective for those purposes? When do governments succeed and when do they fail? The debate, in short, is now openly political, involving government decisions more over when than whether to assert power over land.

Evaluative Criteria

There is no single definition of performance, or of success and failure, that could contain the assessments of several scholars or satisfy the peculiarities of every case. Each of the essays here in effect offers its own definitions. Nevertheless, there are some common notions that prevail.

Performance is difficult to measure. Government objectives are not always clear or congruent. Governments may act to increase the efficiency of land use, to achieve equity and other social goals or, in some cases, to maximize both objectives. One approach to measurement would focus exclusively on policy outcomes or results; another might concentrate on statutes and common law, and still another might look strictly to rises or declines in property values. An analyst might examine bureaucratic politics, looking for the competing objectives among government actors.

The authors here, coming from several disciplines, agree that these measures would be inadequate. Although each may emphasize one or another of these approaches (Michael Goldberg, for example, looks strongly to economic outcomes, Christopher Leman to economic conditions, and Gordon Clark and John Brigham to judicial decisions), they all discuss the process by which choices are made, for the process often makes outcomes inevitable and it helps explain national differences. And a focus on process enables the authors to embrace the competing goals of agencies and of the private sector.

Users of land set their own goals and enunciate policies for their achievement. One measure of performance looks inevitably to how well goals are achieved. However, performance implies more than merely the achievement of goals. By asking "how well" they are achieved, the authors here ask also about consequences—spillover, side effects, unanticipated (or ignored) outcomes, for the authors measure success according to the bureaucratic goals of governments and private corporations, but also according to related effects. Performance, then, measures success *and* failure, where failure refers not merely to shortcomings in an agency (or corporation's) own enunciated goals.[11]

Leman, for example, does not consider it sufficient to ask whether the harvest goals for a certain number of trees are achieved; he asks, too, about the cost of the achievement, about the program to restore the forest and perpetuate it. Brigham is not content with determining whether the public sector succeeds in having the private sector build as planned; he also inquires about the social cost of the effort. Frank Colcord refines the broad picture of Boston's planning achievements to note the protection of the neighborhoods as a success offset by the failure of the transportation system and the decline of the retail and entertainment sectors; by contrast, applause for Montreal's monumental public works must be accompanied by mourning for the city's neighborhoods and housing.

The Structure of the Book

The research project leading to this book was organized around three areas of concern designed to address empirically, theoretically, and analytically the debate over the capacities of government and the invisible genius of the market: (1) public/private sector comparisons; (2) land use comparisons in four principal government and private sector functions: acquisition, management, regulation, and disposal, where management and regulation may be regarded as the major "use" parameters; and (3) Canadian-United States comparisons. In effect, we are examining two types of actors (from the two sectors), as they operate in four functional areas regarding land, in two countries. Frank Colcord, moreover, characterizes four types of government intervention in the land market: facilitative (e.g. improving traffic flow); public works (e.g. highways, or the Montreal Metro); private construction (with particular public help, whether through the provision of infrastructure or tax incentives, zoning, and other such instruments); and control (i.e. express limits on private sector choices and behavior).

Public and Private Sectors

The public/private distinction, "seamless and forbidding,"[12] is difficult to make and sustain. A major problem in law is that the distinction requires an assessment of state action. The reaction to the 1905 Supreme Court decision of *Lochner* v. *New York*[13] destroyed simple notions of state action and with them the conventional public/private distinctions.[14] Critical legal scholars deny the distinction on the left,[15] and lawyer-economists deny it on the right.[16] But in politics perception of a private sphere insulated from state intervention remains.[17]

The authors agree that private–sector control over land use decisions often leads to equitable policies, despite the presumption that government intervention is required because of frequently inequitable private–sector priorities. Too often, however, private–sector efforts organized on short term criteria do neglect legitimate social and political goals. Only state intervention can assure responsible social policy.

The authors are not able to judge whether the goals of governments eventually may have been achieved through private initiative, or whether the private sector might ultimately have pursued policies with a sense of social responsibility. The authors judge, however, that on several issues state intervention at the time it occurred was essential in the pursuit of social policy, even when government efforts themselves have failed. (Boston neighborhoods would have been destroyed; American forests would not be replenished.) And because the protection of private property is a pillar of the liberal democratic state, assessment of a legitimate state role in this policy sphere is at the heart of the policy sciences.

A central difficulty in these evaluations is that there are no reliable patterns within the public and private sectors. Indeed, Leman observes that in some instances there is more in common within a country across sectors than there is within the sectors themselves. Governments at different levels may have competing objectives, more readily aligning at the local level with developers, for example, and with professional planners at the state or provincial level. Large companies may employ professional foresters and formulate policies consonant with the American federal government; smaller companies that can ill-afford such professionalism may align with a clearer profit motive that is also manifest in some Canadian provinces. A Boston mayor may perceive neighborhood preservation as a priority because of the electoral system; a Montreal mayor may find no decisive neighborhood pressure in a system that prefers a grander vision. Because the public/private distinction depends so much on organization and circumstance, the achievement of equitable goals may depend in some instances as much or more on the private sector. But if equity is an objective, then there must be flexibility about the appropriate agents and instruments for its achievement.

Functional Framework

The Concept. One way of conceptualizing land activities is through a simple typology based on the ownership of land and the focus of government controls:

Focus of Control

Locus of Ownership	*Use*	*Transfer*
Private	Regulation	Acquisition
Public	Management	Disposal

Land may be owned by private citizens or by the state, and governments can adopt policies with respect to the use of land or its transfer between the public and private sectors. The use of private land is *regulated* by a variety of policy instruments, urban service requirements, and taxation policies. Public lands are *managed* by governments in pursuit of particular objectives (e.g. recreation, economic growth, or conservation) and, at least in some instances, on behalf of private interests (e.g. loggers or developers). Governments may *acquire* private land for public purposes (although not necessarily for public uses), whether through voluntary purchase or through expropriation; they may also *dispose* of surplus lands to private individuals.

Land tenure systems usually are more complex than the simple distinction between public and private ownership suggests. Private individuals, for example, may possess title to land while portions of the "bundle of rights" are retained by governments. Nor is the distinction between the use and transfer of land absolute, for government acquisition, often land banking, is thought by many to be merely a radical form of control over use. Nevertheless, the typology does reduce a complex array of government polices to four distinct functions that enable the authors to enter detailed empirical analysis.

The typology also invites questions central to the concept of the liberal democratic state. Government land taking, even with compensation, is, next to military conscription, the most extreme exercise of unprovoked state authority;[18] when may government exercise this power? What are the justifications? How do governments decide when to use such power? Economists have been especially interested in such questions because of their impact on the operation of the market, but decisions that restrict individual property rights are of concern to other social scientists and to all citizens.[19]

Both regulatory activities and the involuntary sale of private property deprive citizens of fundamental rights as defined by liberal theory. By contrast, the disposal of public property through the sale of land confers benefits on individuals (or, typically, corporations).[20] During their early years, governments in North America provided cheap land in order to attract settlers, but the sale of public property did not terminate with the end of the frontier. Declining school-age populations, for example, have mandated the closing and sale of school property in many communities throughout the United States and Canada. Western cities in the United States, moreover, have complained about the quantities of land owned by the federal government on their metropolitan fringes; many state and city officials want Washington to surrender land for development. Similar concerns have arisen in Canadian cities where government land banking has supplanted individual ownership and development. Yet the sale of public property raises many of the same equity issues as the acquisition of private land.

Similar concerns apply, too, to the management of public lands. The colonization of the state by organized interest groups is a common theme in criticisms of the pluralist literature; much of the discussion centers on regulatory agencies, but agencies controlling public lands raise like issues.[21] How do governments determine the proper use of public property?[22] How are decisions reached when both private interests and public officials disagree over the use of a particular tract of land? How does resource allocation under public stewardship differ from land use under private ownership? The management of public lands, like the sale of public property, may confer benefits on individuals, and it is important to know what interests governments favor under such circumstances.

The Colcord typology characterizing four types of government intervention advances this functional framework by detailing the possibilities within each category. Whether buying, selling, taking or regulating land, governments are acting to facilitate, build, or control. These choices, often ends in themselves but also strategic means, are important because they help explain public purpose, which any judgment of performance requires.

Decision Making Processes. The key to utilizing the Colcord typology within the functional framework of the overall study is to focus on decision making. Past research on land use originated primarily in urban and regional planning, economics, and law. Planners have developed tools for the use and allocation of land resources, but the technical analyses are normatively derived. Economists have developed universalistic standards of efficiency and equity to evaluate particular land use policies, but they have paid little attention to how decisions are actually made.[23] Government, from the perspective of economics, is an external actor that intervenes in the market; whereas it is necessary to understand the impact of government actions, there is little reason to focus on governmental processes in order to apply universal standards. And lawyers have explored the doctrines and procedures that determine the legal status of land, but they have devoted little attention to either the social and political bases of law or the substantive impact of legal norms on decision making outside the courts.[24]

The decision making focus activates the Colcord typology and helps the authors explain why policies succeed or fail to achieve the objectives of policy makers. Economic, political, or social constraints often are responsible for government failure, but their impact is discernible only through an appreciation of the decision process, locating the point at which the elements of failure emerge.

The concern of each case study with decision making emphasizes the political character of public choice, the role of participation, and the interaction of government agencies at various levels. Moreover, important decisions are taken in all branches of government, for each of the essays focuses on different primary actors precisely because the decision process is so varied and the players so abundant. Colcord looks to mayors shaping cities, but Goldberg looks more to financial institutions; Leman says captains of industry and government bureaucrats shape the hinterland, whereas Mario Ristoratore looks more to local politicians; Feldman sees legislatures defining urban growth, whereas Clark looks to judges and Brigham looks to constitutional fathers. All are conscious of external forces and internal complications, but each detects different principal actors in different problem areas.

The Role of Experts. Policies that affect land are not inherently technical, but governments often act on land issues in response to the judgment of experts, and experts are integral to the decision process. The size and precise location of a land parcel expropriated for the construction of a toxic waste facility, for example, is justified in terms of technical requirements; the decision to permit logging on particular sites in public lands or to restrict development rights on private property may be explained in technical terms; the decision to clear a large area of deficient low-cost housing for luxury apartments or offices is justified usually by economic (often public finance) criteria. Each of the case studies involving expert advice includes an assessment of the political character of expertise.

The role of experts varies in the cases here. Professional foresters plainly influence conservation and harvesting decisions; they also are found working in both the public and private sectors. Scientists rallied to industrial, government, and citizen action causes in the siting of toxic waste facilities. Planners were abundant in revamping the Halifax and Portland ports. In every instance the experts were available to all sides in disputes; they were for hire, and however technically valuable they may have been (and the foresters especially are applauded here), their role is political.

The authors vary their emphases, but all touch on each of the concerns animating the research. Brigham, Clark, and Ristoratore concentrate most on the acquisition and disposal of land; Colcord, Feldman and Leman focus more on uses, particularly with reference to planning, control, and the distinctions between management (implying public sector ownership) and regulation (implying private sector ownership). All the essays examine a range of government instruments intervening in the land market, and they all discuss both the public and private sectors, making some assessment of their relative performance.

Canada-United States Comparisons

The introduction of comparison into the analysis of public policy helps expand the range of choice available to societies whose perception of choice may be bound by tradition, institutions, economic practices, social structure, and culture. Comparison can illuminate the role of institutions by exposing parallel institutions operating in other systems. And a comparative approach can facilitate the development of theory about politics as well as policy, beyond the boundaries erected by the details of systems, because it helps establish norms for judgment and helps distinguish the essential from the trivial.[25]

All the essays in this book are comparative, dealing at least with the two countries and often with several units of government in each, an analytical tool enhanced by the method of structured, focused comparison.[26] Clark's and Colcord's comparisons each focus on pairs of cities, Brigham's on two ports; Ristoratore examines four cases, two in each country, and Feldman and Leman each consider several provinces and states. Goldberg evaluates the universe of major cities in the two countries, and he and Leman devote the most attention to the roles of central governments.

Each of the comparisons maximizes similarities and highlights differences. Explanations for outcomes then profit from the comparisons in the processes, institutions, cultures, and external forces. The test for performance is founded in a systematic screening of variables across two or more political systems.

Goldberg emphasizes differences in use in Canada and the United States as a way of explaining more general differences between the two countries and societies. Leman, by contrast, suggests that national differences define how uses will vary between the two countries. There is more here than a disagreement about which came first, the identities or the uses. Rather, Goldberg is defining a universe in which urban differences manifest a larger reality of different national identities; Leman sees different national identities more as a product of different institutions and political systems. The logic of Goldberg's vision is continuous national divergence between the two countries; Leman's vision would allow for greater convergence.

This subtle dialectic runs throughout the book. Clark and Feldman see similar values at work in both countries, although Clark detects a more sinister ideological force affecting the judiciary. Colcord hypothesized certain cultural and ideological differences that did not materialize empirically, although they do help in explaining specific policies. By contrast, Goldberg argues that the national values are highly distinct throughout the two countries. Feldman and Ristoratore see political systems defining outcomes; Goldberg sees cultures as more dominant, and Leman looks more to a combination of forces, especially economic conditions.

There is no reason, of course, for the authors to agree on the national differences and similarities, although in certain conclusions they do. The authors agree that the public and private sectors cannot easily be distinguished in either country, and they agree that successes are marked by cooperation between the sectors in both Canada and the United States. They agree that the role of government is essential and omnipresent in the allocation of land. They agree that policies governing land use are emblematic of national values and institutions.

In preparing his research in this project, John Brigham observed:

> A comparison of Canada and the United States is a little like a controlled experiment, the kind laboratory scientists try to achieve. At least in parts of Canada one finds cultures and economies very close to those in the United States. This allows much of the variation one usually finds between two countries to be held constant. It is possible to avoid extreme differences in climate, language and history. The result is the prospect of focusing on a limited number of variables, a situation rare in the social sciences.

Brigham went on to observe, however, that there are great variations within the two countries, and that:

> the choice of province or city can skew an otherwise controlled international study. The extremes of Ontario and Quebec make it difficult for a comparative perspective to be grounded in only one province. In order to emphasize the differences between the two countries, it is important to keep the differences between the cases to a minimum. If one were to compare Quebec City and New York City, the differences of culture and condition would be so great as to draw attention [away] from the differences between the two countries within which the cities reside.

These sage observations about equivalence arose from one of the few authors in the project who had not yet published extensively about the merits of comparative analysis or about Canada and the United States.[27]

Despite the many apparent national similarities, the essential historical settings for analyzing land use choices in Canada and the United States are different. Liberal ideas are not as entrenched in Canada as they have been in the United States. Canada's central political philosophy was spawned by British royal doctrine seasoned by the Puritan Revolution and the perceived national and strategic need for collective action in the development of a large land mass with a sparse population. American political philosophy, by contrast, was born of opposition to Britain and the Crown. The two nonrebellious North American colonies supported the state; the thirteen rebels created government to hold back state powers.

Until 1982 there were no entrenched rights of any kind in Canada's constitution, and even after the adoption of the Charter of Rights and Freedoms, Canada's constitution still does not recognize individual property rights. They surely exist by tradition and statute in both countries, but the legal foundations of the two systems have important consequences for public policy, and they are decidedly different. Canada's traditions support a collective vision of property through the authority of the Crown; American tradition celebrates private property free from the state, although that public philosophy clearly has been abolished by American courts.

In the essays here there is substantial evidence of the traditional Canadian and American differences in approaching the role of the state. Goldberg, Leman, and Brigham all emphasize the Canadian inclination to favor state intervention and the American preference for the free market. However, Leman does not find consistent policy or implementation differences explicable by country, and Colcord, hypothesizing that Canadians will rely more on the state, concludes that the comparison of Montreal and Boston is counterintuitive: serious planning and government control prevailed in the development of Boston's urban core, whereas in Montreal the private sector prevailed. Clark contends that similar liberal values are at work in both systems, and Feldman discounts the arithmetic difference in the number of government units trying to control land use comprehensively: although of fifty states only three have legislated statewide controls, only three of the ten Canadian provinces have approved similar measures. A percentage of American states may be less inclined to act, but they are no less able, nor are they inherently less successful.

Ristoratore also finds similarities in the role of the state dominant over differences between Canada and the United States. The key systemic differences, he argues, may be found between examples of success and failure, not among successes or among failures. Hence, his cases of New York and Ontario are similar in the values of market choice and, as a pair, are different from Louisiana and Quebec which both display preference for state intervention.

Analytical explanation is enhanced, too, by policy opportunities. As Brigham also observed:

> The Canadian comparison opens two kinds of analytical questions: (1) Are there transferable lessons from either side of the forty-ninth parallel? (2) Do profound differences in political systems, especially between congressional and parliamentary arrangements, yield different exercises of power and consequently different policy outcomes? Do variations in democratic political structure alter the relations of individuals or communities to their land and property? Are the conflicts among constituencies worked out differently with different political institutions?

Each of the authors is seeking answers to these questions, and, by implication, predictions for the outcomes of policy choices and options for policy makers.

Canada and the United States, while more similar than perhaps any two advanced industrial countries in their levels of economic development, consumer preferences, and life styles, are a bundle of contrasts in political systems, world roles, and urban styles. Goldberg even argues that Canadians seem to like urban dwelling a good deal more than Americans. Canadians resolve disputes differently, relying more on executive authority; Americans are more litigious (a consistent finding in these cases), and their dispute resolution is monetarily far more expensive. However, Americans welcome more participation, which makes the process ultimately more satisfactory to more citizens and possibly makes dispute resolution more durable.

The broad similarities make the differences all the more critical and all the more helpful for determining the relative effectiveness of public and private sectors. Consequently, the Canada-United States comparisons are the most controlled, perhaps, of those possible among advanced industrial countries and the most susceptible to isolating variables for explanations and predictions. All social science requires standards for judgment, and implicitly, therefore, all social science is comparative. The comparisons here are explicit, the standards explained as they operate empirically.

Presentation. There are many ways to present the essays in this project. They could be assembled according to their perspectives on public sector or private sector performance, linking for example, the Colcord, Leman and Ristoratore essays where considerable merit in private sector initiatives is found. Alternatively, they might be organized around the cross-national comparisons, with those emphasizing similarities (Clark, Feldman, Ristoratore) contrasting with those emphasizing differences (Goldberg, Brigham, Colcord). The essays comparing cases within countries (by Goldberg, Feldman, Leman, and Ristoratore) might be presented together. And yet another way would be according to the analytical typology, linking essays focused on use and control (Feldman, Leman, Ristoratore, Colcord) and those concerned with transfer (Clark, Brigham). To some extent, in fact, this latter scheme is followed. The reader, however, certainly can proceed through the book in any preferred fashion, selecting the essays according to alternative organizational schemes.

The book is organized around a geographical vision of the issues raised, in effect looking at land use from the most to the least dense, or from the heart of the city to beyond the fringe. The introductory section offers a macroscopic comparison of Canada and the United

States in terms of public and private sector differences (Leman) and in terms of urban development (Goldberg). The essays then look at the city, inside (Colcord) and out (Feldman), before reaching beyond the urban fringe to examine the forests (Leman) and to search for toxic waste sites (Ristoratore). Finally, the two chapters concerned primarily with the judiciary (Clark) and with the issues of give and take (Brigham) complete the comparisons and the issues raised by the typology.

The many perspectives manifest among these authors are attributable above all to differences in discipline, nationality (there are four represented), and ideology. Each sees different issues within the empirical cases and each is inclined to different causal explanations. Likely the reader will be more or less persuaded to some extent by compatibility with these perspectives. Yet in the overall picture there is remarkable agreement: the authors reject the denunciation of government as simplistic and ill-informed, but they do not celebrate government performance as a cure for all injustice or market inefficiency. They thus take a first step in contributing cross-national empirical data to the debate over governments and land use in North America.

Notes

1. For a selection of views regarding the relative merits of the private and public sectors, see Walter Goldstein, ed., *Planning, Politics and the Public Interest* (New York: Columbia, 1978), and Lawrence Chickering, ed., *The Politics of Planning* (Sacramento: Institute of Contemporary Studies, 1976).
2. Peter Steinfels, *The Neo-Conservatives* (New York: Simon and Schuster, 1979). See also Charles Schultze, *The Public Use of the Private Interest* (Washington, D.C.: Brookings Institution, 1977).
3. See, for example, James Q. Wilson, ed., *The Politics of Regulation* (New York: Basic Books, 1980); Alan Altshuler, *The City Planning Process* (Ithaca: Cornell University Press, 1965); Theodore J. Lowi, *The End of Liberalism*, Second edition (New York: W.W. Norton, 1979); Martin Meyerson and Edward Banfield, *Politics, Planning and the Public Interest* (Glencoe, Ill.: Free Press, 1955); Jeffrey Pressman and Aaron Wildavsky, *Implementation* (Berkeley: University of California Press, 1979); Grant McConnell, *Private Power and American Democracy* (New York: Alfred Knopf, 1966).
4. For background on the United States, see John Delafons, *Land Use Control in the United States* (Cambridge, Mass.: MIT Press, 1969); and Fred Bosselman and David Callies, *The Quiet Revolution in Land Use Control* (Washington, D.C.: Council on Environmental Quality, 1971).
5. For a discussion of the impact of national markets on the perceptions of land, see Karl Polanyi, *The Great Transformation* (Boston: Beacon Press, 1947); see also John R. Commons, *The Legal Foundations of Capitalism* (Madison: Wisconsin University Press, 1920).
6. On this trend, see Lawrence B. Smith and Michael Walker, eds., *Public Property? The Habitat Debate Continued: Essays on the Price, Ownership and Government of Land* (Vancouver: Fraser Institute, 1977); Rutherford H. Platt, "Space and Authority: The

Dimensions of Institutional Response," in Kenneth A. Hammond, et. al., *Sourcebook on the Environment* (Chicago: University of Chicago Press, 1978); Dalton Kehoe, et. al., *Public Land Ownership: Frameworks for Evaluation* (Lexington, Mass.: Lexington Books, 1976); and Bruce Ackerman, *Private Property and the Constitution* (New Haven: Yale University Press, 1977).

7. *Hawaii Housing Authority* v. *Midkiff*, 104 S.Ct. 2321 (1984).

8. *Poletown Neighborhood Council* v. *City of Detroit*, 410 Mich. 616, 304 N.W.2d 455 (1981).

9. *Southern Burlington County NAACP* v. *Township of Mt. Laurel*, 92 N.J. 158, 456 A.2d 390 (1983); in the original case, 67 N.J. 151, 336 A.2d 713, *appeal dismissed and cert. denied* 423 U.S. 808 (1975), the New Jersey Supreme Court ordered the township to correct its zoning violations and prepare a new plan, but in the 1983 decision the court concluded that the township would not meet these obligations and the court effectively claimed the township's powers; the New Jersey legislature subsequently recovered the powers taken by the court, but retained them at the state level.

10. Critical legal scholars say it was never supportable. See, for example, Duncan Kennedy, "The Stages of the Decline of the Public/Private Distinction," 130 U. Penna. L.Rev. 6 (June 1982), pp. 1349–57.

11. The "Law and Economics" approach also focuses on outcomes but is indifferent to process. See Robert H. Mnookin, "The Public/Private Dichotomy: Political Disagreement and Academic Repudiation," 130 U. Penna. L.Rev. 6 (June 1982), pp. 1429–40.

12. This characterization is offered by Christopher D. Stone, "Corporate Vices and Corporate Virtues: Do Public/Private Distinctions Matter?" 130 U. Penna. L. Rev. 6 (June 1982), p. 1443.

13. 198 U.S. 45 (1905).

14. Morton J. Horwitz, "The History of the Public/Private Distinction," 130 U. Penna. L.Rev. 6 (June 1982), pp. 1423–28.

15. Both a general discussion, and one specific to employment issues and unions, may be found in Karl E. Klare, "The Public/Private Distinction in Labor Law," 130 U. Penna. L.Rev. 6 (June 1982), pp. 1358–1422.

16. Robert C. Ellickson, "Cities and Homeowners Associations," 130 U. Penna. L.Rev. 6 (June 1982), pp. 1519–80.

17. Mnookin, *op. cit.*

18. Incarceration, which deprives liberty, is a punitive response to criminal behavior. Conscription and expropriation assume no transgression by the citizen.

19. A useful discussion among economists of these issues can be found in Smith and Walker, eds., *Public Property?*, *op. cit.*

20. Stone, *op. cit.*, argues that the corporation can variously satisfy public or private criteria for identity, and the law makes different allowances depending on the outcome.

21. See especially Lowi, *The End of Liberalism*, *op. cit.*, and McConnell, *Private Power and American Democracy*, *op. cit.*

22. See Wilson, ed., *The Politics of Regulation*, *op. cit.*

23. See, for example, John Kain and John Meyer, *Essays in Regional Economics* (Cambridge, Mass.: Harvard University Press, 1971); John Kain et. al., *Essays in Urban Spatial Structure* (Cambridge, Mass.: Ballinger, 1975).

24. The movement of Critical Legal Studies seeks to change the direction of legal scholarship by accounting more for the forces that shape legal decisions. See Roberto Mangabeira Unger, *The Critical Legal Studies Movement* (Cambridge, Mass.: Harvard University Press, 1983) and the *Critical Legal Studies Symposium of the Stanford Law Review* 36:1–2 (January 1984), especially Allan C. Hutchinson and Patrick J.

Monahan, "Law, Politics, and the Critical Legal Scholars: The Unfolding Drama of American Legal Thought," pp. 199–245.

25. Elliot J. Feldman, "Comparative Public Policy: Field or Method?" *Comparative Politics* (January 1978).

26. Arend Lijphart, "The Comparable-Cases Strategy in Comparative Research," *Comparative Political Studies* (July 1975); Alexander George, "Case Studies and Theory Development: The Method of Structured, Focused Comparison," in Paul Gordon Lauren, ed., *Diplomacy: New Approaches* (New York: Free Press, 1979); Elliot J. Feldman, "Comparative Politics and Case Studies," in Elliot J. Feldman, *Concorde and Dissent: Explaining High Technology Project Failures in Britain and France* (New York: Cambridge University Press, 1985).

27. The books comparing Canada and the United States by the authors here include: Gordon Clark, *Judges and the cities: interpreting local autonomy* (Chicago: University of Chicago Press, 1985); Elliot J. Feldman and Jerome Milch, *Technocracy versus Democracy: The Comparative Politics of International Airports* (Boston: Auburn House, 1982); a comparison of three Canadian cases, in Elliot J. Feldman and Jerome Milch, *The Politics of Canadian Airport Development: Lessons for Federalism* (Durham: Duke University Press, 1983); Michael Goldberg and John Mercer, *The Myth of the North American City: Continentalism Challenged* (Vancouver: U.B.C. Press, 1986); Christopher Leman, *The Collapse of Welfare Reform: Political Institutions, Policy, and the Poor in Canada and the United States* (Cambridge, Mass.: MIT Press, 1980).

PART I

COMPARING PUBLIC AND PRIVATE IN CANADA AND THE UNITED STATES

2

The Concepts of Public and Private and Their Applicability to North American Lands

Christopher K. Leman

One of the major questions for this book is the difference between the public and private sectors in the management, regulation, acquisition, disposal, and use of land. Each of the cross-national comparative analyses includes a comparative assessment of the role and contribution of the public and private sectors. However, there is great ambiguity in distinguishing public and private activities in North American mixed economies, and it is very difficult to measure or compare performance. Indeed, it is often difficult even to determine whether land is owned privately or publicly and therefore under what kind of control it may be governed.

It is easy to assume that public and private organizations have little in common. As a typical argument goes, the market dictates a private company's choices and objectives, closing it off from public desires. Reliance on the market promotes agreement between managers and their subordinates on standards of performance, but narrows the company's concerns even in cases where public and private desires alike would be served by broader thinking. The private investment perspective rewards planning and the taking of risks, but it also invites volatility and a neglect of organizational vitality.

Governmental organizations, by contrast, are often characterized as lacking a single bottom-line criterion for success or failure. The influence of political leaders and social groups creates an endless debate on objectives and makes it difficult to delegate duties to the field levels where they can most sensibly be carried out. Annual appropriations, symbolism, and the media make a public organization sensitive to political demands, but encourage employees to be averse to risks and to take a short term perspective. Public organizations are seen as having difficulty in implementing decisions once made and in rethinking them when circumstances warrant.

Contrasts of this kind may be theoretically appealing but they often have been abstract and polemical.[1] Empirical research reported in this book, and similar research elsewhere, suggests instead that the differences between public and private organizations are not inherent, and interaction between public and private organizations is more important than the ascription of particular characteristics to either.

Assessing Public and Private Performance

Public/Private Contrasts

Many of the apparent differences between public and private organizations often simply reflect different purposes being pursued. Private corporations generally are involved in producing commercial goods and services for the market, whereas the objectives of many government agencies are more complex and more difficult to define. Because a variety of objectives can be found within the public and private sectors, greater differences sometimes may be discovered within a sector than between them, and growth in the nonprofit sector has yielded organizational hybrids with roots in both the private corporation and the government agency.[2] Corporations and nonprofit organizations that deal in nonmarket goods and services exhibit some characteristics of government, and public agencies that carry on businesslike tasks often follow corporate lines.

It may even be the case that bureaucracy renders many public and private organizations fundamentally similar, especially in the middle and lower organizational levels.[3] "Scientific management" tended to discredit efforts to identify common elements in public and private management because of a commitment to prescription, but much recent descriptive research suggests that common elements exist and are being reinforced by the spread in both sectors of experts, information and automated techniques.[4]

As corporations have grown, their behavior no longer reflects the simple entrepreneurship of an owner in reacting to market forces. A corporation's stockholders may technically own a share of its land and facilities, but they typically have very little say in how these resources are mobilized. A classic 1935 study of U.S.-based corporations, many with operations in Canada, and a 1981 sequel both documented an ongoing separation between ownership and control of capital.[5] Historian Alfred Chandler chides historians and economists alike for ignoring the emergence of the "visible hand"—the major new corporate sector of middle management.[6] He argues that corporations grew by internalizing transactions formerly carried out in a market setting and that they could do so by introducing administrative coordination through an innovative use of bureaucracy tailored to the peculiarities of each industry.

An emerging school of economic theory now recognizes that there is an economics of internal organization just as there is one of market exchange.[7] A classic feature of a market is that buyer and seller have few links beyond the immediate transaction.[8] The freedom exercised by the buyer and seller has important advantages in encouraging them to find efficient bargains, but it also introduces search and transaction costs. These costs are never zero, and to the extent that they produce market frictions and hence have a social cost, there may be advantages in reducing them. For example, the U.S. real estate industry incurs costs of over $8 billion a year to confirm, through title searches and insurance, the ownership of land that is being sold.[9] When the ownership of land does not change, these costs are obviously less; large tracts of public or private land often have never been thoroughly surveyed because so few boundaries needed to be established. The social transaction costs of goods and services other than land are even more significant, as for example with advertising, which absorbs an estimated 2.8 percent of U.S. national wealth; and the tremendous apparatus of commercial law.[10] There are obvious advantages if buyer and seller can enter longer term structured relationships such as are provided within a single organization.[11]

When private sector organizations internalize decisions, they replace the market with bureaucracy and reduce significantly the characteristics that distinguish them from the public sector. The new complexity of corporations and their absorption of hard-to-quantify functions such as research and development have rendered the profit measure less useful as an operational guide. A growing number of management researchers even argue that traditional financial guides for corporate investment, particularly the calculation of discounted return on capital, discourage long term strategies to improve products and assure stable and growing markets.[12] Organizational vitality itself may be valued, encouraging reliance on voice (participation) rather than exit (market) because of a need to retain valued employees and clients and to benefit from their views.[13]

To recognize these important similarities between public and private bureaucracies is not, of course, to deny that these respective bureaucracies have differentiating characteristics that are important to policy. A public agency must address questions of democracy, planning and management control that are usually less critical for a private bureaucracy. Governments may often fail in this effort, but private organizations are not necessarily more successful when measured by the economic tests that are their major challenge.

Effective management of any organization respects its internal character and external context. The public or private nature of an organization can be expected to influence managerial approach. For example, all organizations strive to secure financial accountability, programming and management by objectives, but in many private-sector situations the profit measure, for all its limitations, is a basic tool. Lacking that measure, many public organizations pursue the same goals via other pro- cesses, particularly the annual budget process.[14] Similarly, personnel management is important in both sectors, but because the standards for assessing personnel are often not as clear as in many private organizations, public agencies have come to rely more on a combination of formal and informal instruments of socialization, evaluation and discipline.[15]

Public/Private Interaction

Contrary to abstract contrasts of public and private organizations, the two sectors are constantly interacting. There is no private-sector organization that is not touched in some way by government, nor is there a government agency that does not delegate some responsibilities to the private sector. Although such interaction between public and private organizations is almost universal, it takes many different forms. Hence the real choice among institutional alternatives is probably not between public and private action, but rather among different public/ private relationships.

In different ways, both United States and Canadian governments have long been involved in the private economy. In a statement made about the United States that applies even more to Canada, conservative economist Jonathan Hughes observes that governmental controls on the economy "have existed so long in peaceful conjunction with Anglo-American ideas about property rights [that] their long-lived existence must be considered by the historians as somehow 'natural' within the reality of our own laws and customs."[16] He concludes that these controls "came into existence because, put bluntly, Americans distrust capitalism in its pure form. There is just no other explanation."[17]

The government role in Canada's economy is clear and strong. Usually the question has not been whether government will get involved in the economy, but which level of government will get there first. In recent decades, government aid has been extended to hospitals and doctors, universities, parochial schools and many other nominally private institutions. Today, many business organizations are federally or provincially owned: Seven of the largest fifty Canadian industrial firms and nine of the largest seventy-five banks.[18]

Many government corporations and authorities exist in the United States as well, but typically government involvement has been more indirect, such as in aiding individual health costs, financing military procurement, paying for water projects and highways and bailing out corporations and banks. However indirect, these efforts are extensive. All told, the goods and services produced by federal, state and local governments account for nearly one-quarter of the U.S. gross national product, and governments own about one-fifth of the stock of tangible wealth.[19]

In addition to some overall Canadian-American differences in the relationship between public and private authority, this relationship also varies within each country between different regions and issue areas. Contact between public and private representatives may occur most decisively at higher levels, or it may occur in more decentralized contexts, depending on the structure of government and the structure of the business and nonprofit sectors. Sometimes the public and private sectors interact legalistically, and sometimes their relations are more informal. The complexity of public and private authority over land, as shown in the next section, suggests the existence of a wide range of additional configurations of public and private power in each society. Criticisms of the impact of business upon government or of government upon business may overlook the extent to which some kind of relationship is unavoidable, requiring greater awareness of the different possibilities and their varying consequences for good or ill.

The various regulations and other government influences on private landowners have introduced an important public component in their behavior. Many private landowners in both Canada and the United States adapt to some social demands even when not legally required, because they want to avoid regulation or expropriation. For example, forest products companies that operate in both the United States and Canada actively consider the concerns of not only private stockholders, but also of public "stakeholders."[20]

In some cases, publicly owned resources are actually freer of formal and informal restrictions than are resources whose nominal ownership is private. One order of government sometimes ignores the laws passed by another. The U.S. federal government frequently has chosen not to obey state laws, and the provinces often have defied Canadian federal authority. And as a practical matter, a public agency often disobeys laws passed by its own government. A recent study of six public and private electric utilities in the United States and Canada found a U.S. federal entity, the Tennessee Valley Authority, to be the least responsive to environmental and social concerns. Other government utilities, including Ontario Hydro, had better records, and among the privately owned utilities, the record also was mixed.[21]

It appears that as the public and private sectors interact with increasing intensity, they are coming in some ways to resemble each other. Governments are increasingly conscious of being judged on how businesslike they are, while businesses and nonprofit organizations now recognize the importance of public accountability.

Land Ownership and Use

Lands that are in government hands are referred to generically in this book as "public lands," with government regarded as being the owner. Legally, some of these lands are known by other names, but informally they are often called public lands. In the United States, the Federal Land Policy and Management Act of 1976 defines "public lands" to be only those managed by the Bureau of Land Management, thus excluding such huge tracts of government-owned land as the national forests, national parks, and national refuges. Even so, lands that are owned by national, state, or local governments are widely referred to in the United States as public lands. In Canada, most government-managed lands are legally termed "Crown lands," because title to these lands rests with the Crown (see John Brigham's chapter in this volume)—much as government itself operates in the name of the Crown. However, national and provincial parklands or refuges are rarely referred to as Crown lands. Although this term is often applied to lands that have not been designated as a park, refuge or other special category, many Canadians also refer to them as public lands, especially in Quebec, where provincial governments have de-emphasized references to the Crown. Even in Ontario, a provincial government pamphlet, *Ontario's Public Land: A Guide to Its Use*, observes: "Public land or Crown land? The reader will find the former more appropriate for today in most instances."

The federal governments of Canada and the United States are the single largest land owners in their respective countries. More than 40 percent of all U.S. land is owned by governments; 34 percent of all U.S. land is owned by the federal government. Canada's federal government owns 40 percent of all land there and governments collectively own 92 percent. Most government land in both countries has been in government hands since it was originally taken from the Indians.[22]

Much of the federal land in both countries is subject to severe weather and is remote from services and population. All but a very tiny fraction of the one billion acres owned by the Canadian federal government (the single largest landholder in North America) is in federal territories north of the 60th parallel.[23] The major human use of this northern land (managed by the Ministry of Indian and Northern Affairs) is for native subsistence and for mineral exploration and production. Within provincial boundaries, the Canadian federal government owns only 7.8 million acres, land which consists largely of national parks, defense installations, airports and harbors.[24]

Virtually all of the 637 million acres controlled by the U.S. federal government are located within state boundaries and most (68 percent) of this land is controlled by two agencies: the Bureau of Land Management and the Forest Service.[25] Some of this federal land, like Canada's, is not in high demand because of weather and remoteness, and mining activities often are the main human use. In other areas where trees and grass grow faster, logging and grazing are economically attractive. And areas close to population centers have attracted outdoor recreationists. Recreation is also extensive on other U.S. federal holdings such as the national park system (which has more than twice as much land as its Canadian counterpart) and the national refuge system. Other U.S. federal agencies hold land for such purposes as water, power, research, and defense.

While activities such as logging, grazing and recreation are common on U.S. federal lands, in Canada they most commonly are found on lands owned by the provincial governments. The provinces own, in addition to some northern lands, a great deal of land in more temperate and populated regions. Together, the provinces own 1.23 billion acres, just over half of Canada's land area. Quebec, Ontario and British Columbia each control more land than there is in the entire U.S. national forest system. The provincial parks total 55.8 million acres, nearly twice the area of Canada's national parks.

The U.S. state governments own much less land than Canada's provinces—116 million acres or about 5 percent of the U.S. total.[26] Nevertheless, states that own more than three million acres each include not only relatively thinly populated states (such as Alaska, Arizona, Colorado and Washington), but also more densely populated states (such as Florida, Michigan, New York and Pennsylvania). U.S. state parks are used intensively, attracting to only eight million acres more visitors than do the U.S. and Canadian national park systems together.[27]

Although private owners have a far smaller proportion of all land in Canada (9.6 percent) than in the United States (58 percent), for certain land uses the two countries' patterns of landownership are quite similar.[28] The vast Canadian wilderness accounts for most of the difference, and the American population, ten times greater than Canada's, inevitably occupies more privately owned acres. Geography gave Canada far less agricultural land (170 million acres now in cultivation, almost all in private hands) than the United States, and history has made relatively few (49 million acres) of Canada's forests nominally private.[29] Thus agricultural and forest lands represent only about half of Canada's privately owned land, whereas in the United States they comprise 95 percent of the private total. The primary uses of these U.S. lands are for producing crops (462 million acres), livestock (365 million acres) and timber (420 million acres).[30]

In both countries, housing is the leading use of private land outside agriculture and forests. In the United States, urban and rural residences occupy about 25 million acres, and commercial or industrial uses or vacant lands occupy another 21 million acres.[31] In Canada, built-up areas occupy about 3.9 million acres.[32] Other private land uses in both countries include railroad rights-of-way (more extensive in the United States), institutions (e.g. universities, hospitals, churches, cemeteries), recreation (e.g. resorts and golf courses), and nature preserves (more extensive in the United States, where conservation organizations have set aside between one and two million acres).[33]

More for (the) Less(ee)

The data on land ownership cited so far have focused only on the nominal title to land. But nominal owners often choose to convey an interest in the land to others.

About one-fifth of U.S. private land and probably a somewhat lower proportion of Canadian private land is under lease to other operators.[34] Fully 30 percent of U.S. cropland and a somewhat lower proportion of Canadian cropland is being cultivated by a lessee rather than by the owner.[35] Leasing of private timber land is also common; for example, under leases the International Paper Company manages about one million acres of U.S. land owned by others. Leasing can be particularly complex in urban areas, as in the case of the Empire State Building.

The land under the building is owned by the Prudential Insurance Company, which by a 114-year master lease has conveyed the land to Empire State Building Associates, who own the building and have, by another 114-year lease, delegated its operations to a partnership, Empire State Building Company. The partnership subleases space in the building on a ten year basis to the many organizations actually located there. Some of these businesses in turn sublease space to still other organizations.[36]

The delegation of management responsibilities to others is even more common on public than on private land. Government acts as a *rentier*, a landowner that for a charge allows the land to be developed and used by others.[37] The commercial production from public lands of minerals, timber, livestock and downhill ski recreation is, in both countries, conducted almost entirely by business contractors under leases of varying length. Many noncommercial services on the public lands also are conducted for government by businesses or nonprofit groups, sometimes as a condition for the lease, and sometimes under a separate contract. Functions contracted out by public land agencies include roadbuilding, tree planting, trail maintenance, range monitoring and law enforcement. Arrangements of this kind have allowed the public agencies in both countries to remain small in relation to the vast land area under their nominal ownership, and in relation to the vast supply of commodities and amenities produced there. Thus the Weyerhaeuser Company directly employs about 39,000 personnel in the United States and Canada, more than any land-related public agency, but owns six million acres in the United States and Canada, far less than many of these agencies.[38]

Another limitation on the meaningfulness of nominal ownership is that interests in the land may be separated, some by law and others by owner choice.[39] In both Canada and the United States, for example, as a heritage of medieval legal practice, wildlife are held in trust by the state for the people—but owned by government; the landowner does not have the right to take them without the permission of public authorities. In Canada, subsurface mineral resources have a similar status, whereas in the United States these resources can be owned privately. The U.S. federal government in the South and West, state governments in the Midwest and railroad companies in the West have divested themselves of some land surfaces while retaining subsurface mineral rights. The ownership of flowing water in both countries is often separate from land ownership. In all of these cases, differences of interest can arise between the nominal owner of land and the owner of separated rights to its use.

Many citizens in Canada and the United States have no land, and most landowners have relatively little. The top 0.5 percent of U.S. citizens own 40 percent of the private land, and although no similar surveys have been done in Canada, it seems likely that the distribution is about the same.[40] The largest individual private landholdings in both countries are timberlands. At least nineteen companies each own more than 1 million acres of U.S. land; the largest single landholder is the International Paper Company, which owns 7.1 million acres, an area larger than the size of Maryland. Canadian private landholdings are not quite so large. The largest single landholding is by the Canadian Pacific group with nearly 2 million acres, primarily in the Canadian International Paper Company. Close behind are the J.D. Irving group (with about 1.3 million acres in New Brunswick) and the Noranda group (whose Fraser Company owns 750,000 acres in New Brunswick and whose 49 percent-owned MacMillan Bloedel has about 660,000 in British Columbia). Each of these three ownerships exceed Prince Edward Island in total acreage. Apparently no other private landowner in Canada has more than one million acres.[41]

The leasing of government land, especially for the production of oil, gas and other minerals, is even more concentrated than is private land ownership. Ten energy companies alone control mineral rights on 146 million U.S. federal acres, onshore and offshore, with Eön having more than 40 million acres. In Canada, ten companies—including some of the same ones as in the United States—have leases to or subsurface ownership of 218 million acres onshore and offshore.[42] Large corporations control most of Canada's provincial timber, and although small businesses are given more preference for timber on U.S. federal lands, several hundred companies control the bulk of production. And on 220 million acres of U.S. federal grazing lands, 4,000 individual ranch operations control nearly two-thirds of the grazing capacity.[43] Canada's provincial grazing lands show similar concentration.

Government Influence on Private Use

A variety of government policies further complicate assessing to what extent land is "private", or how much nominal owners actually manage or control it. Many policies help landowners by giving them land, or access to it, to promote government objectives. Virtually all the private land in both Canada and the United States was at one time in government hands, and governments built roads, waterways and railroads to encourage settlement, agriculture, mining and logging. Governments have helped many landowners with urban infrastructure, special tax advantages and preferential zoning and development rights.

Of course, many government actions adversely affect the interest of some landowners. "Private" property in both countries is based on the feudal doctrine of fee-simple, under which land is not owned outright, but rather is held at the sufferance of the government, subject to payment of taxes, discharge of various obligations, and—should overriding social needs arise—expropriation through "eminent domain". Canadian governments have imposed many controls on private lands and have interpreted "just compensation" almost arbitrarily when expropriating land.[44] The fifth amendment of the U.S. Constitution strengthened the rights of private owners by requiring that government seizure of property or the imposition of unwelcome taxes or regulations be for public purposes and be done only with due process and just compensation, rights that in Canada are protected only by statute. Consequently, governments in the United States have been more indirect and somewhat more cautious than their Canadian counterparts in controlling private lands.[45] Yet profound overall impacts have stemmed indirectly from taxation and from piecemeal regulatory efforts regarding zoning, air and water pollution, floodplains, wetlands, coastal areas and so on.

Conclusion

Although comparisons of public and private sector performance in land use are highly desirable, they are not easy. Centuries of political advocacy have tended to caricature the choices, discouraging empirical research. This chapter and much of the evidence in this book argue against a clear public/private distinction. Often the apparent differences are really rooted in different tasks; once these tasks are controlled for, greater similarities emerge. Public and private organizations also show the common influence of bureaucracy, technology and professionalism.

The public/private distinction is confounded as well by the extensive interaction between the two "sectors". Public and private are politically joined and hence analytically are often indistinguishable. As the chapters in this book recognize, the key research question in any particular case is often not how public and private activities differ, but in what way these activities are intertwined. Paradoxes abound: public actors can sometimes behave according to private or individual interest, whereas individuals and corporations may behave in accordance with overall social goals.

Debates in the 1980s on public and private action often have criticized the public sector. Some complaints have been elevated to folklore with galvanizing names such as the "Sagebrush Rebellion." Sometimes in the past, private ownership was the institution more under siege. Yet public and private action each has advantages and disadvantages for certain purposes, and perhaps wisest would be a portfolio that makes the best use of both. The grand questions of liberty, equality, efficiency and effectiveness that are always with us would seem to make some balancing of the public and private realms inescapable. And in practice, public and private are so deeply intertwined that to portray them as mutually exclusive alternatives is to miss the real choices in institutions and land use.

Notes

*Helpful comments were received from Frank Popper and Martha Wagner Weinberg.
  1. Given the amount that has been written separately on public and private organizations, there are surprisingly few efforts to compare the two sectors; recent ones include: Louis C. Gawthorp, *Bureaucratic Behavior in the Executive Branch: An Analysis of Organizational Change* (New York: Free Press, 1969), pp. 249–260; Peter M. Blau and W. Richard Scott, *Formal Organizations: A Comparative Approach* (Scranton, PA: Chandler Publishing Co., 1962), pp. 40–58; Henry Mintzberg, *The Nature of Managerial Work* (New York: Harper, 1973); Hal G. Rainey, Robert W. Blackoff, and Charles N. Levine, "Comparing Public and Private Organizations," in *Public Administration Review* (March-April, 1976); Michael Murray, "Comparing Public and Private Management: An Exploratory Essay," in *Public Administration Review* (July-August, 1975); Richard M. Cyert, ed., *The Management of Nonprofit Organizations* (Lexington, Mass.: D.C. Heath, 1975); Joseph L. Bower, "Effective Public Management: It Isn't the Same as Effective Business Management," in *Harvard Business Review* (March-April 1977); Charles E. Lindblom, *Politics and Markets: The World's Economic Systems* (New York: Basic Books, 1977); Gordon Chase, "Managing Compared," in *The New York Times* (March 14, 1978); Michael Blumenthal, "Candid Reflections of a Businessman in Washington," in *Fortune* (January 29, 1979); Donald Rumsfeld, "A Politician Turned Executive Surveys Both Worlds," in *Fortune* (September 10, 1979); Robert N. Anthony and Regina E. Herzlinger, *Management Control in Nonprofit Organizations* (Homewood, Il: Irwin, 1980), chapter 2; Graham T. Allison, "Public and Private Management: Are They Fundamentally Alike in All Unimportant Respects?" in *Setting Public Management Research Agendas: Integrating the Sponsor, Producer and User* (Washington, D.C.: Office of Personnel Management, 1980); Laurence E. Lynn, Jr., *Managing the Public's Business: The Job of the Government Executive* (New York: Basic Books, 1981), ch. 5; Marc J. Roberts and Jeremy S. Bluhm, *The Choices of Power: Utilities Face the Environmental Challenge* (Cambridge: Harvard University Press, 1981); Marshall W. Meyer, "'Bureaucratic' vs. 'Profit' Organization," in B. Staw and L. L. Cummings, eds., *Research in Organizational Behavior* (Greenwich, Conn.: JAI Press, 1982), vol. 4; Martha Wagner Weinberg, "Public Management and Private Management; A Diminishing Gap?" in *Journal of Policy Analysis and Management* 3:1 (1983);

and Hal G. Rainey, "Public Agencies and Private Firms: Incentive Structures, Goals and Individual Roles," in *Administration and Society* 15:2 (August, 1983).

2. See: Cyert, *The Management of Nonprofit Organizations*; AnnMarie Hauck Walsh, *The Public's Business: The Politics and Practices of Government Corporations* (Cambridge, Mass.: MIT Press, 1978); Allan Tupper and G. Bruce Doern, eds., *Public Corporations and Public Policy in Canada* (Montreal: Institute for Research on Public Policy, 1981).

3. See especially, Mintzberg, *The Nature of Managerial Work, op. cit.*

4. Herbert Simon, *The New Science of Management Decision* (Englewood Cliffs, N.J.: Prentice Hall, rev. ed., 1977); David Nachmias and Ann Lennarson Greer, "Governance Dilemmas in an Age of Ambiguous Authority," in *Policy Sciences* 14 (1982); and Weinberg, "Public Management and Private Management: A Diminishing Gap?". For a critique of scientific management, see: Dwight Waldo, *The Administrative State* (New York: Homes and Meier, 2nd ed., 1984; originally published, 1948).

5. Adolph A. Berle and Gardiner C. Means, *The Modern Corporation and Private Property* (New York: MacMillan, 1935) and Edward S. Herman, *Corporate Control, Corporate Power* (Cambridge: Cambridge University Press, 1981).

6. Alfred D. Chandler, Jr., *The Visible Hand: The Managerial Revolution in American Business* (Cambridge, Mass.: Harvard University Press, 1977), p. 490.

7. Ronald H. Coase, "The Nature of the Firm," in *Economica* 386 (November 1937) and "Industrial Organization: A Proposal for Research," in Victor R. Fuchs, ed., *Policy Issues and Research Opportunities in Industrial Organization* (New York: National Bureau of Economic Research, 1972); Oliver E. Williamson, *Markets and Hierarchies: Analysis and Antitrust Implications* (New York: Free Press, 1975); John Kenneth Galbraith, *The New Industrial State* (Boston: Houghton Mifflin, 2nd ed., 1971); Lindblom, *Politics and Markets*; and Kenneth J. Arrow, *The Limits of Organization* (New York: W.W. Norton, 1974).

8. Richard R. Nelson and Sidney G. Winter, *An Evolutionary Theory of Economic Change* (Cambridge: Harvard University Press, 1982), pp. 266–272.

9. Gene Wunderlich, "Land Ownership: A Status of Facts," in *Natural Resources Journal* 19:1 (January, 1979), p. 113.

10. Charles Lindblom, *Politics and Markets, op. cit.,* p. 214.

11. Williamson, *Markets and Hierarchies, op. cit.,* pp. 135–136, 175–176.

12. Robert H. Hayes and William J. Abernathy, "Managing Our Way to Economic Decline," *Harvard Business Review* (July-August, 1980); Robert H. Hayes and David A. Garvin, "Managing as if Tomorrow Mattered," *Harvard Business Review* (May-June, 1982); Thomas Friedman and Paul Solman, "Is American Management Too Selfish?" in *Forbes* (January 17, 1983).

13. Albert Hirschman, *Exit, Voice and Loyalty: Responses to Decline in Firms, Organizations and States* (Cambridge: Harvard University Press, 1970); Oliver E. Williamson, "The Economics of Internal Organization: Exit and Voice in Relation to Markets and Hierarchies," in *American Economic Review* 66:2, Proceedings Issue (May 1976).

14. Robert N. Anthony and John Dearden, *Management Control Systems* (Homewood, Il: Irwin, 4th ed., 1980), chapter 16; Anthony and Herzlinger, *Management Control in Nonprofit Organizations*.

15. Henry Mintzberg, *The Structuring of Organizations: A Synthesis of the Research* (Englewood Cliffs, NJ: Prentice-Hall, 1979), p. 428; Herbert Kaufman, *The Forest Ranger: A Study in Administrative Behavior* (Baltimore: Johns Hopkins Press for Resources for the Future, 1960).

16. Jonathan R. T. Hughes, *The Governmental Habit: Economic Controls from Colonial Times to the Present* (New York: Basic Books, 1977).

17. *Ibid.*, p. 238.
18. John Mercer and Michael A. Goldberg, "Value Differences and their Meaning for Urban Development in Canada and the U.S.A.," paper presented to the Comparative Urban History Conference on Canadian-American Urban Development, University of Guelph, Guelph, Ontario, August 24–28, 1982.
19. Robert H. Haveman, *The Economics of the Public Sector* (New York: Wiley, 2nd ed., 1976), pp. 4, 8.
20. Jeffrey Sonnenfeld, *Corporate Views of the Public Interest: Perceptions of the Forest Products Industry* (Boston: Auburn House, 1981). See also Frank Schnidman, ed., *The Approval Process: Recreation and Resort Development Experience* (Urban Land Institute and Lincoln Institute of Land Policy, 1983); and the author's other chapter in the present volume.
21. Roberts and Bluhm, *The Choices of Power: Utilities Face the Environmental Challenge, op. cit.*
22. Indian tribes retain title to 0.3 percent of Canada's land area and 2.6 percent of U.S. land areas. For the purposes of discussion here, Indian lands are included in the public category.
23. *Canada Yearbook*, 1981–1982 (Ottawa: Authority of the Minister of Supply and Services), p. 27.
24. Hedley Swan, *Federal Lands: Their Use and Management*, Land Use in Canada Series, no. 11, Lands Directorate, Environment Canada (March 1978), p. 12. This total represents only 2.5 percent of federal lands.
25. Robert H. Nelson, "The Public Lands," chapter 2 in Paul R. Portney, ed., *Current Issues in Natural Resource Policy* (Washington, D.C.: Resources for the Future, 1982), table 2–1.
26. U.S. Department of Commerce, *Statistical Abstract of the United States*; John Pekkanen, "The Land, Part 1: Who Owns America?" *Town and Country* (May, 1983).
27. Figures provided by the National Recreation and Parks Association. Municipal lands are about one percent of U.S. land area, and a considerably smaller proportion of Canadian land area.
28. The figures on private landownership are from: *Canada Yearbook*, 1981–1982, p. 27; and James A. Lewis, *Landownership in the United States, 1978*, Agriculture Information Bulletin no. 435, Economic Research Service, U.S. Department of Agriculture, p. 3.
29. Lands Directorate, Environment Canada, *Land Use in Canada: Report of the Interdepartmental Task Force on Land-Use Policy* (January, 1980), p. 7; G. M. Bonnor, *Canada's Forest Inventory 1981* (Ottawa: Canadian Forestry Service, Environment Canada, 1982); *Canada Yearbook*, 1981–1982, p. 363. About 6 percent of Canada's timberlands are in private hands.
30. Gene Wunderlich, "Landownership: A Status of Facts," *op. cit.*, p. 100; Lewis, *Landownership in the United States*, p. 27; and Forest Service, U.S. Department of Agriculture, *The Private Forest-Land Owners of the United States*, Resource Bulletin WO–1 (1982).
31. Wunderlich, "Landownership," *ibid.*, p. 103.
32. Environment Canada, *For Land's Sake* (1980), p. 26. A similar figure for all urban uses can be found in: Statistics Canada, *Perspective Canada II, A Compendium of Social Statistics*, 1977.
33. Christopher K. Leman, "To Visit is to Preserve," in *Exchange*, Newsletter of the Land Trust Exchange (Winter, 1983–84).
34. Lewis, *Landownership, op. cit.*, p. 3. Equivalent research on Canadian lands has not been done, but see the next footnote.
35. Gene Wunderlich, "The Facts of Agriculture Leasing," in J. Peter De Braal and Gene Wunderlich eds., *Rent and Rental Practices in U.S. Agriculture*, Economic Research

Service, U.S. Department of Agriculture, 1983; Linda K. Lee, *Linkages between Landow-nership and Rural Land*, Agricultural Information Bulletin 454, Economic Research Service, United StatesDA, p. 5; and Arthur B. Daugherty and Robert C. Otte, *Farmland Ownership in the United States*, Economic Research Service, United StatesDA, Staff Report no. AGES 830311, p. 11. Again, equivalent research on Canadian lands has not been done. However, rough estimates by the B.C. Assessment Authority suggest that not more than 10 percent of land there is under lease. The difference is attributable to the relative scarcity of private farmland in Canada.

36. Information provided by Empire State Building Associates.

37. Although public land ownership is sometimes derided as socialism, "rentierism" would be a more accurate, if a less polemically satisfying term. Descriptions of the various arrangements for use of public lands can be found in: Christopher K. Leman, "The Revolution of the Saints: The Ideology of Privatization and its Consequences for the Public Lands," in Adrien Gamache, ed., *Selling the Federal Forests* (Seattle: College of Forest Resources, University of Washington, 1984); and the author's other chapter in the present volume.

38. The Weyerhaeuser Company, *1984 Annual Report*, p. 60.

39. A useful discussion is: Richard Almy, et.al., *Separated Rights in Real Estate*, Economic Research Service, United StatesDA, (1982).

40. Lewis, "Landownership," *op. cit.*, p. 5. Figures on the distribution of wealth and income in the two countries are strikingly similar.

41. The U.S. figures are from Jay O'Laughlin and Paul V. Ellefson, *New Diversified Entrants Among U.S. Wood-Based Companies: A Study of Economic Structure and Corporate Strategy*, Station Bulletin 541-1982, Forestry Series 37, Agriculture Experiment Station, University of Minnesota, pp. 18, 20. The Canadian figures were compiled from the provincial governments or the companies. The largest North American private landowner ever was the Hudson's Bay Company which owned much of the Canadian West. However, governments took back much of this land and most of the rest was sold.

42. John Pekkanen, "The Land, Part 2: What Does the Future Hold?" *Town and Country* (June, 1983), p. 95; O'Laughlin and Ellefson, *New Diversified Entrants, op. cit.*, p. 15; "Canada's Top 100 Oil and Gas Producers," in *Oil Week* (June 17, 1985), p. 14. Landownership figures cited elsewhere in this chapter do not include offshore acres.

43. Nelson, "The Public Lands," *op. cit.*, p. 23.

44. Elliot J. Feldman and Jerome Milch, *The Politics of Canadian Airport Development: Lessons for Federalism* (Durham: Duke University Press, 1982), chapters 3–6; John Brigham's chapter of the present book discusses the weaker constitutional protections for property in Canada.

45. Michael A. Goldberg and Peter Horwood, *Zoning: Its Cost and Relevance for the 1980's* (Vancouver: The Fraser Institute, 1980), pp. 11–19.

3

Evaluating Urban Land Use and Development

Michael A. Goldberg

Land, including the full spectrum of property rights, controls by all levels of government, and associated social and cultural values, differs dramatically between the United States and Canada. Urban areas are salient manifestations of different values and institutions, for they are the products of different patterns in the development, management, and use of land. In this chapter I will identify at the national level critical social, economic and political differences between Canada and the United States before assessing differences at the urban level in form, demography, transportation, and public and private economies. There is a direct correlation between the different values and institutions that govern society and the state and the observed differences in the cities of Canada and the United States.

Despite the vast range of possible comparisons between Canada and the United States, it is possible through judicious selection to suggest the more fundamental and meaningful differences that affect land use and urban development in the two countries. I will summarize these differences under four headings, embracing political institutions and attitudes, social values, economic systems, and approaches to property.

Politics

Canadian and American political and constitutional histories are very different. Thirteen North American colonies rebelled against the United Kingdom. The two other North American colonies, that became Canada, did not. The rebellious colonies wrote a constitution seeking at once to protect their separate identities while providing for a common defense and nationhood. Identities were preserved through federalism; nationhood was created through common rights and a hostility toward government. The colonies that did not rebel continued to accept British rule and adopted federalism only as a convenient reconciliation of French and English antagonism. The supremacy of Parliament guaranteed the repudiation of any written constitution and any entrenchment of individual rights.

The Canadian Fathers of Confederation, convening in 1867 to author the British North America Act, blamed the American Civil War on a federal system that they thought conferred excessive independence upon the several states. They preferred, therefore, a strong central government with weak provinces, and their preoccupation was with creating the Dominion of Canada and in allocating powers between the federal and provincial parliaments. They were not concerned with individual rights.

Although the Canadian and American federal systems appear convergent, especially in view of the 1982 patriation of a written Canadian constitution embracing a charter of rights, their histories have many fundamental elements of contrast. Despite the intentions of the Canadian founders, the provinces emerged as the key sources of power in

Table 3.1
Economic Liberalism, United States v. Canadian Legislators
(in percent)

Economic Liberalism*	United States		Canada	
	Federal	State	Federal	Provincial
High	21	25	56	63
Medium	55	53	43	37
Low	24	22	—	—
	(90)	(147)	(722)	(117)

*"Economic liberalism" is defined here by the following items: 'That government which governs least governs best' (reverse scored); 'Economic security for every man, woman and child is worth striving for, even if it means socialism'; 'if unemployment is high government should spend money to create jobs'; 'A national medicare plan is necessary to ensure that everyone received adequate health care'; 'More federal aid to education desirable if we are going to adequately meet present and future educational needs in this country'.

Source: Robert Presthus, ed., *Cross-National Perspectives: United States and Canada* (Leiden: E. J. Brill, 1977), p. 13.

Canadian politics, and centralizing tendencies in the late twentieth century have encountered important institutional and attitudinal obstacles. The most notable consequence for our purposes is the limited role of the Canadian federal government in urban affairs, which is in contrast to the dominant position of the United States government in shaping cities.[1]

The reign of parliaments has entrusted Canadian provincial legislatures with great urban authority. Other branches of government, including especially the judiciary, have figured more significantly in the United States.[2] Canadians tend to trust government more than Americans, and have greater faith in the integrity and performance of civil servants.[3] Therefore, Canadians more readily accept government involvement in the economy and in urban development,[4] and Canadian politicians are readier to act than their American counterparts (see Table 3.1). Canadians are also inclined to permit public servants to use their own best judgment, whereas Americans engage in heavy lobbying.[5]

Society

Differences in social values inevitably are the product of myth as well as reality. Although one cannot prove or disprove whether Americans are essentially more racist than Canadians, or Canadians more deferential, for example, it is possible to identify what Canadians and Americans believe about themselves, and to some extent about each other.

The abiding Canadian myth of social integration is in the image of a mosaic, or a tapestry of many colors blending into a single national expression while preserving each for its own peculiar and independent beauty. According to this myth, Canadians encourage the preservation of ethnic and racial differences in an expanding multicultural and multiracial society.

The abiding American myth is characterized by the melting pot, with a deep-seated suspicion of differences and puzzlement over the retention of old ways and customs. Immigrants have wanted to fashion themselves into the common culture; those reluctant about such change have had to be remade into Americans. That common culture, moreover, requires rejection of lands, cultures and societies left behind where opportunities are few. In the United States, Horatio Alger promises rewards for hard work.

The Canadian myth has concrete manifestation in state financing of distinct religious and language schools. The American separation of church and state, by contrast, has left fee-paying parents without even a tax break if they choose to educate their children under non-state auspices. There are notable neighborhood differences that result from such contrasts in educational arrangements.

Whereas for many scholars and commentators the United States celebrates the individual,[6] group orientation more closely characterizes Canada's public philosophy.[7] Some believe that the public interest or good has become as important as the individual good in Canadian life.[8]

Whatever the reality, Canadians appear more racially tolerant than Americans.[9] More important, however, is the profound difference in racial mix. American cities, often noted for racial violence, are marked by populations sometimes divided in half demographically by race. The dominant white population of Canadian cities can feel no threat or challenge from other racial groups and therefore may espouse more tolerant views.[10] Canada has escaped much of the American social disruption and violence over race.

The Canadian public philosophy equates antisocial behavior with violence against oneself. Indeed, one reasonable hypothesis is that proper behavior is simply easier to instill in Canadians than in Americans,[11] who seem to require more laws. As Myrdal observed, "To demand and legislate all sorts of laws against this or that is just as much part of American freedom as to disobey the laws when they are enacted."[12] However, an alternative hypothesis advanced by Friedenberg accuses Canadians of being more deferential for no good reason and at the price of freedom.[13]

Whatever theory may provide explanation, there is apparent consensus that Canadians are more deferential than Americans. This social proclivity contributes to an acceptance of an active state perceived as serving the public interest.

Economics

Attitudes and Scale. Whereas in the United States the primacy of private enterprise and initiative in principle is unchallenged, in Canada, government typically is in partnership with private interests. Despite many cases of state intervention in the United States, even under "liberal" Democratic administrations, government's role in economic and social issues has not approached the level it has in Canada. And despite encouragement of private enterprise in Canada, the partnership often is dissolved in favor of market intervention defending the public interest.[14] Still, "big government" is acceptable in the United States under some circumstances—especially military expenditures, infrastructure for regional development, and tax incentives for business*—and private home ownership for two-thirds of all Canadian households is but one indication of the viability of Canada's private sector. Indeed, according to Canadian Ambassador Allan Gotlieb, "The fact is that in Canada as in the United States, the private sector has been and will remain the driving force behind economic development."[15]

The United States' population and gross national product are approximately ten times as large as Canada's; such scale differences allow the American economy to be more self-contained and sustained. American manufacturers can operate plants of sufficient size to realize economies of scale and density from the American marketplace alone. Exports and imports represent less than one-tenth of the gross national product, whereas they comprise more than 25 percent in Canada.

A qualitative consequence of these quantitative differences is in goods traded. Canadian exports are dominated by resource-based materials and imports are dominated by manufactures. The situation is reversed in the United States. Despite its high standard of living and remarkable growth over the past century, Clement calls the Canadian economy still only "semideveloped."[16]

Financial Institutions and Savings. The British North America Act conferred upon the Canadian federal government sole responsibility for money and banking. In the United States, the several states are free to regulate banks.

Whereas in the United States banks can be formed quite easily under state charters, in Canada only Parliament can charter banks. However, Canada's banks are free to create as many branches as they choose anywhere across Canada, while American bank branch expansion is dictated by the U.S. Controller of the Currency. Consequently, there are many more banks in the U.S. (15,412 compared to 15 in Canada), although there are more branches per capita in Canada.[17] And despite the conventional factor of ten when comparing the two economies, American bank assets exceeded Canada's in 1983 by a factor of only 6.6,

---

*Whereas the total of public works expenditures on infrastructure does not rival that on military expenditures (which have been of tremendous importance to the domestic economy and certain cities in the urban system), they are not insignificant. The latest and perhaps most extreme case is the 234-mile Tennessee-Tombigbee Waterway. Its proponents claim that it will be a major asset to regional economic development and urban growth in the Gulf region; the impact on Mobile near the mouth of the Tombigbee is already considerable. By its 1985 opening, the project was estimated to cost $1.9 billion in public expenditures.

Table 3.2
Book Value, Ownership and Control of Capital Employed in Canadian Nonfinancial Industries, Selected Years

	Investment Owned In			Percentage of Capital Employed Owned In		
			Other			
	Canada	*U.S.*	*Countries*			*Other*
	$	*$*	*$*			*Countries*
Item and Year	*billion*	*billion*	*billion*	*Canada*	*U.S.*	
Manufacturing						
1971	12.7	11.7	2.3	47	44	9
1975	20.3	17.0	3.4	50	42	8
1979	32.8	24.3	4.9	53	39	8
1982						
Petroleum & Natural Gas						
1971	5.6	6.5	1.5	41	48	11
1975	9.0	8.6	2.2	46	43	11
1979	18.9	14.1	3.5	52	38	10
1982						
Mining & Smelting						
1971	3.1	3.4	0.7	43	47	10
1975	4.0	4.4	1.1	42	46	12
1979	7.1	5.0	1.9	51	36	13
1982						
Railways						
1971	5.1	0.4	0.5	85	7	8
1975	6.0	0.6	0.5	85	9	6
1979	4.6	1.1	0.7	71	18	11
1982						
Other Utilities						
1971	19.2	3.9	0.5	81	17	2
1975	29.0	6.5	1.9	77	17	6
1979	47.6	11.4	5.0	74	18	8
1982						
Total						
1971	64.6	22.3	6.2	66	28	6
1975	98.1	39.4	9.8	67	27	6
1979	156.4	59.4	17.3	67	26	7
1982						

Sources: a) Statistics Canada, Canada's International Investment Position (1979 and 1980), 1983, Cat. No. 67-202, pp. 96–102.
b) Canada Yearbook, 1980–81 (Ottawa, Ont.: Minister of Supply and Services), 1982, pp. 882–883.

	Control						
Investment Controlled In			Percentage of Capital Employed Controlled In			Total Capital Employed $ billion	
Canada $ billion	U.S. $ billion	Other Countries $ billion	Canada	U.S.	Other Countries		
11.2	11.7	3.8	42	44	14	26.7
18.1	17.2	5.5	44	42	14	40.7
30.5	24.4	7.1	49	39	12	62.1
			51	38	11	
3.1	8.3	2.2	23	61	16	13.6
5.1	11.8	2.9	26	59	15	19.8
17.3	14.7	4.6	47	40	13	36.6
			55	35	10	
2.1	4.3	0.8	29	59	12	7.2
3.8	4.4	1.3	40	46	14	9.5
6.9	5.1	2.0	49	37	14	14.0
			57	31	12	
6.0	0.1	—	98	2	—	6.0
7.0	0.1	—	99	1	—	7.1
6.3	0.1	—	99	1	—	6.4
			99	1	—	
21.9	1.0	0.7	93	4	3	23.6
35.9	1.5	0.1	96	4	—	37.4
61.7	2.2	0.1	96	4	—	64.0
			97	3	—	
62.7	26.9	8.5	64	27	9	98.0
99.2	37.4	10.7	67	26	7	147.3
168.1	50.0	15.0	72	22	6	233.1
			74	20	6	

in part because Canadians since 1974 have been saving more.[18] The key consequence of these differences is the relatively greater importance of banks in the Canadian economy, both as sources of money and as central institutions.

Role of the Public Sector. Governments are important economic actors. In 1982 all levels of government in Canada spent 47.3 percent of GNP or US$5,544 per capita. All levels of governments in the U.S. spent US$5,040 per capita, or in the aggregate 38 percent of GNP. Whereas governments in both countries thus are big spenders, 24.4 percent more is spent proportionally in Canada, and spending patterns differ dramatically. Defense and education accounted for more than one-third of U.S. federal spending in 1980, compared to a 40 percent expenditure on social affairs in Canada (in 1982–83).[19]

Canadian governments at all levels engage in economic activities that would be considered inappropriate in the U.S. Crown corporations such as Air Canada, CNR, Pacific Western Airlines, and PetroCan are salient examples. According to Herschel Hardin, Americans have demon-strated a particular and unparalleled ability in the realm of private enterprise, but Canada's "genius" with respect to economic organization and innovation lies in public enterprise.[20]

Foreign Ownership. The United States is the principal purchaser of Canadian exports (primarily raw and semi-finished materials), the principal seller of Canada's imports (primarily manufactured and finished goods), and the principal foreign owner of Canadian productive capacity. The share of foreign ownership of non-financial corporate businesses in the U.S. is so small that it is scarcely a concern. Tables 3.2 and 3.3 display the contrast with Canada.

Coping with the apparent American control of the Canadian economy has been a constant theme of Canadian nationalism. But whereas Liberal federal governments were anxious to protect Canada against American investments, the Progressive Conservative government elected in 1984 has been trying to attract them. The role of foreign ownership is paramount in the Canadian economy, although the direct impact on the character and governance of urban areas is difficult to specify.

Property. Land tenure (ownership) patterns diverge dramatically between Canada and the United States (see Tables 3.4 and 3.5). In Canada, 90 percent of all land is held by governments (both federal and provincial), whereas in the United States land ownership is largely (58 percent) pri-

Table 3.3
Book Value of Foreign Direct Investment in the U.S., by Source, 1937–1982

Year	Total (millions of dollars)	Percentage		
		Canada	United Kingdom	Netherlands
1937	1,882	24.6	44.3	9.5
1941	2,312	22.9	30.8	14.5
1950	3,391	30.3	34.4	9.8
1955	5,076	30.4	34.5	12.1
1960	6,910	28.0	32.5	13.7
1965	8,797	27.1	32.4	14.8
1970	13,270	23.5	31.1	16.2
1975	27,662	19.3	22.9	19.3
1980	68,351	14.7	17.9	24.7
1982	101,844	9.6	22.9	21.1

Sources: Historical Statistics of the United States, Series U47-74; Statistical Abstract of the United States, 1984 edition.

Table 3.4
Land Tenure, United States, Ownership of Land by Class: 1959 to 1978 (in millions of acres, except percent)

Year	Total[1]	Private Land[2]	Indian Land[3]	Total	Federal[4]	State[4]	County and Municipal
1959	2,271	1,332	53	886	765	103	18
1969	2,264	1,317	50	897	763	114	20
1974	2,264	1,316	51	897	761	116	20
1978	2,264	1,315	52	897	742	135	20
Percent distribution	100.0	58.1	2.3	39.6	32.7	6.0	0.9

[1] Changes in total land area are due to variable methods and materials used in periodic remeasurements, and to the construction of artificial reservoirs.
[2] Land owned by individuals, partnerships, and corporations.
[3] Managed in trust by Bureau of Indian Affairs.
[4] Changes in federal and state land holdings mainly represent federal land grants to the State of Alaska. Part of the change indicated after 1974 may have occurred prior to 1974.
Source: Statistical Abstract of the United States, 1984 Edition, page 203.

vate. As Richard Hofstadter noted, in the minds of the American Founding Fathers, "liberty was linked not to democracy but to property."[21]

Property rights are not vested with the individual property owner in Canada, but rather remain with the Crown. The Fifth and Fourteenth

Table 3.5
Land Tenure, Canada, Ownership of Land by Class, Province, and Territory: 1978

Item		Province or Territory											
	Nfld.	PEI	NS	NB	Que.	Ont.	Man.	Sask.	Alta.	BC	YT	NWT	Canada
Federal Crown lands other than national parks, Indian reserves and forest experiment stations	440	16	181	1,489	1,178[1]	1,158	259	5,452	2,844[5]	904	513,191	3,340,848	3,867,960
National parks	2,339	21	1,331	433	790[2]	1,922	2,978	3,875	54,084	4,690	22,015	35,690	130,168
Indian reserves	—	8	114	168	779[3]	6,703	2,145	6,322	6,566	3,390	5	135	26,335
Federal forest experiment stations	—	—	—	91	28	103	—	—	59	—	—	—	281
Privately owned land or land in process of alienation from the Crown	17,992	4,927	37,354	39,754	119,420	119,023	138,079	246,939	183,521	55,040	170	73	962,292
Provincial or territorial area other than provincial parks and forests[4]	382,638	442	2,652	28,495	674,819	819,261	481,951	35,481	63,313[6]	539,280	943	2,937	3,104,212
Provincial parks	805	32	126	215	130,000	48,412	10,650	4,944	7,700	41,629	—	—	244,513
Provincial forests	303	211	13,732	2,792	613,667	—	14,025	348,887	343,0988[7]	303,663	—	—	1,640,378
Total Area	404,517	5,657	55,490	73,437	1,540,680	1,068,582	650,087	651,900	661,185	948,596	536,324	3,379,683	9,976,138

[1] Includes Gatineau Park (351.1 km²) and Quebec Battlefields Park (0.93 km²) both under federal jurisdiction but not national parks. Excludes harbours of Gaspe, Chicoutimi, Quebec and I'Islet, Trois Rivieres, Montreal and Sorel (under federal-provincial negotiation), and CNR properties.

[2] Includes Forillon and Mauricie parks.

[3] Includes reserves existing before 1851: Maria, Lorette, Becancour, Odanak, Cauchnawaga and Saint-Regis. Excludes land transferred provisionally under the James Bay and Northern Quebec Agreement (November 1975) and North-Eastern Quebec Agreement (January 1978).

[4] Includes freshwater area.

[5] Excludes Department of National Defence agreement areas (Primrose Lake, Camp Wainwright) and areas leased for agricultural experiment stations (Manyberries, Stavely).

[6] Includes lands held by the Department of National Defence under agreement with Alberta (Camp Wainwright) and areas leased for agricultural experiment stations (Manyberries, Stavely).

[7] Includes the area held by the Department of National Defence under agreement with Alberta (Primrose Lake Air Weapons Range).

Source: Canada Yearbook, 1980–81, page 27.

Amendments to the United States Constitution guarantee property rights. The Canadian Charter of Rights and Freedoms (1982) explicitly does not protect property rights (which John Brigham discusses in more detail in Chapter 9, leaving greater and more stringent land controls available to government in Canada than in the U.S.

Local and provincial officials in Canada also exercise greater discretion in interpreting and enforcing land use laws. For example, the British Columbia Limited Access Highways Act gives the Minister of Highways the right to expropriate up to 5 percent of an individual's property fronting on a provincial limited access highway without any right to compensation. Such an act would be unconstitutional in the U.S., yet analogous discretion can be exercised in Canada on zoning, historic and heritage building designation, agricultural lands and even on building design. The only control is self-imposed by the provincial or local government, and there is no appeal to higher authority.

Summary

There is a much greater emphasis in the United States on individual goals and achievements when compared with the generally more collectivist values of Canadian society.[22] These value differences have been associated with a much greater acceptance of the role of government in economic affairs in Canada than in the United States, especially noticeable in the degree of control exercised by local and provincial governments over the urban development process, and the absence of any "constitutional" barriers to such controls.

As the Canadian myth of a mosaic might predict, Canadians seem more tolerant of ethnically mixed neighborhoods than are Americans. Canadians hold cities and city life in generally higher regard than do Americans, doubtless because of differences in crime rates but also because of a strong antiurban strain in the American character.[23] Finally, within this more favorable perception of cities, central areas in Canada hold a special place, being seen as having a higher socioeconomic status when compared with suburbs, again a dramatic contrast with American views of central cities.[24]

Urban Development

The focus here is on metropolitan centers,[25] to overcome problems of comparative equivalence[26] even at the risk of a bias toward large cities. In the United States, the statistical unit most widely used and for which the largest data base is readily available is the standard metropolitan statistical area (SMSA).[27] In Canada, the corresponding unit is the census metropolitan area (CMA). But these units are defined with different core population thresholds of 50,000 and 100,000, respectively. To obtain an equivalent to the SMSAs of between 50,000 to 100,000, selected Canadian census agglomerations (CA) have been included if the core city is over 50,000 in population. This method yielded a total set of 40 CMAs and CAs in Canada (1976) and 277 SMSAs in the United States (1975).[28] Using the municipality as the basic spatial unit, the CMAS and CAs are, in general, smaller in area and more precisely bounded than their U.S. county-defined SMSAs.* This problem is partly offset by analyzing the constituent parts of a metropolitan area—the central city and the suburban ring.

Urban Form and Access

An extensive cross-national analysis of population density gradients in Canadian and American metropolitan areas found that either over time or cross-sectionally, Canadian urban regions exhibited consistently higher central densities (twice as dense, in fact) with density gradients that were at least as steep as those in the U.S. By this measure, at least, Canadian cities are more compact and take a different form from cities in the United States.[29] The population density gradient has been widely employed as an indicator of urban form, measuring population concentrations and dispersion within an urban area by linking the distribution of population to the nature and geography of the housing stock.

Closely related to urban form are the physical characteristics of urban transportation systems and the travel behavior of urban dwellers. The dominant transportation feature of the modern city is the expressway. Using the number of expressway lane miles per capita as a standardized measure of capacity, there were just over four times as many lane miles of urban expressway for each metropolitan resident in the U.S. as there were in Canada.[30] Hence, U.S. metropolitan areas clearly are more oriented to the automobile. Canadians show roughly 2.5 times more transit use per capita than Americans despite roughly similar transit

---

*One alternative would have been to use a different U.S. census geographic unit—the Urbanized Area. This is far less likely to be overbounded than the SMSA. However, the range of data items which are available for Urbanized Areas is far less compared to that for the SMSAs. For this research, we accepted some degree of overbounding in the comparisons to permit access to the desired range of data items. A cross-national comparison on certain variables using Urbanized Areas and the CMAs and CAs would be worthwhile, however.

coverage of the metropolitan area (80 percent in Canada versus 74 percent in the U.S.). Fully one-quarter of the Canadian population uses public transportation, compared to the one-eighth of Americans. Indeed, nearly 80 percent of an American sample rely on automobiles to go to work, compared to 66 percent in Canada, and Americans travel about 25 percent further than Canadians, even if overall commuting times are similar.[31]

Urban Population and Social Characteristics

Decline in metropolitan growth, and even absolute population loss in some instances, have been widely discussed in the United States. In earlier research, a pronounced difference was discovered between the two countries during the 1960s. A greater proportion of Canadian metropolitan areas experienced substantial population increases (over 20 percent) and proportionately fewer places suffered an absolute loss.[32] In the central cities, these differences were even more marked (for

Table 3.6
Distribution of Percentage Change in Dwelling Units (Households)
in Central Cities: 1970/71–1980/81

Percentage Change Cumulative	USA			Canada		
	n	*Percent*	*Cumulative Percent*	*n*	*Percent*	*Cumulative Percent*
100 or	1	0.4		0		
90 to 99	1	0.4	0.8	0		
80 to 89	6	2.2	3.0	0		
70 to 79	3	1.1	4.1	1	2.9	
60 to 69	7	2.5	6.6	0		2.9
50 to 59	13	4.7	11.3	0		2.9
40 to 49	19	6.9	18.2	8	23.5	26.4
30 to 39	27	9.8	28.0	7	20.6	47.0
20 to 29	50	18.1	46.1	9	26.5	73.5
10 to 19	52	18.8	64.9	7	20.6	94.1
0 to 9	72	26.1	91.0	2	5.9	100.0
0 to −9	22	8.0	99.0			
−10 or >	3	1.1	100.1			
		Median 11.5			Median 29.7 (26.7)[a]	
		Mean 22.7			Mean 30.1 (27.1)[a]	

[a] The 1971 base data have not been adjusted to ensure comparable area units with 1981. In some cases, this will inflate the amount of change. Cities where this is a major problem (e.g., Winnipeg) are omitted. To compensate, the median and mean are adjusted downward by a factor of 10 percent. The U.S.-Canadian differences remain striking.

Source: *U.S. Census of Population*, Standard Metropolitan Statistical Areas and Standard Consolidated Statistical Areas PC80–S1–5; Statistics Canada, unpublished data (preliminary).

example, almost 40 percent of U.S. central cities lost population compared to only 8 percent in Canada).*

Such Canadian growth suggests more migration into urban areas, and indeed through the 1970s household change was greater than in the United States (Table 3.6). There is more variability in the American data (except for the suburban ring), but there was an absolute loss of households in 15 percent of the central cities. As households leave, service enterprises follow or fail with a decline in effective demand. The cumulative effect is to erode the fiscal base of central city administrations. Over the 1971–1981 decade, no Canadian city exhibited this loss.

Using a ratio of central city to metropolitan household income, the U.S./Canadian difference in either the mean or the median household income ratios is considerable (see Table 3.7 for distributions). While

Table 3.7
Central City to metropolitan Area Income Ratios

	USA (1970)		Canada (1971)	
Ratio	Median Household Income	Mean Household Income	Median Household Income	Mean Household Income
Under 59	1.4			
60–69	4.3	1.0		
70–79	19.5	8.1		
80–89	22.9	20.5	13.8	10.0
90–99	31.0	41.0	44.8	36.7
100–109	15.2	24.8	41.4	53.3
110–119	1.9	2.4		
120–129	1.4	1.8		
130–139	1.0	0.5		
140–149	0.5			
150–159	1.0			
Mean	91.1	93.2	97.6	98.0
SD	16.3	12.1	5.5	5.1
n	217[a]	217[a]	29[b]	30

[a] Since 23 SMSA's in New England are excluded from the analysis and there are 37 SMSA's formed since 1970, then the n is 277 − 60 or 217.

[b] No data are available for one case.

Sources: U.S. Bureau of the Census, *Census of Population and Housing: 1970*, Census Tracts, Final Reports, PHC (1) Series, Table P–4. Statistics Canada, *Census of Canada: 1971*; Population and Housing Characteristics by Census Tracts, Catalogue 95-700 Series.

*While experience in the mid-1980s in some U.S. cities, such as Boston, may appear to negate this assertion, there has not been any general return to the central city in the United States despite selective and hopeful individual exceptions to the contrary.

the Canadian cities form almost equal groups, they are clustered around the value of 98. Spatial disparities in affluence are far more sharply defined in the U.S., where 30 percent of cities have ratios of less than 90 for mean household income, rising to 48 percent for median household income. In Canada, the equivalents are 10 and 14 percent, respectively.

The demand for specific types of housing in particular locations varies according to stages in a life cycle, comparing the distribution of one and two person households (encompassing the elderly and a high proportion of young adults) and households of families with children still at home (Table 3.8). Family households are more prevalent in Canadian cities, particularly the central cities; the difference in the means for the metropolitan areas is statistically significant.

Of course, a dominant difference in urban populations is defined racially, but it may be important to consider two related features. First, the largely French-speaking cities of Quebec have attracted relatively few foreign immigrants, leaving them among the most homogeneous

Table 3.8
Household Structure

	USA (1970)			Canada (1971)		
Type	*Metro*	*Central City*	*Balance*	*Metro*	*Central City*	*Balance*
% of One Person Households:						
Mean	15.7	20.5	11.6	12.5	15.4	7.8
SD	3.3	4.5	3.8	3.4	5.7	3.9
n	217	217	215	32	32	27
$ of Two or Fewer Person Households:						
Mean	43.6	50.0	38.1	37.5	42.4	28.5
SD	6.0	6.6	10.4	6.1	9.4	11.9
n	217	217	215	32	32	28
$ of Households — Families with Children at Home:						
Mean	43.7	40.1	47.2	59.4	57.0	63.1
SD	5.6	6.7	11.3	5.4	11.5	17.5
n	217	217	215	32	32	29

Sources: U.S. Bureau of the Census, *Census of Population and Housing: 1970*, Census Tracts, Final Reports, PHC (1) Series, Table P–1, H–1. Statistics Canada, *Census of Canada: 1971*, Volume 2, Part 1, Catalogue 93-762, Tables 4 and 5, and Volume 2, Part 2, Catalogue 93-715, Tables 16 and 17.

of cities in Canada. And second, immigration has transformed some Canadian cities. Toronto, for example must now be characterized as multicultural.*[33]

The Urban Private Economy

Manufacturing. Within metropolitan areas, manufacturing plants and employment are proportionately more concentrated in Canadian central cities as a whole than in the U.S. (see Table 3.9). This difference is particularly marked in the medium sized urban areas of between 100,000 and one million people. In the million plus category, the differences are again small, with a slight tendency for manufacturing to be more concentrated in the U.S. central cities. Of course, manufacturing activity has been decentralizing within metropolitan areas in advanced market economies for some time, and urban Canada and the U.S. are no exception (see Table 3.10).

In Canada, manufacturing remains a predominantly metropolitan activity, with decentralization to suburban locations. In the U.S., however, substantial economic activity is relocating across regions and beyond metropolitan boundaries. There is obviously considerable central city growth, especially in smaller cities in regions favored by new investment.

Wholesaling. The need for low-cost land on which to expand and the increase in servicing by truck transportation rather than by rail have accelerated manufacturing decentralization. They also have affected wholesaling activity long associated with central cities, such as waterfronts and railroad terminals. Huge new suburban warehouses attest to the new locations of wholesaling throughout North America.

---

*What needs to be recognized, however, is that numerous immigrants are skilled, educated, and employable. This class of immigrant, favored by recent immigration policies, has no initial need of cheap housing in the inner city accessible to unskilled work in the city core, the traditional destination of the stereotypical immigrant and one from which he or she was expected to struggle up and out, both socially and geographically. Rather they head directly to the housing and employment opportunities afforded by the outer city.

The Canadian Census data illustrate this point. In 1981, for example, in three big city suburbs (Scarborough-Toronto, Surrey-Vancouver and Burlington-Hamilton) the percentage of the foreign born population that had entered Canada in the last two years was 6.0, 7.8 and 4.5 percent respectively. It is not unreasonable to infer that a substantial number moved immediately into these suburban municipalities, though this cannot be proven without survey evidence.

Table 3.9
Manufacturing Plants and Employment Showing Central City Share as Percent of Metropolitan Total (1972)

	Manufacturing Plants (City % Metro)		Manufacturing Employment (City % Metro)	
	$\bar{X}^1$	Median	$\bar{X}^1$	Median
Maritime	75.0	76.0	82.0^2	77.0^2
Quebec	59.0	56.0	54.3^2	54.5^2
Ontario	70.7	63.5	68.2^2	71.5^2
Prairie	97.0	95.0	88.3^2	79.5^2
British Columbia	58.0	50.0	57.7^2	45.6^2
New England	37.3	37.0	39.8	31.0
Mid-Atlantic	36.5	35.5	37.4	35.5
East North Central	53.8	53.7	64.9	62.5
West North Central	68.0	77.8	73.3	73.0
South Atlantic	50.7	50.5	48.6	47.5
East South Central	59.9	59.0	64.9	64.0
West South Central	71.0	73.0	71.5	72.5
Mountain	65.5	64.0	61.0	63.5
Pacific	49.3	44.3	49.7	46.0

$^1\bar{X}$ = Mean.
^{2}Maritime (3); Quebec (96); Ontario (12); Prairie (4); British Columbia (2).
Source: Michael A. Goldberg and John Mercer, *Continentalism Challenged: The Myth of the North American City* (Vancouver: The University of British Columbia Press, 1986).

Table 3.10
Change in Manufacturing Employment for Metropolitan Area, Central City and Balance, 1967–72, Showing Means ($\bar{X}$) and Medians (Md) Cross-Tabulated by Size of Central Metropolitan Area

		Metro		City		Balance	
		Canada	USA	Canada	USA	Canada	USA
Total	$\bar{X}$	9.6	6.96	−1.3	8.3	53.0	10.5
	Md	1.5	−6.7	−7.8	−10.5	22.0	9.3
Size							
>1M	$\bar{X}$	5.0	−3.0	−9.9	−6.8	16.9	2.4
	Md	6.0	−8.3	−8.0	−14.5	19.0	−3.8
15 to 1M	$\bar{X}$	−0.2	2.1	−9.2	5.4	19.9	11.5
	Md	−1.5	−4.8	−7.3	−9.0	22.0	11.8
.1 to .5	$\bar{X}$	3.7	9.7	−1.2	12.3	78.9	15.3
	Md	0.5	−6.6	−6.0	−9.5	27.5	−9.0
<100,000	$\bar{X}$		10.8	3.1	18.5		15.2
	Md		−7.5	−10.0	−12.0		28.0

Source: Goldberg and Mercer, 1986.

Despite the common trend, metropolitan deconcentration is proceeding at a much faster rate in the United States, leaving the central cities in an especially perilous situation (see Table 3.11). Whether one considers the location of wholesaling establishments, the incidence of sales or the distribution of wholesaling employment, Canadian central cities contain a significantly higher proportion of each than do American central cities.

There is a strong relationship to city size. In cities with population over one million, there is only a marginal difference between the U.S. and Canadian metropolitan areas in the degree of central city share.

Table 3.11
Central City Share (Means, Medians and Standard Deviations) in %. Metropolitan Area Wholesaling Establishments, Sales and Employment Cross-Tabulated by Metropolitan Area Size and by Central City Metropolitan Area Population Ratio

		Wholesaling (1972)					
		Establishments		Sales		Employment	
		C & M as %		C & M as %		C & M as %	
		Canada	USA	Canada	USA	Canada	USA
Total	X	76.8	61.0	80.3	64.2	80.7	65.6
	SD	15.7	18.7	15.6	20.87	15.7	19.4
	Md	72.2	—	80.8	—	78.5	—
Size							
>1M	X	53.4	49.9	56.9	51.7	50.4	53.7
	Md	60.0	—	63.0	—	55.0	—
.5 to 1M	X	66.0	57.3	73.8	62.0	70.7	63.2
	Md	66.5	—	77.5	—	64.5	—
.1 to .5M	X	81.2	61.9	83.8	65.5	85.6	67.1
	Md	81.0	—	82.5	—	86.5	—
<100,000	X	80.2	77.4	83.4	77.3	84.8	78.2
	Md	77.0	—	83.0	—	85.0	—
	Min Value	34.6	5.1	34.1	1.6	28.9	3.2
CC/M Pop. Ratio							
0.0–0.3	X	54.0	40.0	50.9	42.9	51.5	45.1
	Md	—	—	—	—	—	—
0.3–0.5	X	64.6	57.7	66.0	61.7	67.6	62.8
	Md	65.0	—	64.0	—	68.0	—
0.5–0.7	X	75.4	72.2	81.0	75.6	81.3	77.5
	Md	69.3	—	78.0	—	78.0	—
0.7–1.0	X	86.0	84.9	89.8	88.0	89.7	88.2
	Md	88.2	—	93.5	—	90.5	—

Source: Goldberg and Mercer, 1986.

But in each of the other size classes, the Canadian central city share is consistently higher, especially in the intermediate sized metropolitan centers. Furthermore, as city size declines the central city share of wholesaling systematically increases.

Table 3.12
Central City Share of Retail Sales (Both Means and Medians) in %
for 1966 (1967 U.S.) Cross-Tabulated by Metropolitan Area Size

		Sales					% Change in City Sales	
		Canada		USA			Canada, 1966–71	USA, 1967–72
		1966	1971	1967	1972			
	$\bar{X}$	78.8	76.3	64.4	60.7		40.9	45.0
	Md	80.5	72.5	65.5	60.8		38.5	43.8
						S	27.9	25.6
						Min	14.2	−4.4
						Max	122.0	150.0
Size								
1) >1M	$\bar{X}$	52.9	43.5	47.4	40.3		16.0	26.9
	Md	56.0	48.0	46.0	38.5		12.0	21.0
						S	8.3	20.8
						Min	10.1	−4.4
						Max	25.4	68.5
2) 0.5–1M	$\bar{X}$	72.4	64.3	56.5	50.1		29.9	35.2
	Md	74.5	64.5	55.0	44.0		21.5	32.0
						S	14.0	20.8
						Min	14.3	1.1
						Max	41.9	69.3
3) 0.1–0.5	$\bar{X}$	85.7	82.5	67.3	64.0		50.0	50.8
	Md	93.0	80.5	67.2	65.3		39.5	48.6
						S	23.8	26.3
						Min	23.8	−3.6
						Max	118.8	150.1
4) <100,000	$\bar{X}$	80.3	80.0	84.4	86.4		40.3	49.6
	Md	85.5	79.0	86.5	89.8		35.0	48.5
						S	27.9	15.6
						Min	14.0	7.1
						Max	122.4	83.8
% City		0.0– 0.3	0.3– 0.5	0.5– 0.7	0.7– 1.0			

Sales $\bar{X}$ (Md)	1966	1971	1967	1972
Canada	21.6(12.5)s=13	34.2(3.90)s=13	40.2(34.5)s=31	47.1(41.0)s=45
USA	40.6(37.3)s=32	51.0(32.3)s=21	55.5(51.8)s=22	56.9(56.0)s=17

Source: Goldberg and Mercer, 1986.

Retailing and Services. Retail outlets in older central residential areas have declined with population. A virtual explosion of new retailing opportunities has followed people into the burgeoning suburbs. In the U.S., this situation is epitomized by the contrast between the rows of empty, boarded-up and sometimes vandalized stores along inner city streets and the up-scale affluence of mammoth suburban shopping centers. These centers, when taken collectively across metropolitan areas, represent a significant challenge to the retailing function of the central business district, and such deconcentration again has progressed much faster in American metropolitan areas (see Table 3.12).

In the U.S., the central city retail share consistently increases as city size decreases. In Canada, however, the smallest cities have retail shares either smaller than or similar to those of larger cities, although this pattern does not follow for the median sales values for outlets. Since these smaller urban centers are overwhelmingly in Quebec and Ontario, one explanation might be that their central city retailing activity is "depressed" by the competitive attractions offered by accessible and much larger metropolitan central business districts such as Montreal

Table 3.13
Central City Share (Both by Means and Medians) in % of Metropolitan Area Service Activities, by Sales and by Establishments, Cross-Tabulated by Size of Metropolitan Area

| | | Sales City Share | | | | Establishments/City Share | |
| | | Canada | | USA | | Canada | USA |
		1966	1971	1967	1972	1971	1972
	$\bar{X}$	82.3	81.9	69.1	65.9	76.4	56.9 (−195)
	Md	83.5	81.0	70.8	67.9	74.0	55.6 (15.4)
Size							
1) >1M	$\bar{X}$	72.3	66.2	60.9	55.6	56.1	43.5 (17.6)
	Md	74.8	69.0	64.8	58.5	58.0	43.8 (14.2)
2) 0.5–1M	$\bar{X}$	75.9	71.6	64.6	61.8	66.1	50.5 (15.6)
	Md	71.5	69.5	63.3	57.0	63.5	44.0 (−19.5)
3) 0.1–0.5	$\bar{X}$	86.1	87.3	69.8	67.1	80.7	58.3 (−22.4)
	Md	92.0	87.8	71.1	68.9	77.0	57.7 (−19.3)
4) <100,000	$\bar{X}$	83.0	82.3	86.0	81.1	79.1	78.8 (−0.3)
	Md	84.5	81.0	89.0	86.2	76.0	82.0 (6)
Aggregate							
SD		14.0	14.0	21.0	19.0	16.0	19.0
Min		53.0	53.6	3.8	3.3	47.8	5.0

Source: Goldberg and Mercer, 1985.

for such smaller cities regardless of location does not support this geographical hypothesis, however, and local particularities are a more likely explanation.

The spatial distribution of business and personal services within metropolitan areas is broadly similar to that for retailing (see Table 3.13). Indeed, services are even more concentrated in the largest Canadian central business districts, although this difference between retailing and services tends to decrease with city size.

The Urban Public Economy

Local Government Structural Reforms. There are many more local governments in metropolitan areas of the U.S. than in Canada which fragment authority. According to an index for fragmentation measuring the number of municipalities in a metropolitan area per thousand population resident in municipally governed areas, the Canadian mean score is substantially lower (see Table 3.14). The scores in Canada are also less widely dispersed (note the standard deviations), indicating a greater homogeneity. The majority of Canadian scores are in the lower ranges of the distribution when compared to the U.S.; only 70 percent of American metropolitan areas have scores less than the maximum Canadian score.

Controlling for city size does not remove the difference. In every size class, the Canadian indices are substantially lower than the American. And, contrary to conventional wisdom, for both countries, municipal fragmentation tends to decline as the metropolitan population increases.

Local government fragmentation is considered an impediment to the successful management of metropolitan areas, but provincial actions since the mid-1960s have reduced fragmentation in Canada with no corresponding state action in the U.S. The two-tier federation of metropolitan Toronto is perhaps the most widely known example, but the most dramatic change came in Winnipeg where twelve municipalities disappeared at midnight on December 31, 1971, to be replaced by a single metropolitan-wide city government. The socialist provincial government in Manitoba did not hesitate to eliminate local units to achieve its own economic and political objectives, just as a nominally Conservative government in Ontario created metro Toronto in 1953 and then eliminated seven autonomous suburbs in a consolidation of the lower tier in 1967.

American political culture, encompassing a pervasive belief in local autonomy, coincides with procedural requirements, ostensibly demo-

Table 3.14
Distribution of Scores on the Index of Municipal Fragmentation[a]

I.M.F. Score	Cumulative Percent of Metropolitan Areas with Scores within the Specified Class	
	USA (1972)	Canada (1971)
0.000 to 0.014	10.0	26.5
0.015 to 0.025	20.0	50.0
0.026 to 0.039	30.0	73.5
0.040 to 0.054	40.0	82.4
0.055 to 0.064	50.0	88.2
0.065 to 0.079	60.0	91.2
0.080 to 0.102	70.0	100.0
0.103 to 0.121	80.0	100.0
0.122 to 0.163	90.0	100.0
0.164 to 0.434	100.0	100.0
	(n =264)[b]	(n = 34)
Mean	0.082*	0.031*
Std. Dev.	0.068	0.033

*Significant at 0.001 level.
[a] The index of municipal fragmentation is the ratio of the number of municipalities in a metropolitan area to the per thousand population resident in municipally governed areas. The higher the score the more fragmented an area is.
[b] There were 264 SMSAs in the U.S. in 1972.
Source: Calculated by authors from U.S. Bureau of the Census, 1972, *Census of Governments*, Volume 1, Governmental Oarganisation, Table 19, Local Governments and Public School Systems in Individual SMSA's: 1972; D. M. Ray et al., *Canadian Urban Trends* (Toronto: Copp Clark, 1976) Volume 1, National Perspective: Table A1.3.

cratic, that prohibit such reform. In contrast, in Canada, party discipline, the supremacy of Parliament and the Canadian belief in "peace, order and good government" combine to make metropolitan government reform much easier and more widespread.

Sources of Revenue. Cities get money through transfers from other governments, through their own taxes and through the sale of services. There is not a great deal of difference between American and Canadian cities in the share of total revenues deriving from intergovernmental sources, although Canadian metropolitan regions have shown a decline in transfer payments while the U.S. proportion was rising. However, there is a dramatic difference in the source of these intergovernmental transfers. Federal transfers as a proportion of total revenues and the federal share of all intergovernmental transfers are negligible in urban Canada, whereas they are of growing importance in the U.S., especially

Table 3.15
All Taxes as a Percentage of Total Revenues, Metropolitan Areas, Central Cities and Suburbs

	Canada				USA			
	1971		1976		1972		1977	
	Metro	*City*	*Metro*	*City*	*Metro*	*City*	*Metro*	*City*
Mean	42.8	63.4	43.0	38.5	45.2	49.4	39.4	41.0
Std. Dev.	7.5	17.5	11.0	15.1	10.2	12.6	10.7	12.2
Median	41.0	68.0	39.0	33.0	44.6	49.4	38.0	39.4
n	37.0	40.0	22.0	35.0	264.0	259.0	258.0	274.0
	Metropolitan Suburbs (or Balance of Metro Areas)							
Mean	30.5		37.6		44.7		39.2	
Std. Dev.	16.3		20.2		12.3		14.7	
Median	25.8		42.0		44.3		38.7	
n	37.0		17.0		259.0		256.0	

Source: Goldberg and Mercer, 1986.

for hard-pressed central cities.[34] Certainly, as a source of revenue, the federal government plays a far more pivotal role in American cities.

Taxes as a proportion of revenues have declined in both American and especially Canadian central cities (see Table 3.15). However, Canadian central cities also have experienced a decline in transfers as a proportion of gross revenues, suggesting that Canadian municipalities are making more use of nontax sources such as sales of services, licensing charges, etc.

Expenditures. Although data sources are inadequate to allow very many reliable comparisons about expenditures, American cities clearly allocate

Table 3.16
Expenditures on Protection as a Percentage of Total Expenditures, Central Cities

	Canada		USA	
	1971	1976	1972	1977
Mean	15.3	14.3	23.3	20.8
Std. Dev.	5.4	6.4	9.9	8.4
Median	14.6	13.3	22.5	20.0
n	37.0	37.0	258.0	275.0

Source: Goldberg and Mercer, 1986.

Table 3.17
Violent Crime Per 100,000 Population

	Canada (1976)			USA (1975)		
	Metro	City	Balance	Metro	City	Balance
Mean	93.3	107.4	58.8	436.4	656.0	275.4
Std. Dev.	51.7	94.4	35.5	232.0	455.3	193.8
n	31.0	26.0	17.0	219.0	243.0	212.0

1. Violent Crime Rates by City Size

Size Class						
Over 1 mil.	181.0	468.0	66.0	611.8	1164.8	327.9
0.5 to 1.0 mil.	139.1	205.0	91.0	453.5	755.9	252.0
0.1 to 0.49 mil.	68.4	94.0	36.0	400.9	571.3	274.3
Under 0.1 mil.	75.7	64.0	61.0	202.3	277.7	136.9

2. Violent Crime Rates by Region, Metropolitan Areas

Atlantic	57.7	New England	228.0	South Atlantic	570.0
Quebec	104.0	Mid-Atlantic	335.0	East-South Central	406.0
Ontario	76.0	East-North Central	407.0	West-South Central	454.0
Prairies	147.0	West-North Central	319.0	Mountain	468.0
British Columbia	105.0	Pacific	470.0		

3. Violent Crime Rates by City to Metropolitan Population Ratio

	Canada (1976)			USA (1975)		
Ratio	Metro	City	Balance	Metro	City	Balance
0.0–0.29	85.4	126.3	19.0	411.0	823.0	297.0
0.3–0.49	129.1	216.3	48.0	450.0	718.0	261.0
0.5–0.69	72.5	69.0	85.0	434.0	523.0	274.0
0.7–1.0	94.3	86.0	53.0	449.0	457.0	277.0

Source: Goldberg and Mercer, 1986.

a higher share of their expenditures for police and fire protection (see Table 3.16). However, on a per capita or per household basis, through the mid-1970s, the Canadian expenditure on protection rose as sharply as the American fell, implying that Canadian cities both have greater per capita revenues and spend more money. Such expenditure may buy Canadians more personal safety, but rates of crime against property are almost the same (Table 3.17).

Fiscal Health. For the ten Canadian cities rated by Moody's in the 1970s, all had some type of "A" credit. Six were in the gilt-edged categories of the "AAA" and "AA." In contrast, the vast majority of the U.S. central cities were in some type of "A" category (just over 90 percent) but not gilt-edged.

Between 1970 and 1980, nowhere in Canada was there a decline in general obligation bond ratings. In the U.S., however, there were declines in 16 percent of the rated cities, concentrated in New England, the Middle Atlantic states, Michigan and to a lesser extent, Ohio—the industrial heartland. Despite trends suggesting that the economies of southern Ontario's cities are suffering some of the same structural problems which beset those in the manufacturing core region in the U.S., there was no corresponding loss of credit rating. Above all, it seems that local governments in numerous instances have been integrated and reorganized by the legislative fiat of the provincial government, thereby placing them on sounder financial footing.

Multivariate Approach to Metropolitan Differences

I have enumerated important cross-national differences between metropolitan areas in Canada and the U.S. However, so far each variable or dimension of comparison has been examined in isolation, despite the fact that there are important interrelationships among these individual variables. In the aggregate, do these many differences yield cities sufficiently different in character to allow us to assert that there are distinct Canadian cities and distinct American cities, however great may be the contrasts among the cities within the same country?[35]

Factor Analysis. Twenty variables (Table 3.18) were factored with a structure of four factors accounting for 86 percent of total variance (the factors are built from different combinations of variables). The principal factor accounted for about 40 percent of the variance with each of the others contributing from 10 to 20 percent. Factor 4, a "suburban demographic change" factor made up of population and household change in the suburban periphery, was loaded strongly and positively. Factor 3, comprising most of the fiscal variables in the analysis, denotes a central city/suburban fiscal contrast that is reinforced by nonfiscal variables. The proportion of foreign-born among the central city population is positively associated with other measures of central city characteristics (higher levels of protection expenditures and the fiscal disparity measure). The suburban end of this dimension is picked out by the proportion of single family units in the housing stock (a proportion that generally rises as one moves into suburbia and one which is higher for American metropolitan areas overall), and the high levels of education expenditure, (an important priority in the suburban U.S. given the perceptions of a disadvantaged city public school system). This factor connotes a relatively disadvantaged central city.

Table 3.18
List of Twenty Variables for Multivariate Analysis: Second Stage

		Variable Acronym
R1	% Single Family Dwell. Units in Metro Housing Stock, 1970	SFDWEL
R2	Expressway Lane Miles Per Capita, 1979	XLMLS
R3	Population Change 1970–75 in Balance	POPCHNG
R4	Household Change 1970–75 in Balance	HSECHNG
R5	% Households—Fam. w/Children at Home, Metro 1970	FAMKIDM
R6	% Households—Fam. w/Children at Home, CC 1970	FAMKIDC
R7	Ratio, CC Mean Income to Metro Mean Income 1970	INCDISP
R8	% Non-White, Metro	NONWHTM
R9	% Non-White, CC	ONWHTCX
R10	% Foreign Born, CC	FORBRN
R13	% Wholesale Employees, City/Metro, 1972	WHSLEMP
R15	% Retail Establishments, City/Metro, 1972	RETEST
R17	% Service Establishments, City/Metro, 1972	SERVEST
R19	Violent Crime, CC 1975	VIOLCRIM
R20	Property Crime, CC 1975	PROPCRIM
R22	Intergov Rev (Feds)/Intergov. Rev. 1977	FEDTRASS
R23	Property Taxes/Total Taxes, CC 1977	PT/TAX
R26	Total General Rev Per Capita, City/Bal. 1977	REVDISP
R27	Education per Total Gen Expenditure, Metro 1977	EDUCEXP
R33	Police and Fire Per Capita, CC 1977	PROTCAP

Notes: All dates are listed for USA DATA SOURCES.
CC = Central City
R1 = Identification for a variable
Source: Goldberg and Mercer, 1986.

Factor 2, which accounted for almost 20 percent of the variance, focused on the presence of a non-white population[36] and was positively associated with measures of violent crime and fiscal transfers from federal sources, which may be interpreted as another facet of central city distress. Finally, Factor 1 measures the central city's share of economic activity with variables that are strongly and positively clustered together, including family structure and central city to metropolitan income disparity. Metropolitan areas with economically weaker central cities (relatively speaking) score negatively on this factor.

In every case, the Canadian mean scores (for normalized factors) have a different sign from the American means (Table 3.19). The magnitude of the differences in the mean values is particularly striking. In each instance, the American mean would have to be increased by about seven to nine times the original value to be equivalent to the Canadian.

Grouping (Cluster) Analyses. Of 40 Canadian metropolitan areas in the North American metropolitan set of 317, 31 (or 77.5 percent)

Table 3.19
Mean Factor Scores: Canadian and American Comparison

	Canada (N = 40)		USA (N = 277)	
	Mean	Std. Dev.	Mean	Std. Dev.
Factor 1	0.831	0.779	−0.106	0.946
Factor 2	−1.383	0.456	0.199	0.826
Factor 3	1.172	0.562	−0.169	0.806
Factor 4	0.355	1.347	−0.051	0.803

Source: Goldberg and Mercer, 1986.

formed a distinct Canadian cluster before being connected to the very large, principally American group.[37] This latter group comprised 257 metropolitan areas (including 92 percent of all American cases and only three Canadian cases) at the time of the linkage. This key linking occurred on step 309, very close to the final step (316). A separate group of six Canadian cities, which was formed by step 293, remained apart until step 314 when it was finally linked to the main group.

These findings demonstrate a distinctive and separate group of Canadian cities within a North American context. For confirmation, the variables themselves were used directly as the data input; thus, instead of each metropolitan center having the four factor scores as their attributes or values, they had twenty attributes. Of the forty Canadian cities, thirty-four (or 85 percent) are joined together in a separate group before joining the dominant U.S. group. The overall conclusion from these cluster analyses is that the Canadian cities emerge as places that have more in common with each other than they do with American cities.*

Discriminant Analysis. Factor analysis revealed the different characteristics of Canadian cities when contrasted to cities in the U.S. Under various grouping procedures Canadian cities emerged as a distinctive group. But which variables are the most important in setting apart the cities?

Discriminant analysis was carried out for the same twenty variables employed in both the factor and cluster analyses. A sequential stepwise

---

*This analysis utilized the BMD PKM algorithm and is known as K-means clustering, where K represents the number of clusters. The other cluster procedure (the centroid linkage method) utilized the BMD P2M algorithm.

Table 3.20
Order of Entry of Variables into the Stepwise Discriminant Analysis and Standardized Discriminant Coefficients

	Order of Entry	Coefficient
	FAMKIDH	1.589
	FORBRN	1.516
	SFDWEL	−0.424
	VIOLCRIM	−0.012
	FEDTRANS	−0.603
	EDUCEXP	−0.435
	WHSLEMPA	0.460
	RETEST	−0.368
	POPCHNG	0.192
	NONWHTM	−0.228

Source: Goldberg and Mercer, 1986.

procedure eliminating variables that contribute little to discriminating between the two groups produced a ten-variable discriminant function.[38] Tables 3.20 and 3.21 rank the variables in order of their importance as discriminators according to the size (independent of sign) of their coefficient. The variables that contribute most to the function are

Table 3.21
Population by Race and Nativity

Type	USA (1970) (Central)			Canada (1971) (Central)		
	Metro	City	Balance	Metro	City	Balance
	Percent Population Nonwhite[a]					
mean	11.5	17.1	7.0	1.2	2.0	0.7
sd	9.7	13.9	8.4	1.0	2.6	0.7
n	217.0	217.0	215.0	36.0	36.0	21.0
	Percent Population Foreign Born					
mean	3.3	4.1	2.7	14.6	16.5	11.3
sd	3.4	4.6	3.0	8.9	11.0	8.9
n	217.0	217.0	215.0	33.0	33.0	31.0

[a] Non-white in Canada is the total of the following: Chinese, Japanese, Negro, Native Indian and West Indian. This approximates as closely as possible the definition of non-white in the U.S.

Sources: U.S. Bureau of the Census, *Census of Population and Housing: 1970,* Census Tracts, Final Reports, PHC (1) Series, Table P-1 and P-2; Statistics Canada, *Census of Canada: 1971,* Volume 1, Part 3, Catalogue 92-723, Tables 5 and 6, and Catalogue 92-727, Tables 40 and 41.

Table 3.22
Group Means for the Discriminant Function: Four Groups

Group	Group Size	Group Mean
Canada	33	5.36
United States	223	−0.79
Not Canada	7	6.01
Not United States	54	−0.86

Source: Goldberg and Mercer, 1986.

the proportion of households which are families with children still at home (FAMKIDH) and the proportion of foreign born (FORBRN). All other variables are secondary.

The utility of the discriminant function was verified through a coefficient of 0.901 (compared with a maximum possible value of 1.0). Through a split sample procedure, a very clear separation of the Canadian and American groups was confirmed (see Table 3.22). Hence, in general terms, one can distinguish between American and Canadian metropolitan centers on the basis of the selected variables, which form a function that discriminates effectively between the groups. And finally, the most important discriminatory variables indicate the relative livability and attractiveness of the central parts of Canadian metropolitan areas when compared to the more disadvantaged and less livable areas of sections in the American metropolis.

Conclusions

Canada and the United States are distinct and distinguishable societies, manifest in their different cities. It is not possible to generalize about "North American" cities in any meaningful way; which raises some doubt about loose continentalist notions. It is at least meaningless and, in the extreme, dangerous and misleading to talk about cities outside of their specific cultural and national contexts.

Those contexts often are not what they may at first seem. Although the American public philosophy emphasizes individual action and minimal government intervention, the federal government spends tens of billions of dollars annually in cities, many times per capita the paltry direct spending of the Government of Canada. U.S. federal expenditures are also substantial on highways, reclamation, water and flood control, and urban redevelopment.

The obverse holds for Canada, where there is apparent acceptance of aggressive government involvement in a vast range of areas. Yet neither Canadian cities nor private developers have been the recipients of notable federal subsidies. Residential mortgage interest and property taxes are not deductible from income for tax purposes, there are no massive federal power and water diversion projects, and highways and roads are built by provinces and cities as need and funding demand. Where the public philosophy supports free enterprise and minimal government intervention into markets there is in fact massive government involvement for urban purposes, and where government is more accepted, there has been minimal federal involvement and the provinces and the cities have been left to fend for themselves. It is at least paradoxical to find practice so at odds with theory.

In the years to come, urban analysts may need to abandon simplified country-blind theories about urban growth and population. It will be necessary to be more sensitive to local specifics and contexts (i.e. microdetails); to broader societal issues and contexts so as to be able to place the specific urban setting in its appropriate cultural milieu (i.e. macrodetails); and to spend as much effort on synthesizing these micromacro views as has been spent in the past on rigorous analysis of either micro or macro phenomena. Moreover, the urban analyst must have command of both micro and macro processes and institutions that together shape the city and be more alert to differences than superficial and illusory generalities. Above all, this research contrasting Canadian and American cities amplifies the value of a comparative perspective in which differences and similarities are accorded equal weight. The recent obsession of some social scientists with the derivation of general rules, theories and empirical findings will of necessity be dampened by the reality imposed by the comparative approach. Assumed similarities often must give way on closer analysis to deeper-seated and frequently fundamental differences in urban structure and function, differences that in the end obviate meaningful generalization and force the analyst to appreciate the specifics of the urban setting under study.

Canadian and American cities have been shaped by political and economic institutions, by culture, race, ethnicity and demography. The cities are different because the forces that shaped them are different, and however great are the disparities among cities across Canada, the disparities are of a different order across the forty-ninth parallel.

Different cities with different histories, forms, and designs require different policies to shape their futures. Government officials and private developers watch each other carefully across the border and often borrow or imitate ideas. A consciousness of the dominant differences may help caution them in presuming that all cities are sufficiently similar to warrant common problem definitions and common solutions. Indeed, what has given Canada and the U.S. different character until now has been the choice of different strategies, responding to different diagnoses of urban problems and opportunities.

Notes

1. For a discussion of the problems facing the Canadian federal government in its attempts to become a major player in the urban policy sector in Canada, see: Michael A. Goldberg, "The BNA Act, NHA, CMHC, MSUA, etc.: 'Nymophobia' and the On-Going Search for An Appropriate Canadian Housing and Urban Development Policy," in Michael Walker, ed., *Canadian Confederation at the Crossroads* (Vancouver, B.C.: The Fraser Institute, 1978), pp. 320–361; and Elliot J. Feldman and Jerome Milch, "Coordination and Control: The Life and Death of the Ministry of State for Urban Affairs," in Lionel D. Feldman, ed., *Politics and Government of Urban Canada*, *4th edition* (Toronto: Methuen, 1981), pp. 246–264. For the U.S. Federal role, for example with respect to highway and urban transportation planning, see Transportation Research Board, "State Highway Programs Versus the Spending Powers of Congress" Research Results Digest 136 (Washington, D.C.: Transportation Research Board, 1982).

2. For details about constitutional history and about the respective constitutions of Canada and the United States, including parliamentary authority, see for Canada: W. L. Morton, *The Critical Years* (Toronto: McClelland and Stewart, 1964); Elmer A. Driedger, *The British North America Acts of 1867 to 1975* (Ottawa: Minister of Supply and Services, 1976); Peter H. Russell, *Leading Constitutional Decisions* (Toronto: The Macmillan Company of Canada, 1978); and *The Constitution Act, 1982* (Ottawa: Minister of Supply and Services, 1982). For the United States, see: Richard Hofstadter, *The American Political Tradition* (New York: Alfred A. Knopf, 1948); Henry Steele Commager, *Freedom and Order* (Cleveland: World Publishing Company, 1966); and *The Constitution of the United States, 11th Edition* (New York: Harper and Row, 1979).

3. For supporting evidence see: Nathaniel Beck and John Pierce, "Political Involvement and Party Allegiances in Canada and the United States," in Robert Presthus, ed., *Cross-National Perspectives: United States and Canada* (Leiden, Ont.: E.J. Brill, 1977), pp. 23–43.

4. Stephen J. Arnold and Douglas J. Tigert, "Canadians and Americans: A Comparative Analysis," in K. Ishwaran, ed., *International Journal of Comparative Sociology* XV (Leiden, Ont.: E.J. Brill, 1974), pp. 68–83.

5. Robert Presthus, "Aspects of Political Culture and Legislative Behavior: United States and Canada," in Robert Presthus, *op. cit.*, pp. 7–22.

6. Daniel J. Elazar and Joseph Zikmund, eds., *The Ecology of American Political Culture* (New York: T. Crowell Co., 1975).

7. Leslie Armour, *The Idea of Canada and the Crisis of Community* (Ottawa: Steel Rail Publishing, 1981).

8. J. W. Berry and G. J. S. Wilde, eds., *Social Psychology: The Canadian Context* (Toronto: McClelland and Stewart, 1972), p. 43. See also Mason Wade, ed., *Canadian Dualism* (Toronto: University of Toronto Press, 1960).

9. Anthony H. Richmond, "Immigration and Racial Prejudice in Britain and Canada," in Jean Leonard Elliott, ed., *Two Nations, Many Cultures: Ethnic Groups in Canada* (Scarborough, Ont.: Prentice Hall, 1979), pp. 290–310.

70 • Land Rites and Wrongs

10. Racism and housing discrimination nevertheless are present in Canada; see: Frances Henry, *The Dynamics of Racism in Toronto*, Research Report (Downsview: York University, 1978); Dorothy Quann, *Racial Discrimination in Housing*, Discussion Paper: Canadian Council on Social Development (Ottawa: C.C.S.D., 1979).

11. Carl Berger, *The Sense of Power: Studies on the Ideas of Canadian Imperialism, 1867–1914* (Toronto: University of Toronto Press, 1970).

12. Gunnar Myrdal, *An American Dilemma: The Negro Problem and Modern Democracy* (New York: Harper and Row, 1944) pp. 16–17, cited in Alex C. Michalos, *North American Social Report, Vol. 2* (Boston: D. Reidel, 1980), p. 4.

13. Edgar Z. Friedenberg, *Deference to Authority: The Case of Canada* (Armonk, NY: M.E. Sharpe, 1980).

14. It is important to maintain a sense of perspective on this for individual self-interest is an integral socio-psychological element of Canadian life. Smith provides a salutary reminder that this has been part of Canadian thinking about the nature of society. Allan Smith, "The Myth of the Self-Made Man in English Canada, 1850–1914," *Canadian Historical Review* 59 (1978), pp. 189–219; also Michael Bliss, *A Living Profit: Studies in Social History of Canadian Business, 1883–1911* (Toronto: McClelland and Stewart 1974).

15. "Sensible handling of issues needed to manage Canadian-American relations," *Canada Weekly* 9 (Dec. 2, 1981). Report of a speech made by Allan Gotlieb to the sixth biennial conference of the Association of Canadian Studies in the United States.

16. Wallace Clement, *Continental Corporate Power: Economic Linkages between Canada and the United States* (Toronto: McClelland and Stewart, 1977), esp. Chapters 1–4.

17. These data come from the *Statistical Abstract of the United States, 1984, 104th Edition* (Washington, D.C.: U.S. Government Printing Office, 1984), and from *Canada Yearbook 1980–81* (Ottawa: Ministry of Supply and Services, 1981).

18. A detailed analysis of these changes in savings behavior concludes that they can in fact be explained by changes in income (appropriately defined) in Canada and the United States. For details, see Ronald G. Wirick, "Paradoxes in Recent Canadian-American Personal Savings Behavior: Toward a 'Permanent' Resolution" (London, Ont.: Department of Economics, University of Western Ontario, May 1982), mimeographed.

19. For details see Michael A. Goldberg and John Mercer, *Continentalism Challenged: The Myth of the North American City* (Vancouver: The University of British Columbia Press, 1986).

20. Herschel Hardin, *A Nation Unaware: The Canadian Economic Culture* (Vancouver, B.C.: J.J. Douglas, 1974). An analysis of the efficiency of public and private enterprises in five countries (Canada and the United States included) provides evidence extending Hardin's argument. See Thomas E. Borcherding, Werner W. Pommerehne, and Friedrich Schneider, "Comparing the Efficiency of Private and Public Production: The Evidence from Five Countries" (Burnaby, B.C.: Department of Economics, Simon Fraser University, 1982), mimeographed. A uniquely Canadian public enterprise should also be noted here, local government land banking. See J. Piper, "Saskatoon Robs the Bank," *Ekistics* 233 (1975), pp. 265–267.

21. Richard Hofstadter, *op. cit.*, p. 10.

22. This interest in private as opposed to public action has been documented and analyzed in two classic studies by Sam Bass Warner dealing with Boston and with Philadelphia; see: *Streetcar Suburbs* (Cambridge, Mass.: Harvard University Press, 1962); and *The Private City* (Philadelphia: University of Pennsylvania Press, 1968).

23. The antiurban sentiment in the United States is well documented in Morton and Lucia White, *The Intellectual Versus the City* (Cambridge, Mass.: Harvard University Press,

1962). Empirical evidence to support antiurban public views in the United States can be found in Stephen J. Arnold and James G. Barnes, "Canadian and American National Character as a Basis for Market Segmentation," in Jagdish N. Sheth, ed., *Research in Marketing: Volume 2* (Greenwich, Conn.: JAI Press, 1979), pp. 1–35. Gallup polls over the years have revealed similar discontent in the U.S. with urban living.

24. Survey details can be found in Canada Mortgage and Housing Corporation, *Public Priorities in Urban Canada: A Survey of Community Concerns* (Ottawa, Ont.: Canada Mortgage and Housing Corporation, 1979). T. R. Balakrishnan and G. K. Jarvis, "Changing Patterns of Spatial Differentiation in Urban Canada, 1961–71," *Canadian Review of Sociology and Anthropology* 16:2 (1979), pp. 218–227.

25. William Bunge and Ronald Bordessa (1975), *The Canadian Alternative: Survival, Expeditions and Urban Change* (York Geographical Monographs, No. 2, Toronto: York University); William Coffey (1978), "Income Relationships in Boston and Toronto: A Tale of Two Countries," *The Canadian Geographer* 22, 112–129; Michael A. Goldberg, "Housing and Land Prices in Canada and the U.S.," in L. B. Smith and M. Walker, eds., *Public Property: The Habitat Debate Continued* (Vancouver: Fraser Institute, 1977).

26. See the Methodological Appendix on comparative policy and equivalence in Elliot J. Feldman, *Concorde and Dissent: Explaining High Technology Project Failures in Britain and France* (New York: Cambridge University Press, 1985).

27. James W. Simmons and Larry S. Bourne (1978), "Defining Urban Places: Differing Concepts of the Urban System," in L. S. Bourne and J. W. Simmons, eds., *Systems of Cities* (New York: Oxford University Press, 1978).

28. The most recent census data in Canada available for this research when we collected our data base are for 1976 when Statistics Canada conducted a mid-decade national census. No such equivalent census is carried out in the United States, but where possible, 1975 data are employed as the corresponding year. The use of data for a noncensus year in the United States does create some problems. In the primary data source, *The City and County Data Book, 1977*, 1975 data for New England urban areas are reported for a new spatial unit—the New England County Metropolitan Area—and not for SMSAs. Thus, without a large-scale reconstruction of this new unit for 1970 data, we must exclude 20 New England SMSAs from the analysis. The U.S. cases are therefore 257 rather than 277 for many variables; for certain other variables from different sources the number of cases may vary, sometimes greater, sometimes fewer. One effect is to deflate the amount of population decline in the United States, since many of the excluded areas were already in a loss situation in 1960–70.

29. Barry Edmonston, Michael A. Goldberg and John Mercer, "Urban Form in Canada and the United States: An Examination of Urban Density Gradients," *Urban Studies* 22 (1985).

30. Public Transit Data: American Public Transit Association, Transit Operating Report, for Calendar/Fiscal year 1976 (APTA: Washington, D.C.); J. Sewell, "Public Transit in Canada: A Primer," in *City Magazine* 3 (May-June, 1978), pp. 40–55. Expressway Lane Miles: U.S. Department of Transportation, Federal Highway Administration, Highway Statistics Division, Washington, D.C., personal communication, January, 1979. Author's survey of provincial Departments of Highways, 1978 and maps estimates.

31. *Ward's 1976 Automotive yearbook*; Automotive Industries Statistical Issue, March 1962; Statistics Canada, Household Facilities and Equipment, Catalogue 64–202; Statistical Abstract of the U.S. (1984), p. 617. U.S. Bureau of the Census, Current Population Reports, Series P–23, No. 68, "Selected Characteristics of Travel to Work in 21 Metropolitan Areas, 1975," and Series P–23 No. 72, "Selected Characteristics of Travel to

Work in 20 Metropolitan Areas, 1976," (Washington, 1978). Statistics Canada, Education, Science and Culture Division, "Travel to Work Survey, November, 1976," Catalogue 81–001, (November, 1977) and "Travel to Work Survey, November 1977," Catalogue 87–001 (September, 1978).

32. For more detail, see John Mercer, "On Continentalism, Distinctiveness and Comparative Urban Geography: Canadian American Cities," *The Canadian Geographer* 23 (1979), pp. 119–139. Stelter has also noted striking differences in the population growth experience of Canadian and American cities in the first half of the nineteenth century. Even earlier, in the eighteenth century, he identifies an imperial presence (British colonial authority) as important in the siting and development of urban settlements; this centralized direction was largely absent in the neighboring republic. Gilbert Stelter, "The City-Building Process in Canada," in Gilbert A. Stelter and Alan F. J. Artibise, eds., *Shaping the Urban Landscape: Aspects of the Canadian City-Building Process*, (Ottawa: Carleton University Press, 1982) pp. 1–29, especially p. 12–13.

33. Introductory statements on the techniques used here are available for the interested reader. For factor analysis, see Jae-On Kim and Charles W. Mueller, *Introduction to Factor Analysis*, Sage University Paper series on Quantitative Applications in the Social Sciences, 07–013 (Beverly Hills, Calif.: Sage Publications, 1978); for cluster analysis, see Maurice Lorr, *Cluster Analysis for Social Scientists* (San Francisco: Jossey-Bass, 1983); for discriminant analysis, see William R. Klecka, *Discriminant Analysis*, Sage University Paper series on Quantitative Applications in the Social Sciences, 07–019 (Beverly Hills, Calif.:Sage Publications, 1980).

34. Jan Morris, "Flat City," *Saturday Night* 99:6 (1984) p. 44.

35. Although this study does not reach into the 1980s, it is worth noting that the Reagan Administration, through budget cuts, is shifting more of the urban fiscal aid burden to the states. Given the traditional composition and outlook of state legislatures, this has worked against the interest of central cities and their residents. According to one commentator, Reagan sees this as a realignment of administrative structure with a traditional American political culture. Donald Devine, "American Culture and Public Administration," *Policy Studies Journal* 11:2 (1982), pp. 255–260.

36. See B. J. L. Berry, *City Classification Handbook, Methods and Applications* (New York: J. Wiley and Sons, 1972).

37. Our selection of particular types of cluster analysis was guided by the findings of a careful comparison of a range of such procedures. See Juan E. Mezzich and Herbert Solomon, *Taxonomy and Behavioral Science: Comparative Performance of Grouping Methods* (New York: Academic Press, 1980).

38. It is hard to improve on Klecka's straightforward summary of the *stepwise* procedure: "A forward stepwise procedure begins by selecting the individual variable which provides the greatest univariate discrimination. The procedure than pairs this first variable with each of the remaining variables, one at a time, to locate the combination which produces the greatest discrimination. The variable which contributed to the best pair is selected. The procedure goes on to combine the first two with each of the remaining variables to form triplets. The best triplet determines the third variable to be entered. This procedure of selecting variables on the basis of the one which adds the most discrimination to those already selected continues until all possible variables have been selected or the remaining variables do not contribute a sufficient increment," William R. Klecka, *Discriminant Analysis*, Sage University Paper series on Quantitative Applications in the Social Sciences, 07–019 (Beverly Hills, Calif.: Sage Publications, 1980).

PART II

PLANNING AND CONTROLLING CITIES

4

Saving the Center City

Frank C. Colcord, Jr.

The period since the second world war has been marked by a powerful process by which functions formerly concentrated primarily in the center cities of North American metropolitan areas have been decentralizing. Technological changes in transportation, plus the belated arrival of prosperity and peace, made it possible for residents, workplaces and services to move to suburbia. The steady growth of the central business districts was reversed, and they were now in decline. Challenged by this universal movement, cities could save the centers only by identifying new functions for both business districts and central neighborhoods. Knowledge about these processes and theories about appropriate future directions were limited and often faulty. Thus it is not surprising that urban decision makers felt compelled to take action, but were uncertain about appropriate responsible strategies.

The assumption of continuing growth of the central business district (CBD) lay at the heart of the dominant theories of urban change that had prevailed before the war. Although these theories had never been fully accepted in all their detail, they were the most widely known; indeed, they are still cited as important explanations of urban change. According to these theories, the central business district was the source of the dynamic of the whole metropolis; its growth sent off continuing waves of change all the way to the fringe. Its impact on the center city neighborhoods was inevitably destructive, reducing their livability and transforming the surrounding "zone of transition" into a locale for poor immigrants, fleshpots, lofts for young industries, suppliers to businesses, and a myriad of incompatible uses that reduce the area's attractiveness for residents who could afford to live elsewhere. The transition zone ultimately would be absorbed into the expanding downtown while reducing the attractiveness of the neighboring districts and encouraging the classic "trickle down" process for housing.[1]

This is the theory of Edward Burgess; he perceived the whole metropolis as a series of concentric circles, with the CBD at its heart, and a succession of ever more affluent residential circles as one moves to the fringe. The other important one—the "Sector Theory"—was devised by Homer Hoyt. Here the neat concentric circles were replaced by sectors extending from center to fringe, rather like a pie. But the growth and the effect of the center were essentially the same in both theories.[2]

These theories have been subjected to continuing criticism ever since their creation, but they have had a way of living on, perhaps because of their simplicity and intuitive logic. No persuasive new body of theory has replaced them.

Such theories are rational-economic in character. They derive from a time when the private sector almost totally dominated physical change in cities. The public sector lacked the means for effecting change, and except for a few (largely academic) planners, nobody really expected city governments to intervene, other than perhaps to participate in the "spoils."

An early and significant work that used Boston as its example asserted that these natural forces could be subdued by neighborhoods with a strong cultural identity. In *Land Use in Central Boston*, Walter Firey reported after extensive empirical, longitudinal research, that such different neighborhoods as Beacon Hill (high-income "Yankee") and the North End (working class Italo-American) could deflect the forces that lead to a zone of transition because of their cultural homogeneity.[3]

In addition to the major change in the natural forces at work from centralizing to decentralizing after the war, the public sector also began to emerge as a force itself in developmental policy making. All larger cities saw the growth and professionalization of planning staffs and development administrators. New mayors were elected on the promise of saving the center from the forces of decentralization. And parent governments, federal and state or provincial, began to develop programs of assistance to encourage the healthy adaptation of the center to changing technological and economic realities.[4]

The natural forces described by Burgess, Hoyt, and their colleagues did not vanish, but they were certainly weakened by suburban growth. And they became competitors with the public sector as explanations of physical change.

The Analytical Problem

In this chapter I seek to test the older theories in this modern context and to identify and define the changed process that has developed with the emergence of the public sector as an important force. The cross-national comparison tests the extent of public sector impact. Despite many similarities in the variables, differences in outcome over time appear attributable to political and structural differences—related especially to the extent of private sector control. My hypothesis is consistent with the arguments in the chapters by Michael Goldberg and John Brigham[5]—that the private sector would play a larger role in the bastion of liberalism, the USA, and that in Canada there would be a greater acceptance of government intervention.[6]

This hypothesis is tested by comparing Boston and Montreal. Both were founded in the seventeenth century and have been important urban centers (relative to their respective countries) ever since. Because of their historic origins, both are the easternmost principal cities in their countries and thus became increasingly remote from the geographic center as their countries expanded westward. Both have been great seaports, and continue to be major centers of culture, education, medicine, finance, and manufacturing. Both today are based heavily on a tertiary economy. And both metropolises are today approximately the same size (2.8 million). Both cities became large and important centers long before the advent of the automobile, a fact which is reflected in the physical character of their center cities.

I am not focusing on the central city, i.e., the major municipality of the metropolis, but rather on the center city, a functioning area common to all cities and a concept that allows for more effective comparison. The center city is the urban part of the metropolis, encompassing the downtown and its surrounding urban neighborhoods. It is a particularly important area in any metropolis because it almost always includes the city's distinctive historic buildings and monuments. This definition provides a way to compare Boston and Montreal that is more valid than comparing the municipalities. Montreal has 42.3 percent more land area than Boston and has 74 percent more inhabitants; their center cities are more similar in size and serve identical functions. The maps following identify the two center cities. (Figures 4.1 and 4.2).

Principal Developmental Outcomes:
Summary of Findings

If the rational-economic theories of natural forces explained and predicted the process of change, the numerous similarities of Boston and

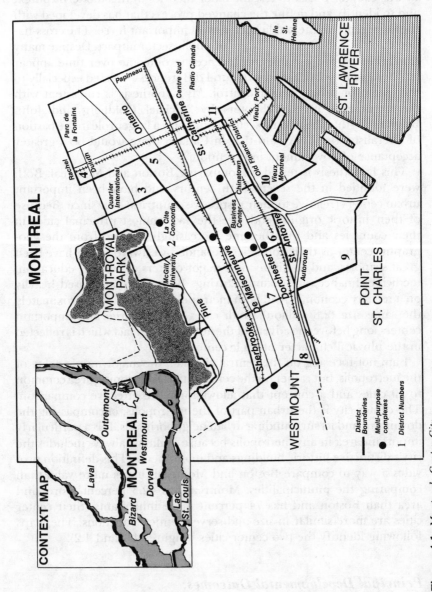

Figure 4.1. *Montreal: Center City.*

Montreal ought to have assumed largely the same outcome after about forty years of postwar development. Yet, there have been significantly different developments in the business districts and the urban neighborhoods, most of which are attributable to differences in public sector variables.

Both cities began this period with very strong downtowns (Montreal's the largest in Canada; Boston's the fourth or fifth largest in the U.S. as measured by their working populations), and with large center city residential populations (Montreal 197 thousand and Boston 156 thousand). Developmental outcomes can be summarized in four sectors: retail and entertainment; offices; housing and neighborhoods; and transportation.

In Boston

Retail and entertainment: This sector declined very severely from 1947 until well into the 1970s; it seems to have stabilized at a much reduced level in the 1980s. An important specific development beginning in the late 1970s has been the surge of growth in hotel construction, after three decades of decline.

Offices: After a long period of decline, office construction resumed in the mid-1960s and has remained steady and strong ever since. The working population of the center has grown as a result.

Housing and neighborhoods: The total number of housing units in the center has remained about the same since 1947, despite many urban renewal-related and private demolitions in the 1950s and 1960s. There has been massive rehabilitation and upgrading with significant new private construction (mostly high-rise) and subsidized housing (mostly low-rise). The identities of Boston's neighborhoods have remained strong, well protected from commercial incursions, and they have been upgraded, thus altering their own socioeconomic mix and that of the center city. Population declined into the 1970s, but it is growing again in the 1980s for the first time in over forty years.

Transportation: The center city began the post war period with one of the best-developed public transportation systems on the continent. The center was connected to the inner suburbs by an extensive subway system and to the outer suburbs by numerous commuter rail lines. The street system was hopelessly inadequate to meet modern traffic needs, but a freeway system was built connecting most fringe areas to the center. It is now seriously overutilized with no real prospect of enlargement due to political opposition and resource limitations. The public transport system, despite some important additions, has not met the

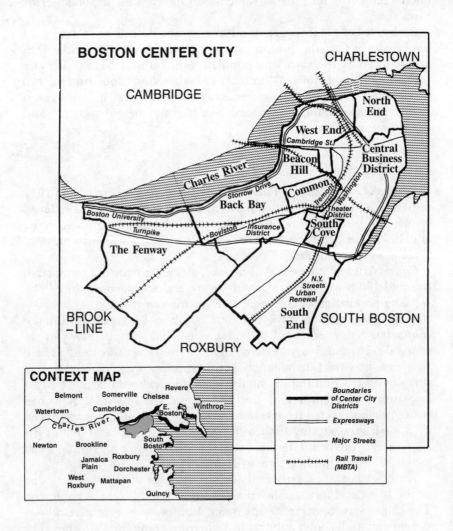

Figure 4.2. *Boston: Center City.*

needs of the community. Parking is a very serious problem and is growing worse.

In Montreal

Retailing and entertainment: As in Boston, retailing has experienced an absolute decline, but the present concentration remains much larger than Boston's, in part because of the successful invention and development of the underground mall, tied in with the new subway system. Entertainment activities have grown substantially, including hotels.

Offices: Postwar construction took off in the mid-1950s, earlier than in Boston; there have been several boom and bust periods since then. The working population has grown modestly, but Montreal's rank, in terms of both workers and office space, although still in the second tier of North American cities (like Boston), has fallen far behind Toronto's.

Housing and neighborhoods: Numerous demolitions continue, although the net loss in numbers of units has been small because of substantial new construction, mostly high-rise, and mostly in the more affluent West End. Although there have been very large losses of low-rent housing, especially in areas surrounding the expanding downtown, there remains a substantial inventory of such housing, particularly in the East End. Population has dropped dramatically in the center, with many residential districts severely damaged by demolitions and commercial incursions.

Transportation: The city street system is a gridiron that has proved remarkably adaptable to modern traffic needs. In 1947, a good commuter rail system existed and an excellent and heavily used public transit system has been built since. The freeway system is adequate, and in general the transportation system meets the needs of the center and the metropolis.

Public Policy in the Two Cities

There are four basic elements defining the nature of public policy in Montreal and Boston:

1. Ideology.
2. Government structure.
3. Political style and process.
4. Formal policies and programs.

Montreal

Ideology. Canada, like the United States, embraces a dominantly liberal-capitalist ideological tradition. However, while the U.S. is often characterized as holding to this ideology exclusively, in Canada there exist as well within the political system significant conservative and socialist ideological elements. Many scholars have argued that their presence in Canada explains the historical propensity of Canada to embrace statist or collectivist solutions to public and economic problems, regardless of which party is in power. Furthermore, there has existed since the founding of the nation a strong fear of the overwhelming economic and political power of the United States, which has generated a powerful sense of nationalism, which in turn has encouraged state intervention.[7]

Quebec has been dominantly conservative through most of its existence because of the stage of political development in which its mother country found itself at the time of conquest by the British (i.e., the pre-revolutionary *ancien regime*). Because of its status as a conquered "nation," it has directed its nationalism toward English Canada rather than the United States. In recent years, as a byproduct of Quebec's "quiet revolution," the region has increasingly accepted liberalism-capitalism as its dominant ideology; as a result of these developments, it resembles more and more the dominant Anglo-Canadian ideological model.[8]

Montreal, within the limits of its political powers, also has accepted these principles. The long-standing political leadership of Jean Drapeau (1958-present) has been profoundly liberal-capitalist in orientation, but has intervened in the economy often for two main reasons: "Franco-nationalism" (i.e., projects to demonstrate visibly the supremacy of the French culture over the English); and "the politics of grandeur," or what might be called "boosterism" in the United States (i.e., to demonstrate and elevate Montreal's position as a world-class city, especially vis-a-vis its major rival, Toronto).

Another important element of ideology to be emphasized is the powerful force of devolution to the provincial level. Although Canada's constitution, the British North America Act, was intended to promote a strong central government, Canada's history, especially since World War II, has elevated the province as the major "parent" government over cities.[9] Quebec took the lead in that movement, although most other provinces have followed. A result is that the central government is relatively much weaker and much more limited in its powers and functions than that of the U.S., which has seen the opposite evolution. This aspect of ideology relates directly to the second element defining public policy.

Government Structure. The structure of government reflects the constitutional command that the municipality is the "creature" of the province. (The American constitutional theory is the same, but it has been eroded by the growth and power of the central government.) In Quebec, highways and all important social policies, notably welfare, education and health, are now the responsibility of the province. The city does not administer these functions, nor does it provide for them through its own tax resources. Police, water, sewerage, environment and public transport are the responsibilities of a metropolitan government (the Montreal Urban Community) supported by financial contributions from the cities and the province. The seaport and airports are federally owned and operated. The city's direct responsibilities are of two basic types: normal city services (e.g., public works, parks, fire, libraries, traffic and parking) and planning, housing, and development.

The city receives financial assistance in these areas from both the provincial and federal governments. It is with these functions, in which the city's role is central, plus transportation, that we are most concerned.

Political Style and Process. With respect to political style and process, Montreal is unique in Canada. Elsewhere mayorships tend to be rather weak. The council bears a heavy responsibility for decision making, a fact which tends to place great emphasis on due process and high visibility. In Montreal, the mayor has been dominant for many years especially while Drapeau was in office. He succeeded in building a machine, operated through his own Civic party, which he totally dominated. In only one election was there a serious threat by a competing party. This fact has allowed for a secretive decision making process; serious debates by the council are infrequent. The mayor had an executive officer and executive committee with whom he consulted, but otherwise his decisions were highly personal.[10]

Policies and Programs. Policies and programs have been oriented toward development at almost any cost, and toward massive and dramatic projects that keep Montreal visible to the outside world, e.g., the 1967 Expo, the 1976 Olympics, the Place des Arts (cultural center), the Palais de Congres (convention center), the Metro, etc. While these projects are expensive, they all unquestionably enliven the city center and contribute to it vitality and attractiveness. They, of course, also help to keep the Mayor firmly in the hearts and minds of his constituents.

Planning in the conventional sense is not a part of the mayor's style. Obviously he has something of a master plan and makes the most of opportunities that present themselves, but he does not wish to be straitjacketed by bureaucratic plans or by the complementary obligation that goes with planning or extensive consultation with community leadership. In this sense, he was not one of the new mayors described in the American literature.[11]

Both Montreal and the Province of Quebec were transformed in another respect during the period of study, and for the same reason. Both governments, in the 1940s and 1950s, were backward, corrupt, and conservative. At the end of the 1950s, both were the subjects of reform, and in both cases (especially the province), the government was seen as a means by which Francophones could lift themselves from a primarily tradition-oriented, peasant society, to that of a modern middle class. The provincial government was quickly modernized[12] and is today the equal of just about any province or state on the continent. Drapeau entered Montreal politics to reform it and did indeed modernize the city government and greatly reduce the most obvious forms of corruption.

A strategic manifestation of Drapeau's ideological commitment to grandeur was the symbolic placement of important new developments in the French part of town. The Place des Arts, several quasi-public retail/office/hotel complexes, the new Federal building, the University of Quebec, the Maison du Radio Canada, the Olympic facilities and the Palais de Congres, are all located to the east of downtown, i.e., in the French quarter. Several are in what has come to be called the Axis Publique (or less benignly, the Axis Imperiale) a public urban renewal area that parallels in the east the private axis in the west, including the Place Ville Marie, Place Bonaventure, and other spectacular multiplexes.

Public housing was anathema to the mayor. It violated the private enterprise system, in his view, as indeed did the planning process. He was reluctant to intervene in the "natural" process described by Burgess in which the private sector demolishes buildings in the expectation of speculative development. But, he was reluctant to facilitate such developments in various ways, as in the case of Place Ville Marie, the project developed by William Zeckendorf.[13]

Boston

Ideology. One might expect Boston to embrace in its development process the prevailing American ideology of liberalism, consistent with the theories of Burgess and Hoyt. Development should be kept to the private sector, and the public sector should facilitate and cooperate. Indeed, such is approximately the prevailing ideology in Montreal. Yet, in Boston, active development planning is clearly the mechanism through which the municipality (the public sector) intervenes and even controls the activities of the private sector, and such planning has been characteristic of Boston in most of the period since World War II. While free enterprise seems to have been totally dominant in some American cities, such as Houston, planning has been accepted as an appropriate role in many others, of which Boston is clearly one. What ideological precepts have intervened? Three seem most clear:

1. A "conservative" determination to protect and preserve the heritage of an old city, especially its neighborhoods

2. A pragmatic acceptance of planning as the only means by which the center city might be saved in the depressing era of the 1950s

3. A powerful insistence on self-determination in the neighborhoods. Boston shares with the New England towns a belief that government (or decision making) at the lowest possible level is government at its best.

In important pieces of legislation at both the federal and state levels, American government has embraced the concept of urban planning. The U.S. and Massachusetts in fact require it for cities to be eligible for developmental grants; clearly, pressure from these higher level governments has contributed to the proliferation of professional planning bodies in most U.S. cities. Yet this influence has been contradicted by intense opposition to serious physical or economic planning at either the federal or the state levels, where the private enterprise system still dominates the rhetoric as the established ideology.

Another contradiction in the American ideology has been the ever-growing (until recently) centralizing process in the face of a stated ideology of decentralization. Some results have been:

1. a strong federal government

2. weak and underdeveloped state governments, which do not effectively provide for and protect their municipalities

3. cities that have looked increasingly to the national government for help while criticizing state governments for unsympathetic meddling

Massachusetts has been especially unresponsive in two important areas of policy: metropolitan structural reform and tax reform. This stands in dramatic contrast to most Canadian provinces, including Quebec. The present national administration has cut many of its urban programs, but there is little evidence yet of states moving into the breach.

Government Structure. In Massachusetts, the city remains responsible (administratively and fiscally) for many functions over which it has little control, notably education and health. Boston harbors a high proportion of the metropolitan area's poor and minorities in an extraordinarily small geographic area (forty-three square miles), making it now, in terms of per capita earnings, one of the poorest cities in America, despite the relative affluence of its metropolitan area.

The state has refused to recognize this impoverishment by enlarging the city's borders to encompass wealthy suburbs, by establishing a metropolitan government that might accept some of these functions and burdens, or by assuming social and other costs (except welfare). Although in 1985 the Commonwealth authorized two relatively small new taxes for the city, an airport jet fuel tax and a hotel/motel excise tax, Boston remains more heavily dependent upon the property tax than any other major city in the United States. Furthermore, all Massachusetts cities have had a tax lid known as "Proposition 2½" imposed upon them by referendum. This has severely limited their ability to increase property taxes. In Boston, the referendum required significant reductions in property taxes. The city subsisted through the 1960s and 1970s by aggressively seeking federal grants, but now much of that assistance has been terminated. The present (Flynn) administration has taken important steps to reduce former extravagances and to economize. These factors all contribute to a severe difficulty in rendering a satisfactory level of services.[14]

Political Style and Process. Boston's political style and process cannot be distinguished clearly from that of Massachusetts. Both governments have been following a slow and painful road of transformation from ramshackle entities of incompetence and corruption, distrusted profoundly by their citizens, to modernization. Both are still a long way from completing that process, relative to the most progressive states and cities of North America. Since James Michael Curley retired in 1947, Boston has had a succession of mayors who have contributed toward a more effective and professional government, especially in the area of development. But there is still a way to go.

In the period 1960–68, under Mayor John Collins, Boston had one of the most professional and creative development programs and staffs in the country, with Edward Logue at the helm of the Boston Redevelopment Authority (BRA). A strong planning orientation with a heavy emphasis on rehabilitation was established then and has continued, particularly in the neighborhoods.[15] Strong community programs with major inputs from local citizenry were developed and continue today in the center city neighborhoods. Mayor Kevin White's stated devotion to neighborhoods (1968–1984) was later displaced somewhat by an attraction to downtown development, a game in which he took a strong personal role, but the tradition of neighborhood planning survived, at least within the center city.

During the Collins administration (1960–68), the city's politics remained very patronage-oriented outside the BRA. This situation deteriorated further during White's sixteen year regime, when he used patronage effectively to maintain power. The present mayor, Raymond Flynn, has entered office as a reformer, specifically oriented toward the outer neighborhoods (which have been neglected) and the poor. However, although there have been appointments of high quality to head public agencies, the civil service remains rather non-professional. The mayor and his BRA director have made many statements about the need for quality planning, and studies have been issued supporting such a policy, but it remains to be seen whether these will be transformed into effective policy.

Formal Policies and Programs. As early as the mid-1950s, Boston sought vigorously to improve its depressed economic state and its severely obsolete physical plant through federal funding. After some serious policy missteps, notably the total urban renewal clearance of the West End[16], the BRA designed in the 1960s a comprehensive planning and development program for the CBD that designated specific areas for redevelopment. The program emphasized housing rehabilitation, new housing (subsidized and otherwise), and selective clearance (to eliminate incompatible uses) for several of the most dilapidated neighborhoods; it also called for improvements in transportation and the tax base. Massive federal funding was used creatively to modernize the city and sustain attractive, viable neighborhoods, while in higher income areas the strategy was preservation and the improvement of neighborhood facilities.

Outcomes of Development and Public Policy Compared

These two cities began the postwar period in similar conditions. They both had problems of poverty, dilapidated housing, deteriorated downtowns and industrial areas, and transportation systems inadequate for modern needs. But both had strong downtowns with large working populations and vigorous retail districts and entertainment areas. Most of their populations and neighborhoods were poor, although they both contained long-standing, surviving high income districts.

Retail and Entertainment

Montreal. In Montreal, retailing and entertainment shifted their focal points in the 1890s from the old downtown (now Vieux Montreal) along the waterfront to St. Catherine Street and associated side streets on the upper terrace. St. Catherine Street enters Montreal at the Westmount boundary and runs for seven miles through the English downtown, the French downtown, and into the East End. The two downtowns were traditionally separated by St. Lawrence Boulevard, although for several blocks west of that artery, the shops were primarily French in orientation. Four big department stores were located in the English CBD and one in the French. The entertainment districts (hotels, restaurants, bars, taverns, night clubs, etc.) were found in two main areas: the first, in the vicinity of St. Catherine and Peel, close to the railroad stations and interspersed with the English retail district; the second, largely French in orientation, was in the vicinity of St. Catherine, St. Lawrence, and St. Denis[17] (see Figure 4.3).

At the end of the 1950s, with the development of the huge Place Ville Marie complex, Montreal (and North America) got its first urban indoor shopping mall. In addition to shops, banks, restaurants, and theaters, the Place also contains two large office buildings and a parking garage. In the next fifteen years or so, nine more such complexes were built, several of them connected underground to each other and to the new Metro, the first ones of which were completed in 1966. By 1983, almost 30 percent of the retail shops in downtown Montreal, i.e., close to 700 in total, were enclosed.[18] Thus, in contrast to Boston, many new shops were opened in the Montreal CBD in the 1960s.

The four anglophone department stores are still in place (one with a name change) and one experienced a substantial expansion. Three of the four are local branches of large national chains. The French store closed in the 1970s in part, one suspects, because the stronger "English" stores learned better how to serve the dominant francophone population. The total number of shops actually declined in the CBD, but this seems to have occurred through a contraction around the periphery, rather than in the center, as in Boston.

In the late 1960s, Montreal saw the beginning of the rebirth of St. Paul Street. Thanks to the statutory designation of Vieux Montreal and the special financial assistance that followed, this ancient main street made a comeback through the extensive recycling of warehouse buildings

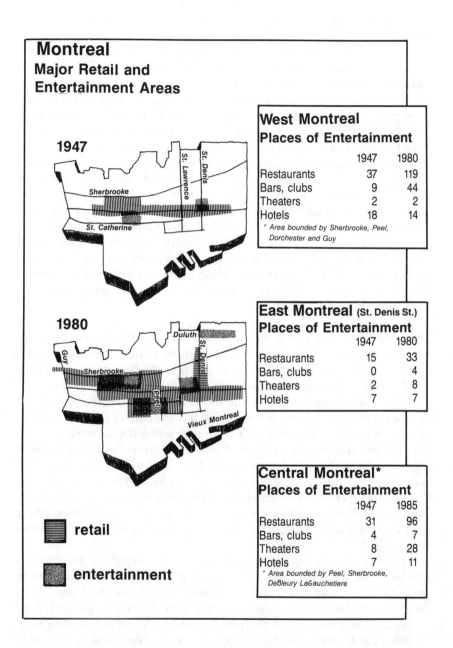

Montreal
Major Retail and Entertainment Areas

1947

Sherbrooke

St. Catherine

St. Lawrence

St. Denis

1980

Duluth

Guy

Sherbrooke

Peel

St. Denis

Vieux Montreal

▓ retail

▓ entertainment

West Montreal
Places of Entertainment

	1947	1980
Restaurants	37	119
Bars, clubs	9	44
Theaters	2	2
Hotels	18	14

* Area bounded by Sherbrooke, Peel, Dorchester and Guy

East Montreal (St. Denis St.)
Places of Entertainment

	1947	1980
Restaurants	15	33
Bars, clubs	0	4
Theaters	2	8
Hotels	7	7

Central Montreal*
Places of Entertainment

	1947	1985
Restaurants	31	96
Bars, clubs	4	7
Theaters	8	28
Hotels	7	11

* Area bounded by Peel, Sherbrooke, DeBleury LaGauchetiere

Figure 4.3. *Montreal: Major retail and entertainment areas.*
Source: *Lovell's Directory* (Montreal: John Lovell, 1947) and the author's own research.

into boutiques, restaurants, bars, and clubs, as well as offices and condominiums.[19]

All evidence suggests that Montreal's entertainment activities grew substantially during this postwar period. Beginning in the 1960s, there were several spurts of hotel construction, particularly energized by the world's fair (Expo 1967) and the Olympics (1976). Four of the complexes contain major hotels, as well as shopping, offices and restaurants. Entertainment activities are now concentrated in several center locations. The two original areas (St. Denis and Crescent Streets) have substantially expanded in numbers and contain the largest concentration of activities (see Figure 4.3). The number of restaurants and clubs in the Crescent St. area grew from 48 to 163. These areas have been augmented by Vieux Montreal and two entirely new restaurant areas at Duluth and Prince Arthur Streets. There seems little question that Montreal is one of the liveliest centers of night life in North America. In addition to private growth, the city built the large Place des Arts in the 1960s, giving Montreal at last a strong cultural center. Further development of this sector is currently underway, reinforcing the other nighttime activities.

Boston. Boston has had a very different postwar experience. Retailing was concentrated in the downtown retail district, with seven department stores and very large numbers of shops, plus the "chic" shopping area in the Back Bay that had begun to develop in the 1920s. Boston experienced a continuing decline in the old downtown from the end of the war until the late 1970s, with the Back Bay remaining relatively stable. In the late 1940s, Boston had a large and active theater district (both movies and legitimate) on lower Washington Street, and an associated entertainment district of restaurants, bars, and night clubs. A second entertainment district, seedy but active, was located in Scollay Square. The district was totally eliminated by urban renewal—along with a large number of mostly rundown shops. The theater district and its support activities diminished considerably, as did retailing within this district (Figure 4.4).

Much of this change in Boston was clearly a result of the flight to the suburbs. Shopping malls were built all around the metropolis. People took to their automobiles, and downtown did not provide cheap, much less free, parking; traffic was very congested. Television seemed to be replacing the movies, and the pre-Broadway tryouts declined in total numbers as Boston experienced growing competition from other cities and Broadway decreased its out-of-town tryouts overall. By the early 1970s, lower Washington Street replaced Scollay Square as the

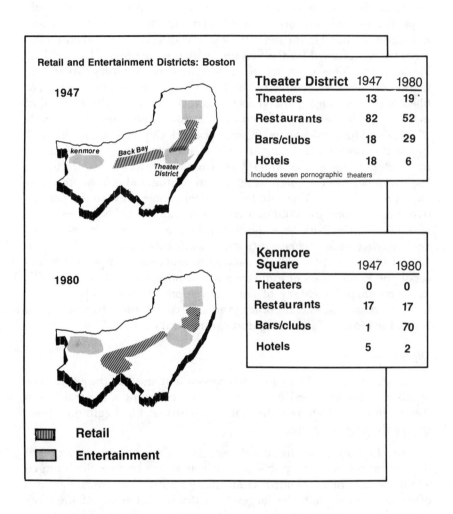

Retail and Entertainment Districts: Boston

1947

kenmore   Back Bay

Theater District

Theater District	1947	1980
Theaters	13	19 *
Restaurants	82	52
Bars/clubs	18	29
Hotels	18	6

Includes seven pornographic theaters

1980

Kenmore Square	1947	1980
Theaters	0	0
Restaurants	17	17
Bars/clubs	1	70
Hotels	5	2

Retail

Entertainment

Figure 4.4. *Retail and entertainment districts: Boston.*
Source: *Polk's Directory* (Boston: Polk, 1947) and the author's own research.

"combat zone." Through a landmark zoning ordinance in the late 1970s, it was made the only area where the burgeoning business of pornography could function legally.

Montreal's developers, spurred on by the mayor, were prepared to speculate that the downtown retail and entertainment market would improve; no one in Boston was investing in such things. The turnaround in Boston occurred in the mid-1970s when both retailing and entertainment were expanded for the first time with the opening of Faneuil Hall Marketplace. This complex of early nineteenth century city-owned market buildings was converted by James Rouse into a fabulous bazaar, filled with boutiques, bars, and restaurants. (This was the original of many copies Rouse has launched in other American cities.) In the early 1980s, two Montreal-style malls were opened, Copley Place in the Back Bay and Lafayette Place downtown (the latter developed by a Montreal firm). Beginning in the late 1970s, after three decades of decline, a large number of new hotels were built in Boston, in both the Back Bay and the downtown. The number of hotel rooms grew by 50 percent (from about 6000 to 9000) between 1980 and 1986.[20] New centers of entertainment activity have developed in the market area and in the Back Bay/Kenmore Square district, substantially improving Boston as a night-life town. Although the data are not yet clear, it appears Boston's retail and entertainment industry has bottomed out and may again be in a growth phase. Many of these developments were supported by federal urban renewal and other grants, in contrast to a lack of federal funds for Montreal's retailing and commercial districts.

Offices

Office space is the one category of development in which the experience of Boston and Montreal has been parallel, reflecting a general North American urban shift away from manufacturing. The beginning, however, was quite different.

Boston. In Boston, in the first decade after the war, a great mood of depression set in as the public and private sector became discouraged about the lack of new construction. Before 1965, there were only two office structures built, the largest one the headquarters of the city's biggest insurance company, the other a small speculative building downtown. Meanwhile, the city was losing many office tenants to the suburbs, office space was going begging, and buildings were being demolished. Certain types of activities—e.g., the garment trade and associated services, medical practitioners, leather wholesalers, etc., were experiencing severe declines, with nothing taking their places.

The largest space users—finance, legal, and similar services—were holding their own but occupying obsolete space that would have been scoffed at in New York. Numerous studies were done by the private and public sectors about the problem, but no enterprising developers appeared on the scene.[21] The general assumption was that Boston's property taxes were too high to attract any investor, even with the tax deals that had been authorized by the legislature.

In the late 1950s, the Prudential Insurance Company of Newark announced it intended to build its Northeast regional headquarters and a complex of shops, a hotel, and apartments in an obsolete railyard in the Back Bay. After several years of negotiation over taxes and a generous deal provided by the city, construction began on the first major general office building constructed in Boston since 1929. The Prudential Center is architecturally mediocre, but it unquestionably kindled a new optimism.

In 1959, with the election of Mayor Collins, the encouragement of urban renewal began. Since then Boston has been experiencing a more or less continuous office building construction boom—first in Government Center (the old Scollay Square), which had two private buildings as part of the plan, and then in the downtown project. Over forty major office buildings have been built, and the total downtown office space has increased to about 40 million square feet.[22] Indeed, there is now so much construction that worries are being expressed about "Manhattanization"; significant controversies have developed both downtown and in the Back Bay.[23] Boston's business district has seen a growth since the war from about 250,000 workers to around 290,000 today, thus keeping it among the three or four largest American downtowns after New York and Chicago.[24]

Efforts are being made by architects and others to get the city to encourage development in other nearby, underdeveloped commercial areas.[25] It is evident that Boston's downtown growth is a product not of the attraction of new companies but of tertiary sector expansion, and although Boston "meddles" with downtown development (through the BRA and the mayor's office), it has not in recent years enforced effective planning controls on developers.[26] Recent public statements from Mayor Flynn and the Boston Redevelopment Authority suggest a new determination to impose such controls, but the evidence is not yet clear.

Montreal. Montreal's business district has seen a growth since the war from approximately 210,000 to around 257,000 workers.[27] This latter figure dates from 1982, and thus follows the largest "anglo-migration" to Central and Western Canada. Unlike Boston, early postwar Montreal—then the unquestioned national metropolis in all respects—was complacent about its future. There is no evidence that it had any serious worries about its position.

Although the early 1950s saw little construction, Montreal took the initiative to widen Dorchester Street into a major boulevard. During the same period, Canadian National Railways decided to fill in and develop its "ditch"—a famous eyesore. These initiatives soon led to the city's first major office and hotel developments. By 1960, several were in place and Place Ville Marie was underway. Vast development followed, much of it stimulated by the sales of rail lands.

Montreal, with Expo '67 approaching, was developing under full throttle, but by the late 1960s it became evident that Montreal's national position was being surpassed by Toronto. Development slowed after Expo and did not pick up again until well into the 1970s.

Following the election of the Parti Quebecois in 1976 and the francophone legislation emphasizing French signage, French education, and the use of French in business offices, the great English exodus picked up (circa 1977–81), and another economic slump set in. But the early 1980s have seen a new spurt of growth, bringing total office space to over 34 million square feet, an increase from 20 million in 1962.[28] Except for the taking of a few historic townhouses on Sherbrooke, there have been few serious controversies about office construction downtown.

The old financial district (St. James Street) experienced decline during the 1960s and 1970s as companies relocated up the hill to Dorchester Boulevard. Thanks to city subsidies for the renovation of landmark buildings, St. James Street now is receiving substantial renovation investment and is welcoming new occupants.[29]

Housing and Neighborhoods

The history of change in neighborhoods and their housing in the two cities since World War II is substantially different. Much of the difference can be attributed to the respective roles of the public sectors in the two cities.

Both city centers in the late 1940s were comprised for the most part of very large low-income neighborhoods, with deteriorated and overcrowded housing dating back to the nineteenth and early twentieth centuries. In Boston, these neighborhoods were typified by concentrations of ethnic groups; the North and West Ends were heavily Italian, with a smattering of Jews and Poles in the latter district; substantial communities of Blacks, Jews, Syrians, and Lebanese lived in the South End and South Cove; and there was a good-sized Chinatown in the downtown area. In Montreal, the whole East End was francophone; the area just east and west of St. Lawrence Boulevard was heavily Jewish, with many other European immigrant subcommunities as well; the south had Chinatown; and the southwest had a large Irish community, mixed with French. In both of these cities, these neighborhood patterns had existed and been quite stable for about half a century.

In both cities, however, there were substantial higher-income neighborhoods as well. In Boston, the elegant Beacon Hill and Back Bay districts had survived largely intact; the Fenway was a more modest extension of the Back Bay. The populations were quite heavily, but by no means solely, "WASP." Changes were already evident in the Back Bay, where many of the great mansions had been transformed into small apartments, rooming houses, and such nonresidential functions as schools and doctors' offices. Both the Back Bay and Fenway were home to large numbers of college students, attending the schools of the area. In Montreal, the "square mile" (district 1), was largely intact and continuing to be occupied by the most affluent anglophones; districts 2, 7, and 8, were mostly English and middle class, with many rooming houses for the clerks of the downtown occupying the old townhouses. Students were numerous in Milton-Parc, next to McGill (district 2).

Before this time, in neither city had the public sector intervened in these neighborhoods in any significant way. Although Boston had built several public housing projects in the 1930s and 1940s, none were in the center city. Housing remained the responsibility of the private sector, but in neither place had there been any development at all for many years. The private sector in this case meant thousands of small landlords. But, already in the late 1940s, Boston was giving serious consideration to the transformation of its old slums into more economically viable and modern facilities. Its general plan for 1950, which had been in the works for some years, called for radical surgery in several of its large neighborhoods, in accord with the prevailing theory and policy expressed in federal legislation.[30]

Montreal published its first master plan in 1944, emphasizing zoning and transportation, but it did not contemplate the kinds of clearance and reconstruction that the Boston plan provided. Montreal did not begin serious consideration of such ideas until the late 1950s, although federal assistance had become available as early as 1944 and was substantially enhanced in 1949.[31]

In both countries this legislation was consistent with the prevailing theories, generated originally by Burgess, Hoyt, et. al., which assumed that there was no rescuing a neighborhood once it began to slide down-hill. An iron law led it down an inevitable path toward ultimate demolition and eventual reconstruction. Notions of rehabilitation were essentially unknown in the scholarly literature and were not reflected in legislation.

In the 1950s, with these new financial and statutory tools now available, Boston continued planning for its regeneration with the major focus on clearance and redevelopment. The first two targets were the West End and the New York Streets district in the South Cove.[32] As noted earlier, the city's mood at this time was one of despair about its future; it seemed to be dying. Planners felt that replacing the West End slum with luxury high rise apartments would lure the middle class back from suburbia to a location of exceptional amenities along the Charles River.[33] The New York Streets slum would be replaced with modern light industry and service businesses supportive of the downtown next door. These programs were underway by the late 1950s. In both cases, the interests of the central business district dominated the thinking of the planners; without an economically viable heart, there could be no prosperous city. Despite the ancient enmity between the Yankee business community and the Irish political leadership, by the late 1950s there seemed to be a consensus on these priorities.

It was not until the late 1950s that Montreal began to develop the kind of political leadership that could contemplate public intervention in the housing market. The Habitations Jeanne Mance was Montreal's only public housing project of the traditional sort; it was built only because of the temporary absence of Jean Drapeau from the mayor's office for two years. With this lone exception, the city chose to remain out of the housing market except to facilitate private construction.[34] In Boston, two substantial housing projects, preceded by the usual clearance, were built in the 1950s in the center city, but well away from the downtown.

It was in the 1960s when the policies of the two cities seriously diverged. By then, both cities had aggressive mayors with big ideas for development of the center, but the approaches were very different. The fundamental policy was essentially the same—to focus concern on the central business district. But the strategies for the surrounding neighborhoods were considerably different, as have been the end results.

A new policy toward Boston's neighborhoods was forged following the furor over the demolition of the West End and after the election of Mayor Collins. Broadly, the policy was meant to encourage the development of stable communities which would not drain the city's resources and which would be appropriate neighbors for the new, progressive downtown. Under the direction of the BRA's Edward Logue, plans were drawn up for the remaining low-income neighborhoods of the center. The politically strong North End opted out because it feared a West End-style demolition. In the center, only the South End, the newly redefined South Cove, which contained a small white neighborhood now called Bay Village, and Chinatown were targets for the new renewal strategy. That strategy came to emphasize preservation and rehabilitation, with clearance being reserved for areas of non-conforming, conflicting uses and severe dilapidation. Significant spot clearance did occur in the South End during the 1960s and after. The announced goal was to remove or reduce its destabilizing characteristics (e.g. excessive bars, drifters and prostitutes, dope dealing) and improve its amenities.[35]

Boston's planners wanted to correct for the mistakes made in the West End. And the renewal efforts of the 1960s emphasized community participation in planning. There are still debates over whether "planning for the people" was effective and how much community participation—especially by low-income groups—it allowed. But there is no question that immense amounts of energy were expended to engage the community in this task.[36]

In Montreal, the city government remained wedded to private residential development. Through the 1960s, there were numerous demolitions and substantial housing construction. Many of the demolitions were the product of ambitious schemes by the city to the east of the downtown (described above) and speculation by business interests expecting rapid commercial growth. Housing growth was largely in the wealthier West End, and came mostly in the form of highrise apartments with equally high rents. The city did not take steps to impede the demolition of low-income housing units or indeed of high-cost housing in the "square mile." The process was very close to the Burgess model described above; the natural forces of free enterprise were at work as a result of expansionism in the commercial center, including public projects associated with the downtown. There was little concern with community participation in planning; indeed, given the plans that were evolving, such consultation would not have yielded the results desired by the city government.

Three large projects to the east of downtown resulted in massive losses of low-rent housing, two publicly sponsored, one private. The largest was the so-called Axis Publique, described above. This was planned during the 1960s to contain the new Place des Arts, the Complexe Desjardins, the Place Guy Favreau (the new federal office building), and the convention hall. All of this was complete by the early 1980s. The second effort was the vast redevelopment project which relocated the Maison Radio Canada (the French broadcasting network's headquarters) from the West End to the east. Both of these areas had been occupied mostly by modest-income Francophones. The third was the private development of La Cité Concordia—the reaction to it belied its name. This was built, with the strong support of the city government, in the anglophone and allophone (not English or French) area east of McGill University. This was an area of handsome though somewhat dowdy grey stone townhouses, and the development project also required clearance. Between 1957 and 1980 these three projects, plus several miscellaneous transport and other public projects, resulted in the loss of 12,000 housing units in center city Montreal.[37]

In the 1970s, as a result of protest movements in many Canadian cities, the federal government terminated the conventional urban renewal programs involving clearance and submitted the question to a major policy review. A new program emphasizing neighborhood improvement was established in 1973, aimed at stabilizing rather than destroying neighborhoods.[38] At about the same time, the Ministry of State for Urban Affairs, the body charged with the development of urban policies at the federal level, was abolished. The remaining programs were administered by the Canada Mortgage and Housing Corporation, which in the case of Montreal worked through the Province of Quebec.

In the mid-1970s, the city of Montreal became concerned over the heavy population losses within the center city and began to consider ways to bring stability to these neighborhoods. The programs that developed focused on the East End. A major neighborhood improvement program called Terrasses Ontario (district 5) emphasized residential rehabilitation and improvement of amenities in this area.[39] Simultaneously, citizens' groups developed an improvement plan in the Milton Parc area east of McGill. The plan's goal was to save and improve those townhouses still remaining after the construction of La Cité Concordia.[40]

In the period covered by this study, many more houses have been built and demolished in Montreal than in Boston; Boston's emphasis has been on rehabilitation. More of Montreal's new housing units have been built in affluent districts than in Boston (65 percent vs. 53 percent). In both cities, the affluent neighborhoods have seen growth in total units and the poorer neighborhoods have experienced losses (Figure 4.5). An exception in Boston is the North End, thanks to the development of the waterfront wharf buildings as luxury housing. In both cities, affluent area housing growth was largely the result of private development.

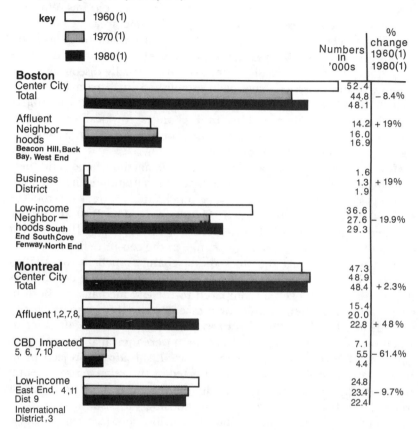

Figure 4.5. *Occupied housing stock, Boston and Montreal Center Cities, 1960(1), 1970(1), 1980(1).*

Source: U.S. Department of Commerce, Bureau of the Census, *Census of Housing,* 1960, 1970, 1980, Boston, Mass.

While private demolitions continued unabated in Montreal until the early 1980s, there has been little of this in Boston since the early 1960s and the development of the neighborhood plans. Most demolitions in Boston have been by public action as part of renewal programs. Whereas demolitions have been common in higher income areas in Montreal, these have been very rare in Boston thanks to vigilant neighborhood organizations. Until a few years ago, Montreal's laws encouraged private demolitions through subsidies; they are now formally discouraged. In Boston, historic districts have been established in Beacon Hill (early 1950s), Back Bay (1966), and the South End (1984), which subject demolitions and other architectural changes to local control. In Montreal, the only such district is Vieux Montreal, primarily a commercial district protected by an ordinance of 1966.

How have these public policies affected the neighborhoods and their housing stock in the two cities? The first generalization is that the total housing stock has not changed very much. In Montreal the total in 1981 is slightly lower than the 1951 inventory. The Boston number declined slightly from 1960 to 1980. (It is necessary to use 1960 instead of 1950 because of an important change in the census definition; however, it is evident that the stock didn't change much in the 1950s.) Another important indicator of residential change in the two cities is the trends in rent levels as compared to the city medians. In Boston, 64 percent of the rental units of the center city were under the city median in 1950. By 1980, this proportion had shrunk to 40 percent, and a very substantial proportion of these were unavailable to the general market because they were in restricted, subsidized projects or in college dormitories. All areas were affected by this relative rise in rental costs, although it was much less evident in the North End, now the last (relative) bastion of low-rent private housing—a bastion soon to be conquered by the prevailing trend of gentrification. (see Figure 4.6.)

In Montreal, the overall picture for the center city is different; here, the percentage of units below the city median is almost exactly the same in 1981 as it was in 1951, i.e. 54 percent. For the most part, the East End plays the same role as a locale of low-rent housing as it did thirty years before. Only Vieux Montreal has moved from low to high rent status. There are fewer extremes in Montreal than in 1951; in 1981, the proportion of housing units lying between 20 percent above and 20 percent below the city median has increased from 37 percent to 47 percent of the total housing stock of the city center. (See Figure 4.7).

The same contrast in trends in income levels of the center city populations is evident as with rents. At the beginning of the 1950s, Boston's center city was home to a much lower-income population than Mon-

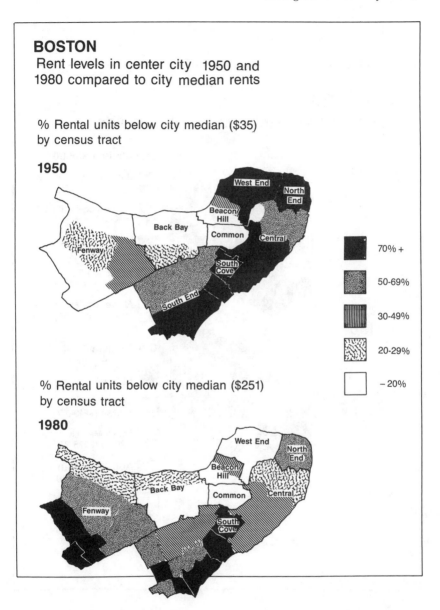

Figure 4.6. *Boston: Rent levels in center city, 1950 and 1980, compared to city median rents.*

Source: U.S. Department of Commerce, Bureau of the Census, *Census of Housing,* 1950 and 1980, Boston, Mass.

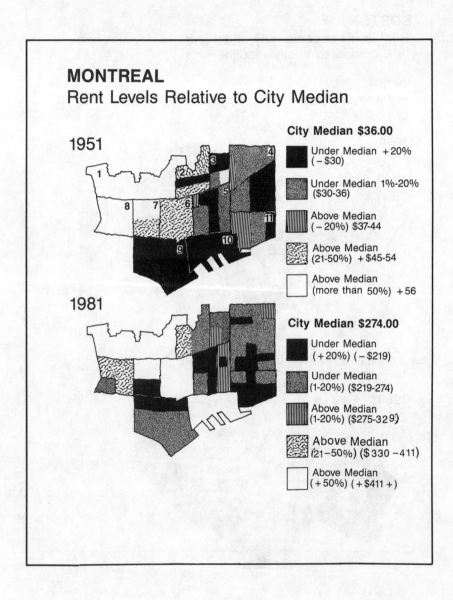

Figure 4.7. *Montreal: Rent levels relative to city median.*
Source: Canadian Census, Census Tracts, *Montreal: Censuses of Housing*, 1951 and 1981 (Ottawa: Statistics Canada).

treal's, relative to the metropolitan medians. In 1950, there were no tracts in Boston's center city higher than the metropolitan median, and none within 20 percent of that median. In Montreal, the "square mile" and one tract in district 7 were above the metropolitan median, but in fact most center city tracts were within 20 percent of that median.

By the beginning of the 1980s, the situation had reversed. All of the Back Bay, Beacon Hill, central, and West End, and several tracts in the Fenway and South End were above the metropolitan median; the whole center was only 3.2 percent below the metropolitan median, and much higher than the city. The areas of low income were tracts associated with subsidized housing and college dormitories, with the sole exception of the North End. Center city was clearly becoming an almost completely high-income district. (See Figure 4.8.)

In contrast, by 1981, most of Montreal's eastern tracts were more than 20 percent under the metropolitan (CMA) level. None in the east was above the CMA median, in contrast to 1951. The picture in the West End was about the same as in 1951, except that Vieux Montreal (district 10) was now above the CMA figure. As with rents, it had moved from low to high status. Data are not available, but it is likely the CBD also moved to that status. Thus Montreal's center, with a median income 15.2 percent below the metropolitan median, remains home to substantial numbers of less affluent residents, mostly in the east, and in district 9. (See Figure 4.9.)

Despite these differences between the two cities, some common changes occurred in the character of the center city populations. Both populations were becoming much better educated and more professional relative to their respective cities and metropolitan areas. In Montreal, the differences were narrowing between the east and west. While there were proportionately six times as many university graduates in the "square mile" as in the St. Louis district (district 4) in 1951, by 1981 there were only about three times as many. Similarly, whereas in 1951 the proportion of professionals in the four East End districts (3, 4, 5, 11) ranged from six to eleven percent, by 1981, this proportion (led by district 4) had grown to between 17 and 33 percent (see Tables 4.1 and 4.2).

Boston's center was already more professional and better educated than the city in 1951, and about the same proportion professional as the metropolitan area. (The metropolitan data are not available with respect to education). Although the proportion of college graduates in Boston's center was considerably higher than in Montreal in 1980(1)*

*Censuses for U.S. are in 1970, 1980, etc.; censuses for Canada are in 1971, 1981, etc.

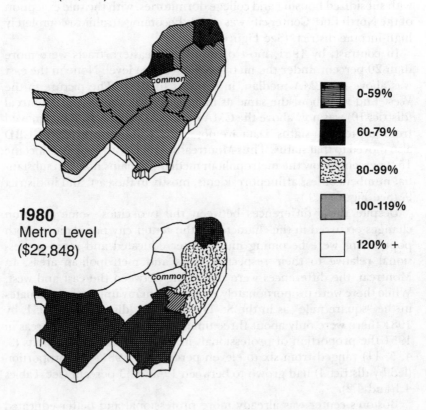

1950
Family Median Income by District
as a Percentage of the Metro
Level ($3,516): Boston

0-59%

60-79%

80-99%

100-119%

120% +

1980
Metro Level
($22,848)

Figure 4.8. *Boston: Family median income by district as a percentage of the metro level, 1950.*

Source: U.S. Department of Commerce, Bureau of the Census, *Census of Housing 1950 and 1980.*

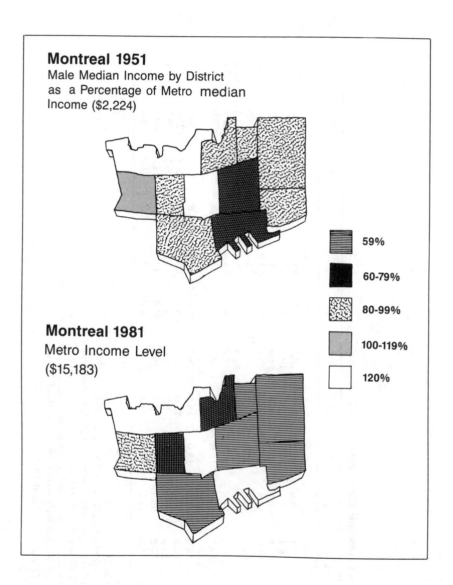

Figure 4.9. *Montreal 1951: Male median income by district as a percentage of metro median income.*

Source: Canadian Census, Census Tracts: Montreal, *Census of Housing 1951 and 1981* (Ottawa: Statistics Canada).

Table 4.1
Montreal: Socio-Economic Characteristics, 1951

District	1	7	8	2	3	4	11	5	9	10	6	C.C.*
POP:												
1941	7.3	8.6	12.8	21.2	20.4	66.5	21.3	27.4	10.8	1.7	7.6	206
1951	8.4	8.1	13.7	20.7	19.1	62.7	20.2	25.2	9.8	2.9	6.4	197
CHNG	+1.1	-0.5	+0.9	-0.5	-1.3	-3.8	-1.1	-2.2	-1.0	+1.2	-1.0	-9
% FR	23.9	31.8	31.1	30.7	45.0	93.3	93.0	67.8	55.3	87.9	41.4	65.3
% BR	62.2	48.0	53.0	27.6	5.1	2.9	3.5	11.2	32.6	8.5	45.9	17.7
% OTH	13.8	20.0	4.4	41.5	51.4	3.7	3.3	22.0	11.9	3.4	12.5	17.2
& PRF	58.5	21.8	27.1	19.1	7.6	10.3	8.4	9.1	5.0	11.1	7.7	13.7
% H.S. ED.+	32.1	15.9	15.6	11.8	3.5	5.0	3.5	3.2	1.7	3.0	10.0	6.5
AGE:												
% -19	18.9	11.2	12.0	18.5	28.7	33.6	29.6	25.6	34.5	20.7	12.5	26.6
% 20-34	26.2	31.0	27.4	25.0	27.4	25.1	25.3	25.0	24.4	25.8	24.9	26.5
% 65+	13.5	9.8	14.5	8.7	5.4	7.1	7.1	7.1	6.1	18.1	13.1	8.5
% SGL	57.2	56.1	57.3	42.4	40.0	46.0	47.0	41.4	44.2	60.1	55.5	—
MED. MALE INC.	3.2	2.2	2.2	2.1	1.9	2.0	1.8	1.7	1.8	1.7	1.8	2.0

*C.C. = City center.
POP = Population in 1000's.
CHNG = Change in population between 1941 and 1951.
% PRF = % of total occupied males classified as professional/technical.
% H.S. ED. + = % of population over 5 with 13 or more years schooling.
% SGL = % of population 15 years and over who are single, divorced or widowed.
MED. MALE INC. = Median male income in thousands of Canadian $.

Source: Censuses of Canada, 1941 and 1951.

Table 4.2
Montreal: Socio-Economic Characteristics, 1981

District	1	7	8	2	3	4	11	5	9	10	6	C.C.
POP:												
1961	8.9	4.7	11.4	17.8	17.0	53.6	18.7	15.3	6.0	1.5	2.8	158
1971	11.9	3.5	12.2	18.5	14.0	42.3	6.2	8.3	1.9	1.1	1.0	121
1981	11.6	2.0	12.3	14.4	12.9	27.9	3.6	5.2	0.8	1.0	0.3	92
% CHNG	+38.0	−73.0	−11.0	−31.0	−32.0	−56.0	−82.0	−79.0	−92.0	−65.0	−95.0	−53.0
% FR	26.0	29.0	36.0	32.0	43.0	87.0	87.0	63.0	53.0	72.0	38.0	53.7
% BR	32.0	26.0	29.0	19.0	6.0	4.0	4.0	7.0	26.0	15.0	28.0	14.0
% OTH	34.0	37.0	29.0	44.0	48.0	8.0	7.0	26.0	17.0	8.0	24.0	26.0
% MTP	1.0	8.0	6.0	5.0	3.0	1.0	1.0	4.0	4.0	4.0	10.0	4.0
% PRF	64.4	32.9	45.8	40.2	21.2	29.1	12.7	23.0	27.5	76.1	63.6	37.5
% H.S. ED.+	65.7	34.7	44.9	51.8	24.7	22.1	14.7	10.9	22.4	51.2	56.1	36.9
AGE:												
% −19	8.4	6.4	6.5	12.9	25.1	17.3	8.6	14.5	16.1	6.9	8.5	14.5
% 20–34	30.9	41.7	41.7	41.3	32.3	33.2	23.6	21.6	34.7	25.1	30.7	34.3
% 65+	18.0	15.6	18.6	14.1	9.6	15.2	15.2	28.7	9.9	26.1	15.4	15.9
% SGL	55.0	74.4	70.7	63.9	52.3	60.1	67.9	65.6	70.3	59.3	60.0	n.a.
CHNG* 51–81	−4.0	+25.0	+23.0	+51.0	+31.0	+31.0	+45.0	+59.0	+59.0	−1.0	−8.0	—
MED. MALE INC.	22.3	9.6	12.1	10.8	8.6	7.7	5.6	5.3	10.3	18.8	(n.a.)	10.9

POP = Population in 1000's.
CHNG = Change in population between 1951 and 1981.
% MTP = % of population from mixed ethnic background.
% PRF = % of total occupied males classified as professional/technical.
% H.S. ED. + = % of population over 14 with 13 years of school or more.
% SGL = % of population 15 years and over who are single, divorced or widowed.
CHNG* = Change in % of single population between 1951 and 1981.
MED. MALE INC. = Median male income in thousands of Canadian $.
Source: Censuses of Canada, 1961, 1971 and 1981 (Ottawa: Statistics Canada).

the percentage increase in Montreal was larger than in Boston, reflecting dramatic improvements in the status of the francophone and "new Canadian" populations.

No review of center city change in the United States can ignore the changes in ethnicity and race. While the contrast in the two cities is interesting, perhaps even more interesting is the difference in the aspects of this question that concern these two urban societies. These differences in concern are mirrored in the data available in the two censuses.

In Boston, minorities are the major consideration. In the center city, the South End, South Cove, and the Fenway have been most heavily affected. That impact has been quite different from the experience of many other American cities, where the city center has commonly received the heaviest growth. Although Boston saw a 215 percent increase in its black population between 1950–80, the center city's black community grew by only 8 percent (see Tables 4.3 and 4.4). The South End, where most of the center city's blacks lived in 1950, actually experienced a 33 percent decline in the absolute numbers in the succeeding thirty years and an increase from 23 to 32 percent of its total population. The heaviest growth in the center occurred in the Fenway, although it began from a very small base. Part of the Fenway is immediately adjacent

Table 4.3
Boston: Socio-Economic Characteristics, 1950

District	Middle Income			Lower Income			Renewal Areas		
	Fenway	Back Bay	Beacon Hill	North End	South End	South Cove	West End	Central	City Center
POP	39.5	17.0	10.5	16.1	49.6	3.8	16.1	3.4	156.0
% BLK	2.0	1.0	0.8	0.3	23.0	1.7	1.0	0.8	7.6
% PRF	27.1	36.1	35.7	8.2	12.3	16.9	17.1	16.9	21.2
% H.S. ED. +	58.3	64.6	66.8	15.0	29.7	21.2	27.5	24.1	—
AGE:									
% 20–34	23.4	33.4	32.1	29.2	20.1	22.9	7.6	24.0	25.0
% 65+	10.8	16.0	12.7	8.1	13.3	10.6	9.1	12.8	11.9
% SGL	54.9	64.2	57.8	43.9	54.3	54.4	5.8	51.0	54.0
MED. FAM. INC.	1.7	1.9	2.2	2.3	1.5	1.5	1.9	1.4	2.1

POP = Population in 1000's.
BLK = Black/IRS = Irish/ITA = Italian.
% PRF = % of total male and female occupied persons classified as professional/technical.
H.S. ED. + = Persons 25 years and older with high school degree or more.
SGL = % of persons over 14 who are single, divorced, or widowed.
MED. FAM. INC. = Median family income in thousands of U.S. $s.

Source: U.S. Department of Commerce, Bureau of the Census, Census Tracts: Boston, 1950.

Table 4.4
Boston: Socio-Economic Characteristics, 1980

District	Middle Income			Lower Income			Renewal Areas		City Center
	Fenway	Back Bay	Beacon Hill	North End	South End	South Cove	West End	Central	
POP:									
1960	36.0	15.2	9.2	11.8	31.3	3.1	4.5	2.2	112.8
1970	39.3	15.5	9.3	9.1	21.7	1.6	4.3	2.2	102.9
1980	35.8	15.7	9.1	8.5	24.1	3.6	5.8	4.8	107.3
% CH 1	−9.5	−7.7	−13.2	−47.0	−51.5	−6.5	−65.4	−43.5	−31.0
% BLK	13.7	3.6	2.0	1.8	31.7	4.7	4.5	3.4	13.1
% PRF	30.1	54.2	52.4	26.5	34.9	15.2	62.6	49.2	39.9
% CH 2	10.1	50.1	46.7	223.2	183.7	−10.1	266.1	191.1	88.2
% H.S. ED. +	81.4	86.8	95.2	54.5	65.8	36.8	89.7	81.4	76.0
AGE:									
& 20–34	52.2	54.8	54.9	36.9	37.5	30.8	41.8	35.0	46.4
% 65	10.1	15.9	12.6	22.6	16.8	19.6	25.3	26.0	15.5
% SGL	90.2	79.0	77.3	65.9	73.6	54.5	71.7	67.6	79.0
% CH 4	64.2	23.1	33.7	50.1	35.5	0.0	56.6	32.5	46.3
MED. FAM. INC.	14.2	37.7	30.3	15.4	15.0	10.6	32.0	21.8	22.1

POP = Population in 1000's.
% CH 11 − % of change in population between 1950 and 1980.
BLK = Black
% PRF = % of all occupied males and females classified as professional or technical.
& CH ¼ − % of change in number of professionals between 1950 and 1980.
% H.S. ED. + = % of persons 25 years or older with high school degree or more.
% CH 3 = % of change in no.'s of persons with h.s.ed.+ between 1950 and 1980.
% SGL = % of persons over 15 single, divorced, or widowed.
% CH 4 = % of change in no.'s of unmarried persons between 1950 and 1980.
MED. FAM. INC. = Median family income in thousands of U.S. $s.

Source: U.S. Department of Commerce, Bureau of the Census, Census, 1960, 1970 and 1980.

to Boston's principal black community, Roxbury. The South End/South Cove/central districts were in 1950 home to most of Boston's Chinese community; in 1980, Chinatown still exists and now includes many Indochinese, but the Asian community has dispersed outside the center to a considerable extent. Since 1950, a whole new community, the Puerto Ricans, have entered the South End, and an important contingent remains now, but most of them have also dispersed elsewhere. The only remaining European neighborhood of consequence is the North End Italian community, which as of 1980 was still about 80 percent Italian. Unlike Montreal, however, it is estimated that all but about 11 percent of the center city population can be described as foreign ethnic.

In Montreal, the key ethnic difference that concerns the community is English versus French, despite the fact that the most important demographic change that occurred in center city Montreal from 1951–81 was the very substantial growth in the proportion of new Canadians living in the center and the concomitant major declines in both of the host populations. The English population declined by 63 percent and the French by 62 percent; the new Canadians, the vast majority of whom are Europeans, increased from 17 to 27 percent of the total.

Within the center city, the once predominantly British West End (districts 1, 7, 8, 9) became far more diverse, dropping from 55 to 30 percent British, with most of the increase in proportion and absolute numbers being new Canadians, rather than French. The French East End, in contrast, remained overwhelmingly French in 1981, although there has been a small influx of new Canadians. Unlike Boston, essentially all of whose neighborhoods have become more heterogeneous, a large part of Montreal's center city has resisted this change and remains predominantly native.

To what degree are these demographic changes the product of deliberate public action, as opposed to natural forces emanating from the economy? Obviously, it is not possible to measure this with exactitude, but one can identify rather clear impacts of the two forces.

In Montreal, public intervention has been both direct and indirect, and it has been very potent, despite the obvious attraction to free enterprise of the city administration. The direct involvement in the planning and construction of the Axis Publique in district 5 and the further intervention in Centre Sud (district 11) for Maison Radio Canada have devastated large areas of working class housing and displaced thousands of residents. The encouragement of private construction initiatives and, for many years, of speculative demolitions through zoning and subsidy in the vicinity of downtown have wiped out many more houses.[41] The effects of these policies on districts of historic interest (notably 1, 2, 7, 8) also have been damaging.

Only since the late 1970s has Montreal's government taken steps to slow private demolition (especially north of Sherbrooke St.) to encourage rehabilitation of older housing and stabilization of neighborhoods, and to stem the decline of population. Important programs are under way in the southern part of Terrasses Ontario and in Milton Parc (district 2) to rehabilitate housing on a large scale, and reduce population loss.[42] Boston terminated its emphasis on land clearance and wholesale demolitions of housing and gained control over private demolitions in the 1960s.

In both cities the private sector has built substantial amounts of luxury housing in affluent districts, often facilitated by the city government; in Boston, such housing (particularly rehabilitated, as opposed to new construction) has also been introduced into formerly low-income neighborhoods. This higher-cost housing has been in response to significant growth in the service sector jobs of the downtown, as well as changes in the demographic characteristics of urban workers.

The major difference in the policies of the two cities has been the degree of control by the city over demolitions. The major difference in social outcome has been the continued presence in Montreal of large areas (in the east) of low-rent housing and thus relatively low-income people; in Boston, this sector is being increasingly priced out of the market.

Transportation

As in all large North American metropolitan areas, urban transportation policy in Montreal and Boston is the product of a complicated array of interconnected but often poorly coordinated public agencies at all levels of government. Given this fact, it is difficult to derive the policy solely from public statements; instead it is necessary to impute it from observations of the sum total of program decisions.

Transportation policy in the two center cities, includes freeways, highways, and urban street systems; parking, off- and on-street; traffic management; and public transportation. The outcomes of transportation policy will be reviewed from two perspectives: the degree to which policy and programs have led to the comfortable and efficient movement of large masses of people to and from the center, and the degree to which transportation policies have avoided damage to the livability of the center city neighborhoods. Both cities have faced a formidable task in this respect, given the need to move each working day between 250,000 and 300,000 workers to and from their homes and the business districts.

For much of the post-war period, neither political system recognized the second concern as a matter for policy consideration. Slowly both have come to accept some governmental responsibility for the social and environmental impacts of transportation. In both cities this responsibility resulted in considerable part from public opposition to transport facility construction. Boston became conscious of this responsibility earlier than Montreal and Boston's greater attraction to city planning as a central process in neighborhood development and preservation inevitably led to such concern.

The issue is particularly complex because of the very complicated and diffuse organizational structure through which transportation decisions are made. The planning of major highways long has been the primary responsibility of the states and provinces, although the U.S.

federal government also plays a powerful role, particularly since the 1956 Federal Aid Highway Act that provided for a 90 percent contribution to freeway costs. In Canada, the federal contribution is much less significant generally, although it has been greater than usual in Montreal. Generally, the federal role has been restricted to the Trans-Canada Highway and highways associated with airports and seaports, both federal responsibilities.

Montreal

Throughout the post-war period, the city of Montreal has been highly influential in the planning of freeways. The concentration of power in Mayor Drapeau made this possible despite the fact that formal authority rests in the parent governments. Only one major controversy occurred in the center city—it was over the demolitions required for the construction of the depressed Autoroute Ville Marie. Although its construction was delayed, Drapeau ultimately won that battle. The broad policy of the city has been that both freeways and a good rapid transit system are required to serve the central business district, and the effects of these policies on the neighborhoods abutting the CBD have not been a primary concern.

Montreal's rail transit system, the Metro, was built in a remarkably short time (1962–1967 for the first sector). It had been discussed for many decades but had not been a priority until Mayor Drapeau took office. He wanted to have it in place by Expo '67. The transit system was a city responsibility; as long as it could find the financing, it did not need to negotiate with the province and the suburban communities. The money was borrowed, and the first sector was entirely financed by the city at a cost of C$213.7 million, including vehicles. As of 1985, the system has 32.8 miles of underground track, built at a total capital cost of C$860 million, including rolling stock. Construction is underway on 9.7 additional miles at a cost of C$302.3 million.[43] In 1982, 52.9 percent of all work-day travelers to the center came by public transportation, compared to 38.4 percent by car.[44] The Metro carried over 197 million passengers in 1984.[45]

There has been a gradual change in responsibility for public transportation in Montreal. The change began with a transfer to the Montreal Urban Community (MUC) in 1972, and in 1975 provincial subsidies were granted to transportation commissions for construction (60 percent) and to alleviate operating deficits (45 to 55 percent). This arrangement was modified in 1980 to finance 100 percent of construction and 40 percent of operating deficits for Metro.[46] While Metro continues to be operated by MUC, whose board is dominated by Montreal representatives, forward planning has been assumed by the Quebec Ministry of Transport which, of course, also plans highways.

The street pattern in center city Montreal is basically gridiron. Two major east-west arteries, Dorchester and Sherbrooke, are wide, as are many of the major north-south streets. The pattern, on the whole, has served well contemporary needs for automobile movement. Commuting destinations in the CBD for the most part are along these several major east-west arteries. Major public projects—the widening of Dorchester Boulevard, the construction of the autoroutes, and especially the building of the Metro—have succeeded (so far) in keeping the problem of congestion manageable. The city and the private sector together have provided 25,000 on- and off-street parking spaces in the center. So, it can be argued that Montreal's transport policies generally have been successful in satisfying contemporary needs.

Boston

Boston's street pattern has a very different configuration. Except for the Back Bay, its business district is located in the oldest part of the city and suffers from a completely unplanned street system. (It is often said the streets in this section were laid out by cows, but in fact they originally served as perfectly logical pedestrian paths, roughly circular with numerous spokes into the center.) Most of the streets are very narrow, with a few exceptions that were widened in the nineteenth and early twentieth centuries (Atlantic, Commercial, Tremont, and Cambridge Streets, especially). Even Boston's main street (Washington) is very narrow and only roughly straight. Congestion was a serious problem in Boston long before the advent of the automobile. It was the nearly unmoving nineteenth century traffic jams on Tremont Street that led to the construction in 1897 of the country's first underground rail line—the start of Boston's subway system.[47]

Boston now has an extensive subway system, with four lines connecting the center to the inner suburbs. It has been extended gradually since the turn of the century, with several new extensions built since the Second World War. The most recent one, 3.7 miles from Harvard Square to outer Cambridge, cost 537 million (mostly federal) dollars. The rapid transit system totals 46 miles, with 4.7 miles more under construction, plus 34.8 miles of streetcar lines, under and on the ground. Although considerably more extensive than Montreal's, the system does not serve adequately the outer suburbs, where most of the downtown workers now live. It carried 153.7 million passengers in 1983 (rail transit and buses) and is augmented by a commuter rail system that carried 11,300 people. By the most recent count, some 59.5 percent of morning rush hour travelers to Boston come by car, while only 36.5 percent are carried by all modes of public transportation.[48]

Transit is provided by a state agency, the Massachusetts Bay Transportation Authority. Operating deficits are shared between the state and the more than seventy cities and towns served, and since the mid-seventies the federal government has contributed between 5 percent and 12 percent. The deficits are very high, running at $307 million in 1984, or 73 percent of the annual budget. Capital costs are shared by the three levels of government, with the federal government paying 75 percent. The present federal administration has sought to eliminate its participation in local transit costs. Congress has insisted on continuing federal contributions, but the elimination of support remains a threat hanging over Boston and other major U.S. cities. In 1983, capital expenditures were about $224 million.[49]

Boston's basic policy from 1945 to about 1970 was to build limited access expressways to connect the center city to the suburbs and to relieve congestion in the city. Storrow Drive was built along the Charles River in the late 1940s (after great controversy), and the elevated and depressed Central Artery and Southeast Expressway were constructed in the mid-1950s through the center of the downtown, connecting to freeways north and south of the city. After passage of the Federal Interstate and Defense Highway Act of 1956, the Boston area, like all American cities, developed a grand plan for a regional freeway system. It called for an "inner belt" across Cambridge, Brookline, and Roxbury and an artery called the Southwest Expressway running from the inner belt.[50] In the mid-1960s, another major expressway, the Massachusetts Turnpike Extension, was built into the center city. It was to be the last.

Meanwhile, the transit system (then called the MTA) was extended west to Newton and north to Revere in the 1950s. But MTA deficits were increasing rapidly. Since all of the cost of such deficits and of new construction had to be covered by the fourteen cities then in the district, political pressures not to build further money-losing extensions become extremely strong. In 1964, this bottleneck was eased by state legislation that expanded the district to include the whole urban area and provided a state subsidy for capital expenditures.[51] Federal legislation providing substantial assistance for transit capital expenditures became effective in 1964.[52] These two changes encouraged the MBTA to plan more ambitiously for further growth.

In the late 1960s, strong opposition developed in Boston, Cambridge, and other cities against several of the links in the freeway plan, including both the inner belt and the Southwest Expressway.[53] After an extensive restudy, Governor Francis Sargent and his transportation secretary, Alan Altshuler, deleted these and other roads, thus forging a new policy that emphasized public transit and banned further freeway construction in the center city.

Three other important policies must be mentioned. First, the federal Environmental Protection Agency in 1975 imposed a plan to reduce exhaust pollution in the city. The plan included a freeze on the construction of added off-street parking facilities downtown. As of 1983, the number of off-street parking spaces was 54,513, of which 35,000 were open to the public. On-street parking is limited to temporary parkers.[54] Second, the BRA instituted strong measures in most of the neighborhoods to eliminate or reduce through traffic on residential streets. Some streets were narrowed and many others were made one-way. And finally, in the 1980s, Boston established a resident parking policy in most center city neighborhoods, preventing commuters and other visitors from parking on residential streets. There is effective enforcement.

By 1985, these policies had combined to make automobile commuting both very unpleasant and very expensive—about $8 a day to park downtown. Yet public transportation remained too unattractive, unreliable and slow an alternative to entice most commuters out of their cars.

Two other non-transportation policies have exacerbated the problem still further. Boston continues to encourage new office construction downtown and gentrification in the center city neighborhoods, both of which encourage the introduction of more cars into the center.

Clearly the only solution within these parameters is to take drastic steps to encourage a shift to the under-utilized public transit system. If Boston were able to reverse the bi-modal split and achieve the same distribution as Montreal, it would greatly relieve the traffic and parking problem. Even if this alternative were feasible, it would rely upon the MBTA. And despite the expenditure of over $2.6 billion since 1965 to improve its tracks and stations and to extend the system, the MBTA has been a very poorly run and unreliable operation for at least forty years. It has been the victim of Massachusetts' highly patronage-oriented political system and of continuous meddling from the legislature. Although there have been periods when management has become fairly professional, new state administrations have tended to disrupt management continuity and reduce efficiency as cronies have been awarded high level jobs. Even in the best of Massachusetts administrations, it remains a major target for low-level patronage jobs.

The most recent example of this approach was the administration of Governor Edward King (1980–84), from which the system still suffers two years later. Until the system can overcome its reputation for unreliability and incompetence, it is difficult to imagine major increases in ridership. Yet the other theoretical alternative—deliberately stemming downtown business growth—remains unimaginable given the long memories of downtown decline in the 1950s.

Transportation Compared

Boston's major achievement in transport has been in the second goal, protecting the livability of the neighborhoods. Its major failure, for forty years, has been its inability to develop an adequate public transport system that might deter or even reduce use of the automobile for commuting to the center city. Boston has failed in this area because patronage politics have been valued more highly than effective public transport. The result is clearly detrimental to the viability of the center city.

Montreal's experience has been almost the opposite. Its great success has been the construction, *and reliable operation*, of the Metro subway system, carrying over half of Montreal's daily commuters to and from the center. The Metro system is a joy to ride—clean, beautiful, and predictable. The management and employees are professional, competent and courteous. And the entire present system has been constructed at a cost of C$658.4 million compared to the US$2.6 billion Boston has spent merely to improve its system since 1965 (figures exclude rolling stock).[55]

Montreal's freeway system is adequate to the job, helped along by numerous straight, wide arteries leading to the center from all parts of the island. Parking in the center is relatively plentiful and relatively cheap.

The parking advantage in Montreal's transportation policy is also its principal flaw. The "frame" area surrounding the central business district on the south and east, once largely occupied by housing, is now pock-marked with open and inexpensive parking lots from demolitions that incorrectly anticipated commercial development. The neighborhoods are continuous losers with such unimproved land, and they also lost the one major controversy over freeway construction when Mayor Drapeau built the extension of the east-west autoroute in East Montreal.

Montreal's transport policies have served the commuter well and probably have contributed to the strength of downtown. As with other policies in this city, the neighborhoods close to the center have been sacrificed, but since that appears to have been a deliberate policy, it is difficult to call it a failure. The neighborhoods to the west and north of the center have not been damaged by these policies (although parking there in the daytime is difficult), and those farther east, out of the downtown orbit, are not seriously affected.

Montreal's transportation policies have been much more successful than Boston's in the first transport goal—moving downtown commuters and others travelling downtown, efficiently and comfortably. Boston's policies, by contrast, have confronted successfully unpleasant social and environmental side effects in the neighborhoods but have failed to meet transport needs.

Conclusions

It is evident that the theories of the 1930s offer only a partial explanation of the evolution and transformation of the center cities of Boston and Montreal since the Second World War. These theories were based in the assumption that expansion of the central business district through private initiatives was the engine of change in our cities. They did not consider public sector intervention or the power of community activism as additional explanations of change or as mechanisms for counting the kinds of changes ascribed to the private sector. Nor did they predict that the central business district might no longer require new land, or might even reduce its requirements, and thus might not need a zone of transition, and have deleterious effects on surrounding neighborhoods.

In the late 1940s, before public sector involvement in development had emerged as a serious factor, both Montreal and Boston had communities that had successfully resisted commercial incursions from the center. In Montreal, the old elite neighborhood, the "square mile" (our district 1) had seen little commercial development. In Boston, as described by Firey, Beacon Hill and the North End had strong enough cultural identities to resist the growth of commerce and to remain essentially intact as strong neighborhoods.

However, the forces from the center, as described by Burgess and Hoyt, clearly had affected the other neighborhoods surrounding the business districts of both cities. Mixed and often incompatible land uses were evident in the predominantly residential areas. And, those areas tended to be rather transient, with many rooming houses, populated by students, elderly, young working people, as well as "psychopathic" segments of the population such as criminals, prostitutes, drifters, alcoholics, etc. Even Boston's Back Bay and Fenway neighborhoods had experienced some elements of this transformation. Thus, both cities had a zone of transition surrounding their downtowns, although there were exceptional districts that had resisted this impact.

By 1947, neither city had seen significant public interventions into real estate, except for a few small public housing projects in Boston; Montreal had none at that time. Neither city had developed a forceful, professional city planning or urban development capability. To the extent there was any development, it was left to the private sector. But it must be recalled that for about twenty years of depression and war, North American cities were relatively stagnant. New construction investment during the depression was not available—and during the war, not possible.

In the period under study, the development process and the participants in that process changed substantially from what they had been in earlier years. The two key changes were the development of and acceptance of a strong role for the public sector and the growth of neighborhood groups and/or citizens' groups as important participants. The extent and character of these two changes were different in the two cities.

Public sector, i.e., city, involvement in development was at least as important in Montreal as in Boston, but citizen and neighborhood group participation was much less effective. Both of these in Boston were strengthened by major financial contributions and by statutory requirements of the federal government. Montreal had greater financial self-sufficiency than Boston. And since Montreal left housing largely to the private sector, the Canadian federal requirements regarding citizen participation, which were comparable to those in U.S. law, were less relevant. Such requirements were inconsistent with the highly centralized decision making tradition of Montreal, and thus did not easily transform the process. U.S. requirements were in fact consistent with Boston's tradition of highly distinguishable, and often ethnically distinctive neighborhoods, and thus supported and strengthened that tradition.

Boston has been governed by strong mayors during this period, and the public sector has been very active in guiding the redevelopment of the center city. This guidance has been rendered possible in large part by the dollars and the statutory tools emanating from federal legislation. The traditional American liberal-capitalist ideology, granting to the private sector the major or exclusive responsibility for urban development, has been modified substantially in Boston by a combination of federal dollars, effective public leadership, and acquiescence of the private sector.

Both the private and public sectors have seen their goals adjusted by strong grassroots citizens' groups, with the result that the neighborhoods have been protected from commercial incursions from the downtown. Although the natural forces described by Burgess and Hoyt regained dynamism by the mid-1960s in Boston, they have been tempered by the power residing in the neighborhoods, now largely supported by the city's zoning, development, and other regulations.

In Montreal, the public sector role has reflected almost wholly city objectives, untroubled for the most part by the goals of higher level governments. The underlying ideologies governing the public sector dynamic were liberalism modified by nationalism. These ideologies were reflective in major part of the powerful and durable mayor, Jean Drapeau. Liberalism, much more strongly than in Boston, determined the private sector development role, a laissez-faire process in both the business district and in the neighborhoods. Few controls were exercised by the city, and as noted, it was quite deliberately facilitative of private development.

Public sector initiatives were aimed at the provision of conventional "public" facilities (transit, highways, convention center, public office buildings, cultural center, sports facilities, amusement park, etc.) dramatically and rapidly developed, which did not seriously intrude upon private sector initiatives. All of these have added to the new image of Montreal as a world-class city, a major goal of the mayor. Nationalism played out its role in the geographic placement of these facilities, always in the eastern part of the city. Except for these very important projects, private sector initiatives determined the shape and form of the city, in the manner suggested by the older model of Burgess and Hoyt.

The guiding principles that have governed the post-war redevelopment of the Boston and Montreal center cities have produced differing balance sheets of successes and failures.

Montreal has been most successful in its downtown-oriented policies. The central business district has prospered and improved not only as an office center but also as a center of cultural, amusement, and retail activities. The city government has facilitated this evolution, largely financed by the private sector, and has encouraged it by adding important new public facilities. The recycling of the old port district into the multifunctional Vieux Montreal has added to the boundaries and interest of the central district, while preserving important historic buildings. The center is provided with well developed, efficient transport and parking programs.

Montreal's major failures have been in its residential policies and in the interface between the commercial and residential districts. Commercial speculation and public sector renewal programs have led to heavy losses of housing units, ranging from great mansions to tenements. The results have been drastic. Attractive, historically important homes have been replaced by high-rise apartments of little architectural interest and inconsistent with the city's traditions. In addition, thousands of housing units have been demolished by public action with little serious consideration of the needs and interests of the dislocated people. Finally, thousands of low-rent units have been destroyed by private speculators, again with no assistance to the dislocated. These demolitions have frequently resulted in a wasteland of empty lots for which there is no foreseeable commercial use. Such open areas would seem to be prime targets for future housing developments. An important byproduct of these policies has been a decline in the center city population of about 100,000; this decline continues unabated. Other obvious effects are heavy losses of low-rent housing in the face of a persistent shortage of affordable housing and added pressure to move to the suburbs. The only really positive aspect of public residential policies has been the continued presence of substantial low-cost housing in the East End.

Boston's balance sheet is quite different. On the positive side, the city's old neighborhoods have been well preserved (except for the West End), and indeed one (the Waterfront) has been added, effectively recycling obsolete historic buildings into a valuable new use. These neighborhoods have been improved deliberately by important public investments in infrastructure and by innovative traffic and parking regulations aimed at excluding undesirable impacts of the central business districts. The quality of housing has been upgraded throughout the center. Commercial investments associated with the downtown have been rigorously excluded from the neighborhoods. The population decline of the center city has been reversed, as these neighborhoods become increasingly attractive.

All these achievements have been at significant cost to the traditional residents of the formerly low-income neighborhoods. Minorities, the elderly, and others of modest means have been gradually excluded from these neighborhoods because of the conversions and the rising cost of housing (except in the publicly subsidized units). No provision was made to assist their relocation in cases of private sector displacement.

In the business district, two positive developments have been dynamic growth as an employment center and the recycling of the old and obsolete Quincy Market area into a great new retail and entertainment district for the city. But there have been several failures. There has been an inability or lack of will through most of this period to control and guide effectively the growth of the business district and the bulk and architectural character of the new additions to downtown. The problem is not one of interface with residential districts, but rather the desire of investors to build in the heart of the financial district and the Back Bay. Further, the city and state have been unable to provide effective transport and parking policies for the business center. Finally, the period from the 1950s to the 1970s has witnessed a serious decline in the center's retail and entertainment facilities. There is some evidence that this has finally bottomed out and may be improving.

To sum up, the major differences in the accomplishments of the two cities are twofold. First, Montreal has been reluctant to use the tools of city planning, zoning, and other public instruments to achieve clear goals for its residential neighborhoods but has left the fate of those areas to the private sector, while Boston has played a strong role in league with neighborhood and community organizations. Second, while both cities have placed great emphasis on their business districts, with policies of growth at almost any price, Montreal has been more success-ful at channeling that growth (along three major east-west streets) and at sustaining a high level of diversity of activity in the downtown, notably retail and amusement functions. Boston is only beginning now to at-tempt to channel future development outside the congested financial district and to avoid overdevelopment of the commercial sector of the Back Bay. Boston's policies have stabilized the neighborhoods and led to a renewed population growth in the center; Montreal's policies have stabilized the downtown.

Despite these differences, Boston and Montreal remain two of the relatively few North American cities that have succeeded in retaining at their core functioning, combined commercial/cultural/ entertainment and residential centers. Their strengths and weaknesses are somewhat different, but at bottom, they both continue to be exciting centers that attract many people by the display of their respective heritages and their continued interest as activity centers.

Notes

*The author wishes to acknowledge the help of the following Tufts University students: David Rueff, James Heidell, Miltiades Toptsikiotis, Philip Swain, Thomas Alperin, Mark Ferri, Stephen Conant, Douglas Hardy, Brian Wyatt, John Fulginiti. Also, I wish to thank the administration and researchers of the Institut National de Recherche Scientifique—Urbanisation, Montréal, especially Francine Dansereau, Gérard Divay, Jean-Pierre Collin, and Georges Mathews; Professor Marc Choko, of the Université de Québec à Montréal (UQAM), and my office associates Catherine Doheney and Bernice Siegel.

1. Ernest Burgess, "The Growth of the City: An Introduction to a Research Project," in Robert E. Park et. al., ed., *The City* (Chicago: The University of Chicago Press, 1925), pp. 47–62.

2. Homer Hoyt, *The Structure and Growth of Residential Neighborhoods in American Cities* (Washington, D.C.: U.S. Federal Housing Administration, 1939), pp. 76, 112–122.

3. Walter Firey, *Land Use in Central Boston* (Cambridge, Mass.: Harvard University Press, 1947), pp. 323–331.

4. Robert Salisbury, "Urban Politics: The New Convergence of Power," *The Journal of Politics* 26 (November 1964), pp. 775–797.

5. Michael Goldberg, chapter 3 in this volume; John Brigham, chapter 9 in this volume.

6. Louis Hartz, *The Liberal Tradition in America* (New York: Harcourt Brace and Co., 1955), Ch. I, pp. 3–32.

7. William Christian and Colin Campbell, *Political Parties and Ideologies in Canada: Liberals, Conservatives, Socialists, and Nationalists* (Toronto: McGraw-Hill Ryerson, 1974), pp. 23–31.

8. *Ibid*, pp. 28–30.

9. D. V. Smiley, *Canada in Question: Federalism in the Eighties* (3rd Edition) (Toronto: McGraw-Hill Ryerson, 1980), see especially chapters 5 and 8.

10. Andrew Sancton, "Montreal," in Warren Magnusson, and Andrew Sancton, eds., *City Politics in Canada* (Toronto: University of Toronto Press, 1983), pp. 58–93. Brian McKenna and Susan Purcell, *Drapeau: Love Him, Hate Him, Fear Him, Admire Him.— He's Still the Boss!* (Markham, Ont.: Penguin Books Canada, Ltd., 1981), pp. 140–141.

11. George A. Nader, *Cities of Canada* (Toronto: MacMillan of Canada, 1975–6), pp. 153. Magnusson and Sancton, *op. cit.*, pp. 71–72.

12. Martin Robin, *Canadian Provincial Politics*, (2nd Edition), (Scarborough, Ont.: Prentice-Hall of Canada, 1978), pp. 275–277. Daniel Latouche, "Quebec," in David Bellamy, Jon H. Pammett, and Donald C. Rowat, *The Provincial Political Systems* (Toronto: Methuen, Ltd., 1976), pp. 19–30. Magnusson and Sancton, *op. cit.*, pp. 66–69.

13. Magnusson and Sancton, *op. cit.*, pp. 69–71. McKenna and Purcell, *op. cit.*, p. 108.

14. Katherine L. Bradbury and John Yinger, "Making Ends Meet: Boston's Budget in the 1980's," *New England Economic Review* (March/April 1984), pp. 18–28.

15. *Architectural Forum* (Special Issue): "Boston." Volume 120, No. 6 (June, 1964), p. 124. Walter McQuade, "Boston: What Can A Sick City Do?" *Fortune* LXIX: 6 (June, 1964), pp. 132–4. Langley C. Keyes Jr., *The Rehabilitation Planning Game: A Study in the Diversity of Neighborhood* (Cambridge, Mass.: M.I.T. Press, 1969), pp. 22, 27–34.

16. Herbert J. Gans, *The Urban Villagers: Group and Class in the Life of Italian-Americans* (New York: The Free Press, 1962), pp. 281–335.

17. Nader, *op. cit.*, pp. 137–147. Service d'Urbanisme, Ville de Montréal, "Centre Ville," Bulletin Technique no. 3 (August 1964), pp. 10–12.

18. Laboratoire d'Urbanisme, "La Fonction Commerciale au Centre-Ville de Montreal," winter, 1983 (unpaged).

19. Nader, *op. cit.*, pp. 155–6.

20. Boston Hotel and Motor Inn Association, interview.

21. Boston City Planning Board, "Preliminary Report, 1950: General Plan for Boston," Boston, December, 1950. Greater Boston Economic Study Committee, "A Report on Downtown Boston," Boston: The Committee, 1959.

22. Maurice Yeates and Barry Garner, *The North American City* (New York: Harper & Row, 1980), p. 338.

23. Anthony J. Yudis, "1984: A Year to Plan, Take Stock," *Boston Globe*, December 30, 1984, pp. A29–30.

24. BRA interview.

25. Boston Society of Architects and Greater Boston Chamber of Commerce, "Change & Growth in Central Boston," Boston, May 1984. *Boston Globe*, "The Livable City: Surging Growth Confronts Boston's Legacy," (Special Magazine section), November 11, 1984, pp. 11–13, 39–42.

26. BRA interview.

27. Nader, *op. cit.*, p. 147. Commission de Transport, Communauté Urbaine de Montréal, 1982; Enquete origine-destination régionale exécutée à l'automne 1982," December 1983.

28. Royal LePage Services Mobilières, interview 1985. Service d'Urbanisme, *op. cit.*

29. *Montreal Gazette*, "New Wave of activity Hits Old Montreal," by Shirley Won, August 18, 1984, pp. H1–2.

30. Boston City Planning Board, "Preliminary Report, 1950: General Plan for Boston," pp. 31–32, 40–41.

31. Francine Dansereau, "La rénovation urbaine comme pratique d'exception," Montreal, 1974 (unpublished), pp. 7–9. Jean-Claude Marsan, *Montreal in Evolution* (Montreal: McGill-Queen's University Press, 1981), pp. 329–330.

32. Boston Housing Authority, Urban Redevelopment Division, New York Streets Redevelopment Project, "Expressways to Everywhere," (Boston, January 1955). Boston Housing Authority, "The West End Project Report" (Boston, 1953).

33. Herbert Gans, *The Urban Villagers* (New York: The Free Press, 1962), pp. 282–285.

34. Brian McKenna and Susan Purcell, *op. cit.*, pp. 108–113.

35. Langley C. Keyes, *op. cit.*, p. 82.

36. *Ibid.*, pp. 82–86. John H. Mollenkopf, *The Contested City*. (Princeton, N.J.: Princeton University Press, 1983), pp. 185–193.

37. Marc H. Choko, "Pour une analyse comparative des conséquences de la restauration et de la démolition-reconstruction," *Actualité Immobilière* 8:3 (fall 1984), p. 24.

38. Dansereau, *op. cit.*, p. 12.

39. Richard Morin, *Réhabilitation de l'Habitat et Devenir des Quartiers Anciens* (Grenoble: Université de Grenoble Institut de Recherche), unpublished Ph.D. Dissertation, 1983, pp. 67–76.

40. Société de Patrimoine Urbain de Montréal. "Action Plan" (Montreal, 1980), pp. 31–32.

41. Francine Dansereau, "La rénovation urbaine comme pratique d'exception" (Montreal, 1974, unpublished), pp. 25–44; Richard Morin, *op. cit.*, pp. 106–107.

42. Morin, *op. cit.*, pp. 100–107.

43. Interview at CTCUM (Transport Commission, Montreal Urban Community).

44. CTCUM, Mobilité des personnes dans la région de Montréal. Enquête origine-destination régionale exécutée à l'automne 1982. December 1983. Also, CTCUM, *Rapport Annuel T.T.L.* pour l'année 1984.

45. CTCUM, *Rapport Annuel T.T.L., 1984*.

46. Jean-Pierre Collin, "Développement urbain et coût des services publics régionaux," *Institut National de Recherche Scientifique-Urbanisation, Document 28* (March 1982), pp. 93–94.

47. Metropolitan Planning Organization, "The Transportation Plan for the Boston Region" (Boston, February 1983), p. 22.

48. Massachusetts Bay Transportation Authority, 1983 Annual Report, pp. 53–54. Central Transportation Planning Staff, "Transportation Facts for the Metropolitan Boston Region" (Boston, 1983), pp. 44, 46.

49. Massachusetts Bay Transportation Authority, *op. cit.*, Appendix (unpaged).

50. Alan Lupo, Frank Colcord, and Edmund Fowler, *Rites of Way: The Politics of Transportation in Boston and The U.S. City* (Boston: Little Brown & Co., 1971), pp. 192–194.

51. *Ibid.*, p. 193, 223.
52. Urban Mass Transportation Assistance Act of 1964.
53. Lupo et. al., *op. cit.*, pp. 76–79.
54. Environmental Protection Agency, "Transportation Control Plan for the Metropolitan Boston Intrastate Air Quality Region," 1975.
55. MBTA, "Statement of Federal Grants and Loans—Approved HUD/DOT/EDA Projects," 1984, and CTCUM interview.

5

On the Fringe: Controlling Urban Sprawl in Canada and the United States

Elliot J. Feldman

After World War II, demographers projected a series of megalopoleis dominating the advanced industrial world. Population would grow so rapidly by the end of the century that industrial countries would become totally urbanized.

The responses to this projection generally were negative. There was concern, rooted perhaps in pre-industrial culture, that the values of rural life would be lost. The city as the source of sin was a lurking premise. Future self-sufficiency also was called into question. If rural lands were urbanized, industrial countries would lose their ability to produce their own food and become dependent upon the uncertainties of the agricultural third world.

The compact urban community that had evoked the aesthetic pleasures of the Renaissance would give way to a sprawling city without end. The focal core would be sacrificed and rural man, cast into the city of sin, would have no urban anchor.[1]

There was an intellectual, perhaps even analytical, basis for concern. Because cities grew up along waterways or as transportation and trading centers, they inevitably were situated on or adjacent to prime agricultural land. Land near rivers was fertile, and trading centers were more for farmers, hunters, and trappers than for manufacturers. At some point the city's expansion would eat into fine food-producing land.[2]

There was an economic logic for concern. Urban dwellers exchange open space for services. A cardinal rule of planning is that there is greater economic efficiency delivering services in a compact space than in linear extensions. If the city were permitted to sprawl, it would become increasingly expensive to deliver services.

The demographic projections and the cultural and analytic responses inspired a surge of planning. In some instances the focus was on the development of new towns. Whole communities would be created, concentrating urban activities and services and controlling the size of populations. By providing housing and services, governments could channel those leaving the countryside away from the fringe of established urban centers and toward new communities. It was asserted that the construction of an entirely new infrastructure was more efficient economically than the extension of an old one, and abstractly it was asserted that the physical size of the community determined livability.

Although the British opted most powerfully for new towns, followed two decades later by the French, the North American response was slower and different. Some talk of new towns could be heard, some experiments were launched, and land was taken in many places with plans to try, but more generally the vast open spaces of the continent seemed persuasive and the demographic projections, therefore, seemed apocryphal. Nevertheless, there was a mounting pressure for planning in the 1950s and 1960s, as much because of the deterioration of established urban centers as because of the concern for agricultural losses or fringe growth.

Some urban centers were ecologically fragile and readily could be identified with demographic fears. Vancouver, British Columbia, for example, closed in by mountains, the sea, and the U.S. border, physically could grow only on prime farm land. The urban agglomeration of southern Ontario was pushing toward land unique in the region for growing tender fruit. Honolulu might overrun the island of Oahu with tourism, but land ownership patterns threatened to concentrate development on the one island.

The principal alternative to the strategy of the new town was to control urban development, to limit the metropolis. The design of policies effecting such control was premised on the extrapolated demographic growth, the assertion of spatial economic efficiency, and an assumption of static agricultural technology that over time would require the same quantities and qualities of land to afford the same agricultural yield.

Policy instruments have taken several forms. Most essential are the most tried and true: zoning, sewage, water and transportation. However, these policy instruments typically are exercised by local officials, and control of the urban periphery posed a new challenge. Those public authorities in the urban center desiring to control the periphery often did not enjoy these traditional powers for the lands implicated. They reacted in two ways.

First, a deliberate effort was made to gain these powers on the periphery by creating regional or metropolitan governments. In the United States this effort was less successful than in Canada, and the American alternative was to look to a still higher authority, the state. Canadian municipalities answer to provincial governments, and municipalities in the United States are creatures of state governments. However, the urban fringe in the United States usually has been controlled by competing municipalities or by county governments, which in turn have controlled much of American political party machinery. Hence, the political cost of manipulating local power is very high and this alternative is pursued reluctantly.

A second response to the shortage of policy instruments on the periphery was to establish new ones. The federal and provincial governments in Canada are the principal owners of land (in behalf of the Crown), but a full appreciation of the power associated with ownership seemed to emerge with the perceived urgency of planning. Then the further acquisition of land became a powerful tool for the provinces, and in turn the federal government. To a lesser degree, this instrument for determining the fate of the urban fringe also was adopted in the United States.

Direct land acquisition generally has taken three forms:

1. purchase or expropriation for a specific public utility, such as airports (by far the largest single land-using facilities on the periphery)

2. purchase or expropriation of corridors for current or future public services, such as pipelines, power lines, or highways

3. land banking, through purchase or expropriation, for large-scale, ill-defined future use, including new town construction or waste disposal or even controlled industrial development

In every instance this strategy has taken land out of the market and reserved it for government use. It also has induced fluctuations in the valuation of adjacent or nearby land.

Despite four decades of concern, few governments have adopted comprehensive legislation for controlling urban sprawl. The most celebrated North American examples of sprawl, including Los Angeles, New York, and Chicago in the United States and Calgary and Montreal in Canada have not been controlled effectively. The most powerful legislation entrusts a state or provincial government with direct authority to approve or deny a construction or development scheme anywhere on the urban periphery. Such legislation exists only in Hawaii, Oregon, Vermont, British Columbia, Ontario, and Quebec. There are legislated programs for specific cases, such as Calgary, Edmonton, Saskatoon, Regina, and Winnipeg, but in each a regional government ultimately replaces broad provincial government controls.

In those cases where authority has been established, a full panoply of policy instruments, often with very cumbersome procedures, has been developed. The results, at best, are mixed. Clearly it is time to begin taking stock of the attempts to control growth at the urban periphery, and to reflect on the assumptions that stimulated this type of planning. It is time to consider once again whether the public sector's intervention in the private land market leads to outcomes more in the public interest than when the exercise of state power is more restrained or benign.

Defining Terms

The metropolis has no clear boundaries. There are legal limits on the municipality or the county, of course, and on other jurisdictions. Often zoning differences will dramatize crossing such borders, but often not. Incorporated areas inevitably display evidence of urbanization, whether within the principal municipality or beyond its formal borders.

With no clear boundaries, there are no simple ways to define the "periphery," or "fringe." Leonard Gertler has called the area beyond the metropolis the "shadow," referring to land visibly affected by urbanization although not urbanized itself.[3] The shadow is a large area, stretching fifty miles or more beyond the built-up zones.

Some planners and geographers have referred to this area beyond the urbanized core as an "echo," signalling back to the city its potential growth area.[4] In this essay, consideration of the fringe or periphery is based on an essentially visual experience. In whatever direction one travels from a city, at some point scattered dwellings replace subdivisions, open spaces replace factories or businesses, a general store replaces a shopping complex. As one passes into this ill-defined area one moves from the metropolis to the fringe. For analytical purposes, the fringe is defined by the availability of open space and large land parcels ripe for packaging and development, whether as residential subdivisions, shopping malls, scientific facilities or other complex activities. The potential for development is on a scale that implies either an already established urban catchment area, or the emergence of one around new construction. The latter implication, however, suggests exurban development, and the fringe or periphery assumes development ultimately related to the city within those vague boundaries.

The fringe or periphery, then, is the area beckoning development as an extension in some fashion of existing populations and activities inside the established metropolis. It is apparent visually, and it is distinct economically and politically. It is the main arena where developers can perceive options, and where governments perceive opportunities for shaping the future direction of urban life.

The Analytical Dilemma

Available or potentially available land subject to government controls poses a dilemma of analytical level. For the liberal democratic state, the imposition of limitations on the acquisition or disposal of land is a primary concern of the citizen. Western democracies all were founded on an objective of protecting private property. Liberal theory has dictated that state involvement must be confined to restrictions on one's property exclusively for the protection of the property of another.

Democratic theory extended this liberal principle to include restraints on private property to protect a broader community. Liberal theory, for example, would allow the state to restrict ill effects on water from pollution that might harm a neighbor; democratic theory would extend such a restriction where the damaging effect might only occur in common recreational water. But analysis at the level of the individual, or at the level of the community, still is not adequate, for neither liberal nor democratic theory defines the appropriate constituency for decision making.

What is the community that ought to decide how land is to be used? Is it the residents or electors within any given political jurisdiction? In federal systems that allocate authority among different jurisdictions, not always hierarchically, it becomes exceedingly difficult to agree upon a moral rule determining who ought to decide on collective good or the public interest.

The pressure to plan for the metropolis was stimulated by technical projections of demographic growth and agricultural land loss (and in Oregon and Hawaii by desires to open land for more equitable use), but it appeared necessary because no single political jurisdiction could exercise sufficient powers to impose control. Moreover, the interests involved were competing. Those seeking to develop the fringe were at odds with those seeking to limit growth. Often those seeking to develop enjoyed common perspective with political jurisdictions on the fringe. Those opposing development often were within the metropolitan core and without political authority where development would take place. And sometimes financial interests in the core were eager to develop the fringe over local resistance.

The larger population, of course, was already in the metropolitan area. A simple majoritarian formula would provide that population with control of the periphery, which encouraged schemes of metropolitanization or regionalization. In the characteristic North American politics of conquest, annexation has been a popular policy instrument for urban areas seizing control of the periphery.[5] However, if political jurisdictions define active political space, the metropolitan population would be free to govern within its borders; others would control the fringe.

In addition to this inherent conflict, all communities on the fringe are not necessarily in agreement. Some have been countrified oases for the rich; others have been working locations for small farmers. Some of the rich may encourage modest development to improve their tax base while others prefer no development at all. Some farmers may want to guarantee generational continuity working the land; others may want to sell to the highest bidder and assure themselves of substantial retirement income. Can the farmers be denied the right to sell their land for development? Can the exurbanites insulate their oases from a popular demand to share the land? Has the first occupier the right to set all terms for those who arrive in a place thereafter?[6]

In many instances even these local community or constituency conflicts do not adequately define the dilemma of level of analysis. In all Canada there are but four small regions for growing tender fruits, and only two that are considered frequently in jeopardy, the Okanagan in British Columbia and the Niagara Escarpment in Ontario. Is it in the national interest to protect these areas from urban development? Although the product may be precious, would Canadian dependence on other countries for tender fruits be an important national loss? Ontario fruits are not marketed in western Canada; is it in western Canada's interest to contribute to the protection of Ontario's exclusive fruit-bearing land?

More generally the argument concerning the protection of agricultural land derives from a concern about national self-sufficiency. Yet, the laws protecting agricultural land are provincial (or state), and they are designed for the local, not the national, constituency. Is it then important for British Columbia to retain a measure of agricultural self-sufficiency? Might one argue that national unity is better served by a national market, and that the national interest may be represented better by the agricultural production of a single region providing produce nationwide? Surely a similar argument has been made about manufacturing in Canada for nearly a century.

If the state should intervene beyond liberal principles, the definitions of level, jurisdiction, and constituency remain ambiguous. Yet any planning, any restrictive land use laws, express a political preference for one constituency or another, for one set of values or another. As we shall see, many of the technical forecasts of the 1950s and 1960s have not materialized, and enforced land use laws consequently have favored some economic, social, and political interests over others.

The Cases Compared

There are four central conclusions from comparing Canadian and American efforts to control urban sprawl:

1. There are at least as many similarities and differences crossing the forty-ninth parallel as there are similarities and differences within the two federal systems, although there is decidedly more judicial recourse in the United States.

2. Despite hindsight, laws having some effect in controlling urban sprawl were not designed originally for that purpose.

3. Land use controls are weakest on the urban periphery.

4. Times and circumstances change, despite the confident forecasts and projections of planners.

Canada vs. the United States

There are several ways in which Canadian and American cases may be classified. Many states and most provinces have specific land use laws to protect "critical areas," or special zones or flood plains or wetlands, etc., but rare is the statewide or provincewide law designed to bring most land under control through the protection of a single use or characteristic (See Table 5.1 for the jurisdictions and their statutes). Nevertheless, there are state and provincial laws whose primary initial purpose, at least as articulated publicly, was to preserve agricultural or rural land (British Columbia, Ontario, Oregon), or to protect particular land-using industries (Hawaii—pineapple and sugar cane). Other principal motivations included opening local housing opportunities with

Table 5.1
Comparing Land Use Controls

	Key Legislation	Date	Key Deciding Body	Centralized or Local Power
United States				
Hawaii	Hawaii Rev. Statute Ch.205	1961	Land Use Commission	Centralized
Oregon	S.B. 100	1973	Land Conservation & Development Commission	Centralized
Vermont	Act 250	1970	Environmental Board (Environmental District Commissions)	Local
Canada				
Alberta	RDA Regulation Act	1979	Planning Board Dept. of Environment	Centralized
B.C.	Land Commission Act	1972	Agricultural Land Commission	Centralized
Ontario	Planning Act Bill 154	1946/ 1973/ 1983	Ontario Municipal Board	Local
Quebec	Planning & Development Bill 125	1979	Regional County Municipalities	Local

price stability (Oregon) and combatting oligarchic land use restrictions (Hawaii). Most land use laws require local governments to gain approval of their own master plans from state or provincial governments, but Hawaii and Vermont, by contrast, seek statewide plans requiring conformity in all local zoning and planning decisions.

Some states and provinces provide much more guidance to local governments than others. British Columbia, Oregon, and Ontario, for example, by zoning all agricultural land according to soil classification, place a burden of proof for a zoning change on local governments or private owners. By contrast, Vermont's law was expected to be approved in three phases, the last incorporating a state master plan which in 1985 was yet to be passed. The master plan would provide comprehensive criteria for changing land classifications. And despite Hawaii's four broad zoning categories for all land in the state, (urban, agricultural, rural, conservation), no comprehensive state plan guides the Land Use Commission in judging county petitions for reclassification.

Some states or provinces emphasize the process of achieving land use planning. Quebec, Ontario, Alberta, Oregon, and Vermont require elaborate participatory procedures that have consumed many years in the pursuit of approved local and regional plans. In 1983, for example, 127 counties and cities in Oregon still had not completed approved plans; only one region of ten in Alberta had a plan approved. In each case the state or provincial government has invested significant sums providing expertise to local or regional governments to enable them to prepare a plan that will conform with state or provincial guidelines. However, the plan must be approved through local public hearings, and invariably it must compromise the interests of more than one municipality. It is never a merely technical exercise.

The Hawaii Land Use Commission has set out a procedural gauntlet (officials call it a "recipe") for reclassification of land. The process, in the absence of a state plan, has replaced substance, and fulfillment of the recipe merits conversion, typically from agricultural to urban use.

In the absence of approved plans, some governments freeze developments; others continue judging projects as they had in the past, while still others attempt to apply what they anticipate will be new criteria. However, the emphasis on participatory procedures to establish plans has extended the planning process literally into decades, with little actual control being operative or enforceable during the interim. And although some Canadian observers suppose that full-scale participation is an imported American concept that is little accepted in Canada, agencies devoted to land use planning emphasize participation almost everywhere in North America.

Whereas the classifications may be according to emphasis on procedure or an emphasis on criteria (agricultural or rural lands; environmental protections; channeled development; utility or service corridors; special uses), there are also important distinctions according to decision making control. In Florida and British Columbia, for example, the state and provincial cabinets act as super-zoning boards, the final court of appeals for reclassification decisions. Appeals in Oregon and Vermont may exceed the authority of the Land Conservation and Development Commission (LCDC) or the district environmental commissions and enter the judicial system even though one of Oregon's objectives in creating LCDC was to move land use decision out of the courts and into administration. Whereas "Development control is a purely local matter in Alberta,"[7] the appointed statewide Land Use Commission is the key democratic authority over land use in Hawaii. However, even the LUC can be challenged—by the state Department of Planning and Economic Development—in the courts, and there has been pressure building in the 1980s to restore power to county governments. Hence, there is great variety in land use institutional arrangements; there is no pattern corresponding to the United States or Canada, but ultimate reliance on the judiciary is more characteristic of the United States.

The Commitment to Control Sprawl

When Act 250 was passed in Vermont, less than 32 percent of the state's population lived in urban zones. The primary concern of legislators was to protect scenic and mountainous areas from resort and ski developments that might have adverse environmental effects and might harm the state's aesthetic appeal. Urban areas were not of primary concern.

Hawaii was interested in promoting compact urban areas, but primary consideration in 1961 was protection of the pineapple and sugar industries against encroachment from the tourist industry. Indeed, in the United States only Oregon placed much emphasis in enacting major land use legislation, S.B. 100, on controlling urban sprawl. Even then, Oregon's law was directed more against ribbon development and leap-frogging (the phenomenon of developments separated by vacant land) than against growth on the periphery. Oregon wanted to assure contiguous and compatible growth, thus directing where development might take place but not limiting its quantity.

Among the provincewide controls, the problem of urban sprawl was most typically entrusted to newly constituted regional governments. Manitoba created a metropolitan district for Winnipeg that effectively annexed the periphery for planning purposes; Regina and Saskatoon were similar beneficiaries of provincial initiative in Saskatchewan, and regional districts were created for seven areas including Calgary and Edmonton in Alberta. However, the cities on the prairies were unlike cities elsewhere in Canada. They generally had been incorporated with expansive lands, ultimately enabling a single municipality (or region) to determine development. When such conditions did not exist, as in Winnipeg and Edmonton, the creation of new government institutions involved the abolition by the province of competing municipalities. Eastern cities and cities in British Columbia more typically were surrounded by other incorporated areas with competing development agendas.

British Columbia's Agricultural Land Commission Act coincided with mounting pressure within Vancouver to slow down and limit growth. With British Columbia's prime agricultural land in the lower mainland and the Fraser River valley, stretching immediately south and east of Vancouver, growth in the province's principal city by definition would consume the best farmland. Thus, in British Columbia protection of agricultural land necessarily meant limiting growth on the urban periphery to a greater degree than elsewhere in North America, and sentiment in Vancouver was echoed in Victoria and in the Okanagan. Municipal governments on the urban fringe did not find such restrictions desirable, but the regional government, particularly the one embracing Vancouver, was dominated by the city, and the provincial government at the same time was environmentally conscious and keen to protect agriculture. It was an unusual coincidence of view.

Over time the experiences of Hawaii and British Columbia seem especially similar. With no municipal governments outside Honolulu, each of the islands constitutes a county. The Land Use Commission's majority representation comes from Oahu, which means that Honolulu's interests have been dominant. The British Columbian equivalent is the relationship within the Greater Vancouver Regional District of Vancouver to the principal outlying municipalities, especially Burnaby, Richmond, Surrey, and Delta in the lower mainland. Both Oahu and Vancouver in the 1960s wanted to relieve themselves of growth pressures, and both used land commissions emphasizing the protection of agriculture to displace growth from their own peripheries. In Hawaii the strategy was to encourage controlled growth on other islands; in British Columbia the strategy was to restrict all growth south and east. In both cases the original agricultural purpose of the land use laws was made to serve the economic well-being of core cities.

It is clear in application of the Vermont and Ontario land use laws that conservation of prime agricultural land has also meant conservative politics. In particular, in both cases downtown business interests have invoked the preservation of agricultural lands to oppose successfully competitive economic growth on the peripheries, although downtown banking and real estate interests in Toronto are more coincident with growth on that metropolitan fringe.[8] Regional governments have behaved in similar fashion in Manitoba and Saskatchewan, and it seems that objections to the appearance of like policies in Oregon contributed to the efforts to repeal S.B. 100. In Oregon's case there has been an apparent transformation of objectives often involving active assistance to developers to find suitable sites and opportunities and thus designed to balance the interests of new investors and old; only in this way has the law survived popular referenda.

Hence, commitment to controlling growth on the urban periphery generally has been a secondary and highly political effect of laws designed initially to preserve prime agricultural land or to open some land for more diversified use. Application of laws for growth control has been motivated as much by political and economic interests as by sincere commitment to environmental protection, although a theology emerged, especially in Canada, around regional governments combatting sprawl. Nevertheless, "orderly development" is often a code for the legal protection of entrenched interests, whether incorporated in the distant countryside or on the immediate urban fringe.

Success and Failure on the Periphery

The planning record on the urban fringe is not impressive. According to Gunnar Isberg, "Implementation devices used to date have not been overly successful in controlling development in the urban fringe."[9] One technique, "planned unit development," merely pushes the fringe further out, for as Daniel R. Mandelker observes, "Short of a major reshaping of underlying doctrine in the field of zoning jurisprudence, control techniques which can deal effectively with the problem of development adjacent to planned unit projects are difficult to construct."[10] And Richard P. Fishman, making a vigorous and extreme case for land banking, proposes removing land from any use: "A more effective way [than zoning] to combat urban sprawl and promote orderly development is to ensure the non-use of land for an indefinite period of time by acquiring or leasing the land."[11]

The need to control sprawl by eliminating the market altogether is an ultimate *cri de coeur* of failure. Perhaps the boldest effort to control sprawl in North America took place in Ontario, where the "golden age" of planning between 1966 and 1975 bore witness to the combined forces of the provincial government and the regional government of Toronto. Two senior Ontario officials responsible for programs in the period have concluded:

> The grandiose Design for Development promised further rationalization of regional political and planning powers, but unfortunately resulted in the creation of half-baked regional governments, the emasculation of Metropolitan Toronto planning efforts and a return to an uncoordinated planning system which cannot produce a coherent planning philosophy for the region.[12]

Design for Development was the grand scheme for the Toronto-centered region, eventually enabled by the Ontario Planning and Development Act of 1973 that conveyed unlimited municipal planning powers to the province.

Because the Toronto-Centered schemes involved the most massive governmental intervention, their failures are perhaps the most monumental, but they are not unique. Nor are the explanations for failure. According to the geographer Larry Bourne, Metro Toronto planning was destined to fail precisely because the urban center's boundaries were separated legally through suburban regional governments that "make[s no] sense in social, economic, or functional terms; nor are they suitable areas for planning purposes."[13] That essentially political problem of controlling the competing interests of jurisdictions has plagued all metropolitan planning and has been observed at least since Robert Wood wrote *1400 Governments.*[14]

Planning on the urban periphery has not been without success. Alberta's principal cities have guaranteed corridors for pipelines and utilities in a province vitally dependent upon the movement of petroleum. Protection of the Niagara Escarpment has begun modestly, although according to Barry Cullingworth politically unrealistic plans and proposals did not help advance environmental concerns.[15] The federal government has carved out of Ontario and Quebec Ottawa's national capital region, whose nearly unidimensional character has simplified growth patterns while helping the government to achieve its aesthetic, political and economic objectives. Urban growth boundaries helped stop unpopular developments in Wilsonville and Salem, Oregon,[16] and a large-scale unwanted project, Islandia, was blocked in Florida (although federal intervention in the executive and legislative branches was needed).[17]

More generally, efforts on the periphery remain untested. Oregon crafted S.B. 100 to situate urban growth boundaries to allow the growth and development projected to occur over twenty years.[18] These projections, moreover, were construed generously and assumed continuous economic vitality. In 1982 Oregon was second only to Michigan in unemployment, thus contributing to a general decline in the state's rate of growth. Oregon's urban peripheries now seem well beyond the farthest reach of development. Indeed, despite some effective intervention of the Land Conservation and Development Commission (LCDC), according to H. Jeffrey Leonard, Portland's urban growth boundary was set politically by the Columbia Regional Association of Governments and guarantees urban sprawl. He says, "The Portland area's only hope of retaining its present character lies in developing and implementing a metropolitan area development plan" that in 1983 still did not exist.[19] Moreover, Oregon's various official land use goals are in conflict, especially on the fringes, which are so far beyond the contiguous borders of urbanization that leapfrogging might yet occur within the Urban Growth Boundaries. So far, only the regulating zeal of LCDC stands between peripheral control and earlier growth patterns, and "Into the 1970s, most of Oregon's population growth and accompanying development took place at the urban fringe—in suburban housing, shopping, and commercial developments—or in widely scattered pockets in the countryside."[20]

The authority of LCDC in the presence of ambiguous or contradictory legislation is similar to the situation of the environmental district boards in Vermont and the Land Use Commission in Hawaii. Similar commissions decorate the Canadian planning landscape. In each instance a commission functions effectively like an administrative tribunal, approving, modifying, or rejecting development proposals accor ling to criteria that are not entirely clear to all players and that are forever subject to economic and political change. In the United States, such ambiguity and uncertainty has invited frequent litigation by individuals, corporations, and even state agencies, appealing the decisions of commissions.

Often laws aimed at assuring compatible or contiguous growth merely defend entrenched interests. One of the most celebrated of such cases is surely the frustrating effort of the Pyramid Corporation of New York to build a shopping mall outside Burlington, Vermont. After several years the case made its way to the Vermont Supreme Court, testing the "regional significance" clause in Criterion Ten of Act 250. Objections to development arose from the downtown businessmen in Burlington who feared the mall would contribute to (or accelerate) deterioration of the urban core.[21] Whereas competition often has adverse effects on some competitors, it is not self-evident that the public interest was most compatible with the interests of established businesses.

In less dramatic fashion, there are experiences akin to the Pyramid Mall case in every state and province that has enacted controls on the urban periphery. In every state and province, therefore, there are political cases determining who shall build and who shall leave, who shall flourish and who shall waste away, who shall sell and who shall buy. Such controls have guaranteed responsible use of resources, protecting drainage and water in elevated areas of Vermont,[22] for example, but they also constitute invitations to political corruption, which some earlier advocates of control think has taken place in British Columbia and Hawaii. In both places there is zoning, not planning, and exceptions to zoning are granted politically.

There are instances, too, where the formation of metropolitan or regional government was designed to encourage growth. Dade County in Florida acquired significant planning powers in 1956 and put them to work to assist development.[23] No comprehensive plan was ever articulated. Toronto's Design for Development was featured by a policy of "Go East," building infrastructure at public expense to persuade developers to work on the eastern edge of the metropolitan area.[24] Montreal's regional planning, in similar fashion, has been highlighted by public investment in infrastructure, thereby lowering costs to private developers. Regionalization has been devoted as often to the marshalling of resources as to the protection of the environment. In Florida, cities have never been designated critical areas; projects within them have never been classified of "regional interest," and state agencies, in the absence of a comprehensive plan, are expected to assist local and county governments in stimulating growth.[25]

The record is not much more impressive elsewhere. The restricted development areas in Alberta assured service corridors, but the metropolitan areas have spread beyond those boundaries. Quebec's land use program, so heavily committed to the process of writing and approving plans, is far from any test of enforcement and therefore no effective controls yet exist. Vermont's flirtation with transfer development rights (TDR) to assure farmers compensation when a public agency restricts land values by forbidding change of use opened more questions than could be answered, and there are still no examples of successful implementation.[26] Honolulu may have reached its limits simply because water resources on Oahu are near exhaustion.

Conclusions and Trends

Policy Instruments

Policy instruments for controlling urban sprawl were summoned and refined when many planners and decision makers thought population would grow exponentially, agricultural technology would be static, and economic conditions would guarantee progressive transportation improvements and increasing affluence. Often they were ready to be used only when the demographic surge had ended, agricultural commodities were in surplus, and the economic conditions had left many governments without the means to follow through on their own development schemes for highways and new towns. The demand for land on the urban fringe simply declined.

The policy of setting boundaries to control growth may be tested only when growth reaches those boundaries. Although Oregon's laws have discouraged some developments while encouraging growth in particular locations, it has not been tested on the urban fringe precisely because urban growth boundaries assure a robust projected growth. "Urbanizable" land, typically vacant or farmed, may even stimulate leapfrogging within the urban boundaries.

Tests of Vermont's Act 250 on the urban fringe have exposed the law as highly political and peculiarly burdensome for developers, a complaint now heard more frequently also in Hawaii. The exploration of TDRs indicates the protest of farmers who want to sell and raises doubts about the beneficiaries of the law's provisions.

In addition to setting boundaries and zoning against urbanization, state and provincial governments most frequently have turned to taxes and land banking to control urban sprawl. Tax policies generate incentives and disincentives for particular land uses, and have been employed often to facilitate the continuation of farming from one generation to the next. But as Fishman argued, no policy is as powerful as the direct acquisition of land (unless, of course, governments abdicate responsibility for management). When governments own land, they surely have the power to determine how it will be used.

State and provincial governments have acquired land often, particularly to secure rights-of-way for highways and utilities. Sometimes such land acquisition supports a projected use for public facilities to be built in the distant future. The policy is prudent socially, reducing the likelihood of displacing settled populations, and fiscally, for unoccupied land is cheaper. But when governments fail to use acquired land, the policy becomes more expensive. The land must be managed, and the investment is sunk. There is an opportunity cost in removing the land from the market where some alternative use might generate tax revenue, and governments can only speculate on the future value of perhaps strategically located but unused land.

Land banking for green belt or rights-of-way is qualitatively different from land banking for major concentrated projects. Undeveloped strips of land may go unnoticed in the urban landscape, and even when intended as boundaries they may be passed over. Large land parcels packaged by governments have a more direct impact on the urban landscape and economy.

Canadian governments have engaged in land banking far more than governments in the United States, perhaps because there has been ambiguity in American law about the constitutionality of seizing land without clear public purpose. In some Canadian experience, governments have operated as businesses for local profit, as in the development investments for resale in Red Deer, Alberta and Saskatoon, Saskatchewan. However, in eastern Canada the experience reflects neither economic acumen nor noble purpose or achievement.

The most celebrated cases are in Ontario where large parcels were acquired for projected new towns and other developments in Pickering, Townsend, Cayuga, and Edwardsburgh. According to Cullingworth, "the land acquisitions probably did more to discredit the image of planning than anything else."[27] Where private enterprise feared to tread, or could not afford to assemble large land packages, the provincial government stepped in, taking land out of the market, often driving up prices, and usually displacing villagers and farmers. In each case, government policy ultimately was to buy dear and sell cheap. When the economy was buoyant and prices high, the provincial government thought it could outdo developers. When projects failed and the economy declined, the government found itself with land it could not sell without acute political embarrassment because of certain financial loss.

The Ontario experience is not unique. The Canadian federal government required a change of political party before it could afford politically to begin surrendering nearly 80,000 "peripheral" acres originally expropriated for Mirabel Airport in Quebec, and it still holds 18,000 prime agricultural acres on the outskirts of Toronto for some future airport construction. Government megaprojects are prone to failure;[28] the assembly of land packages for them typically represents an essentially losing investment.

The Agricultural Argument and Urban Density

With the exception of Oregon, state and provincial land use policies that embraced the urban periphery were fashioned originally for the preservation of agricultural and rural lands. They began with claims about thousands of acres annually giving up the production of food for the construction of homes and businesses, and they forecast a loss of agricultural independence in North America.

These projections were based on a Malthusian principle of exponential growth in population exceeding food supply. However, as Dallas Miner reported in 1976, "food production has more than kept pace with population growth . . . between now and 2000 there is little need for concern over the availability of food in the U.S."[29] Indeed a veritable revolution in agricultural technology has increased crop production radically, at the very time that population growth on the continent has declined.*

There are moral and economic arguments defining the preservation of agricultural lands, but they are not obviously appropriate to regional, state, or provincial governments. Serious food shortages can be expected in other areas of the world, and there is certainly a moral logic to sharing North American abundance to feed the world's hungry. Furthermore, overseas demand for food can be expected to remain high, making agriculture an important export industry. However, the laws protecting agricultural land have neither national nor international visions, and they have notable local costs.

In Ontario, as elsewhere, the question raised among policy makers is why farmland should be protected when the surplus crops need to

---

*However, conversion of agricultural land may be irreversible and in Ontario, for example, crop rotation has declined, signalling a need for more fertilizer to maintain production.

be subsidized. Land use and agricultural policies are intertwined, and although perhaps inseparable, this essay unfortunately cannot address agricultural policy. Nevertheless, small farmers, the object of considerable political affection in the past, are far less enamored of laws preserving agricultural land than are the spokesmen of agribusiness. Indeed, the very introduction of the concept of TDRs signalled the disenchantment of small farmers who want to profit from lifelong investments in farming and farmland.

State and provincial laws to protect agriculture thus typically defend the interests of agribusiness while assuring urban dwellers of open and green space. The economic benefit of this arrangement may accrue to those with investments well within the urban boundaries, for limitations on development on the periphery may raise the value of land approved for development.[30] The social benefit of open space may be more aesthetic and cultural. It may be, however, that accusations of corruption in Hawaii and British Columbia zoning decisions are encouraged by the misleading public rationale for agricultural defense.

The sister argument of agricultural protection is the promotion of urban density. Here, too, the argument may be misleading. Although it is commonly asserted that economic efficiency is promoted through the intensification of use in compact urban areas, the argument is not self-evident. Because land at or near the center inevitably is more valuable than land on the periphery, especially in the presence of policies that raise doubt about the potential use of peripheral lands, the construction of additional facilities to service urban populations will be more expensive than new facilities at the fringe. Thus, for example, the addition of school children requiring more classroom space may precipitate a more cost-effective solution away from the urban core. Similarly, intensified use of old pipes and sewer lines, established roads and power lines, may increase the costs of repair and maintenance beyond the cost of altogether new facilities away from expensive land.

Although the Real Estate Research Corporation concluded that in general urban sprawl is likely to be more expensive than concentrated growth, their research team hastened to warn that every case was unique. They modeled different development mixes and demonstrated that service delivery is less expensive in compact zones, but they did not compare the cost of servicing additional population on the periphery with the cost of servicing and maintaining infrastructure closer to the core. Nor did they distinguish between older and newer facilities and housing stock.[31] It is obvious that it is least expensive to service homes where the services and roads already exist, but such an analysis begs the question. At best there remain uncertainties about the relative economic and social cost of development—long term and short term—in the core or on the fringe in any given North American city.

The provision of new services may be less expensive away from the urban center. It is not mere chance, for example, that the provision of cable television in rural areas preceded urban service by decades in the United States. Thus, planning that discourages sprawl may be protecting established economic interests, raising the land values of early occupiers while preventing newcomers from affording urban land and the services that accompany it. Urban dwellers do not want to pay to service suburbs or exurbs, and suburbanites are content to accept the subsidy in their homes provided through transportation systems and arteries. Not much seems to be known, however, about the trade-off.

Trends

Many of the procedures for land use control seemed to discourage development by requiring paperwork, hearings and permits. However, cumulatively the procedures also could invite development. The incrementalism of Hawaii's Land Use Commission, for example, encourages favorable decisions on reclassification petitions even though the process is burdensome.[32] Whether induced by recession or chastened by unfortunate experience, many governments have loosened land use controls. Responsible agencies in Ontario are seeking to assist investment and development, while Oregon's policy is to channel contiguous development without discouraging growth. Alberta has relaxed control generally. Only Hawaii and Vermont still pursue comprehensive state plans to guide local decisions, and only Hawaii nakedly uses authority to redistribute land and its value from the propertied and the rich to the poor. The British Columbia government has eliminated regional planning, and after appearing to reinstate municipalities as the key decision makers for development, has centralized planning authority in the provincial government, presumably to help investors stimulate growth.

Despite this general retreat from public intervention into the private land market, there is an important legacy from the burst of planning that affected the urban fringe. Much more is known about the quality of soils, and where a choice of land is available for development the burden usually now falls on the developer to demonstrate why the less valuable agricultural land is unsuitable for an urban purpose.

Much more is known about private projects that impose public expense because of demands on infrastructure or because of environmental pressure. In some instances private developers are expected now to meet such expense or at least to prove that they will minimize it. Vermont has established a presumption against construction that would adversely affect mountain drainage or state water supplies.

Whereas the public interest remains ambiguous, and the formulation of provincial or state interests is a continuing exercise of many responsible authorities, private developers are increasingly on notice that they must account for any public expense they may cause in pursuit of private gain. In some cases this awareness has been imposed through onerous approval procedures that have proved damaging to state and provincial economies. Ontario has made notable adjustments in approval procedures since the catastrophe of Design for Development; Vermont's lawmakers remain ambivalent. Oregon's authorities clearly have chosen in favor of helping developers when they seek to comply with state guidelines.

A *modus vivendi* is emerging between the public and private sectors as a result of the planning experience. There are no reliable performance standards because there are no reliable control groups for the few cases where serious attempts have been made to affect urban sprawl. Nevertheless, time and disappointment are forcing planners to bring hidden agendas into the open while obliging entrepreneurs to acknowledge the legitimacy of criteria that compete with profit. One may anticipate, in consequence, a growing partnership between state and provincial governments and private land developing interests. And the experience on each side of the forty-ninth parallel may prove instructive for the other, for the differences in federalism are outweighed by the similarity of policy instruments, planning techniques, social, economic, and cultural objectives.

Notes

1. Apocalyptic visions can be found, for example, in C. A. Doxiodis, *Ecumenopolis: The Settlement of the Future*, Research Report No. 1 (Athens, Greece: Athens Center for Ekistics, 1967); Christopher Tunnard and Boris Pushkarev, *Man-Made America: Chaos or Control* (New Haven: Yale University Press, 1963); Lewis Mumford, *The City in History* (New York: Harcourt, Brace and World, 1961).
2. Leonard O. Gertler and Ron Crowley, *Changing Canadian Cities: The Next 25 Years* (Toronto: McClelland and Stewart, 1977), p. 278.
3. Leonard O. Gertler, *Regional Planning in Canada: A Planner's Testament* (Montreal: Harvest House, 1972), especially pp. 35–41.
4. *Ibid*.
5. Theodore J. Lowi, *American Government: Incomplete Conquest* (New York: Holt, Rinehart and Winston, 1976).

6. For a classic statement of this dilemma, see George Bernard Shaw, ed., *Fabian Essays in Socialism* (Gloucester, Mass.: Peter Smith, 1967).

7. R. Audet and A. Le Henaff, *Land Planning Framework of Canada: An Overview*, Working Paper no. 28, (Ottawa: Ministry of Supply and Services for the Land Use Policy and Research Branch, Lands Directorate, Environment Canada, 1984), p. 32.

8. Leonard O. Gertler, speaking at the Seminar on Canadian-U.S. Relations, University Consortium for Research on North America, Harvard University, Cambridge, Mass., April 29, 1985.

9. Gunnar Isberg, "Controlling Growth in the Urban Fringe," in Randall W. Scott, ed., *Management and Control of Growth, Volume III*, (Washington, D.C.: Urban Land Institute, 1975), p. 34.

10. Daniel R. Mandelker, "PUDs and Growth Control: Procedures and Effects," in Scott, ed., *ibid.*, p. 47.

11. Richard P. Fishman, "Public Land Banking: Examination of Management Technique," in Scott, ed., *ibid.*, p. 62.

12. Wojciech Wronski and John G. Turnbull, "The Toronto-Centered Region," *Plan Canada* 24:3/4 (December '84), Special Issue: *Ontario Planned?*, p. 126.

13. Larry S. Bourne, "Planning for the Toronto Region: By Whom and for Whom," *Plan Canada, ibid.*, p. 139.

14. Robert C. Wood, *1400 Governments: The Political Economy of the New York Metropolitan Region* (New York: Doubleday Anchor Books, 1961).

15. Barry Cullingworth, "The Provincial Role in Planning and Development," *Plan Canada*, Special Issue, *op. cit.*, pp. 145–148.

16. H. Jeffrey Leonard, *Managing Oregon's Growth: The Politics of Development Planning* (Washington, D.C.: The Conservation Foundation, 1983), pp. 16–17.

17. Luther C. Carter, *The Florida Experience: Land and Water Policy in a Growth State* (Baltimore: Johns Hopkins University Press for Resources for the Future, 1974), pp. 160–161.

18. Leonard, *op. cit.*

19. *Ibid.*, p. 98.

20. *Ibid.*, p. 125.

21. Phyllis Myers, *So Goes Vermont: An Account of the Development, Passage and Implementation of State Land-Use Legislation in Vermont* (Washington, D.C.: Conservation Foundation, 1974); Robert G. Healy and John S. Rosenberg, *Land Use and the States*, Second Edition (Washington, D.C.: Resources for the Future, 1979), p. 55.

22. Myers, *ibid.*, p. 23; see also Frank J. Popper, *The Politics of Land-Use Reform*, (Madison: University of Wisconsin Press, 1981), p. 206.

23. Carter, *op. cit.*, p. 157; see also Richard H. Jackson *Land Use in America*, (New York: John Wiley and Sons, 1981), p. 33; Dana D. Minerva, "The Local Government Comprehensive Planning Act: The Issues," paper prepared for "Change, Challenge and Response: Meeting Florida's Future," Saddlebrook Resort, Wesley Chapel, Florida, October 19–21, 1983.

24. Wronski and Turnbull, *op. cit.*, p. 130.

25. Jackson, *op. cit.*

26. A celebrated attempt was made in St. George; see Burley Associates, *People on the Land*, Consulting Report, June 1973, and the town's *New Town Center Project*, Progress Report, July 1977. See also Frank Schnidman, "TDR: A Tool for More Equitable Land Management," in Frank Schnidman, Jane A. Silverman, and Rufus C. Young, Jr., eds., *Management and Control of Growth: Techniques in Application*, Volume IV, (Washington, D.C.: Urban Land Institute, 1978) pp. 52–57.

27. Cullingworth, *op. cit.* p. 151.
28. Elliot J. Feldman, "Patterns of Failure in Government Megaprojects: Economics, Politics, and Participation in Industrial Democracies," in Samuel P. Huntington and Joseph S. Nye, Jr., eds., *Global Dilemmas* (Cambridge, Mass. and Washington, D.C.: Harvard University Center for International Affairs and University Press of America, 1985), pp. 138–158.
29. Dallas D. Miner, "Agricultural Lands Preservation: A Growing Trend in Open Space Planning," in Scott, ed., *Management and Control of Growth, op. cit.*, p. 53.
30. Michael A. Goldberg and Peter Chinloy, *Urban Land Economics*, (New York: John Wiley and Sons, 1984), pp. 328–332.
31. Real Estate Research Corporation, "Costs of Sprawl: Detailed Cost Analysis," in Scott, ed., *Management and Control of Growth, Volume II*, pp. 577–596.
32. Interviews with William Yuen, Chairman, Hawaii Land Use Commission, Honolulu, December 30, 1982, and Gordon Furutani, Executive Officer, Hawaii Land Use Commission, Honolulu, December 29, 1982.

PART III

USING AND ABUSING UNDEVELOPED LAND: BEYOND THE FRINGE

6

A Forest of Institutions: Patterns of Choice on North American Timberlands

Christopher K. Leman

Trees grow in most parts of North America. They grow thickly enough to be called a forest on 1.5 billion acres—fully one-third of the land in both the United States and Canada.[1] Much of this timberland is beyond the fringe of urban development, and it far exceeds all acreage devoted to human settlement, transportation, and other built-up uses. Prior to European settlement, the North American forest was even more extensive; more than 350 million acres have since been cleared for farmland and settlement, and some of the land cleared has returned to trees.[2] Commercial logging is relatively recent as a major reason for the removal of trees. Nearly 700 million cubic meters of wood are now logged annually, about one-quarter of it in Canada and three-quarters in the United States.[3]

North American logging from the 18th to the 20th centuries consumed the primeval forests of one region after another—first New England, then New York and the Atlantic provinces, the lake states and southern Ontario and southern Quebec, the U.S. South, and finally northern Ontario and the far west of both countries.[4] The fires, floods, and illegalities of that era and the depleted forests left behind had by the late 19th century fueled a strong backlash in the United States against commercial logging. The conservation movement helped found the national forests (earlier called the forest reserves), mostly from public land that was previously slated for sale, but partly from cutover or farmed-out private lands; a drive for direct federal regulation of private forests was also strong, but had faltered by the 1950s.[5]

Canada's forests were not depleted as rapidly as those in the United States, and most of them formally remained in public hands. Canadians generally did not share in the U.S. backlash against commercial logging. At the peak of the U.S. conservation movement the Canadian provincial governments were building a lumber and paper industry—often with U.S. capital for U.S. markets—by granting long term cutting rights to massive areas with few restrictions of any kind.[6] A 1984 report of the Canadian Institute of Forestry, a professional association, recalls: "The desire of provincial governments for pulp and paper mill development was usually so great that tenure to the timber land was granted with little or no requirement for forest management."[7] A leading historian has written of one province that government was reduced "to a client of the business community."[8]

These contrasting histories have led to some important differences in how public timberland is managed in the two countries, even though private timberland is managed and regulated with fewer differences. This chapter assesses the performance of two kinds of public ownership (U.S. federal lands and Canadian provincial lands), each of which is respectively characteristic of one country, and two kinds of private ownership (industrial and nonindustrial) that can be found in both the United States and Canada. Although each of these four categories encompasses significant variation, they have distinctive central tendencies in the choices made. The decisions that are explored here, which collectively define public policy, include where to log and where to preserve areas unlogged; how to schedule the timber harvest; whether previously forested areas are regenerated; and how much environmental adjustment is taken in logging.

Most U.S. commercial forest land (nearly three-quarters) is nominally in private ownership; about one-fifth is owned by the federal government, especially in the national forests, and another 7.5 percent is owned by the states, localities, or Indian tribes.[9] U.S. private lands have more than their share of the good growing sites but less than their share of standing timber, especially old growth, as much was logged in recent decades.[10] In Canada the provincial governments control 90 percent of the country's forest land, including many of the best sites and much of the valuable timber.[11] As explained in Chapter 2, government-controlled lands in both countries will be referred to here generically as public lands, even though legally they are sometimes known by other names.

Only 2 percent of Canadian forest land is owned by the federal government, while 8 percent (49 million acres) is privately owned. Ontario and Quebec lead in private acreage, although it is only a fraction of

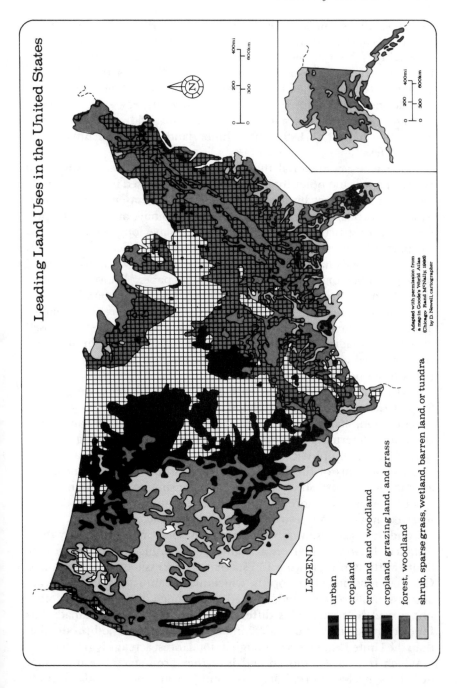

Leading Land Uses in the United States

LEGEND

urban

cropland

cropland and woodland

cropland, grazing land, and grass

forest, woodland

shrub, sparse grass, wetland, barren land, or tundra

Adapted with permission from
a map in Goode's World Atlas
(Chicago: Rand McNally, 1986)
by D. Newell, cartographer

their total timberlands. Only Nova Scotia, New Brunswick, and Prince Edward Island have more than half of their timberlands in private ownership.[12] The largest contiguous blocks of private forest land in both countries, and (especially in the United States) some of the best growing sites, are owned by industrial corporations. However, owners outside the forest industry—including many farmers—have the most acreage and account for more of the volume logged from private lands. More than half of all U.S. private timberland is in ownerships of 500 acres or less.[13]

Wood is a raw material that mills convert into lumber, structural panels, paper, and other forest products; it also is used for fuel, particularly as a byproduct by forest products mills themselves. Softwoods, which grow relatively quickly and are easier to mill, are generally preferred in construction, although hardwoods have long been preferred for particular uses such as flooring, furniture, and decorative panels. But as softwoods have become more scarce, hardwoods are being used more generally for construction panels and in paper.[14] Since the processing of timber presents issues much like those encountered in other manufacturing sectors, these issues are not examined here. This chapter assesses the characteristic economic and environmental questions posed by activities that take place in or near woodlands. Pollution of the forest from external sources, such as by acid rain, is also an important question but will not be covered here.

Silviculture is the art and science of growing and "harvesting" trees. Steps in silviculture taught in schools of forestry include site preparation, regeneration, stand-tending, and logging.[15] Soil, weather, and other conditions determine how well different species of trees will grow on a particular site. Biophysical patterns are no respecter of political boundaries, so sections of the United States and Canada that are near one another—e.g., British Columbia and Washington or Maine and Quebec—can have more in common silviculturally than they do with forested areas farther away in their own countries.

Conditions can also vary within a region, sometimes over a very short distance. However, there is a distinctive difference between the U.S. South with its fast-growing forests that are accessible year-round, and Canada's most northern forests, which may be unusually slow-growing and less easily regenerated, snowed in for much of the year and often not served by roads. This difference helps explain why Canada has fewer commercially exploitable timberlands and less wood production than the United States, even though its total forest acreage is greater.[16]

Which trees are removed and how they are logged are important questions in silviculture. Logging techniques in wide use today include

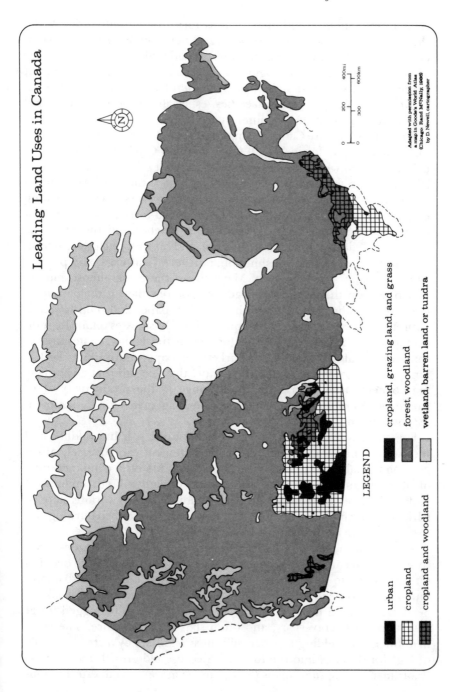

Leading Land Uses in Canada

LEGEND

urban

cropland

cropland and woodland

cropland, grazing land, and grass

forest, woodland

wetland, barren land, or tundra

Adapted with permission from
a map in Goode's World Atlas
(Chicago: Rand McNally, 1986)
by D. Newell, cartographer

clearcutting, shelterwood, and various forms of partial cutting.[17] Although clearcutting sometimes helps regeneration, its real attraction is economic, in that the practice minimizes road building and the number of entries into the forest. Logging has become highly mechanized, but it remains very labor-intensive and is one of the most dangerous of occupations. Yet processing facilities, especially to produce pulp and paper, are unusually capital-intensive.

Forest products are Canada's single largest industry, being the leading manufacturing sector in British Columbia and Quebec and the fourth one in Ontario while accounting for 14 percent of Canada's exports.[18] Although not as dominant in the United States, the industry employs nearly four percent of U.S. manufacturing workers and is a leading employer in several U.S. regions.[19] Commercial forestry is most prominent in the South, Northeast (including Quebec and the Maritime provinces), Midwest (including Ontario), and far west (including British Columbia, Oregon, and Washington, northern California, and parts of Alberta, Idaho and Montana). Many towns there are almost entirely dependent on the industry. Large corporations have a major role in the forest products sector in both countries; paper and pulp is almost entirely processed by such companies.[20] Small businesses retain a significant role in the manufacture of lumber in the United States and to some extent also in Canada.[21] Markets for paper and pulp as well as lumber and structural panels are competitive enough that a company may benefit from even a small advantage in the productivity of its woodland operations, whether in its own management or in its treatment by government.

Forests provide not only wood fiber, but water, fish and wildlife, and recreation; thus commercial timber management can adversely affect environmental quality. Each year logging occurs on a combined total of about eight million acres of U.S. and Canadian land; millions of additional acres are entered for road building and for various steps in silviculture including controversial activities like prescribed burning and the application of pesticides.[22]

Timber management involves one of the longest time horizons faced by either government or business. Since trees grow slowly, the decision on how much to log and how and when to do it can have broad and long-lasting consequences for the economy and the environment alike.[23] Seedlings planted now generally will not be ready to be logged for at least another twenty years, and often sixty years or more. The large investment of building a paper mill must be offset by a steady supply of logs for decades into the future.[24] Because old growth requires extraordinarily long time spans (300 years or more), it is in effect a nonrenewable resource, so its elimination poses profound economic, aesthetic, and ethical questions.[25] The old growth issue is strongest in the West, as much of the old growth in the East and South was eliminated long ago in both countries.

Professional foresters are involved in timber management throughout North America, but their numbers and influence vary. The United States has somewhere over 40,000 foresters and Canada has about 5,000 foresters, a difference that is in rough proportion to the two countries' populations. However, in relation to the amount of wood removed from timberlands, Canada has far fewer foresters—one for every 31,000 cubic meters in contrast to the U.S. ratio of one forester for every 10,500 cubic meters.[26] Thus for example, in a year in which the B.C. Ministry of Forests sold almost exactly the same volume of timber as did the U.S. Forest Service, the ministry employed only 327 foresters while the U.S. agency employed 4,897.[27] U.S. forest products companies employ many foresters to manage private lands, enough to startle a delegation of purchasers of provincial timber who visited the South.[28]

Although trade between Canada and the United States in unprocessed logs and in manufactured goods such as furniture faces some barriers, few barriers exist to trade in lumber, pulp, and paper products.[29] It is natural that since Canada has so much timber and the United States is the world's biggest customer for forest products, Canada is a net exporter in this field largely to the United States, which consequently is a net importer. In the mid-1980s nearly one-third of the lumber and nearly 10 percent of the paper products consumed in the United States came from Canada. The two countries' trade in outdoor recreation, however, favors the United States. Because more U.S. land has been set aside for hiking and camping, a surprising number of Canadians vacation there. Despite Canada's huge forested area, fewer areas are managed for recreation.[30]

Most of the existing studies of North American forest policy have focused on international trade, especially as a result of U.S.-Canadian disputes in the 1980s. This study instead is comparative, examining the two countries not as potential suppliers or customers for one another, but rather as experimenters with varying institutional approaches to a common task. Forestry questions traditionally have been addressed in biological or economic terms, yet the more important issues may well be institutional and political. Despite basic similarities in the biological and economic nature of timber management, North American timberlands are managed by a veritable forest of public and private institutions, with greater diversity probably than found in any other economic or environmental sector. These contrasting institutions—some of which operate in very close proximity to one another—have produced concrete differences in performance, and they are natural candidates for comparison.[31]

The nominal owners of public or private timberland alike frequently delegate various functions to other parties. Public agencies rely substantially for timber operations on private companies, which in turn rely for certain tasks on agency personnel. Some small landowners do none of their own logging and silviculture; in the U.S. South alone, 4.7 million acres of these lands were under long-term management contracts with large companies in 1984, and another 4.2 million acres were under landowner assistance programs (more voluntary in nature).[32] Although the companies that process wood conduct some of their own timber operations, they also often contract out much of the actual logging to small businesses, which in turn sometimes contract out to individuals such specialized tasks as the felling of trees.[33] Thus, whether the land is publicly or privately owned, it often may be logged by the same company or individual. The real choice among institutional approaches is often not between public and private action, but rather among different public/private relationships.

Pressures and Policy Making

The political forces for commodity production from timberlands are stronger in Canada than in the United States, while the forces for protection of forest amenities are weaker. In fact, whereas U.S. forest products interests most often share the stage with environmental activists, in Canada the most prominent groups in addition to the industry are usually forest workers' unions, which generally favor commodity production as much as do the companies. (U.S. forest workers' unions are weaker and less militant).[34]

These pressures are not spread evenly across either country. Because of differences in timber production, procommodity groups are weaker in some provinces than others, and there are many states with almost no procommodity pressures. On national questions, the U.S. forest products industry frequently has been weakened by divisions between regions and between large and small business; similar schisms in Canada have been discouraged by the provincial focus and a greater common dependence on foreign markets. Environmental groups that take positions on forest management are more evenly spread, but they are weaker in some regions. In relation to population, Quebec has fewer environmental groups than any other jurisdiction in either country. In the United States, the South has the fewest environmental groups, although they may be comparable in number with those found in such provinces as Ontario, New Brunswick, and Nova Scotia. The greatest number of environmental groups in either country is in the West, although British Columbia and Alberta do not have quite as many as do the western states.

But what may be more important than the size or distribution of pressure groups is which level of government is in charge of forest policy. A policy determined and administered at the national level will naturally be alert to national publics, including environmental groups in urban areas, thereby diminishing the power of a sector like the forest industry that is concentrated only in certain regions. The U.S. forest industry recognized this fact when in the 1940s and again in the 1970s it countered calls for federal regulation of various practices on private timberlands by securing state regulatory laws which it expected would be administered more sympathetically. Indeed, this chapter will show that the industry has been more influential with state regulators regarding privately owned timberlands than with Congress and federal agencies regarding public timber. In Canada, the management of public timberlands and the regulation of private timberlands are both in the hands of the provincial governments and are carried out with great attention to the preferences of industry in those provinces where it is dominant.[35] Although Canadian forest products companies suffer higher labor costs and more strikes than their U.S. counterparts, they also benefit from union clout in securing government generosity and helping to stave off challenges such as environmental measures that would reduce profits while also inconveniencing workers. Unions are especially weak in the U.S. South, where many states have "right-to-work" laws. The strongest Canadian regulation of public and private timberlands is national, through the Fisheries Act, which was strengthened in 1977 as a part of efforts by the federal government to assert itself against the provinces.

These patterns are reinforced by some other institutional differences. In the United States, laws are comparatively detailed and courts have taken a strong role in interpreting them; in Canada, laws are quite general and courts have more often deferred to administrators and to the political process.[36] Canada has had nothing like the U.S. court decisions (in response to suits by environmental groups) that led Congress to write the National Forest Management Act of 1976 as new guidance for the National Forests.[37] (A very recent exception is that Canadian courts have begun to entertain suits by native peoples regarding aboriginal land claims over some provincial lands.) Another difference is that the prevalence of the parliamentary system in Canada—in contrast to the separation of executive and legislative branches which exists in the United States—seems to discourage citizen activists in Canada and allow closer day-to-day relations between government officials and industry groups. The intermixing of public and private authority in Canada has reached the extent that provincial governments in Quebec, British Columbia, Manitoba, and Saskatchewan have bought stock in some companies that purchase provincial timber.[38]

The effect of these differences, added to the greater power of the forest industry at the provincial level, is to hamper environmental groups in Canada. Thus in British Columbia, the province with the most such groups, an environmental leader wrote in 1984:

> If Rod Serling were here to compose a nightmare for Sierra Club activists in the United States, it might involve transporting them back in time 20 years—to a period when hostile governments could deny them access to significant documents, discriminate against them in employment practices, prevent their representatives from lobbying on an equal footing with business interests, hide behind questions of standing in the courts, and routinely pursue environmentally destructive policies without incurring severe electoral backlash. For Sierra Club activists in British Columbia, however, this is not the Twilight Zone, but everyday reality.[39]

Organization and Management

There are few important U.S.-Canadian differences in the internal organization of private timberland owners but very great differences between large industrial and small nonindustrial owners. Large forest products firms that own timber have much labor and capital, and are oriented to very intensive management. Decisions are based primarily on considerations of investment return as determined by high-level financial officers.[40] However, several other considerations often intervene. Once a mill is installed and staffed, its appetite for a particular volume and mix of wood tends to dictate timber management decisions, sometimes conflicting with larger economic considerations. Foresters also exert a powerful influence, favoring a biological rather than an economic view.[41] Another important factor in industrial decision making—given the large acreage owned—is the political situation. One reaction by the corporations has been to bring public opinion and political leaders over to their way of thinking through lobbying, campaign contributions, and persuasion.[42] But the companies also have recognized a need to adapt, responding to public "stakeholders," not just to their own private stockholders.[43]

Small private timberland owners are organized very differently. Although they are unusually diverse, many lack the financing and the technical forestry and business skills that long-term efforts require. A surprising number are elderly; by one estimate, more than half of U.S. nonindustrial timberlands will be involved in estate proceedings by the end of the century.[44] Many small nonindustrial owners buy the land without planning to manage it actively.[45] Some are quite explicit in valuing the land's amenities over its commodity uses. Yet most sell timber from their land, and tend to do so in response to their particular financial circumstances rather than in response to silvicultural or broader economic conditions. The lack of common feeling among small owners and the lack of political salience of their timberlands—in comparison with industry lands—also reduces the extent that their decisions are swayed by public opinion.

Whereas these contrasts in organization for private timberland management generally apply to the United States and Canada alike, the institutions that manage public lands differ greatly between the two countries. For example, the administration of U.S. federal forest land is quite unified. Agencies like the Forest Service and the Bureau of Land Management largely control the land assigned to them. They are expected to consider not only timber production, but also water, wildlife, recreation, and so forth. In addition to foresters, they employ wildlife biologists, hydrologists, landscape architects, and archeologists, among others. Authority over state forest lands, however, is more fragmented. And Canadian provincial land, except in Ontario, is also subject to fragmentation.[46] A 1976 internal Quebec government report noted that fully fourteen different provincial agencies had a hand in administering its land.[47] For example, forestry, wildlife and pollution were the responsibility of entirely separate ministries. Similarly, in British Columbia, fish and wildlife concerns are assigned to the Ministry of the Environment, which deals with the Ministry of Forests regarding the impacts of timber management. In contrast, Ontario's Ministry of Natural Resources was consolidated in 1962 and now includes branches for forestry, mines, fish and wildlife, range, parks and recreation, and land management and planning.

U.S. federal land agencies traditionally have had decentralized field structures. In the Forest Service, for example, the 649 district rangers, who each may be in charge of up to several hundred thousand acres, have considerable operational authority. They report to the 122 forest supervisors, who have substantial policy discretion in the management of a national forest. Such authority is subject to direction and correction by the nine regional foresters and by the chief, as well as by the Agriculture

Department leadership, the President, and Congress. But field discretion ironically has been enhanced by the very proliferation of rules which, because they often conflict, often leave the ultimate decision to those "on the ground."[48]

The authority of Canadian provincial ministries of forestry traditionally has been more concentrated. Final approval of long-term timber sale contracts must be by the minister rather than by lower level officials. In the past decade, the provinces have carried out reorganizations that deconcentrated personnel and authority to field offices, forty-six in British Columbia, forty-six in Quebec, and forty-nine in Ontario.[49] Annual cutting permits in B.C. formerly were approved by regional offices; now this decision is the responsibility of the district offices. Even so, timber purchasers are able to appeal field decisions to regional offices (of which there are six in British Columbia, eight in Ontario, and nine in Quebec) or to the capital, with well-defined appeal procedures reaching senior levels of government.[50]

The Canadian forest products industry long insisted on this degree of concentrated authority in their dealings with the provincial ministries of forests. However, as the ministries are deconcentrating, so too are the companies. A regional forest engineer in one large company in British Columbia observed in an interview: "I'm deciding things that our head office used to decide, and our head office is having less contact with the Ministry of Forests' regional office in Vancouver. Meanwhile, the Ministry's district office . . . is insisting on having things sent right to them." Thus the Canadian pattern is slowly beginning to resemble the U.S. pattern of lower level company officials working with lower echelon bureaucrats.

Methods of selling public timber vary between the two countries. In the United States, the timber is auctioned to the highest bidder, sometimes with the requirement that the purchaser be a small business. The timber contracts typically extend for from two to five years and do not exceed about thirty million board feet, only a fraction of the amount needed by a mill. Hence, most firms hold more than one contract at a time.[51] In Canada, public timber sales generally are not awarded competitively, but are negotiated between the provincial ministry and the company, with the fee (known as "stumpage") determined (except in British Columbia) by rate schedules that are adjusted to economic conditions. In British Columbia, the fees are set by appraisal of the end-product selling price at the time of removal, minus the logging, hauling, and milling costs, administrative overhead, and an allowance for profit and risk. Although some agreements are short term, the typical one may run for ten or more years, and cover hundreds of millions of board feet, enough to supply a large mill. A company may be granted formal control over thousands of acres of forest land, or may be guaranteed cutting rights to a given volume of timber, without the location being specified. Legislative or administrative measures since 1970 have altered these arrangements in all the provinces, but without dropping their long-term nature. Several provinces have adopted some form of "evergreen license" that seeks to give the companies a greater feeling of "ownership" of a leased area, giving incentives and extracting promises for improved management. Examples are British Columbia's tree farm licenses and Ontario's and Alberta's forest management agreements.

Much of the selection of U.S. public timber to be logged and the planning and administration of the sale is done by public employees. Long-term plans determine the "allowable cut" and lay out a program of sale. More detailed plans lay out road networks and logging sites for five or more years ahead. Further effort goes into preparing each timber sale as the agency "cruises" the timber to determine its volume, marks it for sale, and notes various amenities to be protected. Bidders are provided a detailed prospectus; the contract contains a map showing the exact location of the timber and specifications on how it should be logged, including which logging system to use. Federal timber sale planners calculate the skyline cable deflection that a particular yarder landing will require. One supervisor of a large Oregon logging firm commented in an interview that the companies "don't even ask this of themselves." During logging, government employees administer the contract, inspecting the purchaser's work and often providing supervision. With so much government help and involvement, one Forest Service timber sale administrator says that many loggers "don't even read the contract."

In Canada, the timber purchasers have always played the major role in the planning and administration of the sale of public timber.[52] Since the mid-1970s, the provincial governments have taken a greater part in determining the volume cut through an upper tier of plans, but these plans are not numerous and offer few details on where, when, and how the logging will be conducted.[53] The companies still conduct most of the operational planning, and the current trend in each province is to rely on them more rather than less.[54]

Planning requirements for companies logging on provincial lands are detailed and elaborate. Yet provinces have not always obeyed or enforced these formal procedures. The minister or a deputy must approve a company's long-term management plan before necessary permits can be given and logging or roadbuilding can begin, but some timber operations on provincial lands have continued for decades without such approval. In British Columbia, to obtain an annual cutting permit, companies technically must submit a plan at least three months before harvest operations are to begin, but in some cases this interval has dropped to three weeks. In Ontario, although the requirement for approval of the annual cutting permit is fairly firm, the application and plan are often submitted only weeks before operations are to begin. Changes in some one-year plans have been granted after the year has begun, and after the actual trees in question have been cut. Although in most provinces a woods operation cannot begin until the cutting boundary has been marked or inspected on-site by personnel of the ministry, and until they have given approval in writing, this requirement is not always observed.[55] In a Quebec interview, the ministry district official in charge of the cutting permits and inspection did not know that one company's woods operation was then in progress at a new location.

Politically, the purchasers of Canadian provincial timber are in a stronger position than are the purchasers of U.S. federal timber. The provincial governments are committed, sometimes by law, to supplying the long term timber needs of the companies; if one area is withdrawn from logging, another must be found. Also, purchasers of timber in most of the provinces are not expected to carry out various silvicultural and environmental duties unless compensated, whether by public funds, reductions in charges for the timber, or tax deductions. In some cases, as in British Columbia, this compensation is required by law.[56] A major exception is Alberta, which has long imposed on timber purchasers the full cost of management actions, with no offset against the fees paid for the timber. Newfoundland assesses timber purchasers one-third of the cost of such activities, and Quebec is also moving to require them to pay a share.

In the United States, with rare exceptions (Alaska is one) the purchasers of federal timber have no long term guarantee of supply; they must constantly bid for public timber, with no assurance that the nation-wide volume offered will not decline (as in fact it has declined since the early 1970s). Also, the purchasers of U.S. federal timber are required as a part of the contract to conduct various silvicultural and environmental activities for which they are not directly compensated, except insofar as these requirements reduce the bid value of the offered sale.

A final difference between the United States and Canada is that the presence of a strong national forest service has assured regular inventories of the U.S. timber resource on both public and private lands. Canada lacks such a regular national inventory and consequently has gaps in its data, especially for private lands, and problems as well in the compatibility of data that the provinces have collected on their own lands.[57]

Where to Log and Where to Preserve Areas Unlogged

The pressure to log U.S. and Canadian natural areas at higher elevations generally were traditionally weaker than for lower elevations because in many cases the trees there are not as large or fast-growing and because removing them would require expensive roads and a long haul to the mill. Private owners were less likely to acquire such lands, not considering them financially attractive. The public agencies that ended up with these areas have not been bound by such economic considerations, however, and in some cases they have subsidized timber sales by the construction of forest roads from public funds and by reducing the fees charged. It may be that with the increased value of wood, timber companies would now like to own some of these high-elevation public lands if they had the chance. Nevertheless, it is clear that some of the logging on public lands in such places as Colorado, Wyoming, and Alberta would not occur if the lands were in private hands.[58]

At lower elevations, an area may combine breathtaking natural qualities with extremely valuable timber. In rare cases, as with parts of the California redwoods, private lands that were slated for logging became the subject of successful political campaigns for their donation to non-profit groups or condemnation and purchase by government.[59] Generally, however, private owners have logged their lands freely even when special natural qualities were present, encountering little effective political opposition. Publicly owned timberlands of this kind were themselves in the past rarely set aside from logging. By the 1920s, much of the old growth in the East and the U.S. South had been removed, and by the 1970s much of it at lower elevations in the West was gone. The earliest stands logged were often those close to urban areas where today they could have been enjoyed by large numbers of people.

Natural areas that also are valuable for timber have most been a subject for contention when publicly owned. The national park systems of Canada and the United States were funded in part to block the sale of timber in particularly scenic areas; valuable timberlands that formerly were open to logging are included now in Olympic, North Cascades, Sequoia and Kings Canyon National Parks in the United States, and would be in the proposed Pacific Rim National Park in British Columbia. In addition, some timberlands of the U.S. Forest Service and the Bureau of Land Management have been set aside from logging. Initially these protections resulted from internal innovators such as Aldo Leopold of the Forest Service in the 1920s.[60] Later outside protest and direction from Congress played a greater role—sometimes over the agencies' opposition—leading to the creation of the National Wilderness Preservation System in 1964 and the addition to it of valuable timber areas such as Oregon's French Pete.[61] Even so, prowilderness groups in the 1970s and 1980s lost more battles in the Northwest, where the conflict was with high-value timber, than they did in other parts of the United States, where the conflict was with oil and gas exploration, off-road vehicles, and other uses. In smaller amounts, U.S. federal and state agencies have also by administrative action set aside some valuable timberland as highway corridors, scenic, research, or wildlife areas, and so on.

The preservation story has been quite different on Canada's provincial public lands. Even the provincial parks were traditionally open to logging, and some still are, especially in Quebec. Nonpark provincial lands include much timber that is low in elevation and high in value—lands that in the United States would likely be in private ownership. And since logging is relatively more recent in Canada, some of these lands still have not been logged for the first time. Ironically, the Canadian practice of clearing off an area almost totally before moving on to the next one left some large expanses of timber intact, and some of these areas have become the subject of preservation campaigns in recent years. Because so many other timbered areas were available, provincial land managers for decades deferred the logging of particularly scenic areas, a protection that was generally initiated internally and informally rather than in response to outside pressures or a provincewide policy.[62] Thus in Quebec, field personnel of the Ministry of Energy and Resources in the 1960s and 1970s set aside from logging a breathtaking valley along the Malbaie River, unofficially designating and managing it as Le Parc de la Rivière Malbaie. At about the same time in Ontario's Ministry of Natural Resources, field personnel informally set aside from logging and roadbuilding the area around Northern Light Lake, which is a premier canoeing area and abuts on Quetico Provincial Park and the U.S. Boundary Waters Canoe Area. However, the increasing scarcity of timber on other lands in Quebec and Ontario has created pressures to log these areas. Even now, the pressures to preserve them from logging are coming largely from within government; in contrast to the situation in British Columbia, comparatively few outside groups have advocated the preservation of such areas. In an interview, one Quebec government forester, who had a large role in the development of Le Parc de la Rivière Malbaie, could not remember the office ever having been visited by a delegation of activists about this or any other issue.

Among the provinces, public activism for the preservation of natural areas from logging is greatest in British Columbia, where it approaches levels found in the United States. As in the other provinces, some scenic and untouched areas were for many years left unlogged, partly because of their remoteness but also partly from internal administrative action. Examples were the Stein River Valley (an area with some similarities to Oregon's French Pete), the Tsitika Watershed, the Tahsish area and the Sombrio Forest Trail on Vancouver Island, Meares Island, Windy Bay on South Moresby in the Queen Charlotte Islands, and the Cummins River Valley, Southern Chilcotin Mountains, and Valhalla Mountains in the interior.[63] As these areas came under increasing pressure for logging, activist groups took them up as a cause, helping to prompt the provincial government to study options. In almost every case, the outcome was bitterly disappointing to environmental groups; the logging was to proceed, although with some safeguards. Their only clear victory was in the 1983 decision to establish a provincial park in the Valhallas, and this outcome stemmed largely from the support of many local businesses. Environmental groups in the mid-1980s were welcoming the assertion by native peoples of aboriginal rights to some of these areas, such as Meares Island.[64]

How the Timber Harvest is Scheduled and Utilized

A fundamental question posed in forest management is how much to log and when over the years, a topic known to specialist as timber harvest scheduling.[65] The alternatives vary depending on whether the forest is young or is dominated by old growth. In a young forest, a key issue is rotation age, whether to cut trees at a small size (e.g., 20 or 40 years), largely for pulpwood or structural panels, and thereby make room for regeneration; or allow the trees to grow larger (e.g., 60 to 80 years), increasing their value for dimension lumber. In an old growth forest (with trees often 300 or more years old), the question is largely at what rate to remove the old trees. Their finely grained wood is particularly valuable for use in beams, siding, and so forth, but the extraordinarily long periods needed to produce such trees makes it unlikely that trees planted in their place will be allowed to grow so old.

The question of timber harvest scheduling is, in theory, separable from the questions of whether to log at all, and how much environmental adjustment to make in logging, but politically this separation is not always made. Suggestions that cutting old growth will free up productive sites may hide a more immediate desire to log the valuable old growth.[66] Only an extremely slow rate of cutting will allow old growth to accumulate anew; a moderately slow rate will eventually eliminate all of it just as surely as will a fast rate; but those who advocate a moderately slow rate may hope thereby to maintain more old growth to be saved permanently later. The relatively slow rate at which public agencies in both countries have logged existing old growth has *de facto* protected more of it so far than have formal preservation efforts and has provided decades of added benefits to fish and wildlife and for recreation and scenery.

Untouched old growth forests generally have a static volume of wood. Growth is offset by losses from insects, disease, and the weather. The very conditions that hamper overall increases in volume are part of the beauty and charm of old growth and may be reason enough to preserve it. But to the extent that the continued production of wood is a concern, some old growth stands will be logged. A slow rate of logging will bring a steady flow of valuable wood, gradually freeing up land that can then be regenerated into faster growing trees. A cost of this gradual approach is that many sites that would be ideal for growing large volumes of younger trees will for many decades remain in old growth. Cutting the old growth more quickly in the near term would permit the logging of large volumes of valuable wood and allow the land to be quickly stocked with faster growing trees, but would also mean a subsequent dropoff in timber production pending the maturation of the second forest.

Government Influence: Private Land

Although government has never formally regulated the rate of harvest on private lands in either country, it informally has influenced that rate in several ways.[67] Tax policy undoubtedly has had the biggest impact. Generous U.S. federal tax deductions for the interest on home mortgages and for state and local property taxes promote residential construction and hence wood sales. Canada has no such policy (of course, its wood sales already benefit greatly from U.S. promotion of construction), although it does allow taxpayers to claim more rapid depreciation on wood versus concrete structures (a provision also available in the United States). U.S. timber production is encouraged by a 1944 provision in the Internal Revenue Code taxing lightly as capital gains the returns from logging. The U.S. Department of the Treasury has estimated that in 1985 the forest industry will pay $355 million less in taxes under this law than if the same revenues were taxed at the ordinary income rates applying to corporations. (Economists disagree as to whether this tax provision has much impact on the rate of harvest.)[68]

Another U.S. tax provision that has no parallel in Canada is the 1980 reforestation tax incentive, which allows a ten percent tax credit and a seven-year tax deduction for the first $10,000 invested in reforestation each year.[69] For a small landowner, this provision is likely to promote regeneration more than does the provision on capital gains. Canadian owners of private timberland also enjoy various federal tax concessions, although most are general rather than being aimed at forestry, and they do not seem as large as those found in the United States.[70]

State, provincial, and local taxes also shape the rate of private harvest. Property taxes, which are assessed yearly, led many companies in both countries to forfeit their lands during the Depression.[71] On lands with standing timber, property taxes tend to favor quick harvest, an effect some states and provinces have tried to avoid by reducing them in favor of severance or yield taxes that are paid in the year that logging occurs.

Government Influence: Public Land

Tax policies also influence the rate of harvest on public lands. Favorable U.S. and Canadian treatment of gains from logging are available to the purchasers of public timber, encouraging its sale. Although not a tax, the fees from federal, state, and local timber sales are substantial, an incentive to maintain or increase the volume logged, especially as seen by those states and localities that depend on federal timber revenues for a significant share of their budgets (25 percent of national forest timber sale revenues go to the states to be spent in the counties where they were generated). The provinces place less emphasis on fees from the sale of public timber, relying more on taxes paid by the purchasers.[72] Thus, despite British Columbia's huge timber sales program, the fees collected have usually not exceeded those of its modest oil and gas leasing program.[73]

The government role regarding the volume and rate of timber harvest on public lands is much more direct than on private lands. The volume of U.S. federal timber offered for sale from one year to the next is determined by Congress working with the administration and the land management agencies. Legislators from the affected areas, state and local officials, and other regional interests are highly influential. Oregon's attorney general has pointed out that one of the biggest issues facing the state in recent decades has been how much timber should be sold from federal lands there.[74] The U.S. federal government has not committed itself formally to a particular long-term level of harvest, and thus is freer to reduce it in response to environmental concerns, as gradually occurred after federal timber sales reached their historic peak in the early 1970s. However, informal understandings have lent striking continuity to the volume offered for sale from year to year, despite changes in partisan control of the presidency and Congress and shifts in the relative power of the forest products industry and the environmental movement.

In the United States, government constantly offers tracts of public timber for sale and businesses decide whether to make the purchase. Thus, the volume actually purchased has varied widely; during the recession year of 1982 it fell to a level not seen since the 1950s. U.S. companies in the late 1970s were speculating in western federal and state timber (on a smaller scale, the same thing was occurring in Canada). When the bubble burst and prices began to decline, they could not afford to log the timber for which they had contracted,and they began to default and approach bankruptcy. Pressures were strong for bailout, and in 1984 Congress passed and President Reagan signed a bill allowing companies to buy out of many of their contracts.[75] This law freed up billions of board feet of timber previously under contract, markedly reducing the volume of logging that had been scheduled.

The greater preponderance of public land in Canada makes the decision on volume and rate of timber harvest there even more explicit and important. There is also a major policy difference between Canada and the United States with respect to how public timber is sold. Decades ago, the provincial governments promised various companies the opportunity to log a certain long-term volume of timber from public land. In exchange for being assured of a certain volume of public timber, the companies are expected to keep a certain number of people employed, even if economic conditions may not be favorable. Although these commitments are subject to periodic review and could be revoked, the provinces have been slow to change them and have kept their promise that reductions in the timber available in one area will be made up by increases in another. Only in recent years, as Canada has faced a crisis in the volume actually available for logging, has the prospect emerged of reductions in the timber sold from provincial public lands.

U.S. timber producers felt that the provinces' policy gave Canadian companies an unfair advantage. In 1982, they filed a formal complaint challenging the arrangements for sale of provincial timber.[76] When the U.S. Commerce Department's International Trade Administration rejected this complaint the following year, U.S. timber producers redoubled their efforts, and the agency reversed itself in 1986. Faced with a proposed U.S. 15 percent tariff, the Canadian side submitted to negotiations that produced a 15 percent Canadian surcharge on lumber exports to the United States. U.S. timber producers pressed for additional protection, and the issue has not been resolved at this writing. Lost in the controversy was the extent to which U.S. timber producers as well receive generous public subsidies, including the tax provisions mentioned above; and the major role of the vast U.S. federal deficit and the resulting strong dollar in pricing U.S. timber out of the market.

Other policies have important indirect impacts on the rate of timber harvest on public and private lands. The traditional U.S. policy of free trade in forest products has made it a net importer, relieving some pressures on U.S. timberlands. This same policy has greatly increased U.S. demand for Canadian forest products, as—ironically—has the U.S. Jones Act, which by requiring the use of U.S. flag vessels for shipment from one U.S. port to another makes it cheaper to import similar products from Canada.[77] In the 1980s, the overvalued U.S. dollar slowed U.S. exports while encouraging imports. To assure that timber exports generate more jobs domestically, Canadian federal and provincial governments often have required timber logged from public lands to be processed before export. A similar and more recent requirement exists for U.S. federal timber, which in the far wWest cannot be exported as logs, a policy that has somewhat reduced demand.[78] Logs from private lands and from most state lands can be exported, although only if they cannot be considered a substitute for unexportable federal logs—a restriction that curtails export from nonfederal stocks owned by many of those who also purchase from federal timberlands.

Market Influence and Financing

Modified by these various government measures, the market for forest products and the realities of finance still shape how the harvest is scheduled on U.S. and Canadian private timberlands. Generally, old growth has been cut at a faster rate on private lands, whose owners follow a shorter rotation in younger stands than do public owners. The owners of private timberlands, especially large corporations, are far less concerned than are public land agencies about providing a steady supply of wood to maintain local or regional economic stability. Overall, the private lands in the U.S. Northwest were so extensively cut from the 1950s to the 1970s that the harvest there has dropped off dramatically, causing many mills to close.[79] The South has become the greatest producer of U.S. timber, a shift symbolized by the 1982 move of the Georgia-Pacific Corporation's headquarters from Portland, Oregon to Atlanta, Georgia. While disruptive to particular regions, this mobility of corporate activities contributes to the national economy, and probably creates more jobs overall than a more static approach. But the fluctuations in private supply create a dilemma for public timberlands, which continue to offer for sale a steady supply, although the only way to stabilize some local economies would be to reduce sales in some places and increase them in others.[80]

Yet market considerations encompass significant variety in the scheduling of the harvest from private timberlands. The rapid liquidation of old growth by Georgia-Pacific was a legal condition of the loans under which it rapidly acquired new lands in the 1950s and 1960s.[81] In contrast, many companies—including some from which Georgia-Pacific had bought its lands—have cut their old growth gradually. Weyerhaeuser, for example, has decades of old growth left, reflecting a corporate choice to remain in that business. Similarly, companies vary in the rotation age they observe for younger growth. Some large corporations traditionally strove to maintain steady operations, avoiding layoffs or closures. The recessionary timber economy in the 1970s and 1980s weakened this tradition, however, and now the emphasis is in helping communities deal with the consequences of closures. The International Paper Company has been a leader in this effort.[82] Small companies whose timberland is localized have economic and political incentives and cultural ties motivating them to keep mills operating steadily there. Unfortunately, one price of this strategy has been that some of these smaller companies have gone bankrupt.

Getting More out of Each Tree

The adequacy of timber supplies depends partly on how efficiently forest products companies utilize each tree, avoiding waste in the woods and at the mill and partly on how effectively they market the product, assuring continued demand. Industry traditionally wasted much wood, both on public lands and on its own lands.[83] As the value of timber has increased, companies have improved their utilization of the available wood—particularly on their own lands, but also on U.S. federal lands where increasing fees have forced them to find ways to offset their costs, and where better utilization is required by the contracts under which federal timber is sold. Small nonindustrial private lands have not done as well, lacking the incentives and investment needed to improve utilization.

On Canadian provincial lands, government has done little to require such improvement and—perhaps more important—low fees have encouraged waste. Even the larger Canadian companies that purchase provincial timber have been slow to adapt. H. R. MacMillan, a forester who founded MacMillan Bloedel, Ltd., warned a royal commission in the 1950s that the system by which the provinces were guaranteeing timber supply for a few large companies was creating a monopoly that

> will be managed by professional bureaucrats, fixers with a penthouse viewpoint who, never having had rain in their lunch bucket, would abuse the forest. . . . Public interest would be victimized because vigorous, innovative

citizen businesses needed to provide the efficiency of competition would be denied logs and thereby prevented from penetration of the market.[84]

Thirty years later, a former MacMillan Bloedel and British Columbia trade association executive lamented that the system had created an industry whose "efficiency ranks last among forest areas of the western world."[85] The rare cases where U.S. companies have a guaranteed supply of public timber seem to suffer similar problems.[86] And in this case the companies are relatively small. That the guaranteed supply of timber rather than the size of the company is the root of the problem is also suggested by the fact that when large Canadian companies like MacMillan Bloedel own timberlands in the U.S. South, they manage them more aggressively than the Canadian provincial lands they control.

Whether Previously Forested Areas Are Regenerated

Reforestation is a challenge to any organization because it requires an investment now that will pay off several decades or more in the future. The forest institutions of North America greatly vary in how successfully they have faced this challenge. In Canada and the United States alike, some of the greatest successes and some of the greatest failures are found on private lands. The countries differ more on public lands, with those in the United States being more consistently reforested than their Canadian counterparts.

When trees are logged, new vegetation naturally follows, but not necessarily of the desired species. Since loggers take more of the species they find most valuable, the less valuable species left behind often take over. Thus valuable softwoods often have been succeeded by less valuable softwoods, and softwoods generally by hardwoods or brush. If logging is undertaken with an eye to future regeneration, such as by leaving seed trees of the desired species and preparing the ground for new growth, natural regeneration will be promoted. Natural regeneration generally is slower and less dense than when seedlings are planted artificially, although artificial means like seeding and planting pose the risk that the varieties introduced will not grow well in local conditions. The proportion of trees removed has different implications for regeneration depending on the site. In some areas, clearcutting may produce rapid regeneration, and in others a more selective approach works best. Some cutover areas will support softwood seedlings only if brush or hardwoods that initially compete with them are weeded out, whether manually or with herbicides. Careless or misplaced logging has left some sites virtually incapable of being reforested.

Another issue facing regeneration efforts is whether lands once cut should be retained as timberlands, or be diverted to cropland, urban growth, and other uses. Every year, many sites move out of the timberland category, just as some that are in nontimber uses are regenerated and brought into the timberland base. A new factor for the private owners of forestland in both countries is that a number of states and provinces, directly or through local governments, have adopted zoning systems that restrict forestland owners from putting their land to uses other than timber management. (Most public lands in effect have long been zoned against various urban and farm uses.)

Private Lands

During the early decades of logging, the owners of private forest land had little concern for reforestation because large supplies of valuable old growth stood ready for cutting elsewhere, and because uncontrolled wildfires made it difficult to see a growing forest as an attractive long-term investment. Industry's failure to reforest was a key complaint in the U.S. campaign by Gifford Pinchot and others for federal regulation of private forest lands. Such regulation was briefly introduced under the National Recovery Act (a law ruled unconstitutional by the Supreme Court in 1935), which required, for example, that seed trees be left after logging. Industry concern about further attempts at federal regulation helped in the promotion of cooperative fire protection, in the founding in 1941 of the American Tree Farm System, and in the passage of state laws requiring private owners to make some effort to achieve regeneration. Such changes reflected the industry's self-interest, but only in a broadly political sense; not until privately owned timber stocks began to dwindle in the 1950s did narrower economic self-interest contribute much to industry efforts at regeneration.[87]

Although few of the states require regeneration on private timber lands, some states, especially on the west coast, have strengthened this requirement since 1970.[88] Accordingly, timberland owners are more likely than in the past to seed or plant cutover lands rather than gamble that trees will grow back naturally. But economic incentives rather than legal obligation are most responsible for the aggressive efforts of large U.S. companies to seed or plant promising sites they have logged, with some also acquiring and regenerating cutover or farmed-out land much as did the public agencies in previous decades. They also have worked to improve the genetic makeup and the physical condition of seedlings.

Economic and political incentives matter also to the corporations that own private land in Canada, but these incentives have differed somewhat from those most often found in the United States. Timber remained abundant longer in Canada, with fewer competing uses for the land; thus private timberland owners there have had less economic incentive to manage their lands intensively. Especially in the East, the regeneration of Canadian private industrial timberlands has recently been neglected, much as was once the case in the United States. In British Columbia, where economic conditions more nearly approximate those in the United States, industrial lands are managed more intensively.[89]

Politically, Canada never had a campaign for federal regulation of private forest practices; thus industry did not feel the need to forestall federal regulation by promoting better practices voluntarily and through provincial legislation, as happened in the United States. In some provinces the industry supported mild regeneration requirements as a way to reduce the taxes on private timberlands, but rarely in the past was there much public concern about regeneration expressed at the provincial level. Concerned about scarcities of timber, the provincial governments in recent years have taken steps to require regeneration on private industrial lands. However, they generally have done so not by formal regulation but through informal pressure based on the fact that the same companies are greatly dependent on the purchase of timber from provincial lands and hence can be punished or rewarded by changes in what they are allowed to purchase.

Small private forest landowners in both countries generally have had a poor record in regeneration.[90] In part this performance reflects that some are more resistant to regulation than industrial owners, and are not regulated tightly. But also responsible is lack of basic knowledge in forestry, as in the choice of logging techniques that tend to discourage the return of softwoods.[91] Another problem is that small landowners have been unwilling or unable to invest in planting or other aspects of silviculture, and they have not always taken advantage of government subsidies, tax breaks, and technical assistance.[92] In Canada, the non-industrial owners are not purchasers of provincial timber and hence are not subject to the informal pressures from the provincial governments that are felt by industry.

Public Lands

The U.S. federal land agencies were early leaders in reforestation. Purchasers of federal timber were required contractually to log in a way that would facilitate regeneration. For decades, the Forest Service also was seeding or planting the cutover and farmed-out lands that it had received from the states or from private owners. Federal land managers were committed professionally and politically to bringing back the forest, notwithstanding the absence of economic incentives to do so. The Forest Service made extensive use of Civilian Conservation Corps (CCC) workers. Later it received authority to set aside a fraction of revenues for reforestation, building some regeneration costs into the timber sales process. Today's timber sales in the national forests of the East and South often are from the seedings and plantings of earlier decades.

The Bureau of Land Management also has worked hard at reforestation, assisted on its valuable "O & C" (revested Oregon and California Railroad land grant) timberlands by having a fraction of timber revenues set aside for administrative purposes. In the 1960s and 1970s, as ongoing public timber sales created a backlog of unplanted acres, Congress insisted that planting efforts be increased and that sites not be logged unless they could be reforested. Today, regeneration efforts on U.S. public lands are comparable to those on private lands in magnitude and in the improved quality of the planting stock used.

Public agencies tend to spread the regeneration effort rather evenly on their lands because of a biological conviction that trees should be stocked on every acre regardless of cost and because they recognize a political need to reach a maximum of congressional districts.[93] Industry is freer to concentrate its regeneration investment where growing conditions are best, but here too there is a tendency to spread the effort broadly, reflecting the strong influence of foresters with their often biological orientation.

Prior to the 1950s, many cutover private lands that industry was not reforesting reverted to the states because of failure to pay property taxes. The record of reforestation under state management initially was very poor, with a temporary boost from the CCC. Some state agencies, such as those in Michigan, Oregon, and Washington, were leaders in artificial regeneration. Washington's Department of Natural Resources, whose timberlands are the most valuable among the state agencies, routinely has set aside for reforestation a fraction of timber revenues.

The reforestation problems of Canada's provincial public lands are as serious as those on small, nonindustrial private lands in both countries. For decades, the provincial governments made few efforts to promote natural regeneration, and even now, only about one-quarter of the area of provincial lands cut over each year is being artificially replanted.[94] As a joint report by the provinces and the federal government observed in 1979, "Canada has allowed much of its most productive forestland to revert to a nonproductive state."[95] In 1983, the Science Council of Canada warned: "One-eighth of Canada's productive forest area has deteriorated to the point where huge tracts lie devastated, unable to regenerate a merchantable crop within the next 60 to 80 years. Each year some 200,000 to 400,000 hectares of valuable forest are being added to this shameful waste."[96] This report and others from the Canadian Forestry Service, the Canadian Institute of Forestry, and other groups lament that logging was often carried out in ways that made regeneration more difficult, relatively few efforts were made to improve planting stock, seeding or planting was not carried out on schedule, and regeneration efforts were not sufficiently followed up to ascertain if they had succeeded or new ones were needed.[97]

The traditional division of responsibilities on provincial lands in which the companies were to log and the government was to regenerate meant that government often did not step in even when damage clearly was being done. One Quebec forester interviewed says that the provincial government for decades never

> forced the forest operators, *as the law requires*, to ensure proper natural regeneration of the forests at the time of harvesting. . . . Natural regeneration is easy if some minor precautions are taken such as scarification with harvesting machinery and maintenance of seed trees in the cut areas. Our forest service unfortunately has failed its responsibilities disgustingly.

An Ontario provincial law between 1962 and 1979 even excused the companies explicitly from the task of reforestation. And as explained earlier, most of the provinces have avoided the imposition of requirements on timber purchasers for which the purchasers are not reimbursed by subsidies or a reduction in fees charged.

Even without concrete economic incentives, some Canadian timber purchasers have at least made an effort to log provincial lands in ways that would promote regeneration, thereby reflecting the values of the foresters these companies employ. A forester in one large B.C. company says that even in its less secure forms of tenure, the company tries to log in ways that will promote future regeneration. Thus it follows practices that differ little from those in its tree farm licenses, where it has a contractual obligation to do so.

Provincial political leaders were most responsible for neglect of regeneration, as they ignored frequent warnings from government foresters. Even in the last few years, when the magnitude of the current crisis has become a subject of widespread public discussion, budgetary austerity has led to cutbacks in promised regeneration, most notably in British Columbia. In fact, the government of British Columbia took years to sign an agreement bringing federal government aid for forest renewal, objecting to some of the federal conditions.[98] The agreement was finally signed in May 1985.

The codes of ethics of Canadian and U.S. foresters alike emphasize loyalty to the employer, but such loyalty had more serious consequences in Canada because political leaders were so unsympathetic to investments in regeneration. As one longtime manager in the Ontario Ministry of Natural Resources recalls, "Never once in 28 years did the Management Planning Section say: '. . . you're not doing your job, get with it'."[99] Canadian foresters have been slower than their U.S. counterparts to be political advocates. The code of ethics of the Association of British Columbia Foresters states: "The professional forester will refrain from criticizing other members in public, and will not engage in undignified controversial discussion in public or press."[100]

How Much Environmental Adjustment to Make in Logging

Depending on local conditions and on how and when timber operations are carried out, various environmental impacts are possible.[101] Silt and pesticides in water runoff can reduce stream quality, harming fish and downstream water users. The burning of slash—to reduce the danger of wildfire and to prepare sites for planting—produces smoke that can degrade pure mountain air and worsen urban air pollution. Wildlife, especially small game and nongame species, sometimes lose their habitat to logging; the dwindling of old growth can lead to extinctions, and the decline in diversity of habitat can reduce populations. The storage and movement of logs in streams, estuaries, and lakes often harm water quality and fisheries. Scenery can be dramatically, even irretrievably changed.

The environmental impacts of timber operations vary considerably among regions. The hilly terrain and the soil types of the West increase the land's vulnerability to erosion—but they also draw political attention by making the land more visible than do the flatter areas in the East and South. The shallowness and instability of soils varies from place to place as does the sensitivity of fish and wildlife.

In some cases, logging has environmental benefits and may be encouraged partly for that reason. Elk, moose, and deer often benefit from forest openings so long as timbered cover remains nearby. The removal of trees in certain critical locations can improve scenery by opening up a vista or creating variety.[102] The political compromise of removing old growth slowly has the drawback that constant, repeated entries into the forest may be detrimental; some foresters argue that the massive liquidation of old growth has environmental advantages in that it gives soil, streams, fish and wildlife a long undisturbed period to recover. Loggers in the 19th and early 20th centuries took only the most valuable logs, leaving behind debris that invited fires and harmed streams and fish. But today's effort to utilize more of the tree ("everything but the rustle," as the saying goes) could have the opposite problem of leaving behind insufficient organic matter to anchor and build the soil and provide wildlife habitat.

Because of the devastating appearance that it leaves, clearcutting has suffered more than its share of political backlash. Some of the debris that draws complaints was already on the ground and rotting before the trees were cut, but was previously hidden by them; and after logging, new growth is soon evident to the trained eye. The construction and maintenance of roads, however, has received probably less than its share of criticism, considering that it often does far more environmental damage than the logging activities themselves.

Scenic concerns are in the eye of the beholder. A company timber manager interviewed in British Columbia says: "With the small, staggered clearcuts now done in the U.S., you will never again have the smooth timbered slopes of the past. Here we cut a much wider area of timber at once, leaving it to grow back in a more unbroken expanse." Indeed, decades of logging on the flanks of Oregon's Mount Hood have clearly changed its appearance now and for the foreseeable future.

Environmental concerns present varying implications for timber operations.[103] Impacts are often hard to mitigate when road building and logging are already imminent; they are best addressed several years earlier when roads and logging sites are being designed. In many cases, timber operations can be modified easily and cheaply to prevent or mitigate environmental harm.[104] Relatively small adjustments in timber operations can benefit big game, and public access for hunting on public or private lands can be provided at relatively little cost, especially if directed away from areas of current logging activities.[105] Restrictions on the waterborne transportation of logs present only a moderate inconvenience because land-based alternatives are almost equally economical.[106] Smoke management is complicated because controlled burns can only be conducted on certain days, often on short notice; with sufficient planning, those sites that most need it can be treated, although greater labor costs may be incurred.[107] Restrictions on the use of herbicides in reforestation pose a more serious dilemma—not because brush and hardwoods cannot be cleared manually to release softwood seedlings, but because doing so is much more expensive without herbicides. Efforts to protect smaller animals and fish can also be costly, as they require that merchantable trees be left standing (especially in buffer strips along streams and as old "snags" for nesting) and that downed trees be removed carefully to avoid damage to soil, streams, and the trees that remain. The greatest cost to timber operations is if large amounts of accessible standing timber are left unlogged to protect wildlife, water, or scenery.

U.S. Federal Lands

A number of environmental laws and court decisions of the 1960s and 1970s have greatly affected the administration of U.S. federal lands. Under the National Environmental Policy Act of 1969, federal agencies perform environmental analysis prior to such actions as selling timber, building a road, or applying herbicides. The protection of wildlife, cultural resources, and air and water quality is required by other federal laws, some of which give state governments a say in the administration of federal lands.

In recent decades, U.S. public forest agencies have developed a quite long and complex process for incorporating environmental considerations in the process of selling timber. A typical timber sale contract contains specifications designed to protect wildlife, stream quality, soils, and scenery. Some of these restrictions clearly reduce the volume of timber that can be removed. In fact, a 1979 study found that on the national forests, such cautions in areas to be logged accounted for more loss of timber volume than did the withdrawal of land from logging for preservation as wilderness.[108]

Field personnel, for example, have tended to initiate tighter environmental limitations than have been approved by their agency leadership or political superiors. Although officially the Forest Service and Bureau of Land Management still allow certain herbicides, field decisions in recent years increasingly have de-emphasized their use because of concern about their effects and an awareness of local opposition.[109]

U.S. federal lands in different parts of the country that fall under the same laws and are managed by the same agencies, nevertheless tend to vary in degree of environmental caution depending on the local economic and political situation. Regulations implementing the National Forest Management Act of 1976 in effect authorize different sizes of clearcuts in different parts of the country, from one hundred acres in Alaska to forty acres in the Northeast. By unofficial practice, National Forest clearcuts in the South often directly border on highways, whereas a buffer strip would generally be left in national forests of the West. The federal land agencies are subject to state or local regulation of air and water quality and pesticides, and some states have regulated federal lands more tightly than private lands.

U.S. government contract administrators have significant power over timber purchasers. In fact, the Contract Disputes Act of 1976 requires that they have the final say; only an appeals board or the courts, and not their superiors, can overrule them. Although U.S. timber purchasers can appeal a decision such as an order to shut down operations if they are not living up to the contract, the action in question has already been taken and the burden of proof rests with the company. With many companies, an understanding exists that prevents this situation from arising very frequently. Government field personnel work closely with the loggers—who may not have purchased the timber, but rather may be under contract to the company that purchased the timber—and sometimes provide supervision that the company management would provide if the locations were not so remote and dispersed. The expansion of government offices and skills has actually enhanced the flexibility of administration in many instances. A logger who has long purchased Forest Service timber recalls the district rangers of the 1950s as being bound to rules and subject to rigid guidance from above.[110] Now, the logger says, the ranger has more help, and there are also skilled people at higher levels who may sometimes back up the loggers when they have a complaint against an arbitrary decision by the ranger. Although some authors have argued that a flexible approach to administration inevitably leads an agency to stray from its legislative mandate, the case of U.S. public timber sales suggests that this outcome is not inevitable.[111]

Provincial Lands

Canadian administrators have significant discretion in applying environmental constraints on the purchasers of provincial timber, as the laws are often vague. The environmental assessment laws found in the provinces generally do not apply to public timber management, in contrast to those in the United States. Still, a few laws are quite strict and specific. One of the oldest environmental laws on the continent is Quebec's "three chains law" (1884), which prohibits the cutting of timber within 200 feet of navigable rivers and lakes.[112] Buffer strips of this kind along waterways and highways were once common administratively in U.S. public agencies. However, as the timber became more scarce and as experts became available to remove it more selectively, such blanket measures became less common. The current regulations under which the U.S. national forests are managed suggest, but do not require, that a buffer strip of 100 feet receive special treatment. The Quebec law's impact is restricted in that "navigable" is taken literally, in contrast to the United States, where its legal meaning takes in streams and wetlands that are in no meaningful sense navigable. Under the federal Fisheries

Act, logging and road building on provincial and private lands alike can be halted when they harm fish habitats.

There has been less pressure for environmental protection in Canada than in the United States, with a corresponding difference in public policy. For example, among the suggestions in British Columbia's "Planning Guidelines for Coast Logging Operations" (1972) was a 200-acre limit in clearcuts and a restriction on openings next to streams or lakes.[113] An industry backlash against initial implementation prompted top-level ministry officials to loosen administration of the guidelines, and as a heritage of this episode, the ministry became (as described by one individual who helped write the guidelines) "gun shy" of specific directives regarding timber operations. In January 1985 British Columbia issued a draft of "Coastal Logging Guidelines" written jointly by the provincial government and the federal Department of Fisheries and Oceans, which administers the Fisheries Act. These guidelines specified four classes of streams and the precautions that companies should take in planning timber operations. However, industry protests forced a shelving of the guidelines, at least temporarily. Similarly, Ontario has considered but still has not released guidelines for environmental assessment of cutting practices, road building, stream protection, and other forest management activities.

Given the successful industry opposition to provincewide formal requirements, field-level initiative has emerged as an important influence. For example, each region of Ontario's Ministry of Natural Resources has its own guidelines for reserving timber near streams and roads, and the district managers may impose further restrictions, as in one district where a buffer strip of timber 400 feet wide has been set aside on the shores of lakes where trout are important.

Provincial agencies sometimes seek the voluntary cooperation of timber purchasers, but with negligible success. For example, when Ontario's 1976 proposed clear-cutting policy was getting nowhere, the prov- ince contracted with a consulting firm to prepare a handbook, *Design Guidelines for Forest Management*, suggesting various visual and environmental improvements in timber sale layout and operations.[114] As they were not mandatory, these recommendations provoked little backlash and usually were ignored by company and government personnel alike. Indeed, the chief harvest planner of one large paper company who was interviewed said that he had never heard of the handbook, and even the government forester who oversees that company's operations confessed to not making use of it.

A similar problem arose with a 1977 Quebec forest management handbook, whose visual and environmental suggestions included a restriction in size of 200 acres for clearcuts.[115] There is little evidence that the handbook had any impact on the layout decisions of company foresters or in the supervisory decisions of ministry personnel. In 1982, the B.C. Ministry of Forests published a booklet explaining how timber layouts can be blended better into the landscape; any language on requirements or guidelines was deliberately avoided, and it remains to be seen how much voluntary change will result.[116] A 1981 federal *Handbook for Fish Habitat Protection on Forest Lands in British Columbia* has had considerable impact, probably because the federal authorities wield more authority over fisheries than does the provincial government. The *Handbook* reprints the 1972 planning guidelines for coast logging operations, thereby providing enforcement of prov- incial rules that the province itself treats more loosely.[117]

Sheer geographic size impedes Canadian administrators trying to monitor industry practices on public lands. In north central Ontario, for example, the wildlife biologists who assist in the planning and administration of provincial timber sales are each responsible on the average for 9,090 square miles of territory. Conservation officers from the wildlife branch of B.C.'s Ministry of the Environment are responsible for an average of "only" 1200 square miles, but they also must patrol the area for infractions of the game laws and enforce water and air pollution statutes. When the wildlife branch of the B.C. Ministry of the Environment objected that a proposed timber harvest on the west coast of Vancouver Island would interfere with deer, the Ministry of Forests replied: "If there is a specific problem with deer habitat, we would appreciate your advice as to where these areas exist."

Although the permits required of companies who remove timber from provincial lands were adopted originally to assure an accurate accounting of timber purchases, they stand ready for more consciously environmental purposes. Nevertheless, purchasers of provincial timber have successfully resisted detailed planning for environmental impacts, insisting on a need for flexibility in choosing logging sites for future years. Thus, the five-year development plans they submit to sketch out the location and sequence of logging and road building have remained general and are changed frequently. The annual cutting permits, which are to show the precise boundaries of timber stands to be cut, the location of roads, and needed precautions, are the main lever available to the provinces in pressing for environmental adjustments by timber purchasers. However, the companies typically have requested the permits shortly before woods operations are to begin. By this time the companies have made significant preparations for roads, personnel, camps, equipment, and marketing, and the provincial agencies are under severe pressure not to change them.

In Canada the burden of proof prior to administrative action has rested with agency field personnel, and even when authorization for a shutdown can be obtained, the occasion for action usually has passed. Provincial field inspectors must clear any strong actions with their superiors in the district office, and frequently with high regional authorities, who are receptive to company complaints. As one Ontario regional official has observed:

> A decision that is technically correct and according to all regulations which industry does not agree with is often referred to a higher level in the Ministry in the hope of having it changed . . . the practice of dealing at any level chosen by a company is not efficient, good for morale or good management.[118]

Companies vary in how much they are likely to resist and appeal the decisions of ministry personnel in the field. In one area of British Columbia, a ministry resource assistant oversees the activities of two companies that could hardly be more different. A relatively small company is notorious for its confrontational attitude toward the government: "The woods superintendent always tells me yes, whether or not he intends to do what I say. I have to try to check everything there completely—every stretch of road and every marking of the opening boundary." The other company is one of B.C.'s largest and most progressive, employing many foresters and even some biologists. The resource assistant can always count on its cooperation, and the company has been known to call attention to problems that the resource assistant might otherwise have overlooked.

Out of a combination of professional conscience and political self-interest, some leading Canadian companies have embraced voluntarily certain environmental concerns. Large companies like MacMillan Bloedel and British Columbia Forest Products have developed checklists for the protection of streamside areas that in some cases are more detailed than required by the B.C. Ministry of Forest. A forester of one of these companies observes:

> My company doesn't object if I do something that costs more. In fact, I'll probably get in more trouble if I do something that causes a problem, like in fisheries.

This company's spirit extends beyond immediate economic advantage. The forester suggests that the main effect of the more extensive requirements imposed in British Columbia's tree farm licenses is to moderate the behavior of the worst companies rather than to induce much improvement in the best ones. The company appreciates this impact on other companies for the political reason that it will suffer less public backlash against such practices when it had nothing to do with them, and the economic reason that the company will no longer feel at a competitive disadvantage for being a good citizen.

The tightest regulation on the provincial public lands is probably in the use of pesticides. As on U.S. federal lands, public concern has led to restrictions, although only in some provinces. In the early 1980s, Quebec banned the use of any herbicides on government timberlands. More selective restrictions exist in several other provinces. However, royal commissions in Newfoundland (1981) and Nova Scotia (1984) strongly endorsed the use of herbicides on timberlands, and the herbicide 2,4,5-T was being used in New Brunswick until 1986 when its use was no longer allowed by the federal government.

Private Lands

Despite the failure during his lifetime of Gifford Pinchot's campaign for comprehensive federal regulation of private forest lands, various federal, state, and local laws have in a piecemeal fashion subjected these lands to increasing regulation. Discussed above were regulatory efforts to promote the regeneration of cutover lands. More recent and complex are efforts to promote various other environmental concerns, sometimes through strong federal action but usually through action at other levels of government.

On private forest lands, the degree to which environmental concerns are reflected in logging depends partly on voluntary action by the owners and, even more, on their regulation by government. Certain environmental features—scenery, clean water, and so on—that are threatened by logging are public goods, which benefit all and cannot easily be captured as property rights; hence they are not protected by narrow economic interest. Private owners have little economic incentive to protect common property resources. In any case, they may fear that competitors will not take similar care and thereby gain a competitive advantage in the marketplace. Narrow financial considerations would suggest that logging be done quickly and cheaply, with little consideration for when and how to minimize environmental harm. Owners vary greatly, however, in how they interpret the economic standard. Large companies and small owners alike follow varying philosophies in how far ahead they plan logging sites, how frequently they shift the sites in response to the market and how frequently they re-enter a timber stand for thinning.[119]

Few private owners follow financial considerations exclusively. In summarizing why small owners buy forest land, one leading consulting firm observed: "Timberland is something you can see, feel, smell, walk around on, and enjoy with your family. If you love the woods as much as we do, this is a huge plus."[120] Although forest products companies are less likely to pursue noncommercial objectives explicitly, the foresters who advise in the management of these companies' lands are by training and conviction oriented not only to the production of timber but to the protection of soil, water, fish, and wildlife. Political considerations also dictate a consideration of factors outside the immediate economics of logging. Far-reaching land ownership and regional economic impact have made forest products companies sensitive to the decisions of state and local governments.[121] Environmental precautions are one way, sometimes the cheapest way, to build goodwill.

State taxes are a major cost of doing business. Industrial timberland owners are aware that if they become unpopular because of environmental concern, they could suffer an increased rate of taxation and increased assessment by local elected officials. Also, companies wish to be seen as good citizens in order to stave off greater public pressure, including more restrictive regulations or, at the extreme, vandalism or expropriation of their lands. Many environmental adjustments in timber management, whether they be voluntary or in response to regulation, impose only a low or moderate cost on timber operations. The financial, physical, and human resources of large companies allow them to make this adjustment more easily than smaller owners. State regulators generally have encountered more violations and more resistance in relation to the volume logged on nonindustrial private lands than on industry-owned lands.[122] Of course, some small owners are very cooperative, while some large companies are not. In the 1950s and 1960s, companies that were concerned about the industry's image problems were angered by Georgia-Pacific's unrestrained technique in logging; however, in recent years, that company, too, has sought good citizenship environmentally.[123]

Many industry-owned timberlands are traditional sites for hunting or fishing by local residents. For political reasons, timberland owners must tolerate some of this use and must moderate their logging activities when there is little nearby public land or differently managed private land to provide diversity. When in the late 1970s Weyerhaeuser acquired the huge Dierks tract in eastern Oklahoma and western Arkansas and began to manage it intensively, the company quickly encountered pressure to give more consideration to fish and wildlife. Under a 1980 memorandum of understanding signed with the Oklahoma state wildlife agency, Weyerhaeuser agreed to give special protection to streams, leave snags for wildlife, and keep clearcuts under 350 acres, among other steps.[124] The company soon came under criticism for not observing the terms of this agreement, especially from the National Wildlife Federation, which owns some Weyerhaeuser stock. A blue ribbon panel appointed by the Federation examined the issue, finding that the company indeed was not observing some of the practices to which it had agreed.[125] In 1983 Weyerhaeuser signed a new agreement with the Oklahoma Wildlife Federation essentially restating the 1980 guidelines.[126]

Even if corporate managers may want field activities to adjust to environmental concerns, on-the-ground incentives may thwart this concern, as when field managers are held mainly to financial measures, or loggers look to time, convenience, and safety. Suspending logs while crossing streams, leaving snags and timbered buffer strips, and cleaning up debris are costly, difficult, and thankless tasks. On-the-ground incentives seem to have contributed to Weyerhaeuser's failure to carry out all the terms of its 1980 memorandum of understanding. To help introduce environmental considerations into field situations on private lands when a situation is of critical public or governmental concern, Weyerhaeuser and other large corporations increasingly require logging planners to prepare an environmental assessment that is not dissimilar from those prepared on U.S. public lands.

Some of the tightest regulations faced on private lands stem from action at the federal level. Canada's strong Fisheries Act is federally enforced. Extensive U.S. state efforts to regulate the smoke from timber operations are mandated by a federal law, the Clean Air Act. As a result of a 1979 administrative action of the Environmental Protection Agency, private and public forest managers were denied the use of the herbicides 2,4,5-T and Silvex years before this prohibition was extended to farmers and ranchers.[127] At about the same time, federal action in Canada banned all uses of Silvex, but 2,4,5-T continued to be allowed for timber management until its registration was discontinued in 1986.

State environmental laws that have been passed since 1970 often have been supported by industry as a means to stave off federal regulation, much as was the case with the earlier wave of laws promoting the regeneration of cutover sites.[128] Industry committees traditionally were given a role in such regulation, although state agencies have taken over more of the formal authority in recent decades (sometimes, as in California, pressed to do so by the courts). A more recent motivation for industry support of state laws has been to supersede local regulations as they have begun to proliferate.[129] Even so, most of the states and provinces, especially those in the East, still lack laws that regulate forest practices.[130]

The U.S. Water Pollution Control Amendments Act of 1972 established major new requirements for the reduction of water pollution in urban and rural areas alike. As passed and as interpreted by the courts, this law would have involved the issuance of tens of thousands of permits annually to timber companies for the alteration of wetlands and the crossing of stream courses, and it would have required the states to regulate closely "nonpoint sources" of water pollution. However, in league with agricultural interests, the forest industry fought successfully to loosen the administration of this law and then to alter its text, even as the law's regulation of urban water quality remained firm.[131] Protest from the industry overturned both a 1972 effort by the Environmental Protection Agency to require permits for routine forestry activities and a 1974 effort by EPA to promote a model forest practices act. Then in 1977 the law was amended to exempt routine forestry activities from the need for permits.[132] Throughout the mid-1970s, the EPA moved away from the mandatory enforcement by the states against nonpoint water pollution that it required in most other regulatory programs. As one study sponsored by the forest industry has observed: "Because silvicultural NPS (nonpoint source) control programs departed from this uniform-regulations approach and instead capitalized on the existing informational, regulatory infrastructure of the forestry community, these NPS control programs have generally avoided the resistance reported for other environmental protection programs and have, to the contrary, been supported by both the states and the industry." Industry groups became leading supporters of the program.[133]

In sum, industry has escaped some forms of regulation that would pose large costs to timber operations on private lands. Provincial, state and local regulation of scenic aspects of logging has been largely avoided, although it is beginning to arise in some areas of the United States. Local publics dislike the use of herbicides on public and private land alike, but they have not been as successful at discouraging their use on private lands. After residents of Cape Breton Island obtained an injunction stopping Nova Scotia Forest Industries from spraying 2,4,5-T and Silvex on its private timberlands, the Nova Scotia Supreme Court in 1983 rejected this challenge, praising in its opinion the scientists who had testified on the company's behalf and questioning the objectivity of those who had testified for a ban on herbicides. (Testifying on each side were some U.S. scientists who have contended with each other in U.S. administrative proceedings and political debates, with opposite results.) The court assessed the company's legal costs to those who had sued it; the company forgave most of these costs in exchange for their agreement not to appeal the overall decision.[134]

All but a few state governments rely entirely on voluntary compliance from private timberland owners. This voluntary approach has produced more results in forestry than in agriculture, where the political backlash against pollution is less and where a professional group like foresters does not occupy as strategic a position. But efforts to tighten state regulation of timberlands continue to be resisted by industry. Evaluations of Oregon's regulation of private forest operations find practices that federal land agencies would not allow.[135] The regulators have been plagued by shortages of funds and of experienced, skilled personnel. Although California has perhaps the continent's tightest regulation of private industrial timber lands, one knowledgeable insider gives the state effort a grade of somewhere between "B" and "C."[136] The impact of state regulation on U.S. private land probably has not much altered the behavior of the more progressive companies. Nevertheless, it probably has helped to bring many of the other companies closer to a higher standard, an outcome that the progressive companies appreciate for competitive reasons.

Conclusion

Despite the nominal distinction between public and private ownership, the institutional arrangements for timberland examined here all involve some mix of public and private authority. In no case does government ownership of timberlands mean that public authorities are fully responsible for management; to varying degrees governments have delegated management tasks to private companies. Private landowners, too, delegate some timber management responsibilities to others, as with logging and replanting. Even the most vertically integrated private timberland owner is influenced strongly by such public policies as taxes, international trade, and regulation, as well as by the potential for further government action. Recognizing the mix of public and private authority, this chapter has examined two kinds of nominally public ownerships (U.S. federal lands and Canadian provincial lands) and two kinds of nominally private ownerships (industrial and nonindustrial). The variations within the public and private categories often exceed those between them.

One of the few clear distinctions between public and private ownership is in timber harvest scheduling. Public ownerships in each country are especially concerned to supply from public lands a maximum volume of wood that is steady locally, even where doing so may sacrifice opportunities for higher economic returns. Private landowners, by contrast, place a higher priority on producing more overall economic value over the long term, foregoing the maximum wood volume and allowing periodic scarcities locally. Still, there remains significant variation within the public and private sectors, suggesting that politics and markets respectively are less than conclusive guides to action for them.

In other activities, such as regeneration after logging, the record within public and private ownerships alike is very mixed. Industry's recent successes—especially in contrast to its earlier dismal performance when commercial incentives discouraged regeneration—suggest the contributions of the profit motive. An apparent U.S.-Canadian difference in eastern industrial timberlands is rooted more in the different economic situations than in cultural or institutional differences. Yet the generally disappointing performance of nonindustrial lands suggests that market considerations may be insufficient and sometimes may be a quite misleading guide for action. In fact, this difference arises not from economics, but rather because foresters are far more influential in many large companies than on nonindustrial lands.

The variation among public landholdings is equally great. Canadian provincial lands today face a crisis in timber supply because political leaders and administrators for decades were permissive with timber purchasers and deferred needed seeding and planting. Industry did not perceive an incentive to help because it had the advantages of ownership with few of the responsibilities. A key in Canada was the failure to integrate logging with regeneration. Such an integration has been a trademark of regeneration success on U.S. federal lands, pressed by the professional concerns of foresters and by political demand for results. Also important to U.S. success is that the costs of regeneration have to some extent been hidden in off-budget spending and tax expenditures, whereas they remained explicit in the provinces and hence politically harder to sustain. U.S. federal success confounds the view that government *a priori* lacks the capacity to incur immediate costs for far-off benefits.[137] Institutions clearly matter for forest regeneration, but public and private approaches alike can produce the desired results, while failures can be found in both nominally public and nominally private organizations.[138]

A good record in preserving natural areas from logging and in assuring that logging is conducted in an environmentally sound manner has been compiled by the U.S. federal agencies, which—often under pressure from Congress—sometimes have ignored the market for timber as a commodity when unpriced amenities are at stake. As with regeneration, U.S. timber purchasers have been required to take environmental precautions as part of the contract, making these requirements politically more acceptable than when companies must explicitly be reimbursed for them, as in provincial timber sales. Some of the greatest loss of natural areas and some of the most environmentally damaging logging has occurred on private lands, with industrial lands being managed most intensively and consequently having major environmental impacts but with smaller nonindustrial ownerships having more impact in relation to the volume of timber removed. The market tends to punish companies that take special precautions in logging; thus government regulation such as is found in the U.S. Northwest has prevented some harm that occurs in Canada and the U.S. South where regulation is lighter or nonexistent.

Yet government timberlands have not always served preservation and the environment, while private ownerships sometimes have served them better. The Canadian provincial governments on their lands have not always regulated themselves or assented to federal regulation through the Fisheries Act, while some U.S. private timberland owners have been regulated more. The insulation of government, especially the U.S. federal agencies, from market forces has the drawback that government has subsidized the exploitation of natural areas (such as in the Rocky Mountains) that industry otherwise would find unprofitable to log. Industry intensively manages only a fraction of private timberlands, those it deems most productive. Even on lands that could be logged profitably, some nonindustrial owners have by inaction or conscious choice ignored market concerns and have logged with special concern for amenities or avoided logging altogether.

The performance of private timberlands does not greatly diverge between the United States and Canada, but that of public timberlands varies significantly. The Canadian provincial public lands have been managed very singularly for short run commodity production, while the production of commodities from U.S. federal public timberlands more often has been moderated by concerns for the environment and for preservation. The parliamentary system found in the provinces and in the Canadian federal government tends to discourage citizen involvement; U.S. legislators, administrators, and the courts have granted more access to environmental activists and other groups.[139] But perhaps the more significant difference is that provincial jurisdiction over the Canadian lands strengthens industry and union power in government, lessening the influence of national publics who have more say in the management of U.S. federal lands.

This difference in level of government is not absolute. In the United States, regional concerns in the management of federal forests are voiced by each state's congressional delegation and through lobbying by state and local governments, which are concerned not only indirectly but because they directly receive a share of the revenues from federal lands. The management of Canadian provincial lands has been influenced by such federal activities as taxation, promotion of trade, research, financial aid, and regulation through the Fisheries Act.

Considering the fact that different governments own them, the provincial public lands are impressive in the many similarities in their management, both in the mistakes of the past and in the hopeful reforms currently in progress, whose success cannot yet be fully assessed. This similarity is rooted partly in a common culture, but the economic forces and political institutions that the provinces share seem to explain more of it. U.S. federal lands, which formally are under a national set of laws and administrative arrangements, ironically seem to vary more from region to region in how they are managed.

Notes

*For their comments on an earlier version of this chapter, thanks to the editors and other authors, as well as John H. Beuter, Arthur W. Cooper, K. W. Hearnden, David H. and Kathleen O. Jackson, John V. Krutilla, Guy Lemieux, David F. McCaffrey, Brian W. McCloy, James A. McNutt, Robert H. Nelson, Robert Nixon, F. L. C. Reed, Carl H. Reidel, Tom Roach, William G. Robbins, Debra J. Salazar, Roger A. Sedjo, Henry H. Webster, Graeme Wynn, and John A. Zivnuska. Vivian Papsdorf and Maybelle Frashure provided valuable word processing help.

1. With forest defined as being at least 10 percent stocked with trees, Canada has 766 million acres and the United States has 737 million acres of forest. [Forest Service, U.S. Department of Agriculture, *An Assessment of the Forest and Range Land Situation in the United States*, Forest Resource Report No. 22 (October 1981); and G. M. Bonnor, *Canada's Forest Inventory 1981* (Ottawa: Canadian Forestry Service, Environment Canada, 1982).]

2. Marion Clawson, "America's Forests in the Long Sweep of History," *Science* (June 1979). Clawson estimates that nearly 300 million acres were cleared; adding Canada to this total would probably bring the total to nearly 400 million acres.

3. Averages for the early 1980s were 523 million cubic meters in the United States. [Forest Service, USDA, *U.S. Timber Production, Trade, Consumption, and Price Statistics*. Misc. Pub. #1942 (1984)] and 155 million cubic meters in Canada [Canadian Forestry Service, Environment Canada, *Selected Forestry Statistics for Canada, 1984*].

4. Useful sources on the early history are: William G. Robbins, *Lumberjacks and Legislators: Political Economy of the U.S. Lumber Industry, 1890–1941* (College Station, Texas: Texas A and M Press, 1982); A. R. M. Lower et al., *The North American Assault on the Canadian Forest* (Toronto: Ryerson Press, 1938); and Donald MacKay, *Heritage Lost: The Crisis in Canada's Forests* (Toronto: Macmillan of Canada, 1985).

5. On the conservation movement, see Samuel P. Hays, *Conservation and the Gospel of Efficiency: The Progressive Conservation Movement, 1890–1920* (Cambridge, Mass.: Har-

vard University Press, 1959). On the National Forests and the movement for federal regulation of U.S. private timberlands, see: Harold K. Steen, *The U.S. Forest Service: A History* (Seattle, Wash.: University of Washington Press, 1976).

6. On this period, see Lower, *The North American Assault*; MacKay, *Heritage Lost*; H. V. Nelles, *The Politics of Development: Forest, Mines and Hydroelectric Power in Ontario, 1849–1941* (Toronto: Macmillan of Canada, 1974); and Richard S. Lambert with Paul Pross, *Renewing Nature's Wealth: A Centennial History of Public Management of Lands, Forests, and Wildlife in Ontario, 1763–1967* (Toronto: Province of Ontario, 1967).

7. Canadian Institute of Forestry, "A Case for Improved Forest Management in Canada, *Forestry Chronicle* (February 1984), p. 30.

8. H. V. Nelles, *The Politics of Development*.

9. Congress of the United States, Office of Technology Assessment, *Wood Use" U.S. Competitiveness and Technology* II (1983–4), p. 164. Private ownership totals 347 million acres or 71.4 percent of the total.

10. Forest Service, *An Assessment of the Forest and Range Land Situation in the United States.*

11. Science Council of Canada, *Canada's Threatened Forests* (1983).

12. F.L.C. Reed and Associates, Ltd., *Forest Management in Canada*, Information Report FMR-X-102, Forest Management Institute, Environment Canada (January 1978).

13. Thomas C. Birch, "Private Forestland Owners in the U.S.: Their Numbers and Characteristics," *Nonindustrial Private Forests: A Review of Economic and Policy Studies*, eds., Jack P. Royer and Christopher D. Risbrudt (Durham: School of Forestry and Environmental Studies, Duke University, 1983) p. 74.

14. A useful discussion of the commercial uses of wood can be found in Office of Technology Assessment, *Wood Use* (two volumes).

15. A basic text in silviculture is: David M. Smith, *The Practice of Silviculture* (N.Y., N.Y.: Wiley Publishers, 7th ed., 1962).

16. In terms of productivity, the United States has more commercial forest—507 million acres to Canada's 430 million (from the sources cited in endnote 1). The conditions for growing trees in Canada are discussed in Kenneth O. Higginbotham, "Environmental Constraints in Increasing Canadian Forest Products Supplies," in Frank J. Convery and Boyd R. Strain, *U.S. Dependency on Canadian Natural Resources: Extent and Significance* (Durham, N.C.: Canadian Studies Institute, 1979).

17. Useful background on the physical equipment and methods of logging is: Steven Conway, *Logging Practices: Principles of Timber Harvesting Systems* (San Francisco: Miller Freeman, 1976).

18. I. C. M. Place, "Forestry in Canada," *Journal of Forestry* (September 1978), p. 558; Statistics Canada, *Exports by Commodities* (December 1984). The export figure cited is for 1984.

19. Office of Technology Assessment, *Wood Use*, vol. I, p. 36.

20. In Canada, the top five paper and pulp producers account for nearly half of total capacity, while in the United States the top fifteen account for more than half of total capacity. *1984–85 North American Pulp and Paper Fact Book* (San Francisco: Miller Freeman, 1985), pp. 5, 74. In Canada the top five producers of newsprint and pulp represent 45.8 percent of total production (Canadian figures provided by the Canadian Pulp and Paper Association).

21. The top one hundred lumber and structural panel producers (of which fifty-eight are U.S. companies and forty-two are Canadian companies) account for only 44 percent of the two countries' combined production. ["Lumber Firms Enjoyed '83, but '84 Outlook is Dimmer," *Forest Industries* (July 1984) pp. 14–5.]

22. Logging occurs on about two million acres of Canadian land each year [Science

Council of Canada, *Canada's Threatened Forests*, p. 8]. Although a similar figure on the U.S. area logged has never been compiled, we know that the volume of wood removed from U.S. timberlands is a little over three times that removed in Canada; thus if the same proportion holds, logging should occur on about six million U.S. acres annually. This estimate is supported by the figure that 1.41 million acres in the National Forests were subject to some logging activity in a recent year. (Forest Service, United StatesDA, "Area and Volume Harvested by Cutting Method," 1980.) Since the National Forests supply roughly one-fifth of the U.S. timber removals, the area logged would exceed six million acres annually. U.S. forests generally have more volume of standing timber per acre, so the area logged there per unit of volume may well be less than in Canada. However, various silvicultural activities other than commercial logging, such as pre-commercial thinning, are more common in the United States than in Canada.

23. A useful overview of forest management issues is: William A. Duerr, Dennis Teeguarden, Neils B. Christiansen and Sam Guttenberg, *Forest Resource Management: Decision-Making Principles and Cases* (Philadelphia: Saunders, 1979).

24. Marion Clawson, *Decision-Making in Timber Production, Harvest, and Marketing* (Washington, D.C.: Resources for the Future, 1977), p. 53.

25. John V. Krutilla and Anthony C. Fisher, *The Economics of Natural Environments: Studies in the Valuation of Commodity and Amenity Resources* (Baltimore, Md.: Johns Hopkins University Press for Resources for the Future, 1975). The current chapter's distinction between commodities and amenities is adopted from this book.

26. There are forty-six accredited schools of forestry in the United States: eight states have two each and one (Michigan) has three. Canada has six schools of forestry, two of which were founded in 1970; Ontario is the only province with two of these schools. Estimates of foresters were obtained from the Canadian Institute of Forestry and the Society of American Foresters. Volume of timber production is a better standard for comparison than acreage of commercial timberland because U.S. timberland overall is much more productive.

27. Ministry of Forests, Province of British Columbia, "Forest Resource Planning in British Columbia," a Brief submitted to the Royal Commission on Forest Resources (September, 1975), Appendix A. In the late 1970s, Ontario had only one unit forester (a forester who is involved in field duties) for each one million acres of public land. [K. A. Armson, *Forest Management in Ontario*, Ministry of Natural Resources, Province of Ontario (1976), p. 133].

    On the early struggles of foresters, see A. P. Pross, "The Development of Professions in the Public Service: The Foresters in Ontario," *Canadian Public Administration* X, 3 (September 1967). For recent critiques, see F. L. C. Reed, "Reshaping Forest Policy in British Columbia," Vancouver Institute (February 16, 1985), and three papers by K. W. Hearnden: "The Case of the Unit Forester," *The Professional Forester*, Newsletter of the Ontario Foresters Association 43 (June 1970); "Growing the Second Forest in Ontario," Ministry of Natural Resources, Province of Ontario, *Proceedings of Ontario Conference on Forest Regeneration* (March 29–31, 1978); and "Forestry Practice in Canada: An Ethical Dilemma," paper presented to the Occupational Ethics Workshop, Lakehead University. (March 30, 1985).

28. Canadian Pulp and Paper Association, *Intensive Forest Management Practices in the Southeastern United States, a report on the Forest Management Group's Study Tour of the Southeastern United States*, February 16 to 28, 1975. The report noted: "The southern foresters we met were a very enthusiastic, dedicated, and capable group and it would

seem that this is due, in part, to the fact that, unlike most Canadian foresters, they have been given the opportunity to practice all aspects of their profession" (p. 43).

29. Roger A. Sedjo and Samuel J. Radcliffe, *Postwar Trends in U.S. Forest Products Trade: A Global, National, and Regional View* (Washington, D.C.: Resources for the Future, 1980), Ch. 4. Some barriers do exist to trade in structural panels.

30. Christopher K. Leman, "U.S.-Canadian Outdoor Recreation," *Resources* 71 (Washington, D.C.: Resources for the Future, October, 1982).

31. A pioneering study of U.S. and Canadian approaches is: David H. Jackson and Kathleen O. Jackson, "National Versus Regional Control of Natural Resource Policy: A Comparative Study of the United States and Canada," *Public Land Law Review* 2 (1981).

32. Richard D. Meyer and W. David Klemperer, "Current Status of Long-term Leasing and Cutting Contracts in the South," *Proceedings of the 1984 Southern Forest Economics Workshop*, ed. R. W. Guldin (Memphis, Tenn.) and Jay O'Laughlin, David A. Cleaves, and David J. Skove, "Forest Industry Programs for NIPFs: Management Assistance and Privately Funded Cost-Sharing," in Royer and Risbrudt, eds., *Nonindustrial Private Forests*.

33. For tax reasons and to combat corporate takeovers, some large companies were in the 1980s devolving the ownership of their timberlands to limited partnerships under which the companies no longer owned the land but retained the rights and responsibilities of management. See, e.g., Lazard Frères and Co. et al., *Prospectus, 2,250,000 Class A Depositary Units Representing Class A Limited Partners' Interests, IP Timberlands, Ltd.* (March 7, 1985).

34. In a few cases, especially Ontario and Quebec, a province is large enough to have "national" interests, as Michael Goldberg has pointed out to me in comments on this paragraph.

35. Carlos A. Schwantes, *Radical Heritage: Labor, Socialism, and Reform in Washington and British Columbia, 1885–1917* (Seattle: University of Washington Press, 1979).

36. See Jackson and Jackson, "National Versus Regional Control." Useful accounts of past policymaking in the provinces are provided in a symposium on "Forest Policy Development in British Columbia, Ontario, Quebec and New Brunswick," in *Forestry Chronicle* (April 1984).

37. See, generally, Samuel Trask Dana and Sally K. Fairfax, *Forest and Range Policy* (N.Y., N.Y.: McGraw Hill, 1980); Dennis C. LeMaster, *Decade of Change: The Remaking of Forest Service Statutory Authority During the 1970s* (Westport, CT.: Greenwood Press, 1984); and Christopher K. Leman, *Managing the National Forests* (forthcoming). The distinction in how the courts of the two countries act is brought out by John Brigham's chapter in the current volume.

38. See, e.g.: "New Role in Investing for Quebec," *New York Times* (August 24, 1981).

39. Michael Doherty, "British Columbia: Gray Times for Environmentalists," *Sierra* (September/October, 1984), p. 14. Doherty is the regional representative of the Sierra Club of Western Canada.

40. See Gordon A. Enk, "A Description and Analysis of Strategic and Land-Use Decision-Making by Large Corporations in the Forest Products Industry," Ph.D. Dissertation, School of Forestry and Environmental Studies, Yale University, 1975; and Jay O'Laughlin and Paul V. Ellefson, *New Diversified Entrants Among U.S. Wood-Based Companies: A Study of Economic Structure and Corporate Strategy*, Station Bulletin 541, Agriculture Experiment Station, University of Minnesota (1982).

41. See Kari Juhani Keipi, "Transfer Pricing Alternatives for Allocating Logs in a Forest Products Firm," Ph.D. Dissertation, School of Forestry, Oregon State University, 1976.

194 · *Land Rites and Wrongs*

42. Charles McKinley, "Guildism and the Oregon State Board of Forestry," in his *The Management of Land and Related Water Resources in Oregon: A Study in Administrative Federalism* (Washington, D.C.: Resources for the Future, 1965). The Weyerhaeuser Company's first public education advertisement appeared in 1937. (Charles E. Twining, "Weyerhaeuser and the Clemons Tree Farm: Experimenting with a Theory," in Harold K. Steen, ed. *History of Sustained Yield Forestry: A Symposium* (Forest History Society, 1983, p. 38.)

43. Jeffrey A. Sonnenfeld, *Corporate Views of the Public Interest: Perceptions of the Forest Products Industry* (Boston: Auburn House, 1981). Most of the six companies in Sonnenfeld's study have landholdings in both the United States and Canada.

44. Kenneth E. Smith, "Another View of the South as a Future Timber Source," *Forest Industries* (August 1982), p. 21. A useful general study is Marion Clawson, *The Economics of U.S. Nonindustrial Private Forests* (Washington, D.C.: Resources for the Future, 1979). See also Gunnar Paulsen Knapp, "The Supply of Timber from Nonindustrial Private Forests," Ph.D dissertation, School of Forestry and Environmental Studies, Yale University, 1981.

45. Office of Technology Assessment, *Wood Use: U.S. Competitiveness and Technology*, vol. II, pp. 172–76, 179–83.

46. See Ministry of Natural Resources, Province of Ontario, *Toward the 80s: A Guide to the Organization and Management System* (February 1979), for a description of ministry organization.

47. Ministère des Terres et Forêts, Gouvernement du Québec, *Rapport au comité ministeriel permanent de l'aménagement du territoire* (April 1976); and *Proposition de politique fonciere touchant la gestion du domaine publique* (March 1977).

48. Christopher K. Leman, "The Forgotten Fundamental: Successes and Excesses of Direct Government," in *The Tools of Public Policy*, eds. Michael Lund and Lester Salamon (Washington, D.C.: Urban Institute Press, forthcoming).

49. See, generally, Christopher K. Leman, "The Canadian Forest Ranger: Bureaucratic Centralism and Private Power in Three Provincial Natural Resources Agencies," paper presented at the annual meeting of the Canadian Political Science Association, Halifax, Nova Scotia, May 1981.

50. See *Ibid.*, pp. 20–21.

51. A clear description of the Forest Service timber sales process is provided in Forest Service, United StatesDA, "National Forest Timber Management in the Pacific Southwest Region," *Pacific Southwest Log* (December 1982).

52. Background on provincial timber sales procedures can be found in the symposium on "Forest Policy Development," *Forestry Chronicle* (April 1984) as well as Ministère des Terres et Forêts, Gouvernement du Québec, *Exposé sur la Politique Forestière*, two volumes (1971–72); Province of British Columbia, *Timber Rights and Forest Policy in British Columbia*, Report of the Royal Commission on Forest Resources, (two volumes, 1976); and K. A. Armson, *Forest Management in Ontario*.

53. Louis-Jean Lussier, "The Forest Management Plan Operation in Quebec," *Pulp and Paper Canada* (July 1976); Claude Godbout, *Rapport de fin de mandat du Groupe de conseilliers en gestion des Forêts (COGEF)*, Ministère de l'Energie et des Ressources, Gouvernement du Québec (April 21, 1981); Ministry of Natural Resources, Province of Ontario, *Guidelines for Land Use Planning* (1974); Ministry of Forests, Province of British Columbia, "Planning" (September 1978), and "Forest Resource Planning in British Columbia"; and Leman, "The Canadian Forest Ranger," pp. 9–10.

54. See the symposium on "Forest Policy Development."

55. In some provinces, Quebec for example, even ministry personnel must obtain a permit if they must fell trees in constructing a campground.

56. Anthony H. J. Dorsey, Michael W. McPhee and Sam Sydneysmith, *Salmon Protection and the B.C. Coastal Forest Industry: Environmental Regulation as a Bargaining Process* (Vancouver: Westwater Institute, University of British Columbia, 1980), p. 321.

57. See, e.g., Jamie Swift, *Cut and Run: The Assault on Canada's Forests* (Toronto: Between the Lines, 1983).

58. William F. Hyde, *Timber Supply Land Allocation and Economic Efficiency* (Baltimore: Johns Hopkins University Press for Resources for the Future, 1980). Studies questioning the economics of timber sales in the Rockies and other areas have been done by the Natural Resources Defense Council, Cascade Holistic Economic Consultants, Wilderness Society, General Accounting Office, Congressional Research Service, and House Appropriations Committee staff, among others.

59. Susan Schrepfer, *The Fight to Save the Redwoods: A History of Environmental Reform, 1917–1978* (Madison, Wisconsin: University of Wisconsin Press, 1983).

60. See Dana and Fairfax, *Forest and Range Policy*, pp. 133–4, 155–7, 197–99, 217–22.

61. When their timber values increased in the 1950s and 1960s, the Forest Service removed protections that it had initiated in the 1930s on areas such as French Pete in the Willamette National Forest. During this period, the agency was following a policy of "advance roading," whereby clearcuts were arranged in staggered settings that caused roads to push further into previously unroaded areas. French Pete became the subject of a long campaign that led Congress to include it in the Three Sisters Wilderness area in the 1970s. By one estimate, the area has 700 million board feet of standing timber.

62. The three cases mentioned here are discussed in Leman, "The Canadian Forest Ranger"; and Christopher K. Leman, "Forest Planning and Field Management in Quebec: A Survey and Case Study," a paper presented to the Canadian Study Group, University Consortium for Research on North America, October 1979.

63. See Stein Basin Study Committee, Province of British Columbia, *The Stein Basin Moratorium Study*, a report submitted to the Environmental and Land Use Committee (December 1975) and Tsitika Planning Committee, *Tsitika Watershed Integrated Resource Plan*, a report submitted to the Environment and Land Use Committee (October 1978); Patrick D. Larkey and Chandler Stolp, "Reycoot River Drainage: A Proposed Timber Harvest," Intercollegiate Case Clearing House 9-380-730 (1979) and Diane Swanson, "A Tough Decision on the Tahsis," *ForesTalk* (Summer 1982).

64. See, e.g., Brian Gory, "Appeal Court Prohibits Meares Island Logging," *Globe and Mail* (March 28, 1985), p. 1.

65. A leading textbook in this field is: K. P. Davis, *Forest Management: Regulation and Valuation* (N.Y., N.Y.: McGraw Hill, 1966).

66. Robert H. Nelson and Lucian Pugliaresi, "Timber Harvest Policy Issues on the O&C Lands," ed. Robert T. Deacon and M. Bruce Johnson, *Forestlands: Public and Private*, (San Francisco: Pacific Institute for Public Policy Research, 1985).

67. In a few cases governments have made long-term promises of public timber in exchange for assurances from a private owner on how neighboring lands will be managed; examples are British Columbia's tree farm licenses and the U.S. Forest Service simpson management unit.

68. A useful history of capital gains taxation in forestry is provided in: William C. Siegel, "Historical Development of Federal Income Tax Treatment of Timber," in *Proceedings of the Forest Taxation Symposium* eds. Harry L. Haney, Jr. and John E. Gunter (Blacksburg, VA.: College of Agriculture and Life Sciences, Virginia Polytechnic Institute and State

University, 1978). The Treasury estimate is reported in: Dale Russakoff, "Timber Industry is Rooted in Tax Breaks," *Washington Post* (March 24, 1985). Overviews of U.S. taxation in forestry are: W. D. Klemperer, "A History of United States Forest Taxation," *The Encyclopedia of American Forest and Conservation History* (New York: MacMillan, 1983) and William C. Siegel, "The Impact of Taxation on Private Forest Ownership," in *Timber Supply: Issues and Options* (Madison, Wisc.: Forest Products Research Society, 1979).

69. See D. Lester Holley, Jr., "Financial Analysis of the New Reforestation Tax Incentive (P.L. 96-451)" in *Proceedings of the Forest Taxation Symposium II* eds. Harry L. Haney, Jr. and William C. Siegel (Blacksburg, VA.: VPI, 1982).

70. Canadian federal taxation of forestry is discussed in a symposium on "Forestry Taxes and Tenures in Canada," in *Report of Proceedings of the 28th Tax Conference* (Toronto: Canadian Tax Foundation, 1976).

71. A survey of property taxation in U.S. forestry is: Clifford A. Hickman, "Emerging Patterns of Forest Property and Yield Taxes," in *Proceedings of the Forest Taxation Symposium II.*

72. Provincial forestry taxation is surveyed in "Forestry Taxes and Tenures in Canada."

73. Economic Council of Canada, *Western Transition* (1984) p. 41.

74. Dave Frohnmayer, "A New Look at Federalism: The Theory and Implications of 'Dual Sovereignty,'" *Environmental Law* 12:4 (Summer, 1982), p. 913.

75. Mike Major, "Aftermath of the Timber Relief Act," *Journal of Forestry* (April 1985).

76. A useful summary is: David Leyton-Brown, *Weathering the Storm: Canadian-U.S. Relations, 1980–83* (Toronto and Washington, D.C.: C.D. Howe Institute and National Planning Association, 1985), Ch. 4, "The Softwood Lumber Case." A study comparing timber fees is: David Haley, "A Regional Comparison of Stumpage Values in British Columbia and the United States Pacific Northwest," *The Forestry Chronicle* (October 1980).

77. For a useful summary of the Jones Act, see: Sedjo and Radcliffe, *Postwar Trends in U.S. Forest Products Trade.*

78. A useful survey of log export restrictions is: Gary R. Lindell, *Log Export Restrictions of the Western States and British Columbia* General Technical Report PNW-63 (1978), Forest Service USDA.

79. John H. Beuter, K. Norman Johnson, and H. Lynn Scheurman, *Timber for Oregon's Tomorrow: An Analysis of Reasonably Possible Occurrences*, Research Bulletin 19 (January 1976) (Corvallis, Oregon: Forest Research Laboratory, School of Forestry, Oregon State University) and William G. Robbins, "Timber Town: Market Economics in Coos Bay, Oregon, 1850 to the Present," *Pacific Northwest Quarterly* (October 1984).

80. Con H. Schallau, "Can Regulation Contribute to Economic Stability?" *Journal of Forestry* 72:4 (April 1974).

81. Anthony Bianco, "The Georgia Pacific Story," (four parts) *Willamette Week*, March 12, 19, and 26, April 2, 1979.

82. John C. Rosenthal and Robert T. Don, "International Paper Company: Industry as a Land-Use Planner," *Journal of Forestry* (September 84). Dave Frohnmayer, "A New Look at Federalism: The Theory and Implications of 'Dual Sovereignty,'" *Environmental Law* 12:4 (Summer, 1982), p. 913.

83. Thomas C. Adams and Richard C. Smith, *Review of the Logging Residue Problem and its Reduction Through Marketing Practices*, General Technical Report PNW-48, Forest Service, USDA. (1976).

84. Cited in Patricia Marchak, *Green Gold: The Forest Industry in British Columbia* (Vancouver, B.C.: University of British Columbia Press, 1983), p. 37.

85. Ian Mahood, "Speech to Canadian Institute of Foresters, Duncan Chapter," (1983) pp. 3–4. Similar concerns were expressed by B.C.'s 1976 royal commission report, *Timber Rights and Forest Policy*. A sustained critique of the large companies is: Ken Drushka, *Stumped: The Forest Industry in Transition* (Vancouver and Toronto: Douglas and McIntyre, 1985).

86. See John H. Beuter and Douglas C. Olson, *Lakeview Federal Sustained Field Unit, Fremont National Forest: A Review, 1974–79* (Corvallis, Oregon: School of Forestry, Oregon State University, 1980).

87. See, generally, Henry Clepper, *Professional Forestry in the United States* (Washington, D.C.: Johns Hopkins University Press for Resources for the Future, 1971). Weyerhaeuser Company founded the nation's first tree farm partly in response to the Lumber Code of the National Recovery Administration (Twining, "Weyerhaeuser and the Experimenting with a Theory," Clemons Tree Farm," p. 36). One of the sponsors of the tree farm movement, the Industrial Forestry Association, was established in response to the NRA.

88. A useful survey of the state laws is: Frederick W. Cubbage and Paul V. Ellefson, "State Forest Practice Laws: A Major Policy Force Unique to the Natural Resources Community," *Natural Resources Lawyer* 13:2 (1980) 421–468.

89. See, for example, on Pacific Logging Co., Ltd.: Ted Blackman, "B.C. Firm has a Rare Luxury: Owning 300,000 Timbered Acres," *Forest Industries* (November 1980) and the interview with the company's chief forester in *ForesTalk* (Winter 1981).

90. F.L.C. Reed and Associates, *Forest Management in Canada* and Ministère de l'Energie et des Ressources, Gouvernement du Québec, *Le Point sur le Role et l'Activité du Ministère de l'Energie et des Ressources, Secteur des Terres et Forêts* (May 1981), p. 18.

91. Office of Technology Assessment, *Wood Use*, vol. II, p. 176; H. Fred Kaiser, "Management Practices and Reforestation Decisions in the South," in *Nonindustrial Private Forests*, p. 82

92. Kaiser, "Management Practices," p. 81.

93. Luke Popovich, "Reforestation: Paper Work and Real Work," *Journal of Forestry* (August 1979). Some Canadian observers have complained that recent increases in provincial reforestation have also tended to be spread evenly.

94. Science Council of Canada, *Canada's Threatened Forests*, p. 8.

95. Canadian Council of Resource and Environment Ministers, *Forestry Imperatives for Canada: A Proposal for Forest Policy in Canada* (May 1979), p. 1.

96. Science Council of Canada, *Canada's Threatened Forests*, p. 5.

97. See, e.g., F.L.C. Reed and Associates, *Forest Management in Canada*; Canadian Institute of Forestry, "A Case for Improved Forest Management in Canada." Even the Canadian edition of *Reader's Digest* stepped in. [Donald McKay, "The Silent Emergency in Our Forests," *Reader's Digest* (August 1979)].

98. Peter Griffiths, "Sacrifice: Are the Socreds Kissing Off the B.C. Forests?" *Equity: The Vancouver Business Magazine*, 3:11 (April 1985).

99. Ministry of Natural Resources, Province of Ontario, *Proceedings of Ontario Conference on Forest Regeneration*, p. 16.

100. Cited in Reed, "Reshaping Forest Policy," p. 33.

101. Useful sources on the environmental impacts of timber operations and measures to mitigate them include the following: U.S. Environmental Protection Agency, *Logging Roads and Protection of Water Quality* (March 1975) and *Forest Harvest, Residue Treatment, Reforestation, and Protection of Water Quality* (April 1976); Environmental Council of Alberta, *The Environmental Effects of Forestry Operations in Alberta* (February 1979); and Dorsey, McPhee and Sydneysmith, *Salmon Protection*.

102. Forest Service, U.S. Department of Agriculture, *National Forest Landscape Management*, vols. 1 and 2 (Agriculture Handbooks nos. 434, 462.)
103. Dorsey, McPhee and Sydneysmith, *Salmon Protection*, p. 337.
104. William E. Bruner and Perry R. Hagenstein, *Alternative Forest Policies for the Pacific Northwest*, Pacific Northwest Regional Commission (June 1981), pp. 6–103.
105. Bruner and Hagenstein, *Alternative Forest Policies*, p. 6–103. Thus Mark Rey of the National Forest Products Association observes of water quality regulation: "In forestry you are usually dealing with management practices that aren't capital intensive. . . . You are leaving some trees that you might have otherwise cut. You are locating a road on a different contour." "A Panel Discussion on Nonpoint Source Water Pollution," *Journal of Soil and Water Conservation* (January-February 1985).
106. Dorsey, McPhee and Sydneysmith, *Salmon Protection*, p. 337.
107. Alfred A. Marcus et al, *Improving Forest Productivity: Prescribed Burning in the Light of Clean Air Act Visibility Standards* (Seattle: Batelle Human Affairs Research Centers, 1981).
108. Roger D. Fight, K. Norman Johnson, Kent P. Connaughton, and Robert W. Sassaman, *Roadless Area Intensive Management Tradeoffs on Western National Forests* Forest Service, U.S. Department of Agriculture, (October 1978). See also Robert E. Kemper and Lawrence S. Davis, "Costs of Environmental Constraints on Timber Harvesting and Regeneration," *Journal of Forestry* (November 1976).
109. Based on the author's research on the Forest Service.
110. This logger is referring to one of the ranger districts studied in both Herbert Kaufman, *The Forest Ranger: A Study in Administrative Behavior* (Baltimore: Johns Hopkins University Press for Resources for the Future, 1960); and the author's research on the Forest Service.
111. For the argument against flexibility in administration, see: Theodore J. Lowi, *The End of Liberalism: The Second Republic of the United States* (New York: Norton, 2nd ed., 1979). For the argument in favor of it, see: Eugene Bardach and Robert Kagan, *Going by the Book: The Problem of Regulatory Unreasonableness* (Philadelphia, PA: Temple University Press, 1982). A limitation on flexibility is that U.S. state and federal land agencies are required to award their sales to the highest bidder, even if an unreliable purchaser would be more costly to the government overall.
112. See Christopher K. Leman, "Forest Planning and Field Management in Quebec: A Survey and Case Study," paper presented to the Canadian Study Group, University Consortium for Research on North America, October 1979; "National Forest Land and Resources Management Planning," *Federal Register* 47:190 (September 30, 1982).
113. Ministry of Forests, Province of B.C., "Planning Guidelines for Coast Logging Operation," September 29, 1972.
114. Hough, Stansbury and Associates, Ltd., for Ministry of Natural Resources, Province of Ontario, *Design Guidelines for Forest Management* (1976).
115. Ministère des Terres et Forêts, Gouvernement du Québec, *Guide d'Aménagement du Milieu Forestier* (June 1977). Office de Planification et de Développement du Québec, Gouvernement du Québec, *l'Eau et l'Aménagement du Territoire* (1980), p. 103.
116. Ministry of Forest, Province of British Columbia, *Forest Landscape Handbook* (1981).
117. D. A. A. Toews and M. J. Brownlee, *A Handbook for Fish Habitat Protection on Forest Lands in British Columbia.* Department of Fisheries and Oceans, Government of Canada (1981).
118. Ministry of Natural Resources, Province of Ontario, *Proceedings of Ontario Conference on Forest Regeneration*, p. 18.

119. R. H. Klinoff, "Six Silvicultural Systems Not Studied in College," *Journal of Forestry* (June 1984).

120. James M. Vardaman and Company, Inc., *Timberland: A New System for Buying and Selling* (no date).

121. Sonnenfeld, *Corporate Views of the Public Interest.*

122. Interview with a member of the Private Forestry Division, Department of Natural Resources, State of Washington. See also National Council of the Paper Industry for Air and Stream Improvement, Inc., *Summary of Silvicultural Nonpoint Source Control Programs—1982* (January 1983) p. 21.

123. Bianco, "The Georgia-Pacific Story." A long-term study of the impacts on fish of the 1960s logging practices of Georgia-Pacific is: Research Section, Department of Fish and Wildlife, State of Oregon, *The Alsea Watershed Study: Effects of Logging on the Aquatic Resources of Three Headwater Streams of the Alsea River, Oregon* (three parts) 1975.

124. A memorandum of understanding between the State of Oklahoma and Weyerhaeuser was announced by the state's governor on April 25, 1980. Also at that time, Weyerhaeuser released "Wildlife Management Guidelines" for its Oklahoma Region.

125. Blue Ribbon Panel on Wildlife and Forestry, National Wildlife Federation, *An Assessment of the Weyerhaeuser Company's Forestry Operations in Southwestern Arkansas and Southeastern Oklahoma,* funded under a grant from the Winthrop Rockefeller Foundation (Washington, D.C.: National Wildlife Federation, 1982).

126. Memorandum of Understanding Between Oklahoma Region of Weyerhaeuser Company, National Wildlife Federation, and Oklahoma Wildlife Federation, April 1983. Also at this time, the company released a revision of its wildlife management guidelines. Issues remaining in disagreement included whether to leave softwood trees standing on streambanks, and how much to manage for diverse age classes in cutting blocks.

127. Environmental Protection Agency, "Decision and Emergency Order Suspending Registrations for the Forest, Rights-of-Way, and Pasture Uses of 2,4,5-T" and "Decision and Emergency Order Suspending Registrations for Certain Uses of Silvex," *Federal Register* (March 15, 1979).

128. Debra J. Salazar, "Political Processes and Public Regulation of Private Forest Management," Paper presented at the 1985 Annual Meeting of the Western Political Science Association, La Vegas (March 28–30, 1985).

129. See Fred Cubbage and William Siegel, "Public Regulation of Private Forestry in the East," Paper presented at Western Forest Economists Meeting, Wemme, Oregon (May 6–8, 1985).

130. There are signs of increasing regulation in the East. See Lloyd Irland, "Logging and Water Quality: State Regulation in New England," *Journal of Soil and Water Conservation* 40:1 (January-February 1985); and Cubbage and Siegel, "Public Regulation of Private Forestry in the East."

131. On the politics of water pollution regulation in rural areas, see: Christopher K. Leman and Robert L. Paarlberg, "The Continued Political Power of Agricultural Interests," in *Agricultural and Rural Areas Approaching the 21st Century,* ed. Carl O'Connor (forthcoming).

132. On these struggles, see: Dana and Fairfax, *Forest and Range Policy,* Ch. 10; and Mark Rey, "The Effect of the Clean Water Act on Forestry Practices," Paper presented at a symposium on U.S. Forestry and Water Quality, sponsored by the Water Pollution Control Federation, Richmond, Virginia, June 19–20, 1980.

133. National Council of the Paper Industry for Air and Stream Improvement, *Summary of Silvicultural Nonpoint Source Control Programs*, p. 20. As a representative of the National Forest Products Association has observed: "When was the last time you heard of an industry group supporting appropriations for an EPA program?" Rey, "The Effect of the Clean Water Act," p. 10.

134. Donald D. Lockhart, "A Summary of the Nova Scotia Herbicide Trial," *Forestry Chronicle* (December 1983).

135. Forest Practices Act Technical Work Group, *Meeting Water Quality Objectives on State and Private Forest Lands Through the Oregon Forest Practices Act*, a report prepared for the state forester, Oregon State Department of Forestry (August 1978). One observer concludes, "Oregon simply does not have enough forest practice officers to do the job." George W. Brown, "Oregon's Forest Practices Act: An Early Appraisal," *Journal of Forestry* (December 1978), p. 783.

136. Henry C. Vaux, "State Interventions on Private Forests in California," in Roger A. Sedjo, ed., *Governmental Interventions, Social Needs, and the Management of U.S. Forests* (Washington, D.C.: Resources for the Future, 1983). Vaux is Chairman of the California State Board of Forestry, which has final authority for administration of the forest practices rules.

137. Thus David H. Jackson observes: "Both the capitalist and the public sector invest in reforestation when payoffs are 50 to 100 years away. It is extremely difficult to build investor security into long-term forest leases because they expire long before the leased area becomes reforested." "Canadian Approaches to Forest Land Tenure: An Option for Montana?" *Western Wildlands* (Summer, 1984), p. 23.

138. The "public choice" movement has made claims for inherent public/private differences, with public performance being inferior to private. For a critique, see: Christopher K. Leman, "The Revolution of the Saints: The Ideology of Privatization and its Consequences for the Public Lands," in *Selling the Federal Forest*, Adrien E. Gamache, ed. (Seattle: College of Forest Resources, University of Washington, 1984).

139. The relatively closed nature of decision making in one province is lamented by Dorsey, McPhee, and Sydneysmith, *Salmon Protection*, p. 325. A comparative evaluation of the two countries' politics is: Christopher K. Leman, *The Collapse of Welfare Reform: Political Institutions, Policy, and the Poor in Canada and the United States* (Cambridge, MA.: MIT Press, 1980). As argued there, "The U.S. policymaking circle was much larger and more open to nongovernmental participants than Canada's, but it was not more democratic." (p. 166). This is because the groups that actually participate in U.S. decisions are not necessarily representative of the society at large.

7

Siting Toxic Waste Disposal Facilities: Best and Worst Cases in North America

Mario Ristoratore

The purpose of this essay is to show that siting toxic waste treatment facilities is a political more than a technical problem, and neither private enterprises nor governments alone are able to solve it. A public/private partnership seems to be essential for deploying new technology to address problems posed by toxic waste.

The essay presents the results of a comparative study of four attempts to site toxic waste treatment facilities in the United States and Canada. The different political and economic institutions of the two federal systems did not seem to have affected the outcomes. Siting unwanted facilities is no less difficult in Canada than in the United States; indeed, American states have as much authority and are as capable of solving local/state conflicts as are Canadian provinces. Lessons from the siting experience probably are transferable across the border.

In the two most successful cases examined here—Quebec and Louisiana—personal links between key local and state officials were crucial, and both governments utilized exceptionally centralized authority. These conditions are difficult to replicate elsewhere in North America, due perhaps to the peculiar character of politics in Quebec and Louisiana. Hence, no reliable political model emerges for other states and provinces, although certain patterns of conflict may be predictable.

The Problem of Toxic Waste:
Is it Soluble?

When we call something old by a new name it sometimes indicates little more than a disagreeable connotation. Housewives became domestic managers; janitors became custodians; garbagemen became sanitary engineers. Garbage dumps here became sanitary landfills, and the name change sometimes signified very little. However, the explosion of a new kind of garbage, toxic waste, is the product of sophisticated industrialization, requires new nomenclature and does present new problems.

The garbage dump was a place to isolate odors and vermin. The sanitary landfill meant isolation and burial. Garbage can be dumped and covered, and although an apparently inefficient use of land, the burial of garbage away from habitable places has been a simple solution to a universal and persistent problem. Toxic waste, however, is not susceptible to old solutions. It cannot simply be removed and buried. It has a way to come back, whether from the sky as acid rain or, via underground water, even through a kitchen tap. This new garbage constitutes a new problem, and requires new solutions.

Approximately 100 billion pounds of toxic waste—or 350 pounds per capita—are generated each year in North America by virtually all industries.[1] There are several options for its disposal:

1. reducing the generation of toxic waste at the source
2. recycling and recovering the waste
3. treating the waste before disposal

Large-scale reduction of waste volumes, however, is not possible in the foreseeable future, because it would require major changes in industrial production and probably giving up many goods to which we have become accustomed. Moreover, cleaning up old dumps generates additional quantities of toxic waste.

Waste recycling and recovery is possible in many, but not all, cases. Many major chemical companies already recycle most of the waste that can be recovered; most wastes, however, cannot be recycled economically. Thus, treating toxic waste to neutralize it before disposal is a central component of any hazardous waste management strategy.[2]

Modern toxic waste treatment technology is very reliable, as compared with dumping the waste in landfills. High temperature incinerators destroy 99.99 percent of toxic materials (organic);[3] solidification processes immobilize inorganic waste by mixing it with cement.[4] Yet, releasing to the air .01 percent of large quantities of toxic chemicals contributes to atmospheric pollution, and the solidification technology has not been thoroughly tested for some kinds of waste streams and in very cold climates.[5]

The publicity that surrounded disasters such as Love Canal (U.S.A.), Seveso (Italy) and now Bhopal (India) has heightened the public awareness of the risks associated with toxic chemicals. The siting of new toxic waste facilities has become very difficult: nobody wants them near their homes, even if they allegedly are safe.

The Siting Problem

Governments in Canada and the United States have decided that the solution to the toxic waste problem must include new, safe facilities for the treatment and disposal of toxic waste—even if alternative solutions are pursued. Proposals for large, centralized waste treatment facilities often have been preferred over smaller, regional plants, for the former are easier to control and small plants are no easier to site.

This paper is based on the study of government attempts to site toxic waste treatment and disposal facilities in Quebec, Louisiana, Ontario and New York. The Quebec case has been chosen because it is the first new commercial toxic waste treatment facility built in North America after Love Canal. In the United States, one proposal obtained all necessary construction and operation permits, in Louisiana, although the permit was revoked two years later by the state Supreme Court.

The Quebec and Louisiana waste plant proposals were successful, at least initially, against opponents. In this sense, they constitute the two "best" cases in North America. Ontario and New York have been chosen because they are two large, adjacent political jurisdictions, with a similar industrial and economic base; they share the pollution of the Niagara region. Since the technical dimensions of the two cases are largely the same, important variations allow us to analyze the differences between the two countries. Both Ontario's and New York's siting attempts failed before even reaching public hearings.

Technical Aspects of the Siting Problem

Siting a toxic waste treatment and disposal facility is foremost a political, not a technological problem. It is possible, perhaps, to determine what is the technically best site for such a facility, and technical considerations always enter the decision to choose a certain location as a site for a toxic waste plant. The success or failure of the siting proposal, however, does not depend on its technical merits alone.

Meeting some of the technical criteria employed in the process of siting a toxic waste treatment and disposal facility is necessary for the success of a siting proposal. In addition, advanced waste treatment technology must be used and the disposal site must be located on impermeable soil where no wells or sand drumlins may allow leaching of toxic elements into underground waters.[6]

Proponents of waste disposal sites seem not always to pay enough attention to all necessary technical aspects of their projects, such as the hydrogeological characteristics of the site. In Louisiana, the proposed waste treatment site was chosen because of its proximity to the generators of waste; in Ontario public ownership was the main consideration. In both cases technical issues reemerged at the end of the process. The Louisiana Supreme Court ruled that insufficient consideration had been given to the possible impact of the facility on the nearby water wells and other environmental factors and revoked the permit that had been granted originally to the proponent of the waste facility. In Ontario, the Waste Management Corporation produced a hydrogeological study that declared the site only marginally suitable for a waste disposal plant and withdrew the proposal.

Fulfilling all technical requirements, however, is not sufficient to guarantee success. In New York, a proposed waste disposal facility was to be sited by Lake Ontario, in one of the few areas in the state sitting on an impermeable clay bed. The site had been tested and approved as a potential nuclear plant site. Yet the lack of political support killed the proposal. In Quebec, a government study recommended Laval as the best site to build a waste treatment facility. The developer submitted a proposal that met strong local opposition and rapidly was withdrawn. The plant then was built in a different location—not far from an area that had been considered, by the same government study, unsuitable for a waste facility.

Success is not due, then, to the technical perfection of a proposed site, nor to the reliability of the treatment technology. Some technical drawbacks of a proposed site, such as risk of flooding, closeness to surface sources of potable water, and difficult access to the site, are not considered insurmountable obstacles. The lack of adequate access to a proposed plant was resolved with a new road in Quebec; a plastic lining of the disposal site was required in Louisiana. The solidification technology employed in the Stablex plant in Quebec produces a cement-like, chemically inert, nonsoluble material that emits no odor. The treated waste is not even classified as a toxic substance in Japan, and it is used in Great Britain as construction material for roads. Yet this technology was rejected by the residents of a small town in Quebec, and welcomed, a few weeks later, by a different small town in the same province.

In some cases, technical advantages are an obstacle to successful siting: the proximity of the proposed plant to a large body of water, while useful for the discharge of liquid residues, may be a political liability—as in New York, where the location of the site by Lake Ontario precipitated opposition from the Syracuse Water Board, concerned about the safety of the city's drinking waters.

Technical arguments are always used by governments to justify specific siting proposals, and by the opposition to criticize them. The four cases show that, in fact, the technical merits of a siting proposal usually are not decisive for its success or failure. Rather, determination of who will bear the costs and risks of possible mishaps, whether in transportation of toxic waste to a facility or in accidents at the facility, truly is the decisive, political issue.

Why is it so Difficult to Site a Waste Facility?

Governments and developers who have tried to site toxic waste facilities have a favorite explanation for failure: local opposition. The popularity of acronyms such as LULUs (Locally Unwanted Local Uses)[7] and NIMBY (Not In My Backyard)[8] is an indication of that attitude. Reality, however, is more complex. Governments and developers are not always credible as champions of environmental protection, and there are few incentives for any other group or institution to play a leadership role in promoting waste facility projects. Moreover, local opposition is not always capable, in itself, of defeating a toxic waste facility proposal: it often needs the support of other influential individuals and institutions active at the state or provincial level.

The use of modern, safe facilities for the treatment and disposal of toxic waste benefits society as a whole. Yet government and developers are alone in their attempt to site waste treatment plants, and their records are not always spotless: toxic waste disposal firms often have equated disposal with dumping, and governments occasionally have supported private firms in their attempt to site or expand facilities whose safety was very questionable.[9]

Even when a toxic waste facility proposal is technically sound, few of the actors have any incentive to lead the project to success. Those who generate toxic waste generally favor the construction of safe facilities that avoid the risk of cleanup expenses or damage liability, but they do not want their operating costs raised in the short term. New and dynamic waste disposal firms are very aggressive in their attempt to offer treatment technologies that are much safer than the traditional landfilling methods, but many traditional waste disposal firms, threatened by the use of new technologies, do not lend political support to the siting of new facilities.[10]

Major environmental groups agree that a good waste treatment facility is a big improvement over traditional disposal methods, yet they frequently support local opposition by challenging the safety of most proposed facilities; and federal governments in both Canada and the United States play a very limited role in the siting of non-nuclear waste facilities. Only upon invitation from a province did the Canadian government help by providing land, as in Quebec. Even in this case, the federal government agreed to sell its land only after residents' support was confirmed by the re-election of the local government in Blainville. Because of the controversy associated with waste facilities, state and provincial politicians also have little incentive to support construction. They fear offending either their constituents or industry.

Local opposition often cannot stop toxic waste disposal projects without political influence at the state or provincial level. Local zoning powers can be overridden by state and provincial governments with a legislative act. In most cases opposition begins locally but it spreads to other groups with different agendas. In Ontario and Quebec, local opposition to government-supported waste facility proposals was exploited by opposition parties and used as an electoral issue. In New York, the governor's office and the legislature competed for leadership in the field of environmental protection and proposed different solutions to the problem, the governor favoring a centralized waste treatment plant, the Senate preferring smaller regional plants, and the House recommending on-site reduction and recycling facilities.

The environmental protection movement did not always play an important role. The Ontario government coopted a senior environmental leader, appointing him to head the Ontario Waste Management Corporation. The environmental protection movement was labeled leftist in Quebec and enjoyed only marginal political influence in Louisiana as well. In New York, by contrast, the publisher of the largest Syracuse newspaper and chairman of the local water board feared contamination of the city's water supply and strongly attacked in his paper the government proposal, sited fifty miles upstream.

The Role of the Government

The allocation of costs associated with toxic waste disposal facilities can be accomplished, at the extremes, in two ways: letting market forces decide where a facility is to be sited, or having the government choose. The former approach has been attempted first, but the private sector has been unable to site a single commercial toxic waste facility in North America since the Love Canal disaster.

Pressured by citizens, legislators, or industries unable to get rid of their toxic waste, governments have decided to step in. Public intervention in the field of toxic waste disposal may involve several kinds of action. The government may invite one or more private developers to submit proposals, or plan to build and operate a public facility; the ownership of the disposal site may be public or private; the government may select a site or let the developer choose one. These different forms of government intervention have different economic and political costs.

Public and private proposals for waste disposal facilities are, in many respects, similar. Similar economic considerations, such as realizing economies of scale, result in the preference of public and private developers for large, centralized facilities located near the major centers where waste is generated. The treatment and disposal technologies are usually chosen by governments, either directly or by selecting private companies, on the basis of their reputation and expertise.

Three of the four proposed waste facilities examined in this paper were to be built on government-owned land. The primary reason for the preference given to government ownership is to assure public long term monitoring of the site for the disposal of treated waste. Louisiana is the only case where the proposed disposal site was to be privately owned; yet there, too, thirty years after the closure of the site, the government would become responsible for custodial care.

The disposal of treated waste often requires large sites; finding a sufficiently large parcel of land may be one of the major difficulties in the siting process. In Ontario the availability of a suitable government-owned parcel of land in South Cayuga was the main reason for selecting it as a site for a waste facility. By contrast, the New York state government was unable to find a suitable publicly owned site and tried unsuccessfully to buy a large parcel of land from a utility company.

Public ownership of the waste disposal site, however, does not necessarily speed up the decision process. In Ontario, the Crown corporation decided, a year after the initial proposal, that the site was not suitable and started looking for another location. In Quebec, the federal government had agreed in principle to sell the land to the province, but was concerned about the controversy around the project. The sale agreement was only signed after the re-election of the Blainville local government demonstrated that local citizens supported the waste facility proposal.

Other forms of direct government intervention in a toxic waste facility proposal may be counterproductive because they increase the potential for public opposition. Not only local residents and environmental groups but also political opponents at the state or provincial level are likely to fight against a controversial government proposal for political reasons. The siting controversy becomes more politicized and its outcome more dependent on the interplay of political forces at the local as well as state or provincial government levels.

Often, political opposition to government-supported proposals includes criticizing the government for "taking sides" instead of evaluating a waste facility proposal from a neutral position; the opposition may question basic public policy choices, government's technical expertise, the site selection process, or the use of public funds.

Government support for a waste disposal project often was exploited as an electoral issue, both at the state or provincial and local levels. In Ontario, the opposition to the government siting process was part of the Liberal party campaign; the Liberal incumbent in the South Cayuga district was re-elected. In Quebec the main source of local opposition included a group of former town councilors who were trying a comeback in local politics.

A government-owned and operated waste disposal plant was proposed in Ontario and indicated as a possibility by a public corporation report in New York. In New York, the legislature had directed the state Environmental Facilities Corporation (EFC) to prepare a waste management program, which in its final version recommended the construction of a new central waste treatment facility. The EFC drew plans for the facility, and the commissioner of the Department of Environmental Conservation, who also headed the EFC, proceeded to select a site. But the legislature had never approved the final plan and resented having been excluded from the decision. The assembly also questioned the need for additional waste disposal capacity in the state, suggesting that waste recycling and recovery should be given priority instead. The funds for the waste management program were cut, leading to stalemate.

In Ontario, the option of a public waste facility was suggested by a legislative committee and was fully subscribed by the government because of repeated failures by waste disposal firms to site new facilities. The Ministry of the Environment selected a site and created a Crown corporation to build the waste facility. In the attempt to facilitate the permitting process, the corporation was exempted from local bylaws and public hearing requirements. When the site was announced, the government-backed siting process backfired: the opposition parties accused the government of having chosen the site for political, rather than technical, reasons; the local government and residents protested the powers given to the Crown corporation and demanded full public hearings.

The institution of a public corporation was ruled out by a Quebec government, unwilling to spend the capital and lacking the technical expertise to build a waste facility. The provincial government also believed that a Crown corporation would be less acceptable, politically, than a private waste disposal firm: the opposition would have contended that it is harder for the government to regulate a public corporation than a private developer.

The issue of cost was raised when the government support for a waste facility project involved public expenditures. In all four cases no public agency suggested that the taxpayers pay for waste disposal, yet many forms of government intervention are expensive. The Quebec government refused to finance a Crown corporation. Supporting a private proposal, however, also involved considerable public expense to buy the disposal site, provide it with an access road, and manage an information campaign publicizing the project.

As shown in Table 7.1, greater government involvement in a toxic waste facility proposal is more frequently associated with failure than success.

Yet, the way governments manage the proposal is more important than the degree of government intervention. Early local involvement, the use of geographic and social siting criteria, the exploitation of personal or institutional links between state/provincial and local governments have a great impact on the size and effectiveness of the opposition and hence the success or failure of the effort. The list of elements

Table 7.1
Government Intervention in the Four Cases

	Best Cases		Worst Cases	
	Louisiana	Quebec	New York	Ontario
Ownership of disposal site	private	public	public	public
Operation of facility	private	private	private/public	public
Site selection	private	public/private	public	public

Source: Compiled by the author.

contributing to a successful siting strategy, or a list of mistakes to be avoided, can be very long. Only the most relevant factors will be mentioned here, with a distinction between the formation of opposition and consensus at the local and at the state or provincial levels.

Government Policy and Local Opposition

Local opposition, even if not always decisive, is important. Winning local government support for a waste facility proposal probably is the single most important requisite for success, because it deprives opposition of its most common argument: the imposition of the project against local wishes.

Toxic waste disposal projects elicit local opposition because the concentration of large amounts of toxic waste in one facility, however safe, always involves the possibility, however remote, of disastrous accidents. Still, local sentiment is rarely uniform: some local residents may welcome the opportunity for new jobs or economic growth spurred by the project. Because community opinion can be divided, the response of local government is crucial. The Blainville government was not discouraged by a petition signed by 6,000 citizens (of a total population of 14,500): it helped organize a group of citizens to support the proposal, and conducted meetings with the major social and economic associations in town to present the merits of the waste facility project. In Gonzales, Louisiana, a petition of 10,000 people and the defeat of six town councilors at the local elections were not sufficient to change the basically positive attitudes of the local government towards the proposal.

Some local governments may actively oppose a toxic waste facility project, as in New York and Ontario; others provide continued support and leadership, as in Quebec; and others may evolve from tepid support to mild opposition, as did Gonzales in Louisiana. The outcomes of the four cases here suggest that industrial growth and geographic characteristics of the candidate sites might indicate best the potential for local acceptance of a toxic waste facility project. Sites for the two successful proposals are at the periphery of major centers where toxic waste is generated, in communities that are not fully industrial but in the process of industrial growth. In Blainville, at the periphery of Montreal's metropolitan area, the town council was actively engaged in the creation of an industrial park; in Ascension Parish, on the industrial corridor along the Mississippi between Baton Rouge and New Orleans, the acquisition of a waste treatment plant and the possibility of a hundred new jobs were considered desirable by local politicians.

The two candidate sites in Ontario and New York, by contrast, are located outside any center of industrial growth, in rural areas where a waste treatment plant seems to threaten pollution and the disruption of the local way of life. These sites were chosen by government for their technical characteristics; the governments assumed, furthermore, that public control of the land would speed up the permitting process.

Even when a community indicates an interest in expanding its industrial base, a waste facility project has little chance of local public support if local politicians are not involved from the earliest stages of the proposal. However, because a toxic waste facility project is likely to be controversial, local politicians may need political incentives before providing local leadership. In Louisiana the sale of land for the waste facility site benefitted a local politician and provided electoral contributions for a candidate to state office. In Quebec, the Blainville councillor who first proposed the town as a potential site was working as a consultant at the Ministry for the Environment; a link between provincial and local governments was also provided by common party affiliation, whereas in Ontario the proposed site was located in a predominantly opposition district.

Initial local government interest does not assure continued support, nor local acceptance. Compensating the local community for the imbalance of the geographical distribution of costs and benefits has been suggested as a way to build consensus on a waste facility project.[11] Local consensus may be obtained more easily if the project is not considered a cost, for which compensation is due, but is perceived as part of a package valuable to the local community, which includes, for example, land for an industrial park and a new exit on the main highway to Montreal (Quebec), or the promise of economic development and jobs for local residents (Louisiana). In both cases, moreover, the public hearings were used as an opportunity to improve technical aspects of the waste facility proposal, particularly with regard to its safety.

Building Consensus at the State and Provincial Levels

The likelihood of success for a waste facility proposal increases when a conscious strategy guides the search for consensus at the state or provincial level. A common feature of such strategy is the separation between the roles of developers and regulators, even though the government might be the main supporter of the project. In Quebec and Louisiana the government role was limited formally to deciding on the request for a permit presented by a private developer. In Ontario and

New York the separation of roles was less clear, especially in New York, where the public Environmental Facilities Corporation worked in close contact with the regulating agencies while drawing plans for a toxic waste facility project to be developed probably by a private firm.

In three of the cases governments tried to prevent the eruption of local opposition across the state or province by focusing their efforts on one site alone. This attention, however, gave local residents the impression that a final decision had already been made, and provided a new argument for the opposition. Only in Quebec were developer's permits requested in two localities at the same time and public hearings conducted in both places. This strategy prevented Blainville citizens from feeling singled out and facilitated acceptance of the waste facility proposal.

Quebec's successful strategy also included offering ample information on the proposal and its waste treatment technology in several public meetings, including one in a shopping mall. Trips to a similar plant in England were organized for media and local representatives, with the exclusion of opponents. Weekly meetings with representatives of the developer and of local and provincial governments were organized.

In Louisiana, the lack of a defined strategy did not prevent the proposal from obtaining all the necessary permits, but the conflict of interests involved in several transactions resulted in challenges to the legality of the permits and jeopardized the project financing.

Public and private proposals for siting toxic waste disposal facilities followed different avenues to failure. In Ontario and New York, where government involvement was greatest, failure followed political accusations, financial difficulties and the questioning of policy choices. The New York governor's office narrowed down a list of thirty-one possible sites to one site, without giving any previous indication of the selection criteria and without consulting the owner of the targeted land—a utility company, which eventually refused to sell. In Ontario, the site selection was apparently political and completely unresponsive to local interests. The government was accused of choosing the site to use the land it had purchased a few years earlier for a new town that had never materialized.

In Louisiana, where the government role was limited to awarding a private firm a contract to prepare a study, little political debate accompanied the process. Failure occurred at the end of the process, when a court ruling revoked the permit because some technical aspects of the project had not been given adequate consideration during the permitting process.

In the attempt to avoid causing alarm to residents of all potential sites, governments consistently and mistakenly excluded local representatives from the siting process; often they only learned about the proposal from the newspapers, when the decision appeared to have been made already. The siting process could have been used to marshal local interest and improve the technical aspects of the proposals; instead it was centralized or, in Louisiana, sloppy.

The waste facility proposals were publicized as environmental projects, but environmental groups and local residents were not given the means to conduct studies to assess the environmental consequences of the proposals. In Ontario, utilizing local residents' knowledge of the site, whose allegations were eventually confirmed in a government study, would have avoided a year's delay.

The one fully successful proposal, in Quebec, suggests that cooperation between the public and private sectors may be essential to allow the necessary government support for a waste facility proposal and at the same time minimize political opposition. The provincial government, unconstrained by the profit motive, was in fact able to offer attractive terms in exchange for local consent. The local government, aware of the aspirations and needs of the community, was in a unique position to build local consensus on the project. The constant cooperation between the private developer and government institutions assured that the waste facility project was well documented and enjoyed local support.

Lessons from the Cross-National Comparison: Summary and Conclusions

Solutions to Common Dilemmas

Siting toxic waste disposal facilities is a problem shared by Canada and the United States. The similarities between the two countries—they have similar economic and social structures and they both are federal and liberal-democratic polities—make it possible to learn from each other. Often the U.S. regulatory system, especially in the field of environmental protection, has been considered a model by Canadians (at least, until the explosion of the acid rain controversy). Now Quebec's success in siting the only new commercial toxic waste facility in North America offers an additional opportunity to learn from Canada.

In both countries, governments tended to respond in similar ways to the waste facility siting problem: all four proposals concerned large, centralized facilities supported by state or provincial governments and opposed by a substantial number of local residents. Citizens had little access to decision making, and North American standards of democracy were met by provisions for public hearings. In both countries, governments attempting to site waste facilities encountered two main dilemmas. First, citizens invoked government intervention to solve the toxic waste problem, yet local residents opposed government efforts to create toxic waste treatment and disposal facilities, and governments were exposed to political attack. Secondly, there is always a dilemma in choosing the location—siting toxic waste facilities near the generators of waste arouses local opposition, but siting them away from population centers incurs prohibitive transportation risks and economic costs. The cross-national study of four siting proposals presents a full spectrum of public intervention choices, and shows possible solutions to common dilemmas.

The Government Role. The private sector has been unable to site and build new waste facilities, and companies have asked state and provincial governments to support their proposals. Government intervention is necessary to help waste disposal firms build new waste treatment plants and stop the current practice of hazardous waste dumping. Government support, however, must be very selective to gain citizens' trust and minimize the potential for opposition. Only firms that use the most reliable technology and have proven their expertise, even if on the smaller scale of on-site waste treatment plants, should be encouraged to submit proposals for waste plants, and only the best project should enjoy government support.

All available information on the planned waste treatment technology should be made available by the firm to the regulatory agencies, to require all economically feasible improvements to the safety of the facility. Arrangements should be made to assure continued monitoring of the treatment and disposal processes by a government agent; unlimited access to the plant should also be granted to a local representative. At the same time, governments should be prepared, if necessary, to assist the company and make the project economically viable by providing, for example, land or access roads.

A private firm is unlikely to offer terms that make a waste facility attractive enough to a local community. State or provincial governments, unconstrained by the profit motive, can play an indispensable role by including the waste project in a larger package that meets local interests and demands.

Building a waste treatment facility is not a success unless the facility is in fact used. In Quebec, the waste plant has been operating at a fraction of its capacity and needs to import toxic waste from outside the province in order to function economically. It is hard to persuade the generators of toxic waste to spend considerable amounts of money for proper waste treatment and disposal when they are used to free or low-cost landfilling methods. A system of enforceable regulations might be necessary to create or stabilize a market for the services furnished by the waste treatment facility.

Where to Site. Private developers tend to give primary consideration to economic and technical criteria when selecting a site for a waste facility. Social and political criteria, however, ultimately can be decisive in a siting proposal.

Areas at the periphery of industrial regions, located downstream from large population centers, minimize the potential for political opposition to siting proposals. Communities that are in the process of industrializing are more likely to be interested in a waste disposal plant than congested and probably polluted industrial towns or isolated communities that prefer to conserve their rural character.

Local governments are probably the institutions most legitimized to represent local needs and aspirations, and likely to know if a waste facility is potentially acceptable. They are also in a unique position to mobilize support and strengthen local consensus on a waste facility proposal.

Local government involvement from the initial stages of the siting process is essential to avoid, for local residents, the threat of facing a *fait accompli*. In such conditions, it would be extremely difficult, even for a potentially favorable local government, to build consensus at the local level. Meaningful participation in the process also requires local access to all information on the technical aspects of the projects.

The primary lesson to be learned from the Quebec and Louisiana cases is the need for support from the local government or other politicians with a local base. The challenge for governments in North America is now to institutionalize the local-state/provincial contacts which were provided, in Quebec, by the particular situation of a town councillor, and in Louisiana by the personal advantages of the waste facility proposal for some politicians. An institutional setting where local representatives could be contacted, express their interest and formulate their demands to state/provincial governments and developers would greatly facilitate the search for candidate sites. Local government support is, in fact, likely to be a necessary precondition if the focus of political debate is to shift from local veto-state/provincial preemption towards local participation in siting toxic waste treatment facilities.

Canada and the United States: Special Obstacles and Opportunities

A similar constellation of political forces—local governments and other local politicians, local opposition and environmental groups, legislatures, government bureaucracies and public corporations—were active in siting controversies in Canada and the United States. State governments were not notably weaker than the provinces vis-à-vis the respective federal governments, and Canadian local governments were as able to resist the implementation of provincial policies as were their U.S. counterparts.[12]

Table 7.2 shows that in the two pairs of cases, Quebec/Louisiana and Ontario/New York, there are differences that cut across the national border. In Quebec and Louisiana the legislatures played a lesser role than in Ontario and New York; in Ontario and New York the toxic waste facility proposals were considered purely environmental projects, rather than instruments of economic growth, as in Quebec and Louisiana. The organization of state or provincial coalitions against the projects was more difficult in Quebec and Louisiana. Ontario and New York lacked the special channels of communication and exchange between local and state or provincial governments, which existed in Quebec (party links) and Louisiana (the inclusion of local politicians in business "deals." And the environmental protection movement was kept outside the political process in Quebec and Louisiana, while it played a substantial role in Ontario.

The different outcomes in the four cases correspond to a more general differentiation between the political environments of Quebec/Louisiana and Ontario/New York. Quebec and Louisiana have a tradition of executive rule, priority given to economic development over environmental protection, greater acceptance of government intervention, and more limited citizen participation. Their combination of extensive government intervention and limited citizen participation is probably unique in North America; perhaps it can even be associated with their common French heritage.

By contrast, Ontario and New York's political environments are less tolerant of the centralized decision making process employed by the

Table 7.2
Summary of the Four Cases

	Best Cases		Worst Cases	
	Quebec	Louisiana	Ontario	New York
Early local involvement	Yes	Yes	No	No
State- (or provincial-) local links	institutional and personal links	personal links	No	No
Choice of site	local offer	geographic location	government ownership	technical criteria
Geographic and social characteristic	industrial periphery; economic growth	industrial periphery; economic growth	rural area	rural area
Sources of opposition	local; environmental groups	local; environmental groups	local government; opposition parties; environmental movement	local government; special interests
Sources of support	government party; local government	individual state and local politicians	government party	legislators from Niagara region
Government role	selecting developer; permitting	selecting developer; permitting	selecting site; public corporation	selecting site and developer

Source: Compiled by the author.

two governments in the attempt to site waste facilities. The comparative study shows that, along certain dimensions at least, diversity among states or provinces may be greater than cross-national differences,[13] but the French heritage may associate Quebec and Louisiana as a unique pair contrasted to all other states and provinces in North America.

At the same time, important differences also emerged between the congressional and the parliamentary systems of the t wo countries. These included the sources of institutional opposition—political parties in Canada, legislative assemblies in the United States—and the stronger role played in Canada by political parties, both as potential opponents and as sources of strength for the government in power. Because of the different cultural and institutional contexts, each country faces some special obstacles and has special opportunities to solve the waste facility siting problem.

Lessons for Canada

In the parliamentary systems of Ontario and Quebec, opposition parties may have a vested interest in fighting government decisions regarding waste treatment and disposal sites. Their opposition is especially effective when the government does not command a solid parliamentary majority.

Proposing to build a waste facility in an opposition area reduces the chances for local cooperation on the project; it might be more advisable to propose a site in a progovernment district and count on party loyalty—even if this may involve the risk of losing the seat in the next election.

The strong party organizations in Canada present several advantages. Governments can usually count on legislative support of their decisions regarding basic policy choices and waste facility sites. The party might provide a link between the provincial and the local governments, facilitating the communication of local interest in a waste facility and increasing provincial responsiveness to those demands.

Political scientists have argued that Canadian political culture is more accepting of strong government intervention in the private sector and that deferential attitudes of Canadian citizens toward authority contribute to their relative lack of participation in public policy making.[14] Yet the attempt to exclude local governments and citizen participation in Ontario only delayed the final decision.

The greater centralization of government and the presence of strong party organizations in Canada constitutes an opportunity for a more efficient decision making process, provided that the demand for local participation is not neglected.

Lessons for the United States

In the United States the political context surrounding a waste facility proposal is different from Canada in important ways. The project may be caught in a conflict between the executive and the legislative. The basic policy choices about the waste disposal problem may be questioned. State representatives are most responsive to their local constituency and loyalty to the government, even if they belong to the same party.

Direct government intervention in the private sector often requires more justification and is more likely to be questioned in the United

States. The involvement of private waste disposal firms more clearly defines state intervention as a regulatory function, and is more acceptable politically.

When the government role is limited to permitting a waste facility project, however, the probability of court intervention is higher. The project can be protected from legal challenges if government involvement in the siting process improves the proposal and reduces local opposition.

Utilizing mechanisms for public participation, already present in some states, may cause delays in the siting process. Delay is an affordable price if those mechanisms help to anticipate and respond to objections that could otherwise result in starting the siting process from the beginning again.

A partnership between the public and private sectors, in which the government acts as a facilitator rather than a manager, seems to be essential for the success of toxic waste facilities proposals.

Closeness to industry and water is apparently more acceptable politically than the transportation costs and risks associated with siting a waste facility in rural areas. Early local involvement, however, is very important. This does not necessarily mean securing support from activist groups, but reliance on local governments' ability to assess and exploit the potential for citizen support.

Major private involvement in pursuing a toxic waste facility siting proposal is advantageous, perhaps even essential. This emphasis on the role of the private sector is not a United States bias: the outcomes of the two Canadian cases lead to the same conclusion.

Siting toxic waste facilities is difficult, and even when a facility is built, no final conclusion can be reached about success. The facility must be used. Without strict enforcement of regulations preventing the dumping of toxic waste, a treatment facility may not be worth its political and economic cost. Moreover, why should the public sector pay to solve a problem created by private industries?

The cost of siting waste treatment facilities could be recovered by fines against transgressors of toxic waste disposal regulations or by levying effluent production taxes. In Canada and the United States the federal governments could contribute to reduce disparities between the states or provinces. In both countries the constitutional framework allows them to introduce legislation preventing interstate or interprovince circulation of toxic wastes unless their destination is a certified treatment facility. Such legislation would relieve state and provincial fear of appearing anti-business while providing leverage for the enforcement critical to the economic viability of toxic waste facilities. Thus, although siting is a local and state/provincial problem in partnership with private industry, success of an overall toxic waste program may depend on the legislative intervention of federal governments.

Notes

1. U. S. Environmental Protection Agency, *Hazardous Waste Generation and Commercial Hazardous Waste Management Capacity*, Washington, D.C., 1980, p. III-3, and statement by Vic Niemela, senior officer at the Canadian Department of the Environment, at the 65th Chemical Conference, Ottawa, June 1982.

2. The siting imperative is discussed by David Morell and Christopher Magorian, *Siting Hazardous Waste Facilities. Local Opposition and the Myth of Preemption* (Cambridge: Ballinger, 1982).

3. Peter Williamson, Vice-President, IT Corporation, personal interview, Baton Rouge, Louisiana, February 17, 1983.

4. Stablex Corporation's Technical Director, personal interview, Montreal, Quebec, September 21, 1983.

5. Statements by Joan B. Berkowitz, Vice President, Hazardous Waste Management Section, Arthur D. Little, Inc., at the conference "The Politics of Hazardous Waste," Cambridge Forum, January 16, 1985.

6. Robert B. Pojasek, ed., *New and Promising Ultimate Disposal Options, Toxic and Hazardous Waste Disposal*, Vol. 4 (Ann Arbor: Ann Arbor Science Publishers, Inc., 1980). See also Rensselaer Technical Institute, *Technology for Managing Hazardous Waste*, (Albany, New York: New York State Environmental Facilities Corp., 1979). Technical criteria for siting decisions are reviewed in R. F. Anderson, M. R. Greenberg, and R. J. Nardi, *A Report on Hazardous Waste Management Facility Siting Criteria* (New Brunswick, New Jersey: Middlesex County Planning Board, 1980).

7. This acronym was probably coined by Frank J. Popper, "Siting LULUs," *Planning* 47 (April 1981), pp. 12–15.

8. The failure to site toxic waste facilities is attributed to local opposition in U.S. Environmental Protection Agency, *Siting of Hazardous Waste Management Facilities and Public Opposition* (Washington, D.C., 1979).

9. See David Estrin, "Siting Hazardous Waste Disposal Facilities," in *Proceedings of the 27th Ontario Industrial Waste Conference* (Toronto: Ontario Ministry of the Environment, 1980).

10. A number of large toxic waste disposal firms left the U.S. National Solid Waste Management Association because they advocate stricter toxic waste disposal regulations than the Association. Personal interview with Charles Johnson, National Solid Waste Management Association, Washington, D.C., February 8, 1983.

11. The payment of compensation in connection with the siting of toxic waste disposal and other types of facilities is advocated by Michael O'Hare, Lawrence Bacow and Debra Sanderson, *Facility Siting and Public Opposition*, (New York: Van Nostrand Reinhold Company, 1983).

12. Much political science literature on Canada would have us expect great differences between the Canadian and the United States cases. See, for instance, Donald V.

Smiley, "Federal-Provincial Conflict in Canada," in *Canadian Federalism, Myth or Reality*, J. P. Meekison ed., (Toronto: Methuen, 1977); and C. R. Tindal and S. N. Tindal, *Local Government in Canada*, (Toronto: McGraw-Hill, 1979).

13. In a non-scholarly, fascinating book, journalist Joel Garreau argues that nine regional divisions in North America are more important than the three nation-states of Canada, the United States and Mexico. New York and Ontario are part of the same region, "the foundry." Joel Garreau, *The Nine Nations of North America* (New York: Avon, 1981).

14. Louis Hartz, *The Liberal Tradition in America* (New York: Harcourt, Brace, Jovanovich, 1955). Robert Presthus, "Aspects of Political Culture and Legislative Behavior: United States and Canada," in Robert Presthus, ed., *Cross-National Perspectives* (Leiden: E.J. Brill, 1977), p. 9. Christopher Leman, *The Collapse of Welfare Reform* (Cambridge, Mass.: The MIT Press, 1980), pp. 134–138; Arend Lijphart, "Consociational Democracy," *World Politics*, January 1969; Richard Simeon, *Federal-Provincial Diplomacy*, (Toronto: University of Toronto Press, 1973), pp. 295–296.

PART IV

MAKING CHANGE: GIVE AND TAKE

8

Adjudicating Jurisdictional Disputes in Chicago and Toronto: Legal Formalism and Urban Structure

Gordon L. Clark

Canada and the United States have complex and articulated urban systems, dominated by very large cities and a vast network of smaller cities. There are also close ties between their respective urban systems. For instance, the Canadian metropolitan corridor, stretching from Windsor, Ontario through Quebec City, links Quebec closely to the U.S. midwest urban network (beginning with Detroit), and U.S. Atlantic seaboard cities like Boston and New York.[1] For all these obvious similarities and interrelationships, strong claims have been made for the separate identity and distinctiveness of Canadian cities, compared to American cities.[2] Indeed, it is perhaps because of these interrelationships that leading citizens of both countries (but mostly in Canada) maintain an elaborate rhetorical stance which aims at sustaining the separate integrity of Canadian culture and their cities.* The issues for scholars from both countries are twofold: first, to understand just how similar and dissimilar are the two countries in terms of their urban structures. And, second, how research ought to proceed so that supposed similarities and differences are accorded their appropriate signifi-

---

*Thus, for example, the stance taken by the previous Prime Minister (Trudeau) on such matters as foreign investment is indicative of the importance of this theme in Canadian politics, even if the present government is less strident than the previous government.

cance. In terms of this second issue, several theoretical options can be identified.

One strand of contemporary urban research supposes that cities are much the same the world over. Based on an analytical mode of reasoning, neoclassical economic theorists argue that urban structure can be described by universal principles including land rent, distance costs, and individual preferences. Alonso's model of the internal structure of the city is *the* paradigmatic case.[3] This is a model which allocates competing land uses on the basis of relative prices. Individual location decision makers simply respond to the spatial surface of land values in relation to their own preferences. Local context is eschewed in favor of a standard landscape applicable to all cities, whether Canadian, American or even Latin American.

If it is nevertheless maintained that there are significant differences between different countries' cities, how are such differences to be explained? One strategy is to argue that these so-called "uncomfortable" facts are evidence of the need for further research, a suggestion that has been made by Mills and Hamilton.[4] Another more plausible strategy is to inquire whether the underlying institutional structure of many cities is so different that interurban differences are sustained outside the inherent logic of the neoclassical model. This argument is especially plausible when urban structure is compared between countries. Notice it is an argument which finds favor with a wide variety of scholars, including geographers,[5] sociologists,[6] political scientists and economists.[7]

Thus, there is a second strand of urban research which emphasizes the distinctiveness of countries' urban systems. Commonly, the focus is on how different countries' political systems foster different urban outcomes. Johnston's recent study of the impact of the judiciary on the U.S. urban scene is a good example of this kind of work.[8] Johnston argued that the particular political culture of the U.S., coupled with distinctive institutions like the U.S. Supreme Court, combine to create a peculiarly American spatial organization of capitalism. There have been many other studies of the role of the public sector in structuring urban outcomes. For instance, an early study by Levy, Meltsner, and Wildavsky considered the impact of the bureaucratic structure of policy implementation on local public service provision.[9] And Clark and Dear have more recently linked American urban structure to the role of the state, concentrating on particular ideological underpinnings of the spatial structure of the state.[10] In this mode of urban research, the political sphere of capitalism is considered in its own right; it is presumed to be as important as the economic sphere.[11]

This essay begins with the assumption that this second mode of urban research is basic to any understanding of the differences between countries' urban structures. The essay interprets judicial decision making in Canada and the U.S. as it relates to the resolution of land use disputes.* More specifically, the focus is on how jurisdictional claims for the regulation of urban land use are adjudicated in Chicago and Toronto. The crucial issues in this essay concern the logic and language of decision making and the indeterminacy of structure. In the first instance, this issue involves how adjudication resolved the disputes and how adjudication was itself rationalized in the two cities. In the second instance, the issue is why structure, as in legal and political definitions of local powers, does not provide determinate solutions to conflicts over local responsibilities.

My argument is that whatever the differences between Canada and the U.S. as political entities and whatever the differences between the two cities in terms of their urban structure, there were some similarities in the cases considered here in terms of the legal interpretation of local government powers. The courts used similar decision rules and similar language to justify their decisions. These similarities are argued to be the product of two factors: a common methodological stance in the adjudication of local autonomy and a shared ideological conception of the proper role of decentralized government in society. The causes of structural indeterminacy are found in the nature of judicial reasoning.

Legal Formalism

What is it about the mode of legal reasoning in the U.S. and Canada that encourages similarities in the adjudication of local government powers between the two countries? The answer to this question, I believe, is straightforward. Essentially, the judicial process in both countries, but particularly in Illinois and Ontario, is dominated by what can be termed "legal formalism." Unger identified legal formalism by reference to two basic characteristics of modern North American jurisprudence: objectivism and formalism. He defined objectivism in the following terms: "the belief that the authoritative legal materialism—the

*In this regard I follow the lead of Rabinow and Sullivan (1979) and, more especially, Taylor (1979) in an interpretive mode of analysis. Essentially, my perspective is premised upon a belief that there is no privileged position from which to decide on the truth or otherwise of an argument. Rather, we can only offer interpretations in the hope that they will provide insight as opposed to a determinate conclusion. This argument is developed further in Clark (1985).

system of statutes, cases, and accepted legal ideas—embody and sustain a defensible scheme of human association." He defined formalism as a mode of decision making which "invokes impersonal purposes, policies, and principles as an indispensable component of legal reasoning." And, he suggested that "formalism in the conventional sense—the search for a method of deduction from a gapless system of rules—is merely the anomalous, limited case."[12] Legal formalism is then the combination of these two dimensions of legal practice.

By themselves, objectivism and formalism each presuppose the existence of the other. That is, judges who use objectivism need formalism if they are to sustain their claims of neutral, noncontextual decision making. Similarly, judges who use formalism need objectivism if they are to justify the outcomes of their decisions. Put another way, if judges are to maintain their legitimacy they must claim that the method through which they reach their decisions is above reproach. They must be able to distinguish judicial decision making from "ordinary politics"—because it is the arena of politics which is the origin of disputes that come before them requiring resolution. The status of the judiciary depends on a presumption that the judiciary is *above* politics. Likewise, the judiciary must claim that the logic of their decisions arises from a *principled* adherence to justice, in contrast to "ordinary politics," which is presumed to operate on the basis of subjective self-interest.

To be most crude about it, legal formalism supposes that judges apply neutral rules to contentious situations while appealing to fundamental principles to justify the outcomes of their decisions. As Unger has noted, this combination of neutral rules and fundamental principles seeks to distinguish judicial reasoning from political reasoning, thereby demonstrating that "the laws are not merely the outcome of contingent power struggles or of practical pressures lacking in rightful authority."[13]

Why should the judiciary try to legitimate their decisions using a form of discourse like legal formalism? There are two obvious reasons and one less obvious reason. In contemporary societies like the U.S. and Canada, the judiciary has a great deal of power and status. Whether deserved or not, this power gives the judiciary the right to intercede in the very fabric of society. The fact that so few citizens are qualified (by reason of training in a few elite universities) for the position guarantees that judges will be extraordinarily careful to ensure their elite social positions. Yet this social status is vulnerable precisely because of the elite connotations embodied in the position. Most judges are appointed, not elected. Most judges do not answer to any legislature and have tremendous discretion in how they choose to consider issues. Thus, it is readily apparent that the judiciary must be conscious of their power and vulnerability. These two issues are, of course, quite obvious and have been noted by many scholars of various political persuasions.[14]

More critically, though, the judiciary have a role which is at the very heart of society. That is, they adjudicate disputes in instances where social cohesion is most fragile and where conventional modes of dispute resolution have been unable to deliver a determinant solution to a particular dispute. Here their involvement in social conflict makes the judiciary liable for the resulting conclusion. It is little wonder then that the judiciary cling to devices like legal formalism. It is a means of transforming disputes from their immediate texture to a structured discourse controlled by the judiciary. In this respect legal formalism is a means of protecting the judiciary from the tensions of any one dispute. Thus, the less obvious reason for the significance of legal formalism to the judiciary has to do with the tension within society itself.

One final remark needs to be made concerning the nature of legal formalism before we consider legal formalism in practice in Chicago and Toronto. Unger made the point that formalism involves the application of rules to disputes, in accordance with accepted principles.[15] This remark should not be taken as implying that rules are unambiguous, or fully determined independently of the dispute at hand. Like ordinary language, rules are open textured; meaning is ascribed to rules not found within the fabric of rules. Like J. L. Austin, I contend that there must inevitably be dispute over the very meaning, indeed relevance, of interpretive rules, whether in literature or in the adjudication of disputes.[16] Some legal theorists would debate this point by arguing that as long as these rules were interpreted in a way consistent with principles there need not be any problem of "unbounded judicial discretion."[17] But if rules depend upon principles for meaning, and if these principles require their own interpretation—which is surely the implication of Austin's argument that language is open textured—then the application of legal formalism to any dispute could be a problematic process. Nevertheless, because the judiciary controls the form of legal discourse, how rules are applied and how they are interpreted can radically transform the terms of any dispute.

In the context of legal formalism, what are the rules of local autonomy in the two countries? How are localities treated in Illinois and Ontario? And, can we identify any rule-based similarities or distinctions between Chicago and Toronto in terms of their respective powers? These questions all relate to the formal structure of local government powers in Illinois and Ontario.

The "location" of local government powers in Illinois is the state constitution. In the 1970 state constitution, as in previous constitutions,

Illinois towns and cities are treated generally; that is, the powers of localities are specified in general rules applicable to all communities. This need not mean that all localities have exactly the same powers. There are different classes of localities, all of which have their own enumerated powers. For instance, the constitution makes a distinction between home-rule and nonhome-rule localities and between large and small cities. Nevertheless, localities are not specifically identified; rather, they are treated according to their categorical association.

Ontario towns and cities draw their authority from provincial statutes. Instead of depending upon a provincewide constitutional mandate, localities depend upon the Ontario legislature for their powers. However, the legislature also treats localities generally, not specifically. Broad categories are used to classify Ontario towns and cities, and thus particular localities have the powers of the particular class of community to which they belong. In both instances, a conscious decision was made to avoid enumerating the powers of particular localities.

In Illinois and Ontario, localities are the "creatures" of the immediately higher tier of the state.[18] As Simeon noted for Ontario, localities are the "creatures of the province." And Frug and many others noted in the U.S. that localities are the "creatures of the state."[19] In terms of adjudication, the courts in both instances begin with an assumption that local powers originate at the state or provincial level. While the courts obviously use different materials in interpreting local powers, they nevertheless begin from much the same formal definition of the origin of local powers in the higher tier of the state. A crucial difference, of course, is that the Ontario legislature may revise, amend, or even wholly alter the powers of local governments, whereas the Illinois legislature is bound by the state constitution. But, of course, there remains a formal presumption in both Illinois and Ontario that localities depend upon higher tiers of government for their powers.

Historically, localities in both "states" have been weak and fiscally have depended upon higher tiers for their survival. For instance, in Ontario many municipalities went bankrupt during the late 1890s and again in the 1930s because of what some commentators have termed "local profligacy."[20] The Ontario legislature has had to institute a wide range of controls over local activities in order to assure sound management at the local level. In fact, the Ontario Municipal Board (OMB) owes its existence to the collapse of many municipal streetcar railways at the turn of this century. Similarly, the Illinois constitutional convention of 1870, which severely limited the powers of localities in that state, was based on a strong sentiment against the "extravagance of municipalities."[21] As in Ontario, the financial crisis of many Illinois localities were linked directly to their involvement in dubious street-railway schemes. It was not until very recently that Illinois localities have been able to convince the electorate that they warrant some independence from the state government.[22]

For many years the legal doctrine describing the formal relationship between Illinois and its localities was Dillon's rule. Justice Dillon (1911) held that localities have only those powers expressly delegated by the state government and by implication two further powers:

1. those necessary and incident to carrying out the delegated functions
2. those absolutely necessary for carrying out the expressly noted legislation or constitutional requirements

Essentially, Dillon's rule limits the sphere of local discretion to those powers literally described in enabling legislation and/or in constitutional mandates. Traditionally, Dillon's rule has been the dominant conception of local powers in the U.S. (and Illinois more specifically). Although not explicitly noted as such, Dillon's rule has also been the dominant judicial conception of the formal relationship between Ontario and its localities. Statutes are interpreted literally, and local discretion highly constrained to the letter of the enabling legislation.

More recently, the 1970 Illinois constitutional convention revised the formal decision-rule by declaring that localities may opt to become "home-rule" entities. The essential difference between Dillon's rule and home rule is that localities operating under home rule can claim powers not explicitly detailed in legislation as long as the state has no overriding interest or prior claim to jurisdiction. Many statutes and constitutional requirements still prohibit local discretions, and it is not even clear that the courts acknowledge the differences between Dillon's rule and home-rule requirements.[23] In Ontario, local powers are still highly circumscribed, although the dominant judicial rule is not as explicitly labeled as in Illinois.

Local autonomy in the two "states" can be summarized in the following terms. Local initiative powers are limited, dependent upon higher governmental tiers. Even in instances of home-rule authority, localities in Illinois remain narrowly limited to those areas not already covered by state legislation and those areas explicitly mentioned in the state constitution. Since Illinois local-state relationships have been dominated by state regulation of local activities, it is little wonder that the judiciary have not believed that the formal powers of localities have substantially changed with the introduction of home rule.

In both "states," localities have no immunity from review by higher tier governmental agencies and the courts. In Ontario, the OMB has the right to review any and all local actions. While not initially constituted as a court, the OMB has many of the same functions, especially in terms of its enforcement capacities, and it is formally constituted as the representative of the provincial minister of housing, the minister responsible for local government. Thus it explicitly represents the views and interests of the provincial government. Yet the OMB is itself liable to review in the provincial court system.

Illinois does not have an OMB. State courts play a very important role as "reviewers" of the propriety of local government actions and depend upon the formal rules for guidance in deciding disputes over local actions. Initiative and immunity are so limited in both "states" that I have argued elsewhere that localities in these "states" are often just the administrative arms of higher tier authorities.[24] Rhetoric notwithstanding, the formal control of local powers by higher tiers is so strong in both "states" that we must be wary of how much significance can be attached to claims that cities like Chicago and Toronto are different because of different institutional structures.

Spatial Structure of Liberalism

Legal formalism is more than the application of rules to circumstances. Rules by themselves do not necessarily provide determinant solutions to disputes.[25] The issue is as much the interpretation of rules as their application in particular instances. Likewise, a structured set of rules regarding local authority need not provide an unambiguous blueprint for the allocation of powers between contending agencies and groups. Even Dillon's rule is not complete enough to be noncontentious in certain circumstances.[26] Structures require interpretation; in this regard structures are just like rules.

This much is recognized by those legal theorists who utilize a legal formalist mode of discourse. As Unger noted, legal formalism is actually a pairing of two claims: rule adjudication is a neutral process of applying the law, and rule interpretation depends on a set of principles which embody a fundamental vision of society itself.[27] Thus, legal formalists attempt to have it both ways. If there is debate over the application of certain rules, the legal formalist would justify any interpretation in terms of some higher-order (presumably uncontested) principles. Given that we have been able to identify a set of basic rules which clearly are important in both "states" as the logic of local powers, how would they be interpreted in particular circumstances? To what principles would judges appeal in order to legitimize their decisions?

As there are many rules, there are many principles. Here I wish to concentrate on the principles of liberalism. Remember, Unger noted that the claim of objectivism depends on "a defensible scheme of human association." Thus, although there are many possible principles we could review, practically speaking only those principles which are at the very center of social life would qualify as ground for judicial defense. Notice, however, that there is a great deal of presumption involved in deciding what principles are at the center of society. One could imagine more radical positions than liberalism being claimed to represent the center of society. For instance, Richard Posner has suggested that the appropriate central principles should be economic efficiency and wealth maximization.[28] This is, of course, a fairly conservative "radical" position which has been subject to a great deal of debate.[29] Others might claim social justice as the central principle.[30]

The point is that the judiciary has extraordinary powers in choosing the terrain on which to interpret rules. It is this terrain which is likely to give rules different meanings if different principles are used to interpret them. Thus, we could expect that even if Dillon's rule is common to both Ontario and Illinois, if it is interpreted from markedly different vantage points, then there will be different urban outcomes. So, for example, if a judge were to interpret "necessary powers" from a socialist perspective where private property was not protected, a local government might legitimately appropriate property according to its defined functions. Alternatively, a more conservative judge using a liberal perspective to interpret local powers might hold that any appropriation of private property is illegal—outside a standard interpret ation of "necessary powers." It is quite obvious that urban outcomes would be radically different in both instances even if localities were nominally under the control of Dillon's rule.

In this study I consider the implications of following a liberal perspective in interpreting local powers. Clearly, liberalism has been a favorite set of principles for Canadian and U.S. adjudication. But I do not suppose that liberalism is the only logic which has been used by judges in these two countries to legitimize their decisions. Moreover, I would also accept that liberalism is more problematic as the "central" principle of "human association" in Canada as compared to the United States. Nevertheless, I argue that liberalism is very important in both countries, especially when we come to consider the two case studies in the next section.

Liberalism, as described by theorists such as Lowi,[31] Ely,[32] and Sandel[33] begins with individuals as the very basis for society. In contrast to to structuralist notions of society, liberals assume individuals exist prior (in logical time) to society. Individuals are complete as rational and emotional beings; social context provides a stage in which to act and find fulfillment. More extreme versions of this theory suppose that individual utilities are unstructured by social factors, and that individual self-interest is a natural phenomenon.[34] Of course, this is an ideal image. Once material circumstances are introduced, even the most optimistic liberal is likely to acknowledge that society can radically affect peoples' desires.[35]

In fact, it is precisely this possibility that has led some liberal theorists to argue that individuals are essentially untrustworthy. Choper argued that when an individual's selfish interest is combined in a group, especially a majority, others will inevitably be adversely affected.[36] It is for this reason that liberal theorists often use "original positions" as analytical devices to separate individuals from immediate material interests. Rawls begins his analysis by locating individuals in a nonmaterial context, behind a veil of ignorance.[37] From that vantage point, he then asks individuals to choose a set of rules that would protect them in the event that they end up in an inferior social position. Rawls uses this strategy to ensure a just solution to basic entitlements without recourse to material circumstances. The liberal world is one where individuals have fundamental status, despite their often undesirable behavior.

Not only does liberalism have a highly articulated vision of individual motivations (even though the individuals do not appear to have any social personality);[38] it also claims a particular conception of the proper role of government. Most obviously, a liberal state should protect the rights of individuals. After all, if individuals are so fundamental, their potential for action must be fully realized. If individuals were compromised in the exercise of their rights, their whole integrity would be at risk. Just as obviously, individuals must be protected from those who would not respect the rights of others. But this is not the last word on the role of the liberal state for a number of theorists, past (including de Tocqueville and Locke) and present (including Nozick and Taylor), who have argued for a particular spatial configuration of state powers.

Taking Nozick as the paradigmatic case, some liberals have suggested that government is most appropriately decentralized.[39] At this level, it is argued, human association is most convivial. De Tocqueville suggested that this may be because the small town is closest to nature, man's original position. Nozick suggested that having a set of small towns can allow likeminded people to find and consume their true preferences. As a consequence, decentralized homogeneous communities might also limit the tendencies for individual, selfish exploitative behavior. De Tocqueville invoked God to justify his vision of decentralized life; Nozick justified his spatial geometry by the fundamental assumptions of liberal philosophy—individual self-interest and their fundamental integrity. This liberal vision of community life is what I have termed elsewhere the "imperative of decentralization."[40]

This imperative does not, however, stand alone. It is counterposed by the imperative of centralization. Because liberals do not trust individuals' actions in social groups, isolated individuals must be protected. That is, there must be a mechanism by which those individuals who feel victimized in a community can appeal to some other authority. Also, communities themselves must have protection from other communities which may seek to dominate. Thus, a centralized review agency, like the courts, would be necessary to retain the integrity of the whole system of communities. Inevitably, there is a tension between the two imperatives—decentralization and centralization—and a large role for the courts in adjudicating the relative significance of these two imperatives in different situations. This is a structural feature of liberalism as a mode of social thought[41] and as a logic for a particular spatial configuration of human association.

From where, in a spatial sense, does the state derive its legitimacy in a liberal world? Both de Tocqueville and Nozick would argue that the origins of state legitimacy reside in the local community. Logically, communities *give up* powers to higher tiers in order to facilitate the freedom of all. In the writings of both authors, other more practical reasons are advanced to justify the devolution of powers *up* the spatial hierarchy. Instead of localities being granted powers by state governments, as in a home-rule mode of local autonomy, localities in the liberal model of local autonomy grant powers to the states. This is, after all, the ideological framework which underpins notions like a "commonwealth of communities."[42]

It should be immediately obvious to the reader that any judicial interpretation of local powers in Chicago or Toronto which was justified by reference to liberal principles would be difficult to sustain. In terms of the rules of local powers in the two "states," Chicago and Toronto are granted powers, and are tightly constrained by the review powers (judicial and administrative) of higher tiers. Yet liberal principles, a common basis for the defense of judicial interpretation, assume that localities grant powers to higher tiers, not the other way around. Of course, embedded in liberalism are two counterprinciples, decentralization and centralization, which may provide the judiciary with a means of rationalizing decisions. Nevertheless, the logical locus of state legitimacy in a liberal world resides at the local level, not higher levels. Thus, there is a built-in contradiction in modes of legal formalism that use the language of liberalism to legitimize the current structure of local powers in Chicago and Toronto. In the next section the implications of this contradiction are explored in more depth using two case studies.

Practice of Adjudication

The two cases I wish to consider involve suburban municipalities in metropolitan Chicago and Toronto. The city of Des Plaines is situated in the northwestern suburbs of Chicago, adjacent to and north of O'Hare International Airport. The borough of Scarborough is north of the city of Toronto, adjacent to the major east-west route Highway 400. Both cities (as they will be termed) are composed of middle to upper-class residents who work and live in their larger respective metropolitan areas. These two cities have grown rapidly over the past few decades, and are representative of the postwar suburbanization process so typical of North American cities.[43] Like many such cities, their rapid growth has involved tremendous expansion of their public services and the public and private services of adjacent communities; and both cities have been highly involved in planning the pattern and character of public and private economic development. In these respects, these two cities are two among many similar cities in North America.

Over the course of ten years, from 1966 to 1976, Des Plaines fought a proposal by the Metropolitan Sanitary District of Greater Chicago to locate a water treatment plant in the city. The sewerage authority (the "district" hereafter) planned to locate the plant in an area zoned by the city as an M-1 restricted manufacturing district. In fact, the district did not seek permission from the city; it simply notified the city of its intentions and then proceeded to purchase the property and clear the site. In late 1966, the city filed a complaint in the state circuit asking that the district be forced to acknowledge the city's jurisdiction. The issue here is apparently straightforward: which governmental body had jurisdiction? This issue took some ten years to resolve, partly because of the uncertain status of both entities in terms of the courts and the state constitutional background.[44]

The Scarborough case also involved a question of jurisdiction.[45] In 1972, the city amended its official plan to accommodate a regional shopping center that some developers had proposed for an area close to an adjacent municipality (Pickering Township). The official plan had been approved by the minister of housing in 1957. In accordance with the Ontario Planning Act, the city submitted the amendment to the minister for approval. However, Pickering Township requested that the amendment be reviewed by the OMB, which significantly reduced the scale from a regional to a community shopping center. The OMB also required the city to undertake an impact analysis demonstrating that the regional shopping center would have no detrimental effects on the surrounding area. The city appealed the OMB's decision to the Ontario High Court, claiming that the OMB lacked jurisdiction and had acted improperly.

Both cases involved regional issues. The Des Plaines case involved the site of a regional water treatment plant, while the Scarborough case involved the planning of a regional shopping center. Both cases were related to regional economic growth. The district sought to accommodate the expanding demand for water treatment, and Scarborough sought to accommodate the expanding demand for shopping facilities. Similarly, both cases involved questions of jurisdiction among governmental units. However, in the Scarborough case the issue concerned the reasonable scope of the OMB review powers, especially its requirement that the city change its plans and respond to the OMB's demands for further study. The issue was slightly different in Chicago, for it did not involve the review powers of a higher tier agency so much as the relationship between two nominal municipal entities. How did the courts decide these claims? What rules did they invoke? And, to what principles did they appeal in order to justify their interpretations of the rules?

As we have seen, the powers of municipalities in Ontario are implicitly limited by what jurists in the U.S. legal system would call Dillon's rule. Localities have only those powers expressly given or those powers necessary for the execution of those given powers, which limits initiative and local immunity. Nevertheless, Scarborough appealed to the court arguing that the OMB did not have jurisdiction to modify a plan submitted to the minister of housing. The presiding judge held that the OMB had the same powers as the minister and indeed could act for the minister if requested to do so under the terms of the Ontario Planning Act. Since the minister of housing has the power to amend any local plan, the court held that the OMB had the same power. Moreover, the court held that the OMB's decision constituted the public hearing as stipulated under the Planning Act. Thus, the OMB was within its rightful powers and had acted correctly in a procedural sense.

The city also claimed that the OMB had no right to require the city to undertake an impact analysis before amending the local plan to create a regional shopping center. The court agreed, noting that while the OMB had every right to take into account the regional consequences of any local plan, localities were not so required. The court then removed the requirement that the city undertake an impact analysis. Generally, the court used the notion of express delegation—Dillon's rule in a different guise. Since the city had been expressly delegated the powers to plan, and since the OMB had been expressly given the powers to review, the OMB could not then require localities to plan in a certain manner. Of course, the OMB was nevertheless able to review plans in any manner consistent with its express powers. Thus, it was up to the OMB to undertake an impact analysis if it required one before reaching a decision on the appropriateness of the city's amendment.

To justify its interpretation of the Planning Act, the court argued that local governments have legitimate autonomy in many matters, especially in local planning. The role of the OMB should be that of a coordinator. Local initiative should thus be protected as much as possible. As in other related cases,[46] the court argued for a form of local autonomy. In this regard the court appealed to a liberal conception of the proper spatial division of powers. It emphasized the imperative for decentralization but retained elements of the imperative for centralization by maintaining the legitimacy of the OMB's review powers. Whatever the rhetorical virtues of this argument, there remains the contradiction alluded to in the previous section: in Ontario local governments are expressly delegated powers by the legislature. The origin of local initiative is at the provincial, not the local, level. The courts used liberal principles to justify their interpretation even though the substantive structure of local powers bears little resemblance to the ideological image.

The Des Plaines case is more complex, both in terms of the judicial path the case took and in terms of the logic used to decide the case. There were at least five episodes in this jurisdictional dispute. First, the city took the district to court, claiming that the district should recognize the city's jurisdiction in matters relating to local land use planning. A lower court found in favor of the city and issued an injunction to stop construction.[47] Even on appeal to the next higher court, the city's contention was upheld, despite the claims of the district that it was a separate municipal entity with its own legislatively defined functions. But at the Illinois Supreme Court, the city lost its case when the court held that the district acted within its "corporate purposes" as defined by statute.[48] The court maintained that as both entities were granted powers under the 1870 constitution and were subject to the powers of the legislature, there was no evidence that the city had power over the district.

With the passage of the 1970 Illinois Constitution, the city went back to the courts to establish jurisdiction over the district. Previously, the

Supreme Court had decided the case by invoking a quite narrow and restricted reading of the city's powers based on Dillon's rule. The new constitution allowed localities to claim home-rule status, a presumably wider and less explicit reading. Des Plaines argued that it now had the right to require the district to respect its jurisdiction.

Before dealing with this issue the city had to convince the courts that the previous decision did not continue to hold. At the circuit court level the city lost this procedural argument. But, at the appellate level, the city won both the procedural issue and the substantive claim that the new constitution gave the city expanded powers.[49] Here the court held that home-rule gave the city a broad grant of initiative powers that could be exercised in accordance with matters of local concern, but argued that the district was still bound by Dillon's rule.

Again the Supreme Court held in favor of the district, maintaining that the previous decision still held.[50] The new constitution was not interpreted to have widened the powers of the city, and the court maintained that under statute, the city and the district had different functional responsibilities. Thus, as before, the city could not interfere with the mandate of an agency that owed its powers to the same level to which the city owed its powers. The fact that the constitution had been passed to provide cities with a sphere of initiative not so explicitly conceived was ignored by the court. Home rule was interpreted as Dillon's rule.

Des Plaines would not accept this as the end of the matter. In 1974, it enacted an environmental code for airborne odors and then notified the district that it expected conformity to the standard. The district refused, contending that its license from the state EPA was sufficient. This time the city found favor with the circuit court, but lost again at the Supreme Court.[51] The lower court thought the code reasonable and not in conflict with state requirements. The Supreme Court, however, thought the application of the city's code to the district was outside of the legitimate functions of a home-rule unit. Again the court held to a very narrow reading of home rule, and a wider reading of the responsibilities of the district. The district was argued to fulfill statewide functions as opposed to local functions. Thus the district was not accountable to the city even if the city's regulations were consistent with state regulations. With this ruling the city stopped litigation and accepted the Supreme Court's finding.

Prior to the 1970 constitution, it is quite plausible that the court's decisions were entirely consistent with Dillon's rule. Although the court's decision abides with an exceedingly narrow interpretation of the rule, it is consistent with the rule's formal language. But after the passage of the new constitution, one based deliberately on the liberal rhetoric of local democracy, the court's decisions appear difficult to rationalize.

Here is an instance where liberal principles ought to have been recognized in the interpretation of home-rule, which was conceived to replace Dillon's rule. Yet the court made little attempt to restructure its decision logic in the face of a major democratic revision of local powers. Instead, the court maintained that the legislature was the ultimate source of local powers. Statutes and state regulations were the crucial materials the court used to arrive at decisions. Liberal principles of decentralized democracy were essentially ignored. Rather, the court appealed to the legislature's intent as the means of justifying its interpretations.

Contradictions

Embedded in these two decisions are a couple of related contradictions. In deciding the Scarborough case, the court legitimized its decisions by invoking a liberal, decentralized vision of government. This may have been entirely appropriate at one level. It is clear that Canada has been very much influenced by liberal philosophy, especially the North American kind which draws its inspiration from Locke and de Tocqueville.[52] Thus, appealing to this strand of thought as a rationale for interpretation is legitimate. But at the level of practice the actual rules of local autonomy are inconsistent with this vision of government structure. In fact, localities are granted powers by the legislature, and the scope of these powers are limited by an implicit dependence upon Dillon's rule.

Thus, the first contradiction of interpretation between ideology and practice concerns the Scarborough case. The court used a system of principles antithetical to the structure of the rules to justify an interpretation of them. Whereas localities are empowered rhetorically by the use of these principles, the administrative structure remains the same. One reason for this contradiction involves liberalism's counterprinciples of decentralization and centralization. The contradiction of interpretation identified in the Scarborough case could be explained as an instance where one counterprinciple (decentralization) was used to justify a judicial interpretation while the other counterprinciple (centralization) was used as the legislative basis for allocating powers.

In this explanation of the contradiction, judges are not simply mistaken or somehow inadequate for their tasks. The contradiction is much deeper and involves the incoherence of the particular liberal conception of human association used in this instance as the basis for adjudication.

The prospect for interpretive contradiction is present as long as society designs institutions according to this model. While this explanation has a pleasing theoretical quality, one which involves the whole system, less theoretically minded citizens might easily interpret the contradiction as a failure of the judiciary to deliver a fair determination. After all, this contradiction could be used to suggest that judicial determination is arbitrary and/or capricious. Since there seems to be no rule for determining which counterprinciple should dominate the other in different situations, the judiciary may well be arbitrary.

The second contradiction involves the Des Plaines case. Here the court held to a very narrow reading of local powers. Despite the passage of home-rule provisions in the 1970 constitution, the Supreme Court of Illinois followed the traditional Dillon's rule interpretation of local autonomy. Instead of appealing to a liberal decentralized model of the organization of governmental powers, the judiciary appealed to the intent of the legislature to justify interpretations. The contradiction is that the rules of local autonomy embodied the liberal decentralization imperative, while the appeal to the legislature was an appeal to centralized authority. Compared to the Scarborough case, the interpretive contradiction was exactly reversed.

We could interpret these outcomes as further instances of the inner contradiction of liberal philosophy. In Des Plaines the court chose to base its decision on centralization. The same indeterminacy is implied as before; choice of one counterprinciple may set the stage for an interpretive contradiction if the rules of autonomy are designed in accordance with the other counterprinciple. Here, perhaps more than in the Scarborough case, the judiciary appears vulnerable to political action and invalidated a consciously chosen new rule of local autonomy by asserting the continuing relevance of Dillon's rule. If that interpretation was carried through in other cases one could imagine a crisis of legitimacy in either the judiciary and/or the political coalition that sponsored the home-rule provision.

The principles the judiciary chooses to legitimate interpretations can carry tremendous rhetorical significance. In the previous case, the judiciary chose the decentralization imperative, thereby sustaining a rhetorical claim for strong local autonomy. In the Des Plaines case, the judiciary chose the centralization imperative, thereby sustaining a rhetorical claim for weak local autonomy. Yet, the structural arrangement of local powers in the two cases was reversed. Of course, I do not wish to overemphasize the strength of local powers implied in the home-rule provisions, nor do I wish to imply that Ontario localities have no initiative powers. Rather, the point is one of emphasis and legitimization.

In this regard the logic of the interpretation of local powers has as much importance as the formal design of the powers themselves.

There are, then, at least two explanations for the interpretive contradiction identified above. An obvious explanation is that just as liberal theory is fraught with a fundamental contradiction, so too are judges who attempt to apply liberal principles in practice. This latter explanation seems more satisfactory in that it does not depend on the personalities involved. It suggests that such contradictions are endemic to the whole enterprise.

Are there any other explanations which are relevant in the circumstances? There is another argument relevant here which bears upon the whole notion of legal formalism. Essentially, legal formalism depends on the use of rules and the appeal to principles for legitimization. It could easily be that this model of judicial practice is itself fundamentally flawed. Certainly this is the opinion of Unger.[53] He argued that since rules are indeterminate, legal practice cannot simply be the application of rules to each situation. There must inevitably be an interaction between rules and context, for it is context that gives rules their substance. Similarly, Tushnet has provided a powerful critique of legal theorists who claim that rules are neutral.[54] It can be argued that liberal principles, or any principles, cannot provide a noncontroversial datum point from which to judge the appropriateness of an interpretation. Principles are ideologies, and as such inevitably are controversial.[55]

Perhaps a more crucial argument against the division of legal formalists between principles and practice comes from Quine.[56] He suggested that there is an inevitable dissonance between abstract principles and empirical reality. Because principles depend upon abstraction for their integrity, it is likely that no system of principles will be immediately applicable to specific circumstances. It is their very abstraction which makes principles desirable—but it is precisely this kind of abstraction which makes principles difficult to apply to circumstances. In this sense, the whole project of legal formalism may be miscast from the beginning. There will always be some form of interpretive dilemma as judges move from abstraction to practice and back to abstraction.

This suggests the need for an alternative conception of judicial practice. For present purposes, it is enough to indicate that there are many theorists working on these problems.[57]

Conclusions

Although the two cases considered above began from similar situations, the results were quite different. Both cases involved issues of regional jurisdiction, one between a local government and a review agency, the other between a local government and another governmental entity. Both involved issues of the management of suburban growth. Furthermore, both cases were premised upon nominally similar structural arrangements of local powers. Going from a similar structural arrangement of powers does not necessarily lead to similar outcomes. In the Chicago case, the Illinois Supreme Court denied the city of Des Plaines' claims to regulate local land use. In the Toronto case the Ontario High Court upheld the borough of Scarborough's claim that the OMB did not have the power to require certain planning activities.

Thus, we must be wary of ascribing too much explanatory power to structural theories of urban differentiation. By themselves, structural characteristics of institutional powers do not necessarily provide determinacy. It is one thing to imagine a set of unambiguous decision rules that would structure judicial adjudication; legislation and constitutions attempt to do just that, presuming a wholly ordered world.[58] In practice, such planned determinacy is never achieved. Three kinds of reasons for indeterminacy were identified in the previous sections. The first reason might be termed "judicial incapacity." Despite the desires of legal theorists,[59] judges are not supermen. Applying rules to situations inevitably requires judgment; each new situation is a challenge to the judiciary because rules are general, not specific. Rules are designed to cover many circumstances. It is for this reason that there often are debates over the appropriateness of different rules.

The second kind of reasoning might be termed the "incoherence of principles." Rules require principles for their design and their interpretation as events change, and new circumstances are confronted. That is, there must be some intent behind the design of a rule. Otherwise the rule would be meaningless. Of course, it is plausible that rules are poorly conceived in terms of their justificatory principles. But more problematic are instances where the principles themselves are incoherent. Any system of rules premised upon a confused set of principles inevitably is compromised. In this essay I argued that this was the case for liberal principles; there is a built-in contradiction in liberalism which makes any set of liberal rules appear arbitrary and capricious.

The third—and most powerful—reason for structural indeterminacy has to do with the methodological separation between theory (principles) and practice (rules). This kind of reason might be termed "analytical abstraction." Because principles are conceived as abstract analytical statements, empirical rules will always be distant from their original locations. Rules attempt to provide guidelines for action; principles eschew action for simple clarity. Essentially, rules are the boundaries of principles.[60] There can never be a one-to-one correspondence between the two elements of legal formalism. For these three reasons, just knowing the political structure of different cities or different countries is not enough to derive their likely similarities and differences; structuralism is not a determinate explanation of urban form.

Notes

*Thanks to Meric Gertler and Brad Hudson for comments on a previous draft. All opinions remain the sole responsibility of the author.

1. M. Yeates and B. Garner, *The North American City* (New York: Harper and Row, 1976).
2. J. Mercer and M. Goldberg, "The Fiscal Condition of American Cities," mimeo (Syracuse: Department of Geography, Syracuse University, 1983) and M. Goldberg in this volume.
3. W. Alonso, *Location and Land Use* (Cambridge, Mass.: Harvard University Press, 1964).
4. E. S. Mills and B. W. Hamilton, *Urban Economics*, 3rd Edition (Glenview, IL: Scott, Foresman and Co., 1984).
5. B. J. L. Berry, *Comparative Urbanization: Divergent Paths in the Twentieth Century*, (New York: St. Martin's Press, 1981), and J. Mercer, "On Continentalism, Distinctiveness, and Comparative Urban Geography: Canadian and American Cities," in *Canadian Geographer* 23 (1979): 119–139.
6. M. Castells, *The City and the Grass Roots* (London: Ed. Arnold, 1984).
7. J. Brigham, M. Goldberg and E. Feldman in this volume.
8. R. J. Johnston, *Residential Segregation, the State and Constitutional Conflict in American Urban Areas*, (New York: Academic Press, 1984).
9. F. S. Levy, A. J. Meltsner, and A. Wildausky, *Urban Outcomes* (Berkeley: University of California Press, 1974).
10. G. L. Clark and M. Dear, *State Apparatus: Structures and Language of Legitimacy* (Boston and Hemel Hempstead: Allen and Unwin, 1984).
11. M. Ryan, *Marxism and Deconstruction* (Baltimore: Johns Hopkins University Press, 1982).
12. R. M. Unger, "The Critical Studies Movement," in *Harvard Law Review* 96 (1983): 561–675.
13. *Ibid.*, p. 565.
14. For a radical view, see: R. P. Wolff, ed., *The Rule of Law* (New York: Simon and Schuster, 1971). For a conservative view, see: J. H. Choper, *Judicial Review and the National Political Process* (Chicago: The University of Chicago Press, 1980). For a middle-of-the-road view, see: J. Ely, *Democracy and Distrust: a Theory of Judicial Review* (Cambridge, Mass.: Harvard University Press, 1980).
15. Unger (1983), *op. cit.*

16. J. L. Austin, *How to Do Things With Words*, 3rd Edition (Cambridge, Mass.: Harvard University Press, 1975).
17. For an extended treatment of these issues, see: M. Tushnet, "Following the Rules Laid Down: A Critique of Interpretivism and Neutral Principles," in *Harvard Law Review* 96 (1983): 871–927.
18. R. Simeon, "Current Constitutional Issues," in *Issues and Alternative 1977: Intergovernmental Relations* (Toronto: Ontario Economic Council, 1977).
19. G. E. Frug, "The City as a Legal Concept," in *Harvard Law Review* 93 (1980): 1057–1154.
20. G. L. Clark, *Judges and the Cities: Interpreting Local Autonomy* (Chicago: The University of Chicago Press, 1985).
21. J. W. Lewis, *Constitution of the State of Illinois and United States* (Springfield: State of Illinois, 1971).
22. G. L. Clark (1985) *op. cit.* (the 1970 State Constitutional Convention).
23. G. L. Clark (1985) *op. cit.*
24. *Ibid.*
25. R. Dworkin, "Social Rules and Legal Theory," in *Yale Law Journal* 81 (1972).
26. Clark (1985), *op. cit.*
27. R. M. Unger, *op. cit.*
28. R. Posner, *The Economics of Justice* (Cambridge, Mass.: Harvard University Press, 1981).
29. B. A. Ackerman, *Reconstructing American Law* (Cambridge: Harvard University Press, 1984), and R. Dworkin, "Is Wealth a Value?" in *Journal of Legal Studies* 9 (1980): 191–242.
30. G. L. Clark and M. Dear, 1984, *op. cit.*; and J. Rawls, *A Theory of Justice* (Cambridge, Mass.: Harvard University Press, 1971).
31. T. Lowi, *The End of Liberalism* (New York: W.W. Norton, 1971).
32. J. Ely, *op. cit.*
33. M. Sandel, *Liberalism and the Limits of Justice* (Cambridge: Cambridge University Press, 1982).
34. For a more detailed discussion and critique, see: A. Sen and B. Williams, eds., *Utilitarianism and Beyond* (Cambridge: Cambridge University Press, 1982).
35. J. Rawls, *op. cit.*
36. J. H. Choper, *op. cit.*
37. J. Rawls, *op. cit.*
38. Sandel (1983) *op. cit.* and Clark (1985) *op. cit.*
39. R. Nozick, *Anarchy, State, and Utopia* (New York: Basic Books, 1974).
40. G. L. Clark (1985) *op. cit.*
41. D. Kennedy, "The Structure of Blackstone's Commentaries," in *Buffalo Law Review* 29 (1979): 205–381.
42. M. Dear and G. L. Clark, *op. cit.*
43. M. Yeates and B. Garner, *op. cit.*
44. For more details of the case, see: Clark (1985), *op. cit.*
45. Borough of Scarborough and the Minister of Housing for Ontario, et.al., 67 DLR, 3d 387 (Ont. Div. Ct. 1976).
46. G. L. Clark (1985), *op. cit.*
47. *City of Des Plaines* v. *Metropolitan San. Dist.*, 124, ILL. App. 2d 301 (1970).
48. *City of Des Plaines* v. *Metropolitan San. Dist.*, 48 ILL. 2d 11, 268 NE2d 428 (1971).
49. *City of Des Plaines* v. *Metropolitan San. Dist.*, 16 ILL. App 3d 23 (1973).
50. *City of Des Plaines* v. *Metropolitan San. Dist. of G.*, Chicago, 59 ILL. 2d 29, 319, NE2d 9 (1974).

51. *Metro. San. Dist. of Chicago* v. *City of Des Plaines*, 63 ILL 2d 256, 347 NE2d 716 (1976).
52. G. L. Clark, "Rights, Property and Community," in *Economic Geography* 59 (1982): 120–138.
53. R. M. Unger, *op. cit.*
54. Tushnet (1983) *op. cit.*
55. J. Ely, *op. cit.*
56. W. Quine, *From a Logical Point of View* (Cambridge: Harvard University Press, 1953).
57. J. Ely, *op. cit*; B. A. Ackerman, *op. cit.*; G. L. Clark (1985) *op. cit.*; R. M. Unger, *op. cit.*.
58. N. Goodman, *Of Mind and Other Matters* (Cambridge: Harvard University Press, 1984).
59. D. A. J. Richards, "The Theory of Adjudication and the Task of a Great Judge," in *Cardozo Law Review* 1 (1979): 171–218.
60. Quine (1953), *op. cit.*

9

The "Giving Issue": A View of Land, Property Rights and Industrial Development in Maine and Nova Scotia

John Brigham

Christopher Leman writes in Chapter 2 of this book that much of the once abundant public land in North America has been sold or given away by governments. In the last quarter of the twentieth century public land in North America has begun to seem scarce and expensive, and it is rarely given away. But sometimes governments do actually buy or expropriate land and transfer it to private hands, and sometimes governments even give away land they already own. This transfer of land from public to private hands arises normally as part of economic development policy and depends upon definitions and practices concerning property rights. Thus, it will be referred to here as the "giving issue." Neither the institutions nor the rights are exactly the same in Canada and the United States, but they differ in ways that identify formerly divergent policy processes that show signs of increasing convergence.

The case studies for this essay are drawn from waterfront development in Halifax, Nova Scotia, and Portland, Maine (see Figures 9.1 and 9.2). The two cities and the state/provincial aspects of government will be compared. Their cultural settings and their material conditions, because they are similar, can be held as nearly constant as nonlaboratory social science can make possible; this will allow institutional differences to be observed. Furthermore, the geographical distance from the

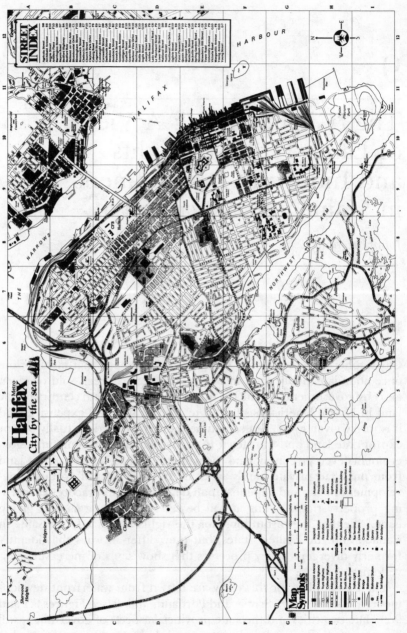

Figure 9.1. *Street map of Halifax.*

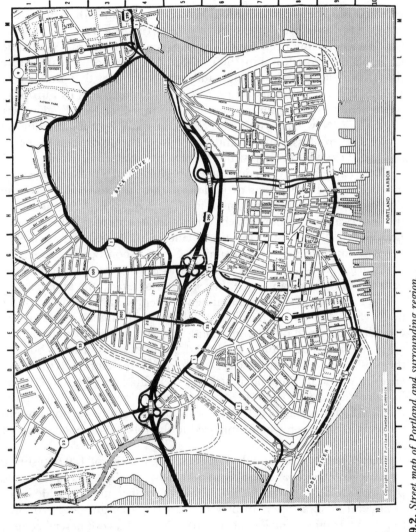

Figure 9.2. Street map of Portland and surrounding region.

"center" of each country and the regional disparities, so closely associated with development policy, are remarkably similar.

Culture

A relationship between Maine and Nova Scotia began in the competitive struggle of European powers for control of the Americas. Nova Scotia was French, having been settled by the Sieur-de-Monts and Samuel de Champlain at Port Royal in 1605. It would be a hundred years before the British established sovereign authority and longer than that before Halifax became a military outpost in 1749. Maine traces its European history from English grants given by the Council for New England for what is now New Hampshire and Maine in 1622. By 1690 the English settlements in Massachusetts and Maine were strong enough to send a successful expedition against the French in Nova Scotia.

These expeditions preceded the establishment of a military presence in Halifax and the brutal expulsion of the French-Acadians by the English in 1755. British dominion in Nova Scotia was strengthened by the American Revolution, which brought thousands of "United Empire Loyalists" to Nova Scotia. The ties of culture and kinship between New England and the maritime region of Canada soon became so strong that during the War of 1812 there is said to have been an agreement between the participants on either side not to attack one another.

The English and the French influences seem to have remained purer in Nova Scotia, but in the fishing villages and lumber towns of the Canadian province on the one hand, and the American state on the other, the material cultures are linked. From the lobsterman's buoy to the lumberman's jacket, these are kindred cultures. Although the influence of Victorian England is striking in Halifax and French Canada has a romantic outpost in the Acadian region along the Bay of Fundy, the values, norms and beliefs that constitute the culture are not substantively different, even when compared to the folksy cosmopolitanism of Maine.

Today Halifax, the capital of Nova Scotia, is a city of 120,000 sitting with English grace and sophistication between the Atlantic and the province's relatively wild interior. Victorian architecture alongside twentieth century skyscrapers display the aspects of culture and economy that make Halifax a major tourist attraction and a commercial center.

Portland, Maine is less than half as big as Halifax, and although its regional significance is comparable, the difference in scale must be taken into account. Forty million dollars of public money are not as important to Halifax as they would be to Portland, even considering rates of exchange. In addition, a good deal of the wealth of Maine and of the city has come from the same rocky shore and rich fishing grounds that touch Halifax. Ferries leave for the islands of Casco Bay and for Nova Scotia—the physical links emphasize the cultural ties.

One apparent difference between Halifax and Portland is in how the city governments are related to the two higher levels of government. The residents of Halifax are Haligonians first, with the province and the country vying for what sometimes appears to be a distant second place. Portland residents value the state of Maine and the U.S. more highly. Some of this difference stems from Nova Scotia's strong regional cultures—like Cape Breton and Acadia—and its local ties.

Material Conditions

The material conditions of life provide the clearest basis for comparison. Maine and Nova Scotia are on the Atlantic coast and Portland and Halifax, by far the largest cities in the state or province, are ports on the fringe of the continent. Although regional centers of population, both have shared hardships due to their distance from the more prosperous urban centers—on the Atlantic coast of the United States and down the St. Lawrence River in Canada.

The orientation of Maine and Nova Scotia and of their urban areas has changed since the Second World War. Boston dominated the trade and finance of Portland until after the war and is still the regional center. But since then, Portland has been integrated into the national economy. Halifax has been drawn south, shifting some of its attention to the United States as an important port of entry for goods from Europe such as Volvo cars and Michelin tires.

Halifax has been growing, adding one-third to its population in the last thirty years, while Portland has been losing people. Due to projects stimulated by the provincial Department of Development, Industrial Estates Ltd., and the Waterfront Development Corporation, Halifax has an attractive and reasonably prosperous waterfront. Whereas neighboring Lunenburgers built the famous schooner Bluenose that appears on the Canadian dime, recent development efforts have included shipbuilding in the plans for Halifax. Yet these days, Haligonians are more likely to take to the sea to drill for oil and the city's economic aspirations reflect the excitement around oil exploration on the Georges Bank.

Portland lost 20 percent of its residents between 1950 and 1980 due to economic stagnation and migration to American cities further south. Recently, however, the city has been undergoing an economic renewal and gentrification. Much of this activity is centered on the waterfront.

The Bath Iron Works, which had its headquarters a few miles down east on the Kennebec River, has begun shipbuilding in the Portland Harbor through a government-financed development project with statewide ramifications. This effort will be the specific reference point for the larger comparison of the way land is transferred from public to private hands.

Canadian and American Institutional Settings

At the extremes of economic policy, a state may maximize individual protection of private property (property rights), or it may emphasize economic development for a perceived collective good (development policy). Consistent with the general characterization of political philosophies offered by Michael Goldberg in Chapter 3, the dominant Canadian practice supports development, while the dominant American approach begins with a defense of property rights. Framed another way, greater recognition appears to be given to individuals and the private sector in the U.S. and to the public sector or state-directed domain in Canada. However, neither Canada nor the U.S. function in fact at the extreme, and an examination of the "giving issue" in both countries exposes the limits and opportunities created by the alternative conventions governing economic policy.

Property Rights

The law on property and the process by which it is determined is a basis for economic policy making. Until 1949, the Judicial Committee of the Privy Council of Great Britain was the supreme legal authority in Canada and British law was the foundation on which provinces entered confederation. Canadian constitutional law, until recently, has been very "British." Canada did not revolt against British rule. Canadians wrote no constitution as a way of establishing the authority of the government. Canadians adopted not only the common law, but also British interpretation and a tradition of parliamentary superiority in the area of fundamental law. There was no Canadian bill of rights until 1960 and the Canadian "Constitution," until 1982, followed the British tradition in that it was a statutory document resting on legislative authority. And even the 1982 Canadian Charter of Rights and Freedoms deliberately does not entrench property rights.

Whereas the British influence in the United States was legally terminated earlier and more completely than in Canada, it was still considerable. The Revolution was justified in terms of natural law influenced by Blackstone, the English jurist who personified the trend toward absolute or vested rights in property. For Blackstone, the Magna Carta was authority for this position. His *Commentaries on the Laws of England* helped to transform the fact of colonial charters into the jurisprudential practice of rights.

Property was "vested" in the United States[1] due to its place in the Fifth Amendment to the Constitution and the use of that document by the judiciary to establish a tradition of rights beyond legislation. The American guarantee that no person be deprived of property without due process of law, nor that it be "taken" without compensation, is the primary legal difference between the United States and Canada on the subject of property.

Property rights in the United States only recently have been recognized as elements of civil libertarian protection.[2] Private property is associated with individual possession and control, and government, with foremost reference to constitutional rights and state laws, defines the extent of a property owner's autonomy.

Property questions, particularly those involving the use of public authority for eminent domain, inevitably involve litigation. Although theoretically open to all, courts are limited in access by the need for a variety of resources determined by lawyers and judges. Because the tradition of property rights inherently prefers the individual to the community, claims are contentious and disputes require institutionalization and perhaps even professional management. Indeed, it could be argued that the American public philosophy of individual rights made the proliferation of lawyers (some 600,000) and the frequency of litigation in the U.S. inescapable.

Expropriation. A link between individual property rights and public interests in both Canada and the United States is in the conditions for expropriating land. In the United States, the parameters for governmental action are in the Fifth Amendment to the Constitution. Constitutional due process in the United States holds that the criteria for evaluating policy should be past interpretations of the document itself and ". . . those settled usages and modes of proceeding existing in the common and statute law of England."[3] Protection of property rights in the United States is an area of constitutional law most dependent on natural or substantive due process interpretations.[4]

The courts in the United States have distinguished regulatory power over property from constitutionally protected "takings." Although the regulatory power often takes some interest in land or property for the public good, it is only the official transfer of property to the public that requires compensation. The "public use" provision is part of the takings standard. It is considered a violation of due process in the United States to use the expropriation power to take property for private use. The tradition has been such that essentially private mills, roads, and railroads were destined for public use.

Jurists after the American Civil War diminished legislative prerogatives. More and more the focus was not only on property but also on the values in property. Concern was expressed over the loss of profits or land value that had not been considered compensable. Property was expanding from the thing lawfully possessed to the expectation of return. The question was, could the government restrict property and radically affect its expected use or exchange value without compensation? In *Mugler* v. *Kansas* (1887) the state outlawed breweries, making Mugler's "facility" worthless. Supreme Court Justice Harlan ruled that "acts done in the proper exercise of government powers, and not directly encroaching upon private property, though these consequences may impair its use, do not constitute a taking . . ." As long as the exercise is a lawful one, then private property is not considered to have been infringed upon, since it was considered to be held subject to the state's need to protect the public well-being.

In 1922, *Pennsylvania Coal Co.* v. *Mahon* changed the takings law. Subsurface mining threatened the Mahon's home but the Pennsylvania legislature had passed an act outlawing the mining of coal where it was dangerous. The Mahons received an injunction based on this law. Justice Oliver Wendell Holmes argued in behalf of the U.S. Supreme Court majority that the act exceeded the police power because of the loss of mineral rights. He stated, "The general rule at least is, that while property may be regulated to a certain extent, if regulation goes too far it will be recognized as a taking." From this point on, property was no longer limited to land but included the money that could be made from it.

The tests that ensued sought to balance the private loss and the public gain. Each case had to be examined with an eye to the positions and expectations of the particular parties. The result, for lawyers attempting to formulate rules, has been called "a crazy-quilt pattern of Supreme Court doctrine"[5] that is "ethically unsatisfying,"[6] but it has been nonetheless the basis for constitutional protection of property in the United States.

Whereas the American citizen may have expectations concerning a parcel of land, property rights must be recognized by the courts. This distinction creates a tension between the everyday idea of property as something protected by the government and the legal practice by which its nature is determined. Despite the general perception, the property claim amounts to an interest that is sanctioned by law, such as a contract or a debt.

Expropriation has a different foundation in Canada. Until recently, except for jurisdictional matters, the law on expropriation has been provincial and statutory. Due process of law is defined as "in accordance with the common and statute law as it exists at any particular time."[7] Parliament, then, can define due process by statute. There are no appeals to the Founding Fathers or the founding document. The familiar American mode of juries, compensation and judicial review are reduced to the question of whether there exist certain statutory provisions for expropriation. When there are, due process requires the fulfillment of these provisions. Failure to follow statutory procedures invalidates the taking, and the individual owner is free to get an injunction, petition to recover possession or take direct action for indemnity.

Expropriation law in Canada is seldom involved in disputes over the scope of governmental authority. If expropriation is properly authorized by legislation it is legitimate; otherwise, it is not. Federal authority stems from the British North America Act, the Expropriation Act, and other empowerments directed to specific situations. The Expropriation Act authorizes any minister "charged with a public work" to "take, directly or through representatives, any land, real property, streams, waters, and water courses necessary to build, improve, or maintain a public work." Each province also has its own statutory basis for expropriation. Courts fix compensation only when other bodies fail, and while compensation has to be provided for by statute, there has been a presumption in favor of compensation, with the intention to withhold having to be stated clearly.[8]

Compensation. The general principles of assessment for the purpose of compensation in Canada are much like those of the United States. In *Cedar Rapids* v. *Lacoste*, Lord Dunedin stated: "The value to be paid for is the value to the owner . . . not the value to the taker . . ." However, there are some elaborations that differ in the two countries. It is generally recognized in Canada that market value is at best a rough guide. The goal is to put the owner in a position similar to that occupied before the expropriation occurred, which may include considerations other than the market value of the property. The standard was formulated as "what would he, as prudent man, at that moment, pay for the property rather than be ejected from it."[9] Judges and administrators generally examine market value, purchase price, municipal valuation, the price of similar land, revenue from the property, and cost of improvements. The basis for the requirements is statutory. Whether any more fundamental provisions may emerge from the new constitutional setting is a subject taken up in the concluding section of this chapter.

Embedded in the structure of expropriation law is a sensitivity to the private landowner which requires that costs associated with public purpose and hence public gain be spread throughout the community by payment of compensation. By requiring the community to bear the costs, the requirements of expropriation law are supposed to contribute to the policy making process.

The mechanism of compensation balances private interests in some parcel of land or property against the general welfare to be served by a public works project. Scholars such as Bruce Ackerman, drawing on modern efficiency concerns, hold that compensation leads to more efficient and more responsible decision making. The rationale proposes that by being required to pay the landowner when property is taken for public use, the legislature will be deterred from enacting inefficient programs. According to this logic of efficiency, public officials will have to weigh the costs and benefits of alternative measures in protecting the public interest. Ackerman has also asserted that compensation, by materially recognizing the private interest of property owners, may minimize resistance to public policies involving expropriation of private property.[10]

The Giving Issue. The modern state "giveth as well as taketh away." Grants to the poor have received a good deal of attention in the past, but in the 1980s, corporate gifts and public generosity to the more well-heeled have merited scrutiny. Policies of the Reagan Administration, such as those implemented by former Secretary of the Interior James Watt, led to the sale of "surplus" land in the West and local movements such as the Sagebrush Rebellion. In Canada, decades of development initiatives are being assessed in an environment referred to gingerly as a "period of industrial 'adjustment.'"[11] All of this activity calls attention to the giving issue.

The link between expropriation and disposal, between taking and giving, stems from the structure of expropriation law. The mirror image of a requirement that the public share costs to private landowners when land is expropriated would be a requirement that when public land is turned over to private hands, the private gain be limited by considerations of public interest. The policy recognizes that the arguments laid down as legal authority in the United States and the policy rationales for compensation apply equally well to cases where public land or property is being sold or transferred to the private sector. Although the giving issue comes out of a legal context in the United States, an analogous policy issue can be examined in the Canadian context by looking at development policy.

The giving issue is generally a function of government intervention itself. The use of eminent domain has brought much closer scrutiny of transfers to private hands. Controversies in the early 1980s developed over lands managed by the U.S. Department of the Interior because of an emphasis on the preservation of the land as well as a sense of the undue enrichment of those able to accumulate wealth from the use of public lands. However, land subject to a taking at some previous time raises constitutional issues in the United States. The public may not have rights in the way that an individual does, but claims of a general nature for deference to the public emerge from the principles of expropriation.

Institutional Operations in Nova Scotia and Maine

Canada and the United States rely on different institutions for land policy and the transfer of wealth from the government to individuals. In the United States, fundamental principles are laid down in the constitution, refined in statutory mandates and ultimately subject to review by the courts through litigation. In Canada, the mandates are laid down by legislatures, are implemented by administrative agencies that rarely are second-guessed by the judiciary. The experiences of the giving issue for waterfront development in Nova Scotia and Maine are portraits of these systematic differences (see Table 9.1).

Administration: The Canadian Way

In Canada, public agencies and civil servants carry out mandated policies consistent with statutory authorization. The tradition is English, and evaluations of contemporary Canadian civil servants have drawn attention to early links with and approximations of the "Whitehall tradition." As John Mercer and Michael Goldberg put it, "Canada demonstrates a Brittanic continuity" in its powerful and generally well-staffed bureaucracies."[12] This form of policy process, distinguishing Canada from the United States, will be amplified here to stand as a comparison with the American process.

Between 1976 and 1985, the waterfront in Halifax was transformed—from a derelict condition in which it was left by the advent of container

Table 9.1
The Atlantic Waterfront: Portland and Halifax, 1975–1985

	Cost to Public	Land Acquisition
Portland		
BIW Expansion	$46.7 million	Transfer and lease
City Fish Pier	25 million	Eminent Domain
Ferry Terminal	.5 million	—
Halifax		
Container Port	$50 million	Nat'l Harbors Board Authorization
Waterfront Development Corporation	37 million	Purchase ($20 mil)
Shipyards	14.5–51.5 million	Negotiated Transfer

Sources: John Ferland, *Portland Press Herald*, May 29, 1982; Ian McAllister, et al., *Projects in Search of Development* (1980).

shipping, bridges and the shift of commercial activity from the city center—to a thriving locus for business and leisure. At about the same time a major shipbuilding operation was rebuilt in the hope of reviving an ailing industry. Both of these projects involved substantial transfer of land and resources from public to private or semiprivate hands.

There are three types of public agencies manifest in the waterfront development in Halifax.[13] The principal assistance has come from a federal department, with implementation and oversight from a provincial department. But the key actors have been provincial Crown corporations. In each instance, employees of government, not private agencies, have been the dominant actors.

Public Enterprise. The management of basic resources in Canada has evolved from the common law and English tradition of royal prerogatives into sophisticated public enterprises acting often with considerable independence. Michael J. Trebilcock and his colleagues described a patchwork of public enterprises across Canada.[14] The telephone system, for example, is owned by the public in Manitoba, Alberta and Saskatchewan, but in the other provinces private phone companies are regulated by government. Capital markets, too, are the domain of Crown corporations and private financial institutions in different provinces. This extensive network of public enterprises is an outgrowth of the administrative power that has long rested in Canadian governments.[15]

Nova Scotia, in the Water Act of 1919, took legal charge of the management of water resources by simply expropriating basic riparian rights, vesting in the provinces the "sole and exclusive right to use, divert and appropriate any and all water." Private rights were replaced by government control, without compensation or recourse to the courts. According to Jennifer Nedelsky, the act "with minor modifications, formed the legal framework for the use and allocation of water until 1963 when the Water Act was modified and expanded to establish the Nova Scotia Water Resources Commission."[16]

Traditional property rights came to be recognized by the end of the nineteenth century as having a built-in antidevelopment bias,[17] to be circumvented in Canada by the creation of public enterprise. Thus, the Nova Scotia Power Company was given the power in 1914 to divert water, to flood lands, and to expropriate.[18]

The Province of Nova Scotia also used land in the early twentieth century to attract settlement, and by 1909 it already had depleted Crown resources. For the next decades the Crown was actively engaged in regaining control of land. In 1920 two cases came before the courts in which defendants had violated traditional property rights but pleaded license under the 1919 water legislation and argued that plaintiff had no right to a remedy in court. The defendants lost, but as Nedelsky pointed out,

> The legislature responded immediately to assure the exclusive control of the cabinet and commissioners over water policy. Section 4(2) was amended to read 'notwithstanding provision for previous users, the Governor-in-council may authorize any water use.'[19]

Moreover, compensation was to be at the discretion of the Crown. Characteristic of prodevelopment legislation, judges in these cases dismantled the last significant impediment to the economic potential of property.[20]

The federal Department of Regional Economic Expansion (DREE), created in 1969, was mandated to reduce regional disparities across Canada through job creation.* It focused considerable attention on the Maritime provinces, within a decade building forty-five industrial parks in the Atlantic region (nine in Nova Scotia costing $8.2 million) and granting $31 million in assistance.[21] And the federal government manages the offshore oil industry that drives Nova Scotia's economy in the 1980s.

The provincial Department of Development and Industrial Estates is Nova Scotia's counterpart to DREE. Much of its activity is conducted

---

*The Department changed its name and its mission in 1983 when it incorporated parts of the Department of Industry, Trade and Commerce to become the Department of Regional Industrial Expansion (DRIE).

by Industrial Estates Limited (IEL), a Crown corporation that epitomizes the authority of the province in economic development. IEL disposes land for purposes other than resource exploitation, uses eminent domain in carrying out economic development projects, and gives small grants (in the range of $2,000) to the rural assistance program. Although IEL has effectively contributed millions of dollars to the private sector in pursuit of jobs, land transactions have been few. The "Auto Port," a development project for importing cars, involved some land banking, but it was built mostly on vacant land within ten miles of the center of Halifax. The Michelin tire plant was built in a rural area outside the capital in Kentville and involved some land accumulation in order to provide a large industrial facility and a port.

On the waterfront in Halifax, one of the major actors was the Waterfront Development Corporation, Ltd., a provincial Crown corporation with $5 million from the Nova Scotia Department of Development and $35 million from DREE. Following demolition of decaying structures, planning, land acquisition and provision of utilities, the corporation sought private developers for the major structures (hotels and condominiums) and private businesses to occupy the renovated "Historic Properties." Another public enterprise active on a different section of the waterfront was a consortium of public and private corporations, Halifax Industries Limited (HIL). In 1980, with the backing of federal departments the province acquired the Halifax Shipyard and constructed a $43.5 million dry dock which it leased to HIL. Under this arrangement, the province issued bonds to pay for the shipyard and then transferred it to HIL through "purchase price loans" and substantial tax benefits. The reduction in assessed valuation by one-third stood up to a legal challenge.[22]

But policies of this sort are coming under closer scrutiny in a more conservative climate, and policy failures are more immediately linked to institutional transformation. In Halifax, the success of the downtown waterfront development is balanced by the failure of the shipyards to generate enough business to remain viable. They went into receivership in 1984, when the consortium members, according to the *Globe and Mail*, walked away from deficits of $7.6 million. Maintained by the province with federal contracts and provincial guarantees, the shipyard had failed to live up to its expectations.

Administration: The American Version

American administration is much weaker, more recent, and everywhere circumscribed by the prerogatives of private property and the role of the courts. In a study prepared for Maine's Bureau of Public Lands, Lloyd Rodwin rejected the idea of public development corporations, preferring local management.[23] His perspective reflects the concern in the United States for local autonomy and very limited state authority.

In Portland, requests to purchase city-owned land go first to the Planning Department for assessment of any conflicts with city projects. The Planning Board acts on the department's recommendation and submits it to the city council. The council, in turn, approves most requests and sends them out to bid.[24] The Economic Development Committee, chaired by a member of the city council, becomes involved when large parcels need to be pieced together.

Most disposal of city-owned land in Portland follows private initiatives to purchase. Only once between 1980 and 1985 did the city initiate a sales campaign and make an inventory of available land. Although this campaign resulted in disposal of approximately forty percent of the available property, the practice did not become established.

Portland has a variety of properties for disposal, and it has used its power on several occasions to assemble land packages for development. However, projects and assembled parcels typically result from private-sector requests or public-sector surplus, not from a government vision of projects worthwhile in the public interest. Because of a change away from neighborhood schools in the 1960s, a number of smaller schools became vacant. The school department notified the city of surplus property and it became available according to the routine described above.[25] The same procedures, also under the economic development mandate, have applied for large parcels of military property, such as a "minifort" in the harbor on George Island. The Economic Development Committee then responds on an *ad hoc* basis to assist private proposals that promise economic benefits to Portland by, for example, initiating improvements in infrastructure.

Litigation: The American Way

In the United States, the legal issues surrounding disposal are closely related to expropriation. The courts are major participants when matters of drafts on the public purse and the disposal of land to profit-making enterprises are approved by governments. Historically, government-sponsored industrial development, particularly that involving private profit-making entities, was highly suspect and generally challenged under the standard that it fulfill a public purpose. The public purpose concept expanded in the late nineteenth century, and the basic proposition that industrial development may meet the public purpose test, often to provide an essential service,[26] became acceptable. Much of the authority for these developments has been judicial and the courts have been the final arbiters of whether public purpose requirements are met when particular industrial development schemes have been challenged.[27] Thus the giving issue in the U.S. typically involves litigation.

Development of the Portland waterfront through the revitalization of the Bath Iron Works exemplifies the American approach. The *Portland Press Herald and Evening Express* described the project on May 29, 1982 in a special issue celebrating Portland's 350th anniversary:

> Today the Maine State Pier sits silently. Gone are even the occasional cargo ships that took loads of paper pulp from Portland. But on this site, Bath Iron Works intends to build a $46.7 million shipyard, two thirds of it financed by taxpayers, that will have a projected annual payroll of $29.5 million by 1986. The yard is expected to create about 1,000 new jobs and spawn 3,500 other jobs throughout the Portland region.

Two legal maneuvers had to take place before the port project could be built. The first was a transfer of title to submerged and intertidal land that had been held in public trust but on which private owners had built. The second maneuver required approval of public funds. In 1982, Maine held a referendum on a bond issue supporting the waterfront development for Bath Iron Works. The courts initially held that the success of the referendum constituted public approval, but there were continuing challenges to the proposition that the public interest was being served by turning the waterfront over to the shipbuilding company.

The final case was brought by taxpayers who alleged that agreements between state, city and the corporation for shipyard development were in violation of state and federal Constitutions. The taxpayers appealed an adverse decision to the Supreme Judicial Court of Maine, where they were heard, on September 21, 1982 for decision January 7 of the next year. They argued that governments as constituted have limited powers, must act reasonably, and must act within constitutional limitations.

Even normally acceptable public expenditures depend on conformity to specific limitations, the plaintiffs argued: ". . . a governmental expenditure for schools (usually permitted) becomes impermissible if the school is a church-owned parochial school; and an expenditure for highways (also usually permissible) would also be impermissible if the proposed road were a private woods road for the exclusive use of one of Maine's forest products firms."[28] They took exception to this example of government-sponsored industrial development, acknowledging instances where the test of public purpose can be met.

The legal maneuver took three years, and despite a referendum, the last word on the project still came from the judicial bench. The challenge was unsuccessful. According to the courts, the bond referendum question was not so clearly misleading as to require setting it aside, and the legislature's determination that the project would benefit the people of Maine by improving the economy, reviving commerce in Portland and enhancing opportunities for employment was not irrational. Government intervention spending public monies for private gains thus was found appropriate in the U.S., but only because the courts said so.

Politics, Economics and the Law

The giving issue, like land policy generally, is impossible to understand if economic or market considerations are not taken into account. The ideological structures that make up the legal environment and the law of property in Canada and the United States affect the economic choices and influence market developments. These structures—and the law—are also subject to market considerations. The results of the comparison suggest that the institutional differences between Canada and the United States are marginal in their effect on economic development and the transfer of public property into private hands.

In isolating the influence of the economic environment, characterized as the particular material interest and advantages associated with a given situation, the institutional differences come into perspective. Demand for economic growth has determined what will be expropriated and the market determines valuation. The economy is the force behind policy-making in land and it must be accounted for in explaining the legal doctrines that emerge. This can be done by separating competitive or market situations from nonmarket disposal contexts.

Administrative practices in the disposal of public land reflect the immediate economic situation. The more lucrative a transaction the more it is treated commercially. In the most common eastern disposal situations, government actually adds value to land and property by refurbishing buildings, providing tax advantages, or by collecting parcels that as a bundle are worth more than they would be individually. Treatment of abandoned schools in Portland, tracking through an urban bureaucracy, stems as much from not knowing what to do with the property as from built-in protections. Larger parcels or projects with an economic interest behind them come immediately under an economic development mandate.

The similarity between Portland and Halifax is striking: two shipbuilding operations, heavily subsidized by governments; gentrification of the waterfront. All the projects reflect contemporary hopes based on nineteenth century romance about what ports are like and what they should do. In the social reality by which such projects are evaluated, it looks as if gentrification is succeeding where shipyard development is not.

In Canada, the government was far more significant. Yet the result, creation of a tenuous shipbuilding operation, was similar. The lesson from this comparison is about form. Development and property disposal are undertaken differently in these two settings. The fact that the outcomes do not seem to differ significantly means simply that outcomes may not be the measure of form. The lesson, perhaps, is that the public trough may be tapped in a variety of ways and those ways are only marginally associated with rational analysis. In the United States, manipulation of government instruments for private advantage has long been associated with development,[29] yet it continues. In Canada, there is a reevaluation of the role of government that seems to have resulted in less emphasis on grants and outright gifts and more emphasis on the provision of services.[30]

Just as "taking" law was the protection government afforded to individuals when it invoked its authority, "giving" is a way of looking at use of public authority for private advantage. These protections are in part a function of eagerness for development and consciousness of the implications. The significance of a corporation like Bath Iron Works in Maine can overcome the relative weakness of the public sector. The profits to be made are related to the influence that can be peddled. In the United States, pragmatism and rights have always maintained a delicate balance.

The promise of jobs, the lure of employment, is so great that institutions have been developing to meet the demand in the United States. In the first half of the 1980s, urban development has become a measure of the success of city and state administration. The transformation of an abandoned waterfront into a private, commercial shipyard is now seen less as a contribution to private wealth, and more as an opportunity for the provision of jobs and development. The public effort in the United States remains small in comparison to the scale of Canadian government authority, but there are signs of a convergence. The experiences on a number of waterfronts point to successes like those in Halifax and fuel visions of new developments.

Toward Convergence?

Rights adjudication in Canada has been characterized by considerable deference to provincial lawmaking. Modern developments leading toward greater centralization began with the Diefenbaker Bill of Rights.

The property issues arising out of this Bill of Rights were secondary to religious and communicative freedoms and freedom from discrimination,[31] although they appeared much as they do in the American Constitution. Because the Bill of Rights was an act of Parliament, the jurisdiction of the Canadian Supreme Court was a function of statutory interpretation.[32]*Indeed, in one of the few cases under the Bill of Rights having an application to the discussion of property, *National Capital Commission* v. *Laponte et al.* (1972), the Supreme Court found no provision in the Expropriation Act for notice of expropriation and, consequently, little opportunity to object or to negotiate compensation. Yet, since the procedures were passed by Parliament, they were by definition due process of law.

The constitutional context changed in 1981 when Prime Minister Trudeau introduced the new constitution. However, property was eliminated from the Charter, at least in part, because of pressure from the New Democratic party which feared the American experience early in this century of judicial activism in defense of corporate interests. Furthermore, the civil law system in Canada has contributed to the belief that the law governing ordinary social relations ought to be provincial.

The 1982 constitutional Charter of Rights and Freedoms has already begun to reveal new levels of judicial activism.[33] Although the right to property was not included, the Charter may affect the role of litigation in the Canadian system. Judicial authority at all levels of government is likely to be greater. Indeed, according to Edward McWhinney, the changes are "all rather American with the courts destined, as in the United States, to be at the heart of the process, whether they like it or not."[34]

Peter Russell, although he is more critical of the jurisprudential shift, agrees that the "main impact of the new constitutional Charter of Rights on the Canadian system of government is to increase the role of the judiciary in deciding how fundamental social and political values should be affected by public policy."[35] Evident in the switch from British to American ancillary graduate training in law, which began in the 1920s,[36] American legal ideas have been making greater and greater headway in Canada. One of the most important is the notion that judges ". . . can, and do, and should make law in the process of decision making."[37] Both those who fear judicial policymaking and those who welcome it recognize that the terrain is new for Canada.

Only a few months after the Charter became law, the New Brunswick Court of Queen's Bench issued a prophetic property decision (*New*

---

*Walter Tarnopolsky tends to minimize the statutory basis while suggesting that the Canadian constitution at that time was simply not the sort of thing where the distinction between being in it or out of it was all that clear.

Brunswick v. *Fisherman's Wharf, Ltd.*). The basis was Section I, the "guarantee clause," and Section 7.1, which reads: "Everyone has the right to life, liberty and security of the person and the right not to be deprived thereof except in accordance with the principles of fundamental justice." Judge Dickson of the New Brunswick court was candid in noting that "the Charter is silent in specific reference to property rights" but he nevertheless asserted that the "right to . . . security of the person must be construed as comprising the right to enjoyment of the ownership of property which extends to 'security of the person.'" This logic is a leap, but coming when it did, the holding supports the contention that the judiciary will be strengthened by the Charter.

There is a paradox stemming from the American experience with due process protections of property. Knowledgeable commentators might assume that judicial protection of property would grow in Canada as it had in American law, yet because of the backlash generated by the American experience, the response may be the reverse.[38] Property protection in the old Bill of Rights incorporated into Canadian law a "due process" phrase that had "long since dropped out of Anglo-Canadian jurisprudence."[39] The significance of the only explicit reference to property in the old Canadian Bill of Rights was not great. Perhaps the best indication of the sensitivity Canadians felt toward due process protection of property, or "substantive due process," is evident in the majority opinion by Chief Justice Bora Laskin in the case of *Curr* v. *The Queen*, in 1972. Laskin discouraged Canadian jurists from following the Americans in this area other than to accept the realization that the American Supreme Court had abandoned economic due process in 1937 because they had entered ". . . a bog of legislative policy making in assuming to enshrine any particular theory . . . which has not been plainly expressed in the Constitution."[40] It was this jurisprudential position that manifested itself in the political give and take during the final days of the drafting of the Charter of Rights in 1981.

Yet, Laskin's opinion still sets up an American past as prologue for the Canadian constitutional future. For as Edward McWhinney said when the political dust had barely cleared from the new text, "The seven English-speaking premiers in the gang of eight who had fought to keep the constitution 'English' and to bar reception of all 'American' constitutional institutions and values, have, in losing so completely and so utterly in the end, simply speeded up the 'Americanization' (or modernization) of Canadian constitutional law."[41]

Notes

1. Edward S. Corwin, *Court Over Constitution* (Princeton: Princeton University Press, 1983).
2. *Goldberg* v. *Kelly* (1970) 397 U.S.254.
3. *Murray's Lessee* v. *Hoboken Land and Improvement Co.* (1855) 18 How. 272.
4. Bernard Siegan, *Planning Without Process* (Lexington, Mass.: Lexington Books, 1977).
5. Allison Dunham, *"Griggs* v. *Allegheny County* in Perspective: 30 Years of Supreme Court Expropriation Law," 63 SUPREME COURT REVIEW 105, 1962.
6. Frank Michelman, "Property, Utility, and Fairness: Comments on the Ethical Foundations of 'Just Compensation' Law," *Harvard Law Review*, 80:1165.
7. *Regina* v. *Martin* (1961) 35 WWR 285.
8. Eric C. E. Todd, *The Law of Expropriation and Compensation in Canada* (Toronto: Carswell: 1976).
9. *Ibid.*
10. Bruce Ackerman, *Private Property and the Constitution* (New Haven: Yale University Press, 1977); Neal A. Roberts, *The Government Land Developers* (Lexington, Mass.: Lexington Books, 1977).
11. James Bickerton and Alain G. Gagnon, "Regional Policy in Historical Perspective: The Federal Role in Regional Economic Development," *American Review of Canadian Studies* (1984), 72–88.
12. Goldberg and Mercer, 1982.
13. For an international comparison, see: Organization for Economic Cooperation and Development, "The Management of Publicly Owned Land in Urban Areas," Paris, 1979.
14. Michael M. Atkinson and Marsha A. Chandler, eds., *The Politics of Canadian Public Policy* (Toronto: University of Toronto Press, 1983).
15. Northrop Frye, "Letters in Canada," in *University of Toronto Quarterly* 22 (April 1953), p. 273.
16. Jennifer Nedelsky, "From Common Law to Commission: The Development of Water Law in Nova Scotia," Proceedings of the Conference on Water and Environmental Law, Dalhousie University, Halifax, N.S., September 14–16, 1979.
17. Morton Horwitz, *The Transformation of American Law: 1780–1860* (Cambridge, Mass.: Harvard University Press, 1977).
18. *Miller* v. *Halifax Power Co.*, (1914) 13 ELR 394.
19. Nedelsky, *op. cit.*
20. *Hanf* v. *Yarmouth Light and Power* 58 NSR 430 (1926).
21. Department of Regional Economic Expansion, "Atlantic Region Industrial Parks: An Assessment of Economic Impact" (Ottawa: Department of Regional Economic Expansion, 1979).
22. *Halifax Industries, Ltd.* v. *Director of Assessment* 55 NSR (2nd) 285 (1982).
23. Lloyd Rodwin, *Economic Development and Resource Conservation: A Strategy for Maine* (Maine: Bureau of Public Lands, 1974); see also Roberts, *op. cit.*, p. 191.
24. Paul Rawlins, Assistant City Manager, Portland, Maine, Interview, March 1982.
25. Ric Knowland, Portland Planning Department, Interview, November, 1981.
26. *Laughlin* v. *City of Portland*, 111, Me. 486, 90 A 318 (1914).
27. Alexander Delogu, Reply Brief for Appellant, August 31, 1982.
28. *Common Cause* v. *The State of Maine* (January 7, 1983) Supreme Judicial Court of Maine, 437 A2d 597 (Me. 1981).

29. Robert C. Fellmeth, *Politics of Land* (New York: Grossman, 1973).

30. Thomas E. Kierans, "Privatization: Strengthening the Market at the Expense of the State," in *Choices*, April 1985.

31. William K. Stevens, "Renaissance Along the Waterfronts of Three Cities Transforms Downtowns," *The New York Times*, May 26, 1985.

32. D. A. Schmeiser, *Civil Liberties in Canada* (London: Oxford University Press, 1964); and Birks, 1955.

33. Walter S. Tarnopolsky, *The Canadian Bill of Rights* (Toronto: McClelland and Stewart Ltd., 1975).

34. Robert Miller, "A New Promise of Equality," *Maclean's*, April 22, 1985. See also *Maclean's*, January 28, May 20, July 9, 1985.

35. Edward McWhinney, *Canada and the Constitution 1979–1982: Patriation and the Charter of Rights* (Toronto: University of Toronto Press, 1982).

36. Peter H. Russell, "The Effect of a Charter of Rights on the Policy-Making Role of Canadian Courts," *Canadian Public Administration* 25:1–33.

37. Edward McWhinney, *Canadian Jurisprudence* (Toronto: Carswell, 1958).

38. William E. Conklin, *In Defense of Fundamental Rights* (The Netherlands: Sitjthoff and Noordhoff, 1979).

39. Peter H. Russell, "Judicial Power in Canada's Political Culture," in M. L. Friedland, ed., *Courts and Trials* (Toronto: University of Toronto Press, 1979).

40. *Ibid.*

41. *Curr* v. *The Queen* (1972) SCR 889.

42. McWhinney, 1982, *op. cit.*

PART V
CONCLUSIONS

10

General Lessons from Diverse Cases

Elliot J. Feldman and Michael A. Goldberg

The central concern of this book is the use of North America's limited (if large) land resource. The authors focus especially on the roles played by the public and private sectors, as summarized in the following schematic of land use decisions and controls:

Ownership	Use	Transfer
Private	Regulation	Acquisition
Public	Management	Disposal

Governments can influence the use of privately owned land through a rich array of land use and development regulations, and they can acquire land directly. Land in public ownership is allocated to alternative uses through disposal to the private sector.

Drawing on the schematic above, the authors devote their primary attention to the following elements:

1. *Government decision making processes* pertaining to land use and land management, including here the openness of these processes and the degree to which affected publics were involved explicitly.

2. *Social equity*, sorting out the beneficiaries and losers of various land use and management decisions.

3. *Efficiency* in using the land under various regimes of ownership and management.

4. *Short run and long run* concerns follow directly from the efficiency issue because questions of efficiency need to be defined over time. Thus, we may reach short run efficient outcomes (such as energy, capital and intensive logging) only to find that there are longer run inefficiencies (inability to reproduce the forest in this example).

5. *Federalism and intergovernmental relations*, making sense of the myriad levels of government influences in North America.

6. The *success and failure* of the diverse land use and management approaches adopted by governments and private actors, in a sense, our "bottom line." Did the various approaches achieve their stated objectives and were these objectives consonant with the generally accepted public interest?

Our comparisons proceed along three levels simultaneously: cross-national Canada-U.S. comparisons, issue by issue, and often region by region. We believe such a comparative method sheds needed light on the complexities of land use, while also providing for the generalization of central findings across issues, regions and national boundaries.

The case studies range over urban uses from city systems in the aggregate (e.g., the product of land using and managing decisions), to specific urban uses such as housing, industrial development and toxic waste, and to urban/rural fringe issues and thus land use decision making under conditions of urbanization and land use change. Finally, remote forest lands, vast in land area and unaffected by urban land use decisions, represent the last case study focus.

Emerging Themes and Consistencies

Certain themes emerge consistently from the chapters of this book, and there are significant differences across national, regional and issue dimensions.

Cities as Wholes (The Product of Land Using Decisions)

At the macro-scale, highly significant differences have been documented using a range of reasonably stringent statistical tests. Canada and the U.S., Goldberg argues, are very different entities at the federal level, and their cities, which are the products of the political, social and economic forces and cultures within the two countries, are distinct. Canadian governments (at all levels) pursue, and Canadians accept, a more vigorous public sector involvement in markets, particularly those relating to land.

According to Goldberg, we should anticipate marked differences between Canada and the United States on land use issues at the more micro level of detailed case studies. If cities, products of the whole complex array of land use and development decisions, are different in Canada and the United States, then behind these differences must be different decision making processes, equity-efficiency trade-offs, federal/provincial-state/local government relations and criteria for success and failure.[1] Sometimes the case studies supported this hypothesis, but often they did not.

Decision Making

There is considerable variation in the management of forest lands: Canada's central government has very little decision making power compared with the U.S. federal government. Provinces, however, exercise the balance of decision making power concerning forests in Canada, whereas the American states are relatively weak in this area. Leman also observes differences in the ways private owners and users of forests approach their roles in the two countries. North American forestry is a private activity in terms of the actual extraction and finishing of the wood resource, but U.S. companies have a good deal more scope for multiple and longer term uses of forest lands than their Canadian counterparts. The Canadians have to deal with provincial governments bent on maximizing short term resource revenues from provincial forest lands.

Leman, Colcord, Feldman and Brigham all find greater public participation in decisions in the United States, but Ristoratore's study of toxic waste disposal turned up a good deal of public input affecting siting decisions in both countries. Clark and Brigham found a more central decision making role for the judiciary in the U.S. Even with the Canadian Charter of Rights and Freedoms, Canadian judges still exercise minor influence in land use decisions in contrast to their U.S. colleagues.

Social Equity

Unlike the contrasts in decision making and participation, the evidence for differences is much less consistent for issues of social equity. Decisional favoritism in agricultural fringe land use and conflicts between local and regional governments are similar in Canada and the United States. Montreal's urban development has consistently favored big enterprises and Boston's has defended neighborhoods, but the specific impact of urban renewal has been to disadvantage low income groups systematically in both cities. Clark reaches an analogous conclusion, arguing that property interests are protected and distributional issues ignored when there are disputes between local and regional governments. Finally, Feldman suggests that attempts to control urban fringe development have worked when they have been consistent with the interests of core businesses (usually central city retailing); they have been a means to maintain capital values of centrally located firms at the expense of the suburbanizing population and the new businesses wanting to open at the fringe.

In contrast, both Leman and Brigham suggest there may be more social equity in the Canadian setting. Strong union and industry interests have teamed up to exert significant pressure on provincial governments to maintain forest yields and with them high paying forest jobs, sustained company profits and large provincial resource rents. The more competitive U.S. forestry environment seems to have led to lower wages and an uneven profit picture although, with the mobility of capital (as in the case of Georgia-Pacific), high profits could be realized by moving to U.S. regions with lower wages and higher short term tree yields. Brigham's work also supports the notion that the general public appears to do better in Halifax, where a Crown corporation handled job creation, than in Portland where a private company stood to be the big gainer in the redevelopment strategy.

Efficiency

The criteria for assessing efficiency are few and narrowly defined economic or technical efficiency is seldom the deciding factor in any land use decision.[2] Ristoratore found in all four toxic waste disposal cases that economic and technical efficiency criteria were often clearly stated, often led to unambiguous results, and never held sway in the end. Political considerations always dominated. Similarly, efficiency in land use and urban development was seldom considered either in the urban renewal cases examined by Colcord or in the industrial development/redevelopment examples treated by Brigham.

In forestry, a somewhat more mixed picture emerges. There were efforts both in the public and private sectors in the United States to maximize sustainable yields over an immediate time period. These strategies were of markedly less concern in Canada where short term yield criteria dominated. However, Leman also observes that the concept of efficiency varies too widely to call any known system efficient in any meaningful long run sense.

Finally, Feldman observes that efficiency of land use and urban development patterns is often a rationale for urban fringe land use regulation, but the body of technical evidence supporting this assertion is mixed. In the particular settings he examined, it is clear that land use efficiency was not achieved or apparently sought with any vigor and conviction.

In sum, therefore, the record does not support policies accomplishing or even expressly designed for efficiency in land use and development. Political considerations consistently prevail over technical or economic notions just as they do in relation to equity. And this conclusion is reached equally for Canada and the United States.

Short Run versus Long Run

Much of the drive to control urban growth, regulate urban and fringe land use and protect the urban, fringe and rural environment stems from a fear that the pressure for short run gains will lead to long run environmental degradation and loss.[3] The short run/long run issue therefore cuts through almost all of the essays in this book, for different groups and institutions have different time horizons and therefore different temporal criteria against which efficiency (and success and failure) are measured.

A clear example of short run and long run considerations is Leman's study. Some large private American forest product firms set out to maximize long run profits by vigorous forest management schemes that would regenerate cutover areas and promote multiple uses of forest lands. In contrast, Leman demonstrated that many Canadian provinces sought to maximize short run resource revenues, exposing themselves to longer run difficulties as the forest resource became exhausted and little reforestation was set in motion to ensure sustained long run yields and revenues.

Feldman also suggests that short run concerns lay beneath many of the fringe controls of the 1960s and 1970s which sought to inhibit growth in response to rapid suburban and exurban expansion. Little in the way of longer run management strategies or monitoring systems were developed and indeed the longer run demographic context for fringe growth was paid scant attention.

In the wholly urban context, Colcord and Brigham find short run concerns especially dominant in Canada. Colcord suggests that Montreal was driven by short run desires to promote core area growth and longer issues relating to social mix and the viability of the housing stock in the core were given short shrift. By contrast, Boston appears to be consistently motivated by long run neighborhood concerns which frequently impede short run gains such as construction jobs and highway investment. Brigham suggests that there was a relatively greater focus on the short run benefits of industrial development in both Halifax and Portland with minimal consideration of long run economic viability and restructuring of these urban economies.

Finally, Ristoratore and Clark deal explicitly with short and long run trade-offs. Ristoratore observes that the one successful toxic waste decision proceeded by balancing longer run fears of pollution from the waste site against shorter run job increase. Clark argues, albeit implicitly, that there is an inherent long run/short run contradiction built into the reliance on legal principles because they arise in a long run process of legal reasoning and dispute adjudication, yet are only given meaning through their application to specific short run issues. Thus, short run dispute resolution relies on long run principles which may or may not be germane in the circumstances.

Federalism and Intergovernmental Relations

By federalism we mean here the relations among governments at various levels, whether those governments be local, regional or special purpose, state/provincial or national.[4] Clear North American differences in the practice of federalism are manifest throughout this volume. Goldberg attributes many of the observed urban differences between the two countries to major differences in the respective urban policy roles of states and provinces and the national governments in Canada and the United States. Similarly, Clark delineates important distinctions in the adjudication of conflicts between local and regional bodies. Colcord supports Goldberg's general observations about greater federal support for cities in the United States, but he argues that federal dollars gave Boston mayors more power to control development; Goldberg's assessment predicts a less productive dependency.

The federal presence in American forests is very substantial. In Canada, the provinces are the key governmental decision makers. Differences in perspective at the different levels of the federal system plainly affect policy choices.

Ristoratore also found the provinces more important than the federal government in Canadian toxic waste decisions; the American balance is more ambiguous. Brigham found a larger federal role in Portland's redevelopment initiatives than in Halifax. And Feldman, in his review of agricultural land preservation and urban fringe controls, found little functional differentiation (and effectiveness, British Columbia and possibly Oregon excepted), despite a proliferation of different statutory and regulatory bases. The differences in federal influence, and the differences between states and provinces, were not significant.

There is, then, no simple pattern. The predictions of greater federal involvement in the U.S. and greater provincial powers when compared to states are supported only occasionally; sometimes when sustained they lead to unforeseen conclusions (as when federal dollars are reported beneficial to local control). Indeed, the reader may be struck by counterintuition and discontinuity here.

Studies of Canada and the U.S. are replete with conclusions and assertions that led to the comparative hypotheses in this project. At the macroscopic level the systemic contrasts are as real as they are apparent. Cities in the two countries are different. They are governed differently, and their populations do seem to reflect different aggregate values. Yet, microscopically, the powerful explanations gag at their foundations: Boston is more planned, controlled, even "governed" than Montreal; Canadian foresters are less environmentally responsible, in part because provincial powers over the private sector are little exercised; Ontario public officials are no more prepared to compromise industry and dense populations for toxic waste control than are officials in New York. And even with metropolitan government, Toronto is no more successful containing the urban fringe than the officials in Oregon trying to preserve the Willamette Valley. The conventional wisdom comparing Canada and the United States, in light of findings here, needs long and hard rethinking.

Success and Failure

Difficulties in evaluating success and failure derived from several sources. There are no broad and consensual criteria against which success and failure can be judged, and where internal criteria were identified, it was often difficult to establish the extent to which they were met. Moreover, the comparison of success and failure across countries, regions and issues, further complicated the chore. Often, different criteria prevail in the two countries.[5]

Generalizations may be impossible, but the authors here have made judgments within their respective studies. Goldberg concludes that Canadian cities are more successful despite great difficulties in defining rigorously "success" in the urban context. He says Canadian cities are safer, that the disparities between central city and suburban residents on income and demographic dimensions is much less, that Canadian urban economies in the core appear healthier (especially retail trade), and that the fiscal condition of Canadian central cities is superior to that of American central cities. It does seem warranted, therefore, to conclude, *on average* (because there are exceptions in both countries), that Canada has been more successful at fostering safe, livable cities.

Colcord and Brigham show more mixed outcomes for North American cities. Public agencies were successful frequently on their own terms with respect to stimulating reinvestment and redevelopment of stagnating or declining urban core neighborhoods and industrial areas in both countries. In Halifax, Brigham suggests, the greater public good may also have been served successfully; he is more skeptical about Portland. Colcord, however, is far more critical of the socioeconomic impact of the Drapeau regime than of any policies in Boston. He sees Boston redevelopment as a qualified success, and Montreal's as a qualified failure.

Ristoratore also finds mixed results. In Quebec, success was achieved because a site was approved; in the three other cases there was failure, although the Louisiana experience most resembled Quebec's. However, even in Quebec the issue is open as to whether the broad public interest is best served: the facility is having trouble operating at efficient levels of throughput and thus is having difficulty justifying its economic costs.

Canadian policy has been more successful at meeting the short term revenue, profit, and employment objectives of provincial governments, forest product firms and the relevant unions. However, on a broader and longer term measure, there has been enormous waste in Canada. There are pending large-scale, long term failures resulting from short term policies that did not restock and carefully manage the forest resource. American policy, by contrast, has yielded longer term success, both from the perspective of the forest companies and of the public managers of forest lands (in terms of profits and resource rents). U.S. forest management also seems more successful relative to protecting the public interest over coming decades, promoting multiple uses of lands and encouraging public participation.

Feldman questions the success of agricultural land preservation efforts and their accompanying attempts to control urban fringe development in both counties. From the evidence he reviews, he leaves open the question as to whether external public interests have in fact been protected, although in the cases of British Columbia and Oregon, it would appear that some internal success has been achieved: workable control programs have been developed and function largely along the original lines.

The diversity of issues raised in this book highlights the need for diversity in evaluation criteria. It is disappointing that no consistent cross-national criteria emerge for judging success and failure, but it is not surprising. Land use analysts have long recognized in the urban land economics tradition that land markets are highly localized. We now tend to doubt the usefulness of universal standards because of the spatial specificity of land use, but we remain persuaded that the cross-national inquiry illuminates a range of choices corresponding to various standards and values.

Synthetic Conclusions

There are at least five conclusions that span the diversity of the essays presented here:

1. There do not appear to be unique "correct" ways of using, managing and regulating land use and development. Rather, there is an extraordinary and rich range of approaches. Ideologues and technocrats will doubtless be very disappointed by this conclusion, for it suggests that in certain circumstances private enterprise (forestry in the U.S.) is capable of looking after long term public interests, whereas in Canada, again using the forestry example, provincial public agencies have not served long term public interests so well. By contrast, public agencies can be effective, as in the case of Canadian urban public transportation and publicly owned industrial development firms (as in Halifax). Accordingly, the public/private dichotomy remains important for defining spheres of protected individual rights, but it is at best disorienting in drawing conclusions about performance.

Technocratic disenchantment with these conclusions is likely to stem from the generally low value placed on purely technical issues, even in such apparently technical areas as toxic waste disposal. Decisions and outcomes typically embrace both public and private elements for both technical and political considerations. Decision making processes are contextual, not formulaic, but the process often dictates the outcome.

2. Virtually all of the papers in this volume have described public/private partnerships which call the public/private dichotomy into question. Many are the public sector agencies seeking to maximize profits, and there are private sector firms seeking to stabilize employment and protect the environment, goals usually associated with government.

More fundamentally, there are so many instances where the public and private sectors form joint ventures or act *de facto* as partners (as in forestry, urban renewal, industrial development, and waste disposal) that the public/private label adds little to descriptive accuracy or functional analysis. The growing interdependence of public institutions and private firms makes the classification of activities as one type or the other misleading; mixed public/private enterprises and actions will of necessity have mixed or even altogether new goals, objectives and methods of operation.[6]

Clearly, a new classifying mechanism is needed that provides greater functional insight and analytic power. Perhaps the long/short run dichotomy is more useful. Alternatively, all generalization may be impossible; different land use issues by their very nature and geographic setting may require different elements to be considered and analyzed. Nevertheless, we have found some generalization possible, and not as futile abstraction.

3. Unambiguous criteria for success and failure are hard to identify. Often it has been difficult to identify an organizational or agency goal for a land use policy or decision, let alone a complementary and consistent public criterion of success. Success and failure are concepts that need to be applied issue by issue, region by region, and country by country, for use issues, as we have emphasized, are highly localized, and criteria for success and failure may be as specific as a case requires.

4. Cross-national research surely broadens the horizons of choice, but it may not deliver so much in the transferability of lessons. Mayors of Boston and Montreal traded off housing, transportation, public works and commercial development; in neither city was it apparent that some strategy might have been available to make all these policy arenas compatible. Nor could the short run supplies of lumber be maintained through long term conservation strategies. Public participation might produce longer term satisfaction with democracy, but it certainly does not help get a toxic waste facility sited. The examples running throughout this volume suggest that different systems, societies or cultures may trade off differently, but there are no clear examples of one or another arriving at "better" choices for all goals at once. Moreover, the characteristics of failure, as in controlling urban sprawl, are more apparent cross-nationally than are the formulas of success.

5. Finally, land use policy has been used often either in lieu of or as an implicit (but rarely explicit) adjunct of social policy. Elements of redistribution are apparent in urban renewal, forest policy, industrial port developments, fringe development controls, toxic waste disposal siting and in the adjudication of intergovernmental land disputes. This political use of control instruments helps explain the difficulty assessing success, failure and efficiency and it relates to our earlier observation about the blurring of the public/private dichotomy: public activities often seek efficiency and private ones are concerned increasingly with equity and redistribution.

It is well known in policy making that one policy can only imperfectly meet more than one objective.[7] Given the implicit redistributive and social elements of land use decisions, it is clear that land use efficiency *and* social equity policies cannot be met simultaneously. Perhaps, as a result, we expect too much from the land and its regulation. To complement our search for better land use policy we might also work diligently to engender more realistic expectations about the social ends that even good land use policy can achieve. Abstractly, it might seem best to assign land use policy to land use issues and social policy to social issues, but it by now surely is obvious that such a choice is unavailable. Land use policies are inherently political, for they involve the essential purposes of the liberal democratic state.[8]

Notes

1. The centrality of culture in studying cities, and in the comparative analysis of social and political systems more generally, is strongly supported by the essays presented in John Agnew, John Mercer and David Sopher, eds., *The City in Cultural Context* (Boston: Allen and Unwin, 1984).

2. Attempts to impose narrowly defined efficiency criteria on complex political issues have generally failed. Work by Aaron Wildavsky in the 1970s details one such fiasco and is instructive for the more general point that tightly specified efficiency is a dubious goal for public policy. See, for example, Aaron Wildavsky, "Rescuing Policy Analysis from PPBS," in Robert H. Haveman and Julius Margolis, eds., *Public Expenditures and Policy Analysis* (Chicago: Markham Publishers, 1970). Another eloquent statement asserting the need for politics (in its broadest sense) to supersede technical efficiency can be found in Bernard Crick, *In Defense of Politics* (Chicago: University of Chicago Press, 1972).

3. The enormous, and still growing, environmental literature of the late 1960s, the 1970s and up through the 1980s focuses very much on issues related to long run and short costs and benefits. Fairly typical of the genre and of the argument being made is Lester Brown, *Building a Sustainable Society* (New York: W.W. Norton and Co., 1981). Brown explicitly considers long and short run land use issues related both to cities and agriculture.

4. An excellent discussion of the nature of federalism in Canada and the United States can be found in Roger Gibbins, *Regionalism: Territorial Politics in Canada and the United States* (Toronto: Butterworths, 1982). An analysis of federalism in Canada and its implications for federal influence over cities (and urban land use) can be found in Elliot J. Feldman and Jerome Milch, "Coordination or Control? The Life and Death of the Ministry of State for Urban Affairs," in Lionel D. Feldman, ed., *Politics and Government in Urban Canada*, Fourth Edition (Toronto: Methuen, 1981), pp. 246–264.

5. An illustration of this point can be found in a challenging work by Herschel Hardin, who suggests that attempts to assess the "failure" of Canadian private sector firms to compete in the way private firms do in the United States is really off the mark. Hardin argues that success in Canada needs to be measured against Canadian values, not against those preferred in the United States. Thus *public*, not *private* enterprise is

Canada's forte and should be the standard against which Canadian economic performance is judged. See Herschel Hardin, *A Nation Unaware: The Canadian Economic Culture* (Vancouver: J.J. Douglas, 1974).

6. The growing mixture of public and private sector activities has spawned a growing body of research into the "mixed" enterprise economy. See, for example: Anthony E. Boardman, Catherine C. Eckel, and Aidan R. Vining, "The Advantages and Disadvantages of Mixed Enterprises," in A. Negandhi and H. Thomas, eds., *State-Owned Multinationals in International Business* (London: John Wiley and Sons, 1985), and Anthony E. Boardman, Catherine C. Eckel, Marianne Linde and Aidan R. Vining, "An Overview of Mixed Enterprises in Canada," *Business Quarterly* 48:2 (1983).

7. The classic statement of the impossibility of simultaneously maximizing two or more interdependent variables (as is almost always the case in actual policy decisions) can be found in John von Newmann and Oskar Morgenstern, *The Mathematical Theory of Games* (Princeton: Princeton University Press, 1963). Similar findings can be found in most policy analysis studies and critiques. See, for example: Wildavsky, *op. cit.*; and Charles E. Lindblom and David K. Cohen, *Usable Knowledge: Social Science and Social Problem Solving* (New Haven: Yale University Press, 1979).

8. On these values, see Ronald Dworkin, *Taking Rights Seriously* (London: Duckworth, 1977).

Bibliography

Part I: Comparing Public and Private in Canada and the United States

Ackerman, Bruce, *Private Property and the Constitution* (New Haven: Yale University Press, 1977).

Agnew, John, John Mercer and David Sopher, eds., *The City in Cultural Context* (Boston: Allen and Unwin, 1984).

Altshuler, Alan, *The City Planning Process* (Ithaca: Cornell University Press, 1965).

Alcaly, Roger E., and David E. Mermelstein, *The Fiscal Crisis of American Cities* (New York: Vintage, 1977).

Allison, Graham T., "Public and Private Management: Are They Fundamentally Alike in All Unimportant Respects?" in *Setting Public Management Research Agendas: Integrating the Sponsor, Producer and User* (Washington, D.C.: Office of Personnel Management, 1980).

Almond, Gabriel and Sydney Verba, *The Civic Culture* (Princeton: Princeton University Press, 1963).

Almy, Richard, et al., *Separated Rights in Real Estate*, Economic Research Service, USDA (1982).

Anderson, Martin, *The Federal Bulldozer* (Cambridge: MIT Press, 1964).

Anthony, Robert N. and Regina E. Herzlinger, *Management Control in Nonprofit Organizations* (Homewood, IL: Irwin, 1980).

——— and John Dearden, *Management Control Systems*, 4th ed. (Homewood, IL: Irwin, 1980).

Armour, Leslie, *The Idea of Canada and the Crisis of Community* (Ottawa: Steel Rail Publishing, 1981).

Arnold, Stephen J., and Douglas J. Tigert, "Canadians and Americans: A Comparative Analysis," in K. Ishwaran, ed., *International Journal of Comparative Sociology*, Vol. XV (Leiden: E.J. Brill, 1974).

———— and James G. Barnes, "Canadian and American National Character as a Basis for Market Segmentation," in Jadgish N. Sheth, ed., *Research in Marketing*, Vol. 2 (Greenwich: JAI Press, 1979).

Arnopolous, Sheila McLeod and Dominique Clift, *The English Fact in Quebec* (Montreal: McGill-Queen's University Press, 1980).

Arrow, Kenneth J., *The Limits of Organization* (New York: W.W. Norton, 1974).

Atkinson, Tom, et al., *Social Change in Canada* (Downsview, Ontario: Institute for Behavioral Research, York University, 1982).

Avery, Robert B., Gregory E. Elliehausen, Glenn B. Canner and Thomas A. Gustafson, "Survey of Consumer Finances, 1983," *Federal Reserve Bulletin* 70:9 (September 1984).

Bahl, Roy E., ed., *The Fiscal Outlook for Cities* (Syracuse: Syracuse University Press, 1978).

Bakvis, Herman, *Federalism and the Organization of Political Life: Canada in Comparative Perspective* (Kingston, Ontario: Institute of Intergovernmental Relations, Queen's University, 1981).

Balakrishnan, T. R. and G. K. Jarvis, "Changing Patterns of Spatial Differentiation in Urban Canada, 1961–71," in *Canadian Review of Sociology and Anthropology* 16:2 (1979).

Banting, Keith and Richard Simeon, eds., *And No One Cheered* (Toronto: Methuen, 1983).

Barger, Harold, *The Transportation Industries, 1889–1956* (New York: National Bureau of Economic Research, 1951).

Bean, D. R., "Forecasting the Future of Federalism," in Advisory Commission on Intergovernmental Relations, *The Future of Federalism* (Washington: U.S. Government Printing Office, 1981).

Beck, Nathaniel and John Pierce, "Political Involvement and Party Allegiances in Canada and the United States," in Robert Presthus, ed., *Cross-National Perspectives: United States and Canada* (Leiden: E.J. Brill, 1977).

Bell, David V. J., "The Loyalist Tradition in Canada," *Journal of Canadian Studies* (1970).

———— and Lorne Tepperman, *The Roots of Disunity: A Look at Canadian Political Culture* (Toronto: McClelland and Stewart, 1979).

Berger, Carl, *The Sense of Power: Studies on the Ideas of Canadian Imperialism, 1867–1914* (Toronto: University of Toronto Press, 1970).

Berle, Adolph A. and Gardiner C. Means, *The Modern Corporation and Private Property* (New York: MacMillan, 1935).

Berry, Brian, J. L., *Comparative Urbanization* (New York: St. Martin's Press, 1981).

————, *City Classification Handbook, Method and Applications* (New York: J. Wiley and Sons, 1972).

————, ed., "Urbanization and Counterurbanization," in *Urban Affairs Annual Review* 11 (Beverly Hills: Sage Publications, 1976).

————, "The Counterurbanization Process: How General," in Niles M. Hansen, ed., *Human Settlement Systems* (Cambridge: Ballinger, 1978).

————, "The Future of the Metropolis: What Lies Ahead for Urban America," in Larry S. Bourne and John Hitchcock, eds., *The Changing Metropolis:*

Essays in Honor of Hans Blumenfeld (Toronto: University of Toronto Press, 1984).

Berry, J. W. and G. J. S. Wilde, eds., *Social Psychology: The Canadian Context* (Toronto: McClelland and Stewart, 1972).

Bettison, David, *The Politics of Canadian Urban Development* (Edmonton: University of Alberta Press, 1975).

Between Friends-Entre Amis (Ottawa: National Film Board of Canada, 1976).

Bibby, Reginald W., "The Delicate Mosaic: A National Examination of Intergroup Relations in Canada," in *Social Indicators Research* 5 (1978).

Bird, Richard M. and Enid Slack, *Urban Public Finance in Canada* (Toronto: Butterworths, 1983).

Bish, Robert L. and Vincent Ostrom, *Understanding Urban Government: Metropolitan Reform Reconsidered* (Washington: American Enterprise Institute for Public Policy Research, 1973).

Blau, Peter M. and W. Richard Scott, *Formal Organizations: A Comparative Approach* (Scranton, PA: Chandler Publishing Co., 1962).

Bliss, Michael, *A Living Profit: Studies in Social History of Canadian Business, 1883– 1911* (Toronto: McClelland and Stewart, 1974).

Blumenthal, Michael, "Candid Reflections of a Businessman in Washington," in *Fortune* (January 29, 1979).

Boardman, Anthony E., Catherine C. Eckel and Aidan R. Vining, "The Advantages and Disadvantages of Mixed Enterprises," in A. Negandhi and H. Thomas, eds., *State-Owned Multinationals in International Business* (London: John Wiley and Sons, 1985).

———, Catherine C. Eckel, Marianne Linde and Aidan R. Vining, "An Overview of Mixed Enterprises in Canada," *Business Quarterly* 48:2 (1983).

Bonner, G. M., *Canada's Forest Inventory 1981* (Ottawa: Canadian Forestry Service, Environment Canada, 1982).

Borcherding, Thomas E., Werner W. Pommerehne and Friedrich Schneider, "Comparing the Efficiency of Private and Public Production: The Evidence from Five Countries," (Burnaby, BC: Department of Economics, Simon Fraser University, 1982).

Bosselman, Fred and David Callies, *The Quiet Revolution in Land Use Control* (Washington, D.C.: Council on Environmental Quality, 1971).

Boston Redevelopment Authority, "1965–1975 General Plan for the City of Boston and the Regional Core," November 1964.

Bourne, Larry S., ed., *Internal Structure of the City*. 2nd ed. (New York: Oxford University Press, 1982).

Bower, Joseph L., "Effective Public Management: It Isn't the Same as Effective Business Management," in *Harvard Business Review* (March–April 1977).

Brown, Lester, *Building a Sustainable Society* (New York: W.W. Norton and Co., 1981).

Bunge, William and Ronald Bordessa, *The Canadian Alternative: Survival, Expeditions and Urban Change*, York Geographical Monographs, No. 2 (Toronto: York University, 1975).

Campbell, Colin, *Governments Under Stress* (Toronto: University of Toronto Press, 1983).

Campbell, Joseph, *Myths to Live By* (New York: Bantam Books, 1972).

Canada Ministry of Finance, *Economic Review* (Ottawa: Minister of Supply and Services, April 1984).

Canada Mortgage and Housing Corporation, *Public Priorities in Urban Canada: A Survey of Community Concerns* (Ottawa: Canada Mortgage and Housing Corporation, 1979).

Canada Yearbook, 1981–1982 (Ottawa: Authority of the Minister of Supply and Services).

Cartwright, Don, *Official Language Populations in Canada: Patterns and Contacts* (Montreal: Institute for Research on Public Policy, 1980).

———, "Language Policy and the Organization of Territory: A Canadian Dilemma," in *Canadian Geographer* 25 (1981).

Chandler, Alfred D. Jr., *The Visible Hand: The Managerial Revolution in American Business* (Cambridge: Harvard University Press, 1977).

Chase, Gordon, "Managing Compared," in *The New York Times*, March 14, 1978.

Chickering, Lawrence, ed., *The Politics of Planning* (Sacramento: Institute of Contemporary Studies, 1976).

Clairmont, D. H. and Dennis W. Magill, *Africville: The Life and Death of a Canadian Black Community* (Toronto: McClelland and Stewart, 1974).

Clark, Gordon, *Judges and the Cities: interpreting local autonomy* (Chicago: University of Chicago Press, 1985).

Clark, Samuel D., ed., *The Developing Canadian Community* (Toronto: University of Toronto Press, 1968).

Clement, Wallace, *Continental Corporate Power: Economic Linkages between Canada and the United States* (Toronto: McClelland and Stewart, 1977).

———, *The Canadian Corporate Elite: An Analysis of Economic Power*, Carleton Library No. 89 (Toronto: McClelland and Stewart, 1975).

Coase, Ronald H., "The Nature of the Firm," in *Economica* 386 (November, 1937).

———, "Industrial Organization: A Proposal for Research," in Victor R. Fuchs, ed., *Policy Issues and Research Opportunities in Industrial Organization* (New York: National Bureau of Economic Research, 1972).

Coffey, William, "Income Relationships in Boston and Toronto: A Tale of Two Countries," in *Canadian Geographer* 22 (1978).

Collier, Robert, *Contemporary Cathedrals* (Montreal: Harvest House, 1975).

Colton, Timothy J., *Big Daddy* (Toronto: University of Toronto Press, 1980).

Commager, Henry Steele, *Freedom and Order* (Cleveland: World Publishing Company, 1966).

Commons, John R., *The Legal Foundations of Capitalism* (Madison: Wisconsin University Press, 1920).

Corke, S. E., *Land Use Controls in British Columbia: A Comparative Analysis of Provincial Planning Legislation*, Land Policy Paper No. 3 (Toronto: Centre for Urban and Community Studies, University of Toronto, 1982).

Critical Legal Studies Symposium of the Stanford Law Review, 36:1 and 2 (January 1984).

Cullen, Dallas, J. D. Jobson and Rodney Schneck, "Towards the Development of a Canadian-American Scale: A Research Note," in *Canadian Journal of Political Science* 11 (1978).

Cyert, Richard M., ed., *The Management of Nonprofit Organizations* (Lexington, MA: D.C. Heath, 1975).

Dahl, Robert A., *A Preface to Democratic Theory* (Chicago: University of Chicago Press, 1956).

Darroch, A. Gordon, "Another Look at Ethnicity, Stratification and Social Mobility in Canada," in *Canadian Journal of Sociology* 4 (1979).

Daugherty, Arthur B. and Robert C. Otte, *Farmland Ownership in the United States*, Economic Research Service, USDA, Staff Report No. AGES 830311.

Davis, Cary, Carl Haub and Joanne Willette, "U.S. Hispanics: Changing the Face of America," in *Population Bulletin* 38:3.

Dear, Michael and Allan J. Scott, eds., *Urbanization and Urban Planning in Capitalist Society* (New York: Methuen, 1981).

Delafons, John, *Land Use Control in the United States* (Cambridge, Mass.: MIT Press, 1969).

DelGuidice, Dominic and Stephen M. Zacks, "The 101 Governments of Metro Toronto," in Lionel D. Feldman and Michael Goldrick, eds., *Politics and Government of Urban Canada*. 2nd ed. (Toronto: Methuen, 1968).

deLeon, P. and J. Enns, *The Impact of Highways on Metropolitan Dispersion: St. Louis*, RAND Report P-5061 (Santa Monica: RAND Corporation, 1973).

Dennis, Michael and Susan Fish, *Programs in Search of a Policy* (Toronto: Hakkert, 1972).

Devine, Donald, "American Culture and Public Administration," in *Policy Studies Journal* 11:2 (1982).

Dommel, Paul, *The Politics of Revenue Sharing* (Bloomington: Indiana University Press, 1974).

Downs, Anthony, *An Economic Theory of Democracy* (New York: Harper, 1957).

Driedger, Elmer A., *The British North America Acts of 1867 to 1975* (Ottawa: Minister of Supply and Services, 1976).

Duncan, Allen and Nancy G. Duncan, "A Cultural Analysis of Urban Residential Landscapes in North America: The Case of the Anglophone Elite," in John A. Agnew, John Mercer and David E. Sopher, eds., *The City in Cultural Context* (Boston: Allan and Unwin, 1984).

Dworkin, Ronald, *Taking Rights Seriously* (London: Duckworth, 1977).

Easterbrook, W. T. and Hugh G. J. Aitken, *Canadian Economic History* (Toronto: Macmillan, 1963).

Edmonston, Barry, Michael A. Goldberg and John Mercer, "Urban Form in Canada and the United States: An Examination of Urban Density Gradients," in *Urban Studies* 22 (1985).

Elazar, Daniel J. and Joseph Zikmund, eds., *The Ecology of American Political Culture* (New York: T. Crowell Co., 1975).

Elkins, David J. and Richard Simeon, *Small Worlds: Provinces and Parties in Canadian Political Life* (Toronto: Methuen, 1980).

Ellickson, Robert C., "Cities and Homeowners Associations," 130 U. Penna. L.Rev. 6 (June 1982), pp. 1519–80.

Environment Canada, *For Land's Sake* (1980).

Fearn, Gordon, F. N.., *Canadian Social Organization* (Toronto: Holt, Rinehart and Winston, 1973).

Elliot J. Feldman, *Concorde and Dissent: Explaining High Technology Project Failures in Britain and France* (New York: Cambridge University Press, 1985).

———, "Comparative Public Policy: Field or Method?" *Comparative Politics* (January 1978).

——— and Jerome Milch, *The Politics of Canadian Airport Development: Lessons for Federalism* (Durham: Duke University Press, 1983).

———, "Coordination and Control: The Life and Death of the Ministry of State for Urban Affairs," in Lionel D. Feldman, ed., *Politics and Government of Urban Canada*. 4th ed. (Toronto: Methuen, 1981).

———, *Technocracy versus Democracy: The Comparative Politics of International Airports* (Boston: Auburn House, 1982).

Friedenberg, Edgar Z., *Deference to Authority: The Case of Canada* (Armonk, NY: M.E. Sharpe, 1980).

Friedman, Thomas and Paul Solman, "Is American Management Too Selfish?" in *Forbes* (January 17, 1983).

Fry, August J., *On the Battle of Stoney Creek and Other Allegories* (Amsterdam: Free University of Amsterdam, 1982).

Galbraith, John Kenneth, *The New Industrial State*. 2nd ed. (Boston: Houghton Mifflin, 1971).

Gawthorp, Louis C., *Bureaucratic Behavior in the Executive Branch: An Analysis of Organizational Change* (New York: Free Press, 1969).

George, Alexander, "Case Studies and Theory Development: The Method of Structured, Focused Comparison," in Paul Gordon Lauren, ed., *Diplomacy: New Approaches* (New York: Free Press, 1979).

Gertler, Len, "The Challenge of Public Policy Research," *Canadian Journal of Regional Science* 2:1 (1979).

Gibbins, Roger, *Regionalism, Territorial Politics in Canada and the United States* (Toronto: Butterworths, 1982).

Glazebrook, G. P. de T., *A History of Transportation in Canada*, Vols. 1–2 (Toronto: University of Toronto Press, 1964).

Glazer, Nathan and Daniel Patrick Moynihan, eds., *Ethnicity: Theory and Experience* (Cambridge: Harvard University Press, 1975).

———, "Individualism and Equality in the United States," in Herbert Gans et al., eds., *On the Making of Americans: Essays in Honor of David Riesman* (Philadelphia: University of Pennsylvania Press, 1979).

Goldberg, Michael A., "The BNA Act, NHA, CMHC, MSUA, etc.: 'Nymophobia' and the On-Going Search for An Appropriate Canadian Housing and Urban Development Policy," in Michael Walker, ed., *Canadian Confederation at the Crossroads* (Vancouver: The Fraser Institute, 1978).

———, "Housing and Land Prices in Canada and the U.S.," in L. B. Smith and

M. Walker, eds., *Public Property: The Habitat Debate Continued* (Vancouver: Fraser Institute, 1977).

—— and John Mercer, "The Fiscal Condition of American and Canadian Cities," in *Urban Studies* 21 (1984).

——, *Continentalism Challenged: The Myth of the North American City* (Vancouver: The University of British Columbia Press, 1986).

—— and Peter Horwood, *Zoning: Its Cost and Relevance for the 1980s* (Vancouver: The Fraser Institute, 1980).

—— and Michael Y. Seelig, "Canadian Cities: The Right Deed for the Wrong Reason," in *Planning* 41:3 (1975).

Goldstein, Walter, ed., *Planning, Politics and the Public Interest* (New York: Columbia, 1978).

Goodsell, Charles T., *The Case for Bureaucracy: A Public Administration Polemic* (Chatham, N.J.: Chatham House, 1983).

Gordon, Milton, *Assimilation in American Life* (New York: Oxford University Press, 1964).

——, *Human Nature, Class and Ethnicity* (New York: Oxford University Press, 1978).

Greenstone, J. David, ed., *Public Values and Private Power in American Politics* (Chicago: University of Chicago Press, 1982).

Guillot, Eliane, "LRT Design Choices: Edmonton and Calgary," in *Traffic Quarterly* 37:3 (1983).

Hardin, Herschel, *A Nation Unaware: The Canadian Economic Culture* (Vancouver: J.J. Douglas, 1974).

Harris, Richard, *Class and Housing Tenure in Modern Canada*, Research Paper No. 153 (Toronto: Centre for Urban and Community Studies, University of Toronto, May 1984).

Harrison, Fred, "U.S. has own set of investment controls, Ottawa points out," in *Financial Post* (July 3, 1982).

Harvey, David, "The Political Economy of Urbanization in Advanced Capitalist Societies," in G. Gappert and H. Rose, eds., *The Social Economy of Cities* (Beverly Hills: Sage Publications, 1975).

Haveman, Robert H., *The Economics of the Public Sector*, 2nd ed. (New York: Wiley, 1976).

Hawaii Housing Authority v. Midkiff, 104 S.Ct. 2321 (1984).

Hayes, Robert H. and William J. Abernathy, "Managing Our Way to Economic Decline," *Harvard Business Review* (July–August, 1980).

—— and David A. Garvin, "Managing as if Tomorrow Mattered," *Harvard Business Review* (May–June 1982).

Hellyer, Paul, *Report of the Task Force on Housing and Urban Development* (Ottawa: Queen's Printer, 1969).

Henry, Frances, *The Dynamics of Racism in Toronto*, Research Report (Downsview: York University, 1978).

Herberg, Will, *Protestant-Catholic-Jew* (Garden City, NY: Anchor Books,1960).

Herman, Edward S., *Corporate Control, Corporate Power* (Cambridge: Cambridge University Press, 1981).

Highbee, Edward, "Centre Cities in Canada and the United States," in J. W. Watson and T. O'Riordan, eds., *The American Environment: Perceptions and Policies* (New York: John Wiley and Sons, 1976).

Hirschman, Albert, *Exit, Voice and Loyalty: Responses to Decline in Firms, Organizations and States* (Cambridge: Harvard University Press, 1970).

Hodge, Gerald D. and Mohammed A. Qadeer, *Towns and Villages in Canada* (Toronto: Butterworths, 1983).

Hofstadter, Richard, *The American Political Tradition* (New York: Alfred A. Knopf, 1948).

Hofstede, Geert, *Culture's Consequences: International Differences in Work-Related Values* (Beverly Hills: Sage Publications, 1980).

Horowitz, Gad, "Conservatism, Liberalism and Socialism in Canada: An Interpretation," in *Canadian Journal of Economics and Political Science* 32:2 (1966).

Horowitz, Irving Louis, "The Hemisphere Connection," in *Queen's Quarterly* 80 (1973).

Horwitz, Morton J., "The History of the Public/Private Distinction," 130 U. Penna. L.Rev. 6 (June 1982), pp. 1423–28.

Hudson, William E., "The New Federalism Paradox," in *Policy Studies Journal* 8:6 (1980).

Hughes, Jonathan R. T., *The Governmental Habit: Economic Controls from Colonial Times to the Present* (New York: Basic Books, 1977).

Hulchanski, D., "St. Lawrence and False Creek," (Vancouver: School of Planning, University of British Columbia, 1984).

Hunter, Alfred A., *Class Tells: On Social Inequality in Canada* (Toronto: Butterworths, 1981).

Hutcheson, John, *Dominance and Dependency* (Toronto: McClelland and Stewart, 1978).

Hutchinson, R. C., "Religion, Morality and Law in Modern Society," in P. Slater, ed., *Religion and Culture in Canada* (Ottawa: Canadian Corporation for Studies in Religion, 1977).

Inglehart, Ronald, *The Silent Revolution: Changing Values and Political Styles Among Western Publics* (Princeton University Press, 1977).

Inkeles, Alex, "Continuity and Change in the American National Character," in Seymour Martin Lipset, ed., *The Third Century: America as a Post-Industrial Society* (Chicago: University of Chicago Press, 1979).

Jacobs, Jane, *Cities and the Wealth of Nations* (New York: Alfred A. Knopf, 1984).

Johnston, Ronald J., *The American Urban System* (New York: St. Martin's Press, 1982).

———, "Residential Area Characteristics: Research Methods for Identifying Sub-Areas," in David Herbert and Ronald J. Johnston, eds., *Social Areas in Cities* 1 (London: J. Wiley and Son, 1976).

Kain, John F., "Black Suburbanization in the Eighties: A New Beginning or a False Hope?" in J. Quigley and D. Rubinfeld, eds., *An Agenda for Metropolitan America* (Berkeley and Los Angeles: University of California Press, 1985).

———— and John Meyer, *Essays in Regional Economics* (Cambridge, Mass.: Harvard University Press, 1971).

————, *Essays in Urban Spatial Structure* (Cambridge, Mass.: Ballinger, 1975).

Kalbach, Warren E. and Wayne W. McVey, *The Demographic Bases of Canadian Society*, 2nd ed. (Toronto: McGraw-Hill Ryerson, 1979).

Kammen, Michael, *People of Paradox: An Inquiry Concerning the Origins of American Civilizations* (New York: Oxford University Press, 1980).

Kaufman, Herbert, *The Forest Ranger: A Study in Administrative Behavior* (Baltimore: Johns Hopkins Press for Resources for the Future, 1960).

Kehoe, Dalton, et al., *Public Land Ownership: Frameworks for Evaluation* (Lexington, Mass.: Lexington Books, 1976).

Kennedy, Duncan, "The Stages of the Decline of the Public/Private Distinction," 130 U. Penna. L.Rev. 6 (June 1982), pp. 1349–57.

Kim Jae-On and Charles W. Mueller, *Introduction to Factor Analysis*, Sage University Paper series on Quantitative Applications in the Social Sciences (Beverly Hills: Sage Publications, 1978).

King, Preston, *Federalism and Federation* (Baltimore: Johns Hopkins University Press, 1982).

Klare, Karl E., "The Public/Private Distinction in Labor Law," 130 U. Penna. L.Rev. 6 (June 1982), pp. 1358–1422.

Klecka, William R., *Discriminant Analysis*, Sage University Paper series on Quantitative Applications in the Social Sciences (Beverly Hills: Sage Publications, 1980).

Knight, David B., "Canada in Crisis: The Power of Regionalisms," in D. G. Bennett, ed., *Tension Areas of the World* (Champaign, IL: Park Press, 1982).

Lands Directorate, Environment Canada, *Land Use in Canada: Report of the Interdepartmental Task Force on Land-Use Policy* (January 1980).

Laponce, Jean A., "The City Centre as Conflictual Space in the Bilingual City: The Case of Montreal," in Jean Gottman, ed., *Centre and Periphery: Spatial Variation in Politics* (Beverly Hills: Sage, 1980).

Lappin, Ben, "Canadian Jewry and the Identity Crisis," in *Viewpoints* 2 (1967).

Leacy, F. H., ed., *Historical Statistics of Canada*, 2nd ed. (Ottawa: Statistics Canada, 1983).

LeDuc, Lawrence and J. Alex Murray, "Public Opinion and North American Integration: Pragmatic Nationalism," in Jon Pammett and Brian Tomlin, eds., *The Integration Question: Political Economy and Public Policy in Canada and North America* (Toronto: Addison-Wesley, 1984).

Lee, Linda K., *Linkages between Landownership and Rural Land*, Agricultural Information Bulletin 454, Economic Research Service, USDA.

Leman, Christopher K., "The Revolution of the Saints: The Ideology of Privatization and its Consequences for the Public Lands," in Adrian Gamache, ed., *Selling the Federal Forests* (Seattle: College of Forest Resources, University of Washington, 1984).

————, "To Visit is to Preserve," in *Exchange*, Newsletter of the Land Trust Exchange (Winter 1983–84).

————, *The Collapse of Welfare Reform: Political Institutions, Policy, and the Poor in Canada and the United States* (Cambridge, Mass.: MIT Press, 1980).

Levitt, Kari, *Silent Surrender* (Toronto: MacMillan, 1970).

Lewis, James A., *Landownership in the United States, 1978*, Agriculture Information Bulletin No. 435, Economic Research Service, U.S. Department of Agriculture.

Ley, David F., *A Social Geography of the City* (New York: Harper and Row, 1983).

Lijphart, Arend, "The Comparable-Cases Strategy in Comparative Research," *Comparative Political Studies* (July 1975).

Lindblom, Charles E., *Politics and Markets: The World's Economic Systems* (New York: Basic Books, 1977).

Lipset, Seymour M., "The Value Patterns of Democracy: A Case Study in Comparative Analysis," in *American Sociological Review* 28:4 (1963).

————, *Revolution and Counterrevolution* (New York: Anchor Books, 1970).

————, "Revolution and Counterrevolution—Some Comments at a Conference Analyzing the Bicentennial of a Celebrated North American Divorce," in Richard A. Preston, ed., *Perspective on Revolution and Evolution* (Durham: Duke University Press, 1979).

————, *The First New Nation* (New York: Norton, 1979).

————, "Canada and the United States: The Cultural Dimension," in Charles F. Doran and John H. Sigler, eds., *Canada and the United States* (Englewood Cliffs: Prentice-Hall, 1985).

Lithwick, N. H., *Urban Canada: Problems and Prospects* (Ottawa: Central Mortgage and Housing Corporation, 1970).

Lorr, Maurice, *Cluster Analysis for Social Scientists* (San Francisco: Jossey-Bass, 1983).

Lowi, Theodore J., *The End of Liberalism*, 2nd ed. (New York: W.W. Norton, 1979).

Lynn, Laurence E. Jr., *Managing the Public's Business: The Job of the Government Executive* (New York: Basic Books, 1981).

Mark, Jonathan and Michael A. Goldberg, "Neighbourhood Change: A Canadian Perspective," in *The Annals of Regional Science* (forthcoming).

Marr, William L. and Donald G. Paterson, *Canada: An Economic History* (Toronto: Macmillan, 1980).

Masser, Ian, Comparative Planning Studies: A Critical Review," *Town and Regional Planning* 33 (Sheffield, England: Department of Town and Regional Planning, University of Sheffield, 1981).

————, "Some Methodological Considerations," in Philip Booth, ed., *Design and Implementation of Cross-National Research Projects, Town and Regional Planning* 44 (Sheffield, England: Department of Town and Regional Planning, University of Sheffield, 1983).

McCarthy, Eugene J., "American Politics and American Character," in Roger L. Shinn, ed., *The Search for Identity* (New York: Harper and Row, 1964).

McConnell, Grant, *Private Power and American Democracy* (New York: Alfred A. Knopf, 1966).

McLelland, David C., *The Achieving Society* (Princeton: Van Nostrand, 1961).

McNaught, Kenneth, *The Pelican History of Canada* (Harmondsworth, England: Penguin, 1982).

McRoberts, Kenneth and Dale Posgate, *Quebec: Social Change and Political Crisis* (Toronto: McClelland and Stewart, 1980).

Meekison, J. Peter, *Canadian Federalism: Myth or Reality*, 3rd ed. (Toronto: Methuen, 1977).

Meisel, John, "Who Are We: Perceptions in English Canada," *Proceedings of the Conference on the Future of the Canadian Confederation* (Toronto: University of Toronto, 1977).

Mercer, John, "On Continentalism, Distinctiveness and Comparative Urban Geography: Canadian American Cities," *Canadian Geographer* 23 (1979).

—— and John Hultquist, "National Progress Toward Housing and Urban Renewal Goals," in John S. Adams, ed., *Urban Policymaking and Metropolitan Dynamics* (Cambridge: Ballinger, 1976).

—— and Deborah A. Phillips, "Attitudes of Homeowners and the Decisions to Rehabilitate Property," in *Urban Geography* 2 (1981).

——, "Comparing the Reform of Metropolitan Fragmentation, Fiscal Dependency and Political Culture in Canada and the United States" (Syracuse: Department of Geography, Syracuse University, 1982, mimeograph).

Meyer, John R. and Jose A. Gomez-Ibanez, *Autos, Traffic and Cities* (Cambridge: Twentieth Century Funds, 1981).

Meyer, Marshall W., "'Bureaucratic' vs. 'Profit' Organization," in B. Staw and L. L. Cummings, eds., *Research in Organizational Behavior* (Greenwich: JAI Press, 1982).

Meyerson, Martin and Edward Banfield, *Politics, Planning and the Public Interest* (Glencoe, IL.: Free Press, 1955).

Mezzich, Juan E. and Herbert Solomon, *Taxonomy and Behavioral Science: Comparative Performance of Grouping Methods* (New York: Academic Press, 1980).

Michalos, Alex C., "Foundations, Population and Health," in *North American Social Report*, 1 (Boston: D. Reidel, 1982).

Mills, C. Wright, *The Power Elite* (New York: Oxford University Press, 1956).

Mills, E. S., *Studies in the Structure of the Urban Economy* (Baltimore: Johns Hopkins University Press, 1972).

Milner, Henry, *Politics in the New Quebec* (Toronto: McClelland and Stewart, 1978).

Mintzberg, Henry, *The Nature of Managerial Work* (New York: Harper, 1973).

——, *The Structuring of Organizations: A Synthesis of the Research* (Englewood Cliffs: Prentice-Hall, 1979).

Mishler, William, *Political Participation in Canada: Prospects for Democratic Citizenship* (Toronto: Macmillan, 1979).

Mnookin, Robert H., "The Public/Private Dichotomy: Political Disagreement and Academic Repudiation," 130 U. Penna. L.Rev. 6 (June 1982), pp. 1429–40.

Moodley, Kogila, "Canadian Ethnicity in Comparative Perspective: Issues in the Literature," in Jorgen Dahlie and Tissa Fernando, eds., *Ethnicity, Power and Politics in Canada* (Toronto: Methuen, 1981).

Morris, Jan, "Flat City," in *Saturday Night* 99:6 (1984).

Morris, Richard S., *Bum Rap on America's Cities: The Real Causes of Urban Decay* (Englewood Cliffs: Prentice-Hall, 1978).

Morton, William L., *The Critical Years* (Toronto: McClelland and Stewart, 1964).

————, *The Kingdom of Canada* (Toronto: McClelland and Stewart, 1969).

————, *The Canadian Identity*, 2nd ed. (Toronto: University of Toronto Press, 1972).

Muller, Peter, *The Outer City: The Geographical Consequences of the Urbanization of the Suburbs* (Washington: Association of American Geographers, Resource Paper No. 75–2, 1976).

Murray, Michael, "Comparing Public and Private Management: An Exploratory Essay," in *Public Administration Review* (July–August, 1975).

Myrdal, Gunnar, *An American Dilemma: The Negro Problem and Modern Democracy* (New York: Harper and Row, 1944).

Nachmias, David and Ann Lennarson Greer, "Governance Dilemmas in an Age of Ambiguous Authority," in *Policy Sciences* 14 (1982).

Nagata, Judith A., "One Vine, Many Branches: Internal Differentiation in Canadian Ethnic Groups," in Jean Leonard Elliott, ed., *Two Nations, Many Cultures: Ethnic Groups in Canada* (Scarborough: Prentice-Hall, 1979).

Nelson, Richard R. and Sidney G. Winter, *An Evolutionary Theory of Economic Change* (Cambridge: Harvard University Press, 1982).

Nelson, Robert H., "The Public Lands," in Paul R. Portney, ed., *Current Issues in Natural Resource Policy* (Washington: Resources for the Future, 1982).

Newman, Peter C., *The Canadian Establishment*, vols. 1 and 2 (Toronto: McClelland and Stewart, 1975).

Niemi, Albert W. Jr., *U.S. Economic History*, 2nd ed. (Chicago: Rand McNally, 1980).

O'Connor, James, *Accumulation Crisis* (New York: Basil Blackwell, 1984).

Office of Policy Development and Research, *A Survey of Citizen Views and Concerns about Urban Life* (Washington: U.S. Department of Housing and Urban Development, HUD-PDR-306, May 1978).

O'Laughlin, Jay and Paul V. Ellefson, *New Diversified Entrants Among U.S. Wood-Based Companies: A Study of Economic Structures and Corporate Strategy*, Station Bulletin 541-1982, Forestry Series 37, Agricultural Experiment Station, University of Minnesota.

Palm, Risa, *The Geography of American Cities* (New York: Oxford University Press, 1981).

————, "Urban Geography: City Structures," *Progress in Human Geography* 6 (1982).

Parry, Robert L., *Galt, U.S.A.* (Toronto: MacLean-Hunt, 1971).

Pekkanen, John, "The Land, Part 1: Who Owns America?" *Town and Country* (May 1983).

————, "The Land, Part 2: What Does the Future Hold?" *Town and Country* (June 1983).

Pineo, Peter C. and John C. Goyder, "Social Class Identification of National Sub-Groups," in James E. Curtis and William G. Scott, eds., *Social Stratification in Canada* (Scarborough, Ontario: Prentice-Hall, 1973).

———, "The Social Standing of Ethnic and Racial Groupings," in *Canadian Review of Social Anthropology* 14 (1977).

Piper, J., "Saskatoon Robs the Bank," *Ekistics* 233 (1975).

Platt, Rutherford H., "Space and Authority: The Dimensions of Institutional Response," in Kenneth A. Hammond, et al., *Sourcebook on the Environment* (Chicago: University of Chicago Press, 1978).

Polanyi, Karl, *The Great Transformation* (Boston: Beacon Press, 1947).

Poletown Neighborhood Council v. City of Detroit, 410 Mich. 616, 304 N.W. 2nd 455 (1981).

Porter, John, *The Vertical Mosaic* (Toronto: University of Toronto Press, 1965).

Pressman, Jeffrey and Aaron Wildavsky, *Implementation* (Berkeley: California University Press, 1979).

Presthus, Robert, "Aspects of Political Culture and Legislative Behavior: United States and Canada," in Robert Presthus, ed., *Cross-National Perspectives: United States and Canada* (Leiden, Netherlands: E.J. Brill, 1977).

———, *Elites in the Policy Process* (London: Cambridge University Press, 1974).

———, ed., *Cross-National Perspectives: United States and Canada* (Leiden: E.J. Brill, 1977).

Preston, Richard A., ed., *Perspectives on Revolution and Evolution* (Durham: Duke University Press, 1979).

Public Transit Data: American Public Transit Association, Transit Operating Report for Calendar/Fiscal Year 1976 (Washington: APTA, 1976).

Purdy, Harry L., *Transportation Competition and Public Policy in Canada* (Vancouver: University of British Columbia Press, 1972).

Quann, Dorothy, *Racial Discrimination in Housing*, Discussion Paper: Canadian Council on Social Development (Ottawa: C.C.S.D., 1979).

Quigley, John and Daniel Rubinfeld, eds., *An Agenda for Metropolitan America* (Berkeley and Los Angeles: University of California Press, 1985).

Rainey, Hal G., "Public Agencies and Private Firms: Incentive Structures, Goals and Individual Roles," in *Administration and Society* 15:2 (August, 1983).

———, Robert W. Blackoff, and Charles N. Levine, "Comparing Public and Private Organizations," in *Public Administration Review* (March–April, 1976).

Ray, D. Michael and Robert A. Murdie, "Canadian and American Urban Differences," in Brian J. L. Berry, ed., *City Classification Handbook: Methods and Applications* (New York: John Wiley and Sons, 1972).

———, *Canadian Urban Trends: Volume 1, National Perspective* (Toronto: Copp-Clark, 1976).

Reid, John, "Black America in the 1980s," in *Population Bulletin* 37:4 (1982).

Resources Task Force on Constitutional Reform, *Municipal Government in a New Canadian Federal System* (Ottawa: Federation of Canadian Municipalities, 1980).

Richards, John and Larry Pratt, *Prairie Capitalism: Power and Influence in the New West* (Toronto: McClelland and Stewart, 1980).

Richardson, Harry, *The New Urban Economics and Alternatives* (London: PION, 1977).

———, *Urban Economics* (Hinsdale, IL: Dryden Press, 1978).

Richmond, Anthony H., "Immigration and Racial Prejudice in Britain and Canada," in Jean Leonard Elliott, ed., *Two Nations, Many Cultures: Ethnic Groups in Canada* (Scarborough, Ont.: Prentice-Hall, 1979).

Richmond, Dale, "Provincial-Municipal Tax and Revenue Sharing: Reforms Accomplished, 1978 Compared with 1971," in Lionel Feldman, ed., *Politics and Government of Urban Canada*, 4th ed. (Toronto: Methuen, 1980).

Roberts, Lance W., and R. A. Clifton, "Exploring the Ideology of Canadian Multiculturalism," in *Canadian Public Policy* 8 (1982).

Roberts, Marc J. and Jeremy S. Bluhm, *The Choices of Power: Utilities Face the Environmental Challenge* (Cambridge: Harvard University Press, 1981).

Robertson, James O., *American Myth, American Reality* (New York: Hill and Wang, 1980).

Robinson, Ira M., *Canadian Urban Growth Trends* (Vancouver: University of British Columbia Press, 1981).

Robinson, L., "The American Sponge," in *The Canadian Forum* 64:743 (November 1984).

Robson, Brian T., *Urban Social Areas* (London: Oxford University Press, 1981).

Rumsfeld, Donald, "A Politician Turned Executive Surveys Both Worlds," in *Fortune* (September 10, 1979).

Russell, Peter H., *Leading Institutional Decisions* (Toronto: The Macmillan Company of Canada, 1978).

Savas, E. S., *Privatizing the Public Sector: How to Shrink Government* (Chatham, NJ: Chatham House, 1982).

Schnidman, Frank, ed., *The Approval Process: Recreation and Resort Development Experience* (Cambridge, Mass.: Urban Land Institute and Lincoln Institute of Land Policy, 1983).

Schultze, Charles, *The Public Use of the Private Interest* (Washington, D.C.: Brookings Institution, 1977).

Schwartz, Mildred A., *Politics and Territory: The Sociology of Regional Persistence in Canada* (Montreal: McGill-Queen's University Press, 1974).

Sewell, J., "Public Transit in Canada: A Primer," in *City Magazine* 3 (May–June 1978).

Shulman, Norman and R. E. Drass, "Motives and Modes of Internal Migration: Relocation in a Canadian City," in *Canadian Review of Sociology and Anthropology* 16:3 (1979).

Simmons, James W. and Larry S. Bourne, "Defining Urban Places: Differing Concepts of the Urban System," in L. S. Bourne and J. W. Simmons, eds., *Systems of Cities* (New York: Oxford University Press, 1978).

————, *Recent Trends and Patterns in Canadian Settlement, 1976–1981*, Major Report No. 23, Centre for Urban and Community Studies, University of Toronto, 1984.

Simon, Herbert, *The New Science of Management Decision*, rev. ed. (Englewood Cliffs: Prentice- Hall, 1977).

————, "The Challenge of Canadian Ambivalence," in *Queen's Quarterly* 88:1 (1981).

Smith, Allan, "Metaphor and Nationality in North America," in *Canadian Historical Review* 51 (1970).

―――, "National Images and National Maintenance: The Ascendancy of the Ethnic Idea in North America," in *Canadian Journal of Political Science* 14 (1981).

―――, "American Culture and the English Canadian Mind at the End of the Nineteenth Century," in *Journal of Popular Culture* 4:3 (1971).

―――, "The Myth of the Self-Made Man in English Canada, 1850–1914," in *Canadian Historical Review* 59 (1978).

Smith, Edward Conrad, ed., *The Constitution of the United States*, 11th ed. (New York: Harper and Row, 1979).

Smith, Lawrence B. and Michael Walker, eds., *Public Property? The Habitat Debate Continued: Essays on the Price, Ownership and Government of Land* (Vancouver: Fraser Institute, 1977).

Smith, Peter J., "Public Goals and the Canadian Environment," in *Plan Canada* 11:1.

Sonnenfeld, Jeffrey, *Corporate Views of the Public Interest: Perceptions of the Forest Products Industry* (Boston: Auburn House, 1981).

Southern Burlington County NAACP v. Township of Mt. Laurel, 92 N.J. 158, 456 A.2n 390 (1983).

Spann, Robert M., "Public Versus Private Provision of Governmental Services," in Thomas E. Borcherding, ed., *Budgets and Bureaucrats: the Sources of Government Growth* (Durham: Duke University Press, 1977).

Stark, Werner, *The Social Bond: An Investigation into the Bases of Law-Abidingness* (New York: Fordham University Press, 1976).

Statistics Canada, *Perspective Canada II, A Compendium of Social Statistics* (1977).

―――, *Canada Yearbook 1980–81* (Ottawa: Ministry of Supply and Services, 1981).

Steinfels, Peter, *The Neo-Conservatives* (New York: Simon and Schuster, 1979).

Stelter, Gilbert, "The City-Building Process in Canada," in Gilbert A. Stelter and Alan F. J. Artibise, eds., *Shaping the Urban Landscape: Aspects of the Canadian City-Building Process* (Ottawa: Carleton University Press, 1982).

Stevenson, Garth, *Unfulfilled Union* (Toronto: Gage Publishing Co., 1982).

Stewart, Walter, *As They See Us* (Toronto: McClelland and Stewart, 1977).

Stone, Christopher D., "Corporate Vices and Corporate Virtues: Do Public/Private Distinctions Matter?" 130 U. Penna. L.Rev. (June 1982), p. 1443.

Swan, Hedley, *Federal Lands: Their Use and Management*, Land Use in Canada Series, No. 11, Lands Directorate, Environment Canada (March 1978).

Taylor, Charles, *Radical Tories: The Conservative Tradition in Canada* (Toronto: Anansi, 1982).

Taylor, D. G., P. B. Sheatsley and A. M. Greeley, "Attitudes Towards Racial Integration," *Scientific American* 238:6 (1978).

The Constitution Act, 1982 (Ottawa: Minister of Supply and Services, 1982).

Thornton, Arlavel and Deborah Freedman, "The Changing American Family," in *Population Bulletin* 38:4 (1983).

Transportation Research Board, "State Highway Programs Versus the Spending Powers of Congress," in *Research Results Digest* no. 136 (Washington: Transportation Research Board, 1982).

Trofimenkoff, Susan Mann, *The Dream of a Nation: A Social and Intellectual History of Quebec* (Toronto: Macmillan, 1983).

Trudeau, Pierre Elliott, *Federalism and the French Canadians* (Toronto: University of Toronto Press, 1968).

Tupper, Allan and G. Bruce Doern, eds., *Public Corporations and Public Policy in Canada* (Montreal: Institute for Research on Public Policy, 1981).

Turkel, G., "Privatism and Orientations Toward Political Action," in *Urban Life* 9:2 (1980).

Truman, Tom, "A Critique of Seymour M. Lipset's Article, 'Value Differences, Absolute or Relative: The English Speaking Democracies,'" *Canadian Journal of Political Science* 4:1 (1971).

———, "A Scale for Measuring a Tory Streak in Canada and the United States," *Canadian Journal of Political Science* 10 (1977).

Unger, Roberto Mangabeira, *The Critical Legal Studies Movement* (Cambridge: Harvard University Press, 1983).

Urbanics Consultants, "A Study of the Market Development Opportunities in the LRT South Corridor" (Calgary: Planning Department, City of Calgary, 1978).

Urquhart, M. C. and K. A. H. Buckley, eds., *Historical Statistics of Canada* (Toronto: Macmillan, 1965).

U.S. Advisory Commission on Intergovernmental Relations, *The Federal Role in the Federal System: The Dynamics of Growth* (Washington: U.S. Government Printing Office, 1980 and 1981).

U.S. Department of Agriculture, Forest Service, *The Private Forest-Land Owners of the United States*, Resource Bulletin WO-1, 1982.

U.S. Department of Commerce, Bureau of the Census, *Historical Statistics of the United States: Colonial Times to 1970*, parts 1 and 2 (Washington: U.S. Government Printing Office, 1975).

———, *Statistical Abstract of the United States*, 104th ed. (Washington: U.S. Government Printing Office, 1984).

Vallee, Frank G. and D. R. Whyte, "Canadian Society: Trends and Perspectives," in B. Blishen et al., eds., *Canadian Society: Sociological Perspectives* (Toronto: Gage, 1968).

Von Newmann, John and Oskar Morgenstern, *The Mathematical Theory of Games* (Princeton: Princeton University Press, 1963).

Wade, Mason, ed., *Canadian Dualism* (Toronto: University of Toronto Press, 1969).

———, *Regionalism and the Canadian Community, 1867–1967* (Toronto: University of Toronto Press, 1960).

Waldo, Dwight, *The Administrative State*, 2nd ed. (New York: Homes and Meier, 1984, orig. published, 1948).

Walsh, Annmarie H., *The Public's Business: The Politics and Practices of Government Corporations* (Cambridge: MIT Press, 1978).

———, *The Urban Challenge to Government* (New York: Praeger, 1969).

Walton, John, "Comparative Urban Studies," in *International Journal of Comparative Sociology* 22.

Ward, Peter, *White Canada Forever* (Montreal: McGill-Queen's University Press, 1978).

Ward's 1976 Automotive Yearbook, Automotive Industries Statistical Issue, (March 1962).

Warner, Sam Bass, *Streetcar Suburbs* (Cambridge: Harvard University Press, 1962).

Weinberg, Martha Wagner, "Public Management and Private Management, A Diminishing Gap?" in *Journal of Policy Analysis and Management* 3:1 (1983).

The Weyerhaeuser Company, *1984 Annual Report*.

Wheare, K. C., *Federal Government* (London, England: Oxford University Press, 1953).

Whitaker, Reg, "Images of the State in Canada," in Leo Pantich, ed., *The Canadian State: Political Economy and Political Power* (Toronto: University of Toronto Press, 1977).

White, Morton and Lucia White, *The Intellectual Versus the City* (Cambridge: Harvard University Press, 1962).

Wildavsky, Aaron, "Rescuing Policy Analysis from PPBS," in Robert H. Haveman and Julius Margolis, eds., *Public Expenditures and Policy Analysis* (Chicago: Markham Publishers, 1970).

Williamson, Oliver E., *Markets and Hierarchies Analysis and Antitrust Implications* (New York: Free Press, 1975).

————, "The Economics of Internal Organization: Exit and Voice in Relation to Markets and Hierarchies," in *American Economic Review* 66:2 Proceedings Issue (May 1976).

Wilson, James Q., ed., *The Politics of Regulation* (New York: Basic Books, 1980).

Winks, Robin W., *The Blacks in Canada: A History* (Montreal: McGill-Queen's University Press, 1971).

Wirick, Ronald G., "Paradoxes in Recent Canadian-American Personal Savings Behavior: Towards a 'Permanent' Resolution," (London, Ontario: Department of Economics, University of Western Ontario, May 1982, mimeograph).

Woodcock, George, *The Canadians* (Cambridge: Harvard University Press, 1979).

Wunderlich, Gene, "Land Ownership: A Status of Facts," in *Natural Resources Journal* 19:1 (January 1979).

————, "The Facts of Agriculture Leasing," in J. Peter De Braal and Gene Wunderlich, eds., *Rents and Rental Practices in U.S. Agriculture*, Economic Research Service, U.S. Department of Agriculture, 1983.

Yearwood, R. M. "Land Speculation and Development: American Attitudes," in *Plan Canada* 9:1 (1968).

Yeates, Maurice, *Main Street: Windsor-Quebec City* (Toronto: Macmillan, 1975).

————, *North American Urban Patterns* (New York: J. Wiley and Sons, 1980).

————, *Main Street: Concentration and Deconcentration in the Windsor-Quebec City Axis* (Ottawa: Lands Directorate, Environment Canada, 1985).

Part II: Planning and Controlling Cities

Anchour, Dominique, *Finances Municipales en Transition* (Chicoutimi, Quebec: Gaetan Morin & Assoc., Ltée., 1978).

Architectural Forum, Special Issue: "Boston," 120:6 (June 1964).

Aubin, Henry, *City for Sale* (Montreal: Editions L'Etincelle with Jos. Lorimer, Toronto, 1972).

Audet, R. and A. Le Henaff, *Land Planning Framework of Canada: An Overview*, Working Paper No. 28, (Ottawa: Ministry of Supply and Services for the Land Use Policy and Research Branch, Lands Directorate, Environment Canada, 1984).

Baltzell, E. Digby, *Puritan Boston and Quaker Philadelphia* (New York: Free Press, 1979).

Bellamy, David, John H. Pammett, and Donald C. Rowat, *Canadian Provincial Politics*, 2nd edition (Toronto: Methuen, Ltd., 1976).

Boston City Planning Board, "Preliminary Report, 1950: General Plan for Boston" (Boston: December 1950).

Boston Globe, Special Edition, "The Livable City? Surging Growth Confronts Boston's Legacy," November 11, 1984.

Boston Housing Authority, Urban Redevelopment Division, New York Streets Redevelopment Project, "Expressways to Everywhere" (Boston: The Authority, January, 1955).

———, "The West End Project Report" (Boston: The Authority, 1953).

Boston Society of Architects and Greater Boston Chamber of Commerce, "Change and Growth in Central Boston," May 1984.

Bourne, Larry S., "Planning for the Toronto Region: By Whom and for Whom," *Plan Canada* 24:3–4 Special Issue: *Ontario Planned?* (December 1984).

Bradbury, Katherine L., "Urban Decline and Distress: An Update," in *New England Economic Review* (July–August 1984).

——— and Anthony Downs, *Urban Decline and the Future of American Cities* (Washington, D.C.: The Brookings Institute, 1982).

——— and John Yinger, "Making Ends Meet: Boston's Budget in the 1980's,": *New England Economic Review* (March/April 1984), pp. 18–28.

Bratt, Rachel G., "Housing for Low Income People: A Preliminary Comparison of Existing and Potential Supply Strategies," *Journal of Urban Affairs* 7:3 (Summer 1985), pp. 1–18.

———, "People and their Neighborhoods: Attitudes and Policy Implications," in Philip Clay and Robert Hollister, *Neighborhood Policy and Planning* (Lexington, Mass.: The Lexington Press, 1983), pp. 133–150.

Burchell, Robert W. and George Sternlieb, eds., *Planning Theory in the 1980's: A Search for Future Directions* (New Brunswick, NJ: Center for Urban Policy Research, 1978).

——— and David Listokin, eds., *Energy and Land Use* (New Brunswick, NJ: Center for Urban Policy Research, 1982).

Burgess, Ernest, "The Growth of the City: An Introduction to a Research Project," in Robert E. Park et al., eds., *The City* (Chicago: The University of Chicago Press, 1925).

Canadian Census, Census Tracts: Montreal (Ottawa: Statistics Canada).

Carter, Luther C., *The Florida Experience: Land and Water Policy in a Growth State* (Baltimore: Johns Hopkins University Press for Resources for the Future, 1974).

Choko, Marc H., "Pour une analyse comparative des conséquences de la restauration et de la démolition-reconstruction," *Actualité immobilière* 8:3 (Autumn 1984), pp. 29–35.

———, *Crise de logement et capitale immobilier à Montréal: le redéveloppement centre ville de 1957 à nos jours et ses conséquences* (Paris: Université de Paris VIII, 1981) (unpublished dissertation).

Christian, William and Colin Campbell, *Political Parties and Ideologies in Canada: Liberals, Conservatives, Socialists and Nationalists* (Toronto: McGraw-Hill Ryerson, 1974).

Clay, Philip, *Neighborhood Revitalization: The Recent Experience in Large American Cities* (Cambridge, Mass.: The MIT Press, 1978).

Collin, Jean-Pierre, "Développement urbain et coût des services publics régionnaux," *Institut National de Recherche Scientifique-Urbanisation*, document #28 (March 1982).

———, "Dossier PIQA: L'Evolution des programmes de rénovation urbaine," (unpublished).

Commission de Transport, Communauté Urbaine de Montréal, "Mobilité des personnes dans la région de Montréal, 1982; enquête origine-destination régionale exécutée à l'automne 1982" (December 1983).

———, "Rapport annuel T.T.L. pour l'année 1984."

Commission des citoyens pour l'avenir de Montréal, "Centre-ville: les gens se prononçent!" (Sauvons Montréal, 1977).

Corporation de Recherches Economiques, Ltée, "Etude générale de rénovation urbaine," June 1961. (Montreal urban renewal plan).

Couzin, Michael and George K. Lewis, *Boston: A Geographical Portrait* (Cambridge, Mass.: Ballinger Publishing Co., 1976).

Cullingworth, Barry, "The Provincial Role in Planning and Development," *Plan Canada* 24:3–4 (December 1984), Special Issue: *Ontario Planned?*

Dansereau, Francine, "La rénovation urbaine comme pratique d'exception," (Montreal: 1974), (unpublished).

———, "Montréal les aléas de la rénovation urbaine," *Neuf 50* (July–August 1974), pp. 28–32.

Doolittle, Fred C. et al., *Future Boston: Patterns and Perspectives* (Cambridge, Mass.: Joint Center for Urban Studies of M.I.T. and Harvard University, 1982).

Doxiodis, C. A., *Ecumenopolis: The Settlement of the Future*, Research Report No. 1 (Athens: Athens Center for Ekistics, 1967).

Environmental Protection Agency, "Transportation Control Plan for the Metropolitan Boston Interstate Air Quality Region" (1975).

Feldman, Elliot J., "Patterns of Failure in Government Megaprojects: Economics, Politics and Participation in Industrial Democracies," in Samuel P. Huntington and Joseph S. Nye, Jr., eds., *Global Dilemmas* (Cambridge and Washington: Harvard University Center for International Affairs and University Press of America, 1985).

Firey, Walter, *Land Use in Central Boston* (Cambridge, Mass.: Harvard University Press, 1947).

Fishman, Richard P., "Public Land Banking: Examination of Management Technique," in Randall W. Scott, ed., *Management and Control of Growth*, Volume III (Washington: Urban Land Institute, 1975).

Gans, Herbert, *The Urban Villagers: Group and Class in the Life of Italian-Americans* (New York: The Free Press, 1962).

Gertler, Len O., *Regional Planning in Canada: A Planner's Testament* (Montreal: Harvest House, 1972).

—— and Ron Crowley, *Changing Canadian Cities: The Next 25 Years* (Toronto: McClelland and Stewart, 1976).

Goldberg, Michael A., "Value Differences and their Meaning for Urban Development in Canada and the U.S.A.," paper presented to the Comparative Urban History Conference on Canadian-American Urban Development, University of Guelph, Guelph, Ontario, August 24–28, 1982.

—— and Peter Chinloy, *Urban Land Economics* (New York: John Wiley and Sons, 1984).

Greater Boston Economic Study Committee, "A Report on Downtown Boston" (Boston: The Committee, 1959).

Grigsby, William G., *Housing Markets and Public Policy* (Philadelphia: University of Pennsylvania Press, 1963).

Halprin, Kenneth, *Downtown USA* (New York: Whitney Library of Design: Architectural Press of London, 1978).

Handlin, Oscar, *Boston's Immigrants* (Cambridge, Mass.: Harvard University Press, revised edition, 1959).

Harris, John, *Historic Walks in Old Boston* (Chester, Conn.: Globe-Pequot Press, 1982).

Hartz, Louis, *The Founding of New Societies* (New York: Harcourt, Brace & World, 1964).

——, *The Liberal Tradition in America* (New York: Harcourt, Brace & Co., 1955).

Healy, Robert G., and John S. Rosenberg, *Land Use and the States*, 2nd ed. (Washington: Resources for the Future, 1979).

Hero, Alfred O. and Marcel Daneau, eds., *Problems and Opportunities in U.S.-Quebec Relations* (Boulder: Westview Press, 1984).

Hoyt, Homer, *The Structure and Growth of Residential Neighborhoods in American Cities* (Washington, D.C.: U.S. Federal Housing Administration, 1939).

Isberg, Gunnar, "Controlling Growth in the Urban Fringe," in Randall W. Scott, ed., *Management and Control of Growth*, Volume III (Washington: Urban Land Institute, 1975).

Keyes, Langley Carleton, Jr., *The Rehabilitation Planning Game: A Study in the Diversity of Neighborhood* (Cambridge, Mass.: M.I.T. Press, 1969).

Knott, Leonard and Huguette Lavigeuer, *Montreal: The Golden Years* (Toronto: McClelland and Stewart, 1965).

Laboratoire d'Urbanisme, "La Fonction commerciale au centre-ville de Montréal," *Montréal* (winter 1983).

Leonard, H. Jeffrey, *Managing Oregon's Growth: The Politics of Development Planning* (Washington: The Conservation Foundation, 1983).

Lipset, Seymour M., *The First New Nation: The U.S. in Historical and Comparative Perspective* (New York: Basic Books, Inc. 1963).

Lovell's Directory, various years (Montreal: John Lovell).

Lowi, Theodore, J., *American Government: Incomplete Conquest* (New York: Holt, Rinehart and Winston, 1976).

Lupo, Alan, Frank Colcord and Edmund Fowler, *Rites of Way: The Politics of Transportation in Boston and the U.S. City* (Boston: Little Brown and Co., 1971).

Magnuson, Warren and Andrew Sancton, eds., *City Politics in Canada* (Toronto: University of Toronto Press, 1983).

Mandelker, Daniel R., "PUDs and Growth Control: Procedures and Effects," in Randall W. Scott, ed., *Management and Control of Growth*, Volume III (Washington: Urban Land Institute, 1975).

Marsan, Jean-Claude, *Montreal in Evolution* (Montreal: McGill-Queen's University Press, 1981).

Massachusetts Bay Transportation Authority, "Statement of Federal Grants and Loans—approved HUD/DOT/EDA Projects," 1984.

———, Annual Report and Appendix, 1983.

McKenna, Brian and Susan Purcell, *Drapeau: Love Him, Hate Him, Fear Him, Admire Him,—He's Still the Boss!* (Markham, Ont.: Penguin Books Canada, Ltd., 1981).

McQuade, Walter, "Boston: What Can a Sick City Do?" *Fortune* 69:6 (June 1964).

Metropolitan Planning Organization, "The Transportation Plan for the Boston Region" (Boston: February 1983).

Miner, Dallas D., "Agricultural Lands Preservation: A Growing Trend in Open Space Planning," in Randall W. Scott, ed., *Management and Control of Growth* Vol. III (Washington: Urban Land Institute, 1975).

Minerva, Dana D., "The Local Government Comprehensive Planning Act: The Issues," paper prepared for "Change, Challenge and Response: Meeting Florida's Future," Saddlebrook Resort, Wesley Chapel, Florida, October 19–21, 1983.

Mollenkopf, John H., *The Congested City* (Princeton: Princeton University Press, 1983).

Montreal Gazette, "New Wave of Activity Hits Old Montreal," by Shirley Won, August 18, 1984, pp. H1–2.

Morin, Richard, "Réhabilitation de l'Habitat et Devenir des Quartiers Anciens" (Grenoble: Université de Grenoble, Institut de Recherche, 1983) (unpublished dissertation).

Muller, Peter O., *Contemporary Suburban America* (Englewood Cliffs, NJ: Prentice-Hall, Inc., 1981).

Mumford, Lewis, *The City in History* (New York: Harcourt, Brace and World, 1961).

Murphy, Raymond E., *The American City: An Urban Geography* (New York: McGraw-Hill, 1966).

Myers, Phyllis, *So Goes Vermont: An Account of the Development, Passage and Implementation of State Land-Use Legislation in Vermont* (Washington: Conservation Foundation, 1974).

Nader, George A., *Cities of Canada* (Toronto: Macmillan of Canada, 1976).

Polk's Directory, various years, 1947–1984 (Boston: Polk).

Popper, Frank J., *The Politics of Land-Use Reform* (Madison: University of Wisconsin Press, 1981).

Real Estate Research Corporation, "Costs of Sprawl: Detailed Cost Analysis," in Randall W. Scott, ed., *Management and Control of Growth*, Vol. II (Washington: Urban Land Institute, 1975).

Redstone, Louis G., *The New Downtowns: Rebuilding Business Districts* (New York: McGraw-Hill, 1976).

Robin, Martin, *Canadian Provincial Politics: The Party System of the Ten Provinces*, 2nd ed. (Scarborough, Ont.: Prentice-Hall of Canada, Ltd., 1978).

Roy, Jean, *Montréal: Ville d'Avenir: Projet Collectif pour Les Montréalais* (Montreal: Quinze, 1978).

Salisbury, Robert, "Urban Politics: The New Convergence of Power," *The Journal of Politics* 26 (Nov. 1964).

Schnidman, Frank and Jane A. Silverman, eds., *Management and Control of Growth, Vol. V: Updating the Law* (Washington: Urban Land Institute, 1980).

—— and Rufus C. Young, Jr., eds., *Management and Control of Growth, Vol. IV: Techniques in Application* (Washington: Urban Land Institute, 1978).

Scott, Randall, David J. Brower and Dallas D. Miner, eds., *Management and Control of Growth, Vols. II, III, and IV: Issues, Techniques, Problems and Trends* (Washington: Urban Land Institute, 1975).

Service d'Urbanisme, "Ville de Montréal," *Centre ville*, Bulletin Technique no. 3 (August 1964).

Shaw, George Bernard, ed., *Fabian Essays in Socialism* (Gloucester, MA: Peter Smith, 1967).

Smiley, Donald V., *Canada in Question: Federalism in the Eighties*, 3rd ed. (Toronto: McGraw-Hill Ryerson, 1980).

La Société d'Architecture de Montréal, *Découvrir Montréal* (Montreal: Les Editions du Jour, Inc., 1975).

La Société de Patrimoine Urbain de Montréal, "Action Plan," (Montreal, 1980).

Tunnard, Christopher and Boris Pushkarev, *Man-Made America: Chaos or Control* (New Haven: Yale University Press, 1963).

U.S. Department of Commerce, Bureau of the Census, Censuses of Population and Housing, Census Tracts: Boston, Standard Metropolitan Statistical Area, 1950, 1960, 1970, 1980.

U.S. Department of Housing and Urban Development, "The Dynamics of Neighborhood Change," prepared for the Office of Policy Development and Research by the Real Estate Research Corporation, Washington, D.C., 1975.

Urban Massachusetts Transportation Act of 1964.

Ward, D., "The Industrial Revolution and the Emergence of Boston's Central Business District," *Economic Geography* 42 (1966), pp. 157–71.

Whitehill, Walter Muir, *Boston: A Topographical History* (Cambridge: Harvard University Press, 1968).

Whyte, William Foote, *Streetcorner Society: The Social Structure of an Italian Slum*, 2nd ed. (Cambridge: Harvard University Press, 1955).

Wood, Robert C., *1400 Governments: The Political Economy of the New York Metropolitan Region* (New York: Doubleday Anchor Books, 1961).

Woods, Robert, ed., *The City Wilderness* (Cambridge, Houghton-Mifflin Co., 1898).

——— and Albert J. Kennedy, *The Zone of Emergence* (Cambridge: MIT Press, 1962).

Wronski, Wojciech and John G. Turnbull, "The Toronto-Centered Region," *Plan Canada* 24:3–4 December 1984, Special Issue: *Ontario Planned?*

Yudis, Anthony J., 1984: A Year to Plan, Take Stock," *Boston Globe* (December 30, 1984), pp. A29–30.

Part III: Using and Abusing Undeveloped Land: Beyond The Fringe

Adams, Thomas C., and Richard C. Smith, *Review of the Logging Residue Problem and its Reduction Through Marketing Practices*, General Technical Report PNW-48, Forest Service, USDA 1976.

Anderson, R. F., M. R. Greenberg and R. J. Nardi, *A Report on Hazardous Waste Management Facility Siting Criteria*, (New Brunswick, NJ: Middlesex County Planning Board, 1980).

Armson, K. A., *Forest Management in Ontario* (Ontario: Ministry of Natural Resources, 1976).

Auerbach, Stuart, "Lumber Imports Complaint Rejected," *Washington Post* (March 9, 1983).

Bacaw, Lawrence S. and James R. Milkey, "Overcoming Local Opposition to Hazardous Waste Facilities: the Massachusetts Approach," in *Harvard Environmental Review* 6 (1982).

Bardach, Eugene and Robert Kagan, *Going by the Book: The Problem of Regulatory Unreasonableness* (Philadelphia: Temple University Press, 1982).

Beuter, John H., K. Norman Johnson and H. Lynn Scheurman, *Timber for Oregon's Tomorrow: An Analysis of Reasonably Possible Occurrences*, Research Bulletin 19, January 1976 (Corvallis, OR: Forest Research Laboratory, School of Forestry, Oregon State University).

Bianco, Anthony, "The Georgia Pacific Story," (four parts) *Willamette Week* (March 12, 19 and 26, April 2, 1979).

Blue Ribbon Panel on Wildlife and Forestry, National Wildlife Federation, *An Assessment of the Weyerhaeuser Company's Forestry Operations in Southwestern Arkansas and Southeastern Oklahoma* (Washington: National Wildlife Federation, 1982).

Bosselman, Fred and David Callies, *The Quiet Revolution in Land Use Controls: Summary Report*, Prepared for the Council on Environmental Quality, (Washington: U.S. Government Printing Office, 1971).

Bowman, Ann O., "Explaining State Responses to the Hazardous Waste Problem,: in *Hazardous Waste* (November 1984).

Brown, George W., "Oregon's Forest Practices Act: An Early Appraisal," *Journal of Forestry* (December 1978).

Bruner, William E., and Perry R. Hagenstein, *Alternative Forest Policies for the Pacific Northwest*, Pacific Northwest Regional Commission, June 1981.

Canadian Council of Resource and Environment Minister, *Forestry Imperatives for Canada: A Proposal for Forest Policy in Canada*, May 1979.

Canadian Institute of Forestry, "A Case for Improved Forest Management in Canada," *Forestry Chronicle* (February 1984).

Canadian Pulp and Paper Association, *Intensive Forest Management Practices in the Southeastern United States*, a report on the Forest Management Group's Study Tour of the Southeastern United States, February 16–28, 1978.

Chandler, Marsha A. and William M. Chandler, *Public Policy and Provincial Politics* (Toronto: McGraw-Hill, 1979).

Clawson, Marion, *Decision-Making in Timber Production, Harvest and Marketing* (Washington: Resources for the Future, 1977).

———, "America's Forests in the Long Sweep of History," in *Science* (June 1979).

Congress of the United States, Office of Technology Assessment, *Wood Use: U.S. Competitiveness and Technology*. vol. 2 (1983–4).

Conway, Steven, *Logging Practices: Principles of Timber Harvesting Systems* (San Francisco: Miller Freeman, 1976).

Dahl, Robert A. and Edward R. Tufte, *Size and Democracy* (Stanford: Stanford University Press, 1973).

Dana, Samuel Trask and Sally K. Fairfax, *Forest and Range Policy* (New York: McGraw-Hill, 1980).

Davis, Kenneth P., *Forest Management: Regulation and Valuation* (New York: McGraw-Hill, 1966).

Day, Robert D., Jr., "The Corporation: Private Forestry's Future?" in *Journal of Forestry* (October 1980).

Doherty, Michael, "British Columbia: Gray Times for Environmentalists," *Sierra* (September/October, 1984).

Dorsey, Anthony H. J., Michael W. McPhee and Sam Sydneysmith, *Salmon Protection and the B.C. Coastal Forest Industry: Environmental Regulations as a Bargaining Process* (Vancouver: Westwater Institute, University of British Columbia, 1980).

Duchacek, Ivo D., *The Territorial Dimension of Politics* (Boulder: Westview, 1976).

Duerr, William A., Dennis Teeguarden, Neils B. Christiansen and Sam Guttenberg, *Forest Resource Management: Decision-Making Principles and Cases* (Philadelphia: Saunders, 1979).

Elazar, Daniel J., *American Federalism, A View From the States* (New York: Thomas Y. Crowell, 1966).

Environmental Council of Alberta, *The Environmental Effects of Forestry Operations in Alberta* (February 1979).

Estrin, David, "Siting Hazardous Waste Disposal Facilities," in *Proceedings of the 27th Ontario Industrial Waste Conference* (Toronto: Ontario Ministry of the Environment, 1980).

Feldman, Elliot J., *A Practical Guide to the Conduct of Field Research in the Social Sciences* (Boulder: Westview Press, 1981).

―――― and Jerome Milch, *Technocracy versus Democracy: The Comparative Politics of International Airports* (Boston: Auburn House, 1982).

――――, "Comparative Public Policy: Field or Method?" *Comparative Politics* (January 1978).

Fight, Roger D., K. Norman Johnson, Kent P. Connaughton and Robert W. Sassaman, *Roadless Area Intensive Management Tradeoffs on Western National Forests*, (Forest Service: USDA, October 1978).

Forest Practices Act Technical Work Group, *Meeting Water Quality Objectives on State and Private Forest Lands Through the Oregon Forest Practices Act*, report prepared for the State Forester, Oregon State Department of Forestry, August 1978.

Forest Service, U.S. Department of Agriculture, *An Assessment of the Forest and Range Land Situation in the United States*, Forest Resource Report, No. 22, October 1982.

――――, "National Forest Timber Management in the Pacific Southwest Region," *Pacific Southwest Log* (December 1982).

――――, *National Forest Landscape Management*, vols. 1 and 2 (Agricultural Handbooks nos. 434, 462).

Forestry Chronicle, "Forest Policy Development" (April 1984).

Frohnmayer, Dave, "A New Look at Federalism: The Theory and Implications of 'Dual Sovereignty,'" in *Environmental Law* 12:4 (Summer 1982).

Garreau, Joel, *The Nine Nations of North America* (New York: Avon, 1981).

Godbout, Claude, *Rapport de fin de mandat du groupe de conseilliers en gestion des forets (COGEF)*, (Ministère de l'Energie et des Ressources, Gouvernement du Québec, April 21, 1981).

Hartz, Louis, *The Liberal Tradition in America*, (New York: Harcourt, Brace, Jovanovich, 1955).

Hays, Samuel P., *Conservation and the Gospel of Efficiency: The Progressive Conservation Movement, 1890–1920* (Cambridge: Harvard University Press, 1959).

Healy, Robert C. and James L. Short, *The Market for Rural Land: Trends, Issues and Policies* (Washington: Conservation Foundation, 1981).

Hearnden, K. W., "The Case of the Unit Forester," *The Professional Forester* 43 (June 1970).

――――, "Growing the Second Forest in Ontario," in *Proceedings of Ontario Conference on Forest Regeneration* (Ontario: Ministry of Natural Resources, 1978).

Higginbotham, "Environmental Constraints in Increasing Canadian Forest Products Supplies," in Frank J. Convery and Boyd R. Strain, *U.S. Dependency on Canadian Natural Resources: Extent and Significance* (Durham, NC: Canadian Studies Institute, 1979).

Hough, Stansbury and Associates, Ltd., for Ministry of Natural Resources, Province of Ontario, *Design Guidelines for Forest Management*, 1976.

Jackson, David H. and Kathleen O. Jackson, "National Versus Regional Control of Natural Resource Policy: A Comparative Study of the United States and Canada," in *Public Land Law Review* 2 (1981).

Kaufman, Herbert, *The Forest Ranger: A Study in Administrative Behavior* (Baltimore: Johns Hopkins University Press for Resources for the Future, 1960).

Kemper, Robert E. and Lawrence S. Davis, "Costs of Environmental Constraints on Timber Harvesting and Regeneration," *Journal of Forestry* (November 1976).

Key, V. O., Jr., *Southern Politics* (New York: Alfred A. Knopf, 1949).

Klinhoff, R. H., "Six Silvicultural Systems Not Studies in College," *Journal of Forestry* (June 1984).

Krutilla, John V. and Anthony C. Fisher, *The Economics of Natural Environments: Studies in the Valuation of Commodity and Amenity Resources* (Baltimore: Johns Hopkins University Press for Resources for the Future, 1975).

Lambert, Richard S. and Paul Pross, *Renewing Nature's Wealth: A Centennial History of Public Management of Lands, Forests and Wildlife in Ontario, 1763– 1967* (Toronto: Province of Ontario, 1967).

Larkey, Patrick D. and Chandler Stolp, "Reycoot River Drainage: A Proposed Timber Harvest," Intercollegiate Case Clearing House 9-380-730, 1979).

Leman, Christopher K., *The Collapse of Welfare Reform: Political Institutions, Policy and the Poor in Canada and the United States* (Cambridge: MIT Press, 1980).

———, "The Canadian Forest Ranger: Bureaucratic Centralism and Private Power in Three Provincial Natural Resources Agencies," paper presented at the annual meeting of the Canadian Political Science Association, Halifax, NS, May 1981.

———, "Forest Planning and Field Management in Quebec: A Survey and Case Study," paper presented to the Canadian Study Group, University Consortium for Research on North America, October, 1979.

———, "The Forgotten Fundamental: Successes and Excesses of Direct Government," in Michael Lund and Lester Salamon, eds., *The Tools of Public Policy* (Washington: Urban Institute Press, forthcoming).

———, "Forest Planning and Field Management in Quebec: A Survey and Case Study," a paper presented to the Canadian Study Group, University Consortium for Research on North America, October 1979.

———, "U.S.-Canadian Outdoor Recreation," in *Resources* (October 1982).

LeMaster, Dennis C., *Decade of Change: The Remaking of Forest Service Statutory Authority During the 1970s* (Westport, CT: Greenwood Press, 1984).

Lembcke, Jerry Lee, "The International Woodworkers of America: an Internal Comparative Study of Two Regions," Ph.D. Thesis, University of Oregon, 1978.

Lester, James P. and Ann O'M. Bowman, *The Politics of Hazardous Waste Management* (Durham: Duke University Press, 1983).

Levin, Martin L. and Barbara Ferman, *The Political Hand: Policy Implementation and Youth Employment Programs* (Elmsord, NY: Pergamon Press, 1985).

Lijphart, Arend, "Consociational Democracy," in *World Politics* (January 1969).

Lindell, Gary R., *Log Export Restrictions of the Western States and British Columbia*, General Technical Report PNW-63, 1978, Forest Service, USDA.

Lockhard, Donald D., "A Summary of the Nova Scotia Herbicide Trial," in *Forestry Chronicle* (December 1983).

Lower, A. R. M., et al., *The North American Assault on the Canadian Forest* (Toronto: Ryerson Press, 1938).

Lowi, Theodore, *The End of Liberalism* (New York: Norton, 1969).

———, "Four Systems of Policy, Politics, and Choice," in *Public Administration Review* 32 (July–August, 1972).

Lundqvist, Lennart J., "Do Political Structures Matter in Environmental Politics: The Case of Air Pollution Controls in Canada, Sweden and the United States," in *Canadian Public Administration* 17 (1974).

Lussier, Louis-Jean, "The Forest Management Plan Operation in Quebec," *Pulp and Paper Canada* (July 1976).

Mahood, Ian, "Speech to Canadian Institute of Foresters, Duncan Chapter," 1983.

Marchak, Patricia, *Green Gold: The Forest Industry in British Columbia* (Vancouver: University of British Columbia Press, 1983).

Marcus, Alfred A. and Associates, *Improving Forest Productivity: Prescribed Burning in the Light of Clean Air Act Visibility Standards* (Seattle: Batelle Human Affairs Research Centers, 1981).

McKinley, Charles, "Guildism and the Oregon State Board of Forestry," in *The Management of Land and Related Water Resources in Oregon: A Study in Administrative Federalism* (Washington: Resources for the Future).

Ministère de L'Energie et des Ressources, Gouvernement du Québec, *Le Point Sur le Rôle et l'Activité du Ministère de l'Energie et des Ressources, Secteur des Terres et Forêts*, May 1981.

Ministère des Terres et Forêts, Gouvernement du Québec, *Rapport au comité ministeriel permanent de l'aménagement du territoire* (April 1976); *Proposition de politique foncière touchant la gestion du domaine publique* (March 1977) and *Exposé Sur la Politique Forestière*, two volumes (1971–72).

———, *Guide d'Aménagement du Milieu Forestier*, June 1977.

Ministry of Forests, Province of British Columbia, "Forest Resource Planning in British Columbia," a brief submitted to the Royal Commission on Forest Resources, September 1975.

———, *Forest Landscape Handbook*, 1981.

———, "Planning Guidelines for Coast Logging Operations," September 29, 1972.

———, "Forest Resource Planning in British Columbia," a brief submitted to the Royal Commission on Forest Resources, September 1975.

Ministry of Natural Resources, Province of Ontario, *Toward the 80s: A Guide to the Organization and Management System* (February 1979).

Morell, David and Christopher Magoiran, *Siting Hazardous Waste Facilities, Local Opposition and the Myth of Preemption* (Cambridge: Ballinger, 1982).

Nelles, H. Vivian, *The Politics of Development: Forest, Mines and Hydroelectric Power in Ontario, 1849–1941* (Toronto: Macmillan of Canada, 1974).

"New Role in Investing for Quebec," in *The New York Times* (August 24, 1981).

Office de Planification et de Développement du Québec, Gouvernement du Québec, *l'Eau et l'Aménagement du Territoire*, 1980.

Office of Technology Assessment, *Wood Use: U.S. Competitiveness and Technology*, 2 vols.

O'Hare, Michael, Lawrence Bacow and Debra Sanderson, *Facility Siting and Public Opposition* (New York: Van Nostrand Reinhold Company, 1983).

———, "Not on My Block You Don't: Facility Siting and the Strategic Importance of Compensation," *Public Policy*, Fall 1977.

O'Laughlin, Jay and Paul V. Ellefson, *New Diversified Entrants Among U.S. Wood-Based Companies: A Study of Economic Structure and Corporate Strategy*, Station Bulletin 541, Agriculture Experiment Station, University of Minnesota, 1982.

Pearse, Peter, "Forest Products," in Carl Beigie and Alfred O. Hero, Jr., eds., *Natural Resources in U.S.-Canadian Relations*, vol. 2 (Boulder: Westview, 1980).

Place, I. C. M., "Forestry in Canada," in *Journal of Forestry* (September 1978).

Pojasek, Robert B., ed., *New and Promising Ultimate Disposal Options, Toxic and Hazardous Waste Disposal*, vol. 4 (Ann Arbor: Ann Arbor Science Publishers, Inc., 1980).

Popovich, Luke, "Reforestation: Paper Work and Real Work," *Journal of Forestry* (August 1979).

Popper, Frank J., "Siting LULUs," *Planning* 47 (April 1981).

Presthus, Robert, "Aspects of Political Culture and Legislative Behavior: United States and Canada," in Robert Presthus, ed., *Cross–National Perspectives* (Leiden, The Netherlands: E.J. Brill, 1977).

Pross, A. P., "The Development of Professions in the Public Service: The Foresters in Ontario," *Canadian Public Administration* 10:3 (September 1967).

Reed, F. L. C., "A Check-up for the Professional Forester," in *Forestry Chronicle* (April 1984).

——— and Associates, Ltd., *Forest Management in Canada*, Information Report FMR-X-102, Forest Management Institute, Environment Canada, January 1978.

Rennsalaer Polytechnic Institute, *Technology for Managing Hazardous Waste* (Albany: New York State Environmental Facilities Corp., 1979).

Robbins, William G., *Lumberjacks and Legislators: Political Economy of the U.S. Lumber Industry, 1890–1941* (College Station, TX: Texas A and M Press, 1982).

———, "Whither the Lumber Industry," address given at Oregon State University, Corvallis, Oregon, March 5, 1985.

Rosenthal, John C. and Robert T. Don, "International Paper Company: Industry as a Land-Use Planner," *Journal of Forestry* (September 1982).

Russakoff, Dale, "Timber Industry is Rooted in Tax Breaks," *Washington Post* (March 24, 1985).

Schallau, Con H., "Can Regulation Contribute to Economic Stability?" *Journal of Forestry* 72:4 (April 1974).

Schattschneider, E. E., *The Semi-Sovereign People: A Realist's View of Democracy in America* (New York: Holt, Rinehart, Winston, 1960).

Schoenfeld, A. Clay, Glen M. Broom and Nancy Bavec, "The Changing Environmental Message of the Forest Industry," *Journal of Forestry* (October 1980).

Schrepfer, Susan, *The Fight to Save the Redwoods: A History of Environmental Reform 1917–1978* (Madison: University of Wisconsin Press, 1983).

Schwantes, Carlos A., *Radical Heritage: Labor, Socialism and Reform in Washington and British Columbia 1855–1917* (Seattle: University of Washington Press, 1979).

Science Council of Canada, *Canada's Threatened Forests*.

Sedjo, Roger A. and Samuel J. Radcliffe, *Postwar Trends in U.S. Forest Products Trade: A Global, National and Regional View* (Washington: Resources for the Future, 1980).

Sharkansky, Ira, *The Maligned States* (New York: McGraw-Hill, 1972).

Simeon, Richard, *Federal-Provincial Diplomacy* (Toronto: University of Toronto Press, 1973).

Smiley, Donald V., "Federal-Provincial Conflict in Canada," in J. P. Meekison, ed., *Canadian Federalism, Myth or Reality?* (Toronto: Methuen, 1977).

Smith, David M., *The Practice of Silviculture* (New York: Wiley Publishers, 7th ed., 1962).

Smith, Kenneth E. "Another View of the South as a Future Timber Source," in *Forest Industries* (August 1982).

Sonnenfeld, Jeffrey A., *Corporate Views of the Public Interest: Perceptions of the Forest Products Industry* (Boston: Auburn House, 1981).

Steen, Harold K., *The U.S. Forest Service: A History* (Seattle: University of Washington Press, 1976).

Stein Basin Study Committee, Province of British Columbia, *The Stein Basin Moratorium Study*, a report submitted to the Environmental and Land Use Committee, December 1975.

Swanson, Diane, "A Tough Decision on the Tahsis," in *ForesTalk* (Summer 1982).

Thurow, Lester, *The Zero-Sum Society* (New York: Basic Books, 1980).

Tsitika Planning Committee, *Tsitika Watershed Integrated Resource Plan*, a report submitted to the Environment and Land Use Committee.

U.S. Environmental Protection Agency, *Logging Roads and Protection of Water Quality*, April 1976.

———, "Decision and Emergency Order Suspending Registrations for the Forest, Rights-of-Way, and Pasture Uses of 2, 4, 5,-T" and "Decision and Emergency Order Suspending Registrations for Certain Uses of Silvex," *Federal Register* (March 15, 1979).

———, *Hazardous Waste Generation and Commercial Hazardous Waste Management Capacity* (Washington, 1980).

———, *Siting of Hazardous Waste Management Facilities and Public Opposition* (Washington, 1979).

Vardaman, James M. and Company, Inc. *Timberland: A New System for Buying and Selling* (no date).

Vaux, Henry C., "State Interventions on Private Forests in California," in Roger A. Sedjo, ed., *Governmental Interventions, Social Needs, and the Management of U.S. Forests* (Washington: Resources for the Future, 1983).

Wilson, James Q., ed., *The Politics of Regulation* (New York: Basic Books, 1980).

Zimmerman, Joseph F., *The Government and Politics of New York State* (New York: New York University Press, 1981).

Part IV. Making Change: Give and Take

Ackerman, B. A., *Reconstructing American Law* (Cambridge: Harvard University Press, 1984).

———, *Private Property and the Constitution* (New Haven: Yale University Press, 1977).

Alonso, W., *Location and Land Use* (Cambridge: Harvard University Press, 1964).

Atkinson, Michael A. and Marsha Chandler, eds., *The Politics of Canadian Public Policy* (Toronto: University of Toronto Press, 1983).

Austin, J. L., *How to do Things with Words*, 3rd ed. (Cambridge: Harvard University Press, 1975).

Bickerton, James and Alain G. Gagnon, "Regional Policy in Historical Perspective: The Federal Role in Regional Economic Development," *American Review of Canadian Studies* (1984).

Borough of Scarborough and the Minister of Housing for Ontario, et al., 67 DLR, 3d 387 (Ont. Div. Ct. 1976).

Castells, M., *The City and the Grass Roots* (London: Edward Arnold, 1984).

Choper, J. H., *Judicial Review and the National Political Process* (Chicago: The University of Chicago Press, 1980).

Clark, Gordon L. and M. Dear, *State Apparatus: Structures and Language of Legitimacy* (Boston and Hemel Hempstead: George Allen and Unwin, 1984).

———, *Judges and the Cities: Interpreting Local Autonomy* (Chicago: The University of Chicago Press, 1985).

——— and M. Dear, "Dimensions of Local State Autonomy," *Environment and Planning* A 13 (1981).

——— "Rights, Property and Community," *Economic Geography* 59 (1982).

Common Cause v. *The State of Maine* (January 7, 1983) Supreme Judicial Court of Maine, 437 A2d 597 (Me. 1981).

Conklin, William E., *In Defense of Fundamental Rights* (The Netherlands: Sitjthoff and Noordhoff, 1979).

Corwin, Edward S., *Court Over Constitution* (Princeton: Princeton University Press, 1983).

Curr v. *The Queen* (1972) SCR 889.

Department of Regional Economic Expansion, Atlantic Region Industrial Parks: An Assessment of Economic Impact," (Ottawa: Department of Regional Economic Expansion, 1979).

Dillon, J., *Commentaries on the Law of Municipal Corporations*, 5th ed. (Boston: Little, Brown, 1911).

Dunham, Allison, "Griggs v. Allegheny County in Perspective: 30 Years of Supreme Court Expropriation Law," 63 *Supreme Court Review* 105 (1962).

Dworkin, R., "Is Wealth a Value?" in *Journal of Legal Studies* 9 (1980).

———, *Taking Rights Seriously* (Cambridge: Harvard University Press, 1978).

Ely, J., *Democracy and Distrust: A Theory of Judicial Review* (Cambridge: Harvard University Press, 1980).

Fellmeth, Robert C., *Politics of Land* (New York: Grossman, 1973).

Frug, G. E., "The City as a Legal Concept," in *Harvard Law Review* 93 (1980).

Frye, Northrop, "Letters in Canada," in *University of Toronto Quarterly* 22 (April 1953).

Goldberg v. *Kelly* (1970) 397 U.S. 254.

Goodman, N., *Of Mind and Other Matters* (Cambridge: Harvard University Press, 1984).

Halifax Industries, Ltd. v. *Director of Assessment* 55 N.S.R. (2d) 285 (1982).

Hanf v. *Yarmouth Light and Power* 58 N.S.R. 430 (1926).

Horwitz, Morton, *The Transformation of American Law: 1780–1860* (Cambridge: Harvard University Press, 1977).

Johnston, R. J., *Residential Segregation, the State and Constitutional Conflict in American Urban Areas* (New York: Academic Press, 1984).

Kennedy, D., "The Structure of Blackstone's Commentaries," in *Buffalo Law Review* 29 (1979).

Kierans, Thomas E., "Privatization: Strengthening the Market at the Expense of the State," in *Choices*, April 1985.

Laughlin v. *City of Portland*, 111, Me. 486, 90 A 318 (1914).

Levy, F. S., A. J. Meltsner, and A. Wildavsky, *Urban Outcomes* (Berkeley: University of California Press, 1974).

Lewis, J. W., *Constitution of the State of Illinois and United States* (Springfield: State of Illinois, 1971).

McWhinney, Edward, *Canada and the Constitution 1979–1982: Patriation and the Charter of Rights* (Toronto: University of Toronto Press, 1982).

———, *Canadian Jurisprudence* (Toronto: Carswell, 1958).

Michelman, Frank, "Property, Utility, and Fairness: Comments on the Ethical Foundations of 'Just Compensation' Law," *Harvard Law Review* 80.

Miller, Robert, "A New Promise of Equality," *MacLean's* (April 22, 1985).

Miller v. *Halifax Power Co.*, (1914) 13 ELR 394.

Mills, E. S. and B. W. Hamilton, *Urban Economics*. 3rd ed., (Glenview, IL: Scott, Foresman and Co., 1984).

Murray's Lessee v. *Hoboken Land and Improvement Co.* (1855) 18 How. 272.

Nedelsky, Jennifer, "From Common Law to Commission: The Development of Water Law in Nova Scotia," Proceedings of the Conference on Water and Environmental Law, Dalhousie University, Halifax, NS, September 14–16, 1979.

Nozick, R., *Anarchy, State and Utopia* (New York: Basic Books, 1974).

Organization for Economic Cooperation and Development, "The Management of Publicly Owned Land in Urban Areas," (Paris, 1979).

Posner, R., *The Economics of Justice* (Cambridge: Harvard University Press, 1978).

Quine, W., *From a Logical Point of View* (Cambridge: Harvard University Press, 1953).

Rabinow, P. and W. Sullivan, eds., *Interpretive Social Science: a Reader* (Berkeley: University of California Press, 1979).

Rawls, J., *A Theory of Justice* (Cambridge: Harvard University Press, 1971).

Regina v. *Martin* (1961) 35 WWR 285.

Richards, D. A. J., "The Theory of Adjudication and the Task of a Great Judge," *Cardozo Law Review* 1 (1979).

Roberts, Neal A. *The Government Land Developers* (Lexington, MA: Lexington Books, 1977).

Rodwin, Lloyd, *Economic Development and Resource Conservation: A Strategy for Maine* (Maine Bureau of Public Lands, 1974).

Russell, Peter H., "Judicial Power in Canada's Political Culture," in L. Friedland, ed., *Courts and Trials* (Toronto: University of Toronto Press, 1975).

Ryan, M., *Marxism and Deconstruction* (Baltimore: Johns Hopkins University Press, 1982).

Sandel, M., *Liberalism and the Limits of Justice* (Cambridge: Cambridge University Press, 1982).

Schmeiser, D. A., *Civil Liberties in Canada* (London: Oxford University Press, 1964).

Sen, A. and B. Williams, eds., *Utilitarianism and Beyond* (Cambridge: Cambridge University Press, 1982).

Siegan, Bernard, *Planning Without Process* (Lexington, MA: Lexington Books, 1977).

Simeon, R., "Current Constitutional Issues," in *Issues and Alternatives 1977: Intergovernmental Relations* (Toronto: Ontario Economic Council, 1977).

Stevens, William K., "Renaissance Along the Waterfronts of Three Cities Transforms Downtowns," *The New York Times*, May 26, 1985.

Tarnopolsky, Walter S., *The Canadian Bill of Rights* (Toronto: McClelland and Stewart Ltd., 1975).

Taylor, C., "Interpretation and the Sciences of Man," in P. Rabinow and W. Sullivan, eds., *Interpretive Social Science: a Reader* (Berkeley: University of California Press, 1979).

Tushnet, M., "Following the Rules Laid Down: A Critique of Interpretivism and Neutral Principles," in *Harvard Law Review* 96 (1983).

Unger, R. M., "The Critical Studies Movement," in *Harvard Law Review* 96 (1983).

Wolff, R. P., ed., *The Rule of Law* (New York: Simon and Schuster, 1971).

World Bank, *Report on Third World Urbanization* (Washington, 1983).

Yeates, Maurice and Barry Garner, *The North American City* (New York: Harper and Row, 1976).

About the Authors

John Brigham is a professor of Political Science at the University of Massachusetts, Amherst. He holds a Ph.D. from the University of California, Santa Barbara. He has published and presented numerous papers on law and land policy, including *Constitutional Language: An Interpretation of Judicial Decision* (1978) and *Policy Implementation: Penalties or Incentives?* (1980).

Gordon L. Clark is Professor of Labor Studies and Urban Policy at Carnegie-Mellon University's School of Urban and Public Affairs. Clark is the author of several books, the most recent being *Judges and the Cities: Interpreting Local Autonomy* (1985). He has taught at the Kennedy School of Government at Harvard University and the University of Chicago. He has also been a National Research Council Fellow at the National Academy of Science.

Frank C. Colcord, Jr. is Dean of the Faculty of Arts and Sciences, Tufts University. Before becoming Dean, he taught political science and urban planning at Tufts and at M.I.T. (where he received his Ph.D.). He is the author of numerous articles on urban planning, zoning and transportation.

Elliot J. Feldman founded the University Consortium for Research on North America and was, for seven years, its director. He is Director of the Consortium's Land-Use Project, Research Director of the Consortium, and Research Associate Professor at Tufts University. He has a Ph.D. from M.I.T. and has taught at universities in the U.S., Canada and Italy. He has published many books and articles on comparative politics and policy, government megaprojects, land use, defense and manpower. His latest book is *Concorde and Dissent: Explaining High-Technology Project Failures in Britain and France* (1985).

Michael A. Goldberg is the Herbert R. Fullerton Professor of Urban Land Policy at the Faculty of Commerce and Business Administration, The University of British Columbia. He has a Ph.D. in economics from The University of California, Berkeley and has published extensively in the fields of economics and land policy. His most recent book is *The Myth of the North American City: Continentalism Challenged* (with John Mercer) (1986).

Christopher K. Leman is an Assistant Professor at the Graduate School of Public Affairs, University of Washington, and previously taught at Brandeis University. After serving as Policy Analyst on the economics staff in the Office of the U.S. Secretary of the Interior, he was a Research Fellow at Resources for the Future, Inc., where he conducted studies of forestry and land use in North America. He holds a Ph.D. in political science from Harvard University and is the author of *The Collapse of Welfare Reform: Political Institutions, Policy, and the Poor in Canada and the United States*.

Mario Ristoratore, former Graduate Student Associate of the Center for International Affairs, Harvard University, recently received his Ph.D. from Brandeis University and is a policy analyst at Italstat in Rome. He has published several articles on political science and land use in Italy and the United States.

Index

Books from the Lincoln Institute of Land Policy

The Story of Land: A World History of Land Tenure and Agrarian Reform
John P. Powelson

The Peasant Betrayed: Agriculture and Land Reform in the Third World
John P. Powelson and Richard Stock

The Zoning Game Revisited
Richard F. Babcock and Charles L. Siemon

The Zoning Game
Richard F. Babcock

Economics and Tax Policy
Karl E. Case

Second World Congress on Land Policy, 1983
Edited by Matthew Cullen and Sharon Woolery

World Congress on Land Policy, 1980
Edited by Matthew Cullen and Sharon Woolery

Advanced Industrial Development: Restructuring, Relocation, and Renewal
Donald Hicks

Introduction to Computer Assisted Valuation
Edited by Arlo Woolery and Sharon Shea

Land Supply Monitoring: A Guide for Improving Public and Private Urban Development Decisions
David R. Godschalk, Scott Bollens, John Hekman, and Mike Miles

Planning with a Small Computer: An Applications Reader
Edited by Mathew MacIver and Jan Schreiber

Urban Planning for Latin America: The Challenge of Metropolitan Growth
Francis Violich, in collaboration with Robert Daughters

Land Markets and Land Policy in a Metropolitan Area: A Case Study of Tokyo
Yuzuru Hanayama

Land Policy in Modern Indonesia
Colin MacAndrews

Land Readjustment: The Japanese System
Luciano Minerbi, Peter Nakamura, Kiyoko Nitz, and Jane Yanai

Land Acquisition in Developing Countries: Policies and Procedures of the Public Sector
Michael G. Kitay

Proposition 2 1/2: Its Impact on Massachusetts
Prepared by the IMPACT: 2 1/2 Project at the Massachusetts Institute of Technology, Lawrence E. Susskind, Director

Measuring Fiscal Capacity
Edited by H. Clyde Reeves

The Urban Caldron: The Second Annual Donald G. Hagman Commemorative Conference
Edited by Joseph DiMento, LeRoy Graymer, and Frank Schnidman

Rental Housing in California: Market Forces and Public Policies The Third Annual Donald G. Hagman Commemorative Conference
Edited by LeRoy Graymer, Joseph DiMento, and Frank Schnidman

1984 Real Estate Valuation Colloquium: A Redefinition of Real Estate Appraisal Precepts and Processes
Edited by William N. Kinnard, Jr.

Retention of Land for Agriculture: Policy, Practice and Potential in New England
Frank Schnidman, Michael Smiley, and Eric G. Woodbury

Constitutions, Taxation, and Land Policy: Abstracts of Federal and State Constitutional Constraints on the Power of Taxation Relating to Land-Planning Policy
Michael M. Bernard

Constitutions, Taxation, and Land Policy: Volume II: Discussion and Analysis of Federal and State Constitutional Constraints on the Use of Taxation as an Instrument of Land-Planning Policy
Michael M. Bernard

Conflicts over Resource Ownership
Albert Church

Taxation and Nonrenewable Resources
Albert Church

Land Readjustment: A Different Approach to Financing Urbanization
Edited by William A. Doebele

Measuring Profitability and Capital Costs: Issues and Prospects
Edited by Daniel M. Holland

Building for Women
Edited by Suzanne Keller

Urban Land Policy for the 1980s: The Message for State and Local Government
Edited by George Lefcoe

Fiscal Federalism and the Taxation of Natural Resources: 1982 TRED Conference
Edited by Charles E. McLure, Jr. and Peter Mieszkowski

The Role of the State in Property Taxation
Edited by H. Clyde Reeves, with Scott Ellsworth

Funding Clean Water
H. Clyde Reeves

Land-Office Business: Land and Housing Prices in Rapidly Growing Metropolitan Areas
Gary Sands

Property Tax Relief
Steven David Gold

State Land Use Planning & Regulation
Thomas G. Pelham

Taxation of Mineral Resources
Robert F. Conrad and R. Bryce Hool

Fiscal Federalism and Taxation of Natural Resources
Edited by Charles E. McLure, Jr. and Peter Mieszkowski

Cities, Law & Social Policy
Charles M. Haar

Heterick Memorial Library
Ohio Northern University

DUE	RETURNED	DUE	RETURNED
1.		13.	
2.		14.	
3.		15.	
4.		16.	
5.		17.	
6.		18.	
7.		19.	
8.		20.	
9.		21.	
10.		22.	
11.		23.	
12.		24.